IT'S CRIMINAL!

About the author

Virginia V Dunn, BA, MA, Barrister began practice in civil and family law and spent most of the last 30 years teaching students training for the Bar at the Inns of Court School of Law, now the City Law School. She taught a range of subjects there, including litigation and evidence. For much of the time, she co-ordinated the civil litigation course, and has first-hand knowledge of how the subjects of litigation and evidence are taught and assessed. She is currently a Visiting Lecturer there. She contributes to the City Law School's Manuals supporting training for the Bar, and has written for the Institute of Legal Executives. This book is the companion to her popular *Be Civil!: A Guide to Learning Civil Litigation and Evidence* (Worth Publishing).

IT'S CRIMINAL!

a guide to learning criminal litigation, evidence and sentencing

Second Edition

VIRGINIA DUNN

Worth Publishing

First published 2013 by Worth Publishing Ltd
worthpublishing.com

Printed and bound in Great Britain by Grosvenor Group

British Library Cataloguing in Publication Data
A catalogue record for this book is available from
the British Library

ISBN 9781903269398

Cover and text design by Anna Murphy

Preface to the first edition

If you are reading this, my guess is you are getting ready to sit a professional examination. Whether you are at the beginning or end of your course or, having already qualified, are embarking on a change of direction in early practice, this book is intended to help. It is a companion to *Be Civil! Guide to Learning Civil Litigation and Evidence* (2011) and aims to perform the same function - to make your exam preparation more effective and perhaps even enjoyable. But this time the sublect is *criminal* litigation, evidence and sentencing.

This is a very large canvas, which could have been the subject of two books. We have kept them as one so you can more easily link up the various aspects of criminal litigation. In any case, on the BPTC, your knowledge will be tested in one single examination.

The fact remains that it is easy to feel overwhelmed by what can seem like an avalanche of principles, rules, (changing) legislation and explanatory case law. The source of criminal procedure and evidence comes from all directions, and this can make it difficult for beginners to get a confident grip on the subject. It is very easy to forget what was learned for class one week in order, as it seems, to 'make room' for what needs to be taken on board in preparation for the next. The danger with this approach is that by the end, you may not remember much at all! This book is intended to make the various aspects of the subject easier to understand and integrate, thereby increasing and consolidating the depth of your knowledge.

One key to the confident learning of criminal litigation and evidence is being able to see the bigger picture. If you have a good grasp of the general purpose and principles underpinning the rules, the detail will be easier to learn and recall. If, for example, you are putting together a jigsaw puzzle, it is much more difficult if you do not know what it should look like when it is completed. This is what I hope to provide. You have been (or are about) to look at all the individual pieces of the evidential and procedural puzzle in some detail on your course. This book is the picture on the box.

It is intended to augment, not replace, your own learning. It can assist with classroom preparation, by allowing you to focus purposefully on the subject matter, research more knowledgeably and contribute intelligently to discussions, rather than merely writing down everything you see and hear. It should be especially helpful as you prepare for examinations by reinforcing the bigger picture, while at the same time, reviewing the essential individual concepts. I provide many revision tips. This book should also remind you of the value of common sense (an under-rated commodity) in learning how to think about, understand and apply any aspect of the law, including procedure and evidence.

This book is the product of many years of helping students to learn and enjoy procedure and evidence. As always, I am grateful to all of them - past and present - for teaching me to teach them better. Many colleagues at City Law School were also very supportive of this enterprise, in particular: Lisa Laurenti (who helps keeps me in the loop), my ex-colleague Barbara Mensah (who has gone on to higher places and very kindly wrote the Foreword), Paul Banks and the library team (for their search and rescue skills, and occasional blind eyes), Paul McKeown (a man of wide horizons and knowing assertions) and Nikki Walsh (who shared both her notes and her know-how). I am particularly grateful to Adrian Keane and Caitriona Hegarty, who very generously spent valuable time reviewing, and thereby improving, my chapters on evidence. Special thanks also go to Robert McPeake, who wears his considerable knowledge with charm and good humour, but whose patience must have been sorely tested as chapters on criminal procedure and sentencing kept appearing randomly on his doorstep like serially abandoned children. Luckily he took them in and returned them in better shape than he found them. The entire manuscript is very much enhanced as a result of all of their efforts. None of them, of course, should be held accountable for any of its content, and any errors which remain are mine alone.

As always I am grateful to Andrea Perry for her caring and highly capable editing of this book, and thank all those at Worth Publishing who assisted in its production, especially the ever patient Anna Murphy, who probably now knows a lot more about litigation than she ever thought possible (or desirable).

Finally, Ray's son, Ollie, and my girls continue to be a source of support, amusement, pride and joy both to me and the memory of their late father. How I wish he were here to see all of them.

VVD
London
July 2013

For Chris, Felix and Charlie,
who were indispensible to my understanding the law of evidence

and

for Eden, Kate and Rachael,
who are simply indispensible

Preface to the second edition

Since *It's Criminal!* was first published in 2013, there have been several important changes, not only to the procedural rules and various resource materials, but also to the way in which knowledge of criminal litigation, sentencing and evidence is examined on the Bar Professional Training Course (BPTC). I have tried to reflect all of these changes in this new edition.

The Criminal Procedural Rules were revised and restructured in 2015, placing even greater emphasis on proactive case management and the use of technology. Efforts to ensure that magistrates try more cases without passing the buck to the Crown Court, have redoubled: low value shoplifting can be tried summarily and legal aid is now means tested in the Crown Court. The long-awaited overhaul of sentencing, however, is not expected before 2018 at the earliest.

Not to be left out, the Bar Standards Board has, since 2013, changed almost everything about how the procedural subjects are examined on the BPTC. The 'short answer' question is dead; long live the 'single best answer' test. I have thus completely re-written Chapter 25 on exam preparation for this edition (which might be worth reading before starting the book, so you know where you want to end up).

I remain grateful to the 'usual suspects' for their continued commitment to this book (all mentioned in the first Preface), in particular Paul McKeown and Robert McPeake, who both cast discerning eyes over this edition. Peter Hungerford-Welch also generously shared his updated knowledge. As usual, however, any errors of content are mine alone. Special mention, of course, goes to Worth Publishing, and especially Andrea Perry (editor) and Anna Murphy (designer) for their support and indefatigable patience. Finally many thanks for the constructive and positive comments from those who have both enjoyed and benefitted from this book - which, after all, is the point of it.

VVD April 2017

Foreword

Law students at undergraduate level will have studied criminal law and may have taken criminal evidence and possibly even criminal procedure as options, but will rarely have had to combine all those topics into one subject.

Very few will have had to consider sentencing principles or practice, or have to understand and apply the guidance from the Sentencing Council. That is why this book is such an important one for the student and aspiring criminal practitioner. In addition, with so many criminal statutes and hundreds of new cases from the higher courts each year dealing with criminal law, practice and procedure, it can be a real challenge for students and practitioners to understand and marry up law, evidence and practice. This is why *It's Criminal!* is so welcome. It is the second book in what is promising to be an excellent series of law guides.

Virginia Dunn has spent many years teaching at the post-graduate BPTC level and has a wealth of experience in getting the information out to students and practitioners in the most user-friendly way. *It's Criminal!* is a very helpful resource book which serves as an introduction to and overview of the subject, and also as a revision aid. It is clearly written, accurate and comprehensive in its presentation of the subject, covering magistrates' courts and the Crown court, evidence, procedure and sentencing. It is different in its presentation as a student text, in the practical way in which it is set out and with helpful revision tips and pointers as to what else is worth reading.

My only regret is that *It's Criminal!* was not around when I was a student myself. I am sure that it will prove itself to be an important addition to the law library of every aspiring legal professional student.

Her Honour Judge Barbara Mensah
Luton Crown Court
July 2013

Glossary of terms

Code of Conduct	Rules and principles governing behaviour of practising barristers (England and Wales)
Criminal Practice Directions	Practice directions governing criminal court procedure
Criminal Procedural Rules	A primary source of procedural law in the criminal courts of England and Wales. Modelled on the civil procedure rules. First published in 2005
Crown Court Compendium	Judicial College Guidance to Crown Court Judges on Trial Management (Pt 1) and Sentencing (Pt 2)
Crown Prosecution Service	Responsible for public prosecution of criminal cases in England and Wales
Farquharson Guidelines	Recommendations on the role of prosecuting counsel, published in 1986
Legal Aid Agency	Government Body providing both civil and criminal legal aid
Overriding Objective	The principal aspiration of the CrPR, which is to deal with cases justly
PACE Codes of Practice	Guidance on various aspects of police procedure, supplementing the statutory provisions of PACE 1984
Practice Form	Form to be used for a particular purpose, as specified by the rules or a practice direction
Privilege	The right of a party to refuse to disclose or produce a document or to answer questions on the ground of some special interest recognised by law
Sentencing Guidelines	Guidance to sentencing judges issued by the Sentencing Council
Stay	A stay imposes a halt on proceedings, apart from taking any steps allowed by the rules or the terms of the stay. Proceedings can continue if, but only if, the stay is lifted

Abbreviations and references

A-G Guidelines	Attorney-General's Guidelines to prosecutors
BCrP	Blackstone's Criminal Practice
BPTC	Bar Professional Training Course
BSB	Bar Standards Board
CJEU	Court of Justice of the European Union
CPS	Crown Prosecution Service
CrimPD	Criminal Practice Directions
CrimPR	Criminal Procedure Rules
DTO	Detention and training order
ECHR	European Convention/Court of Human Rights (depends on context)
RSPCA	Royal Society for the Prevention of Cruelty to Animals
r/rr	Rule/s
s/ss	Section/s
YRO	Youth rehabilitation order

Key case references

AC	Appeal Court
All ER	All England Law Reports
Crim LR	Criminal Law Review
Cr App R/(S)	Criminal Appeal Reports/(Sentencing)
EWCA Crim	Neutral case citation for Court of Appeal case (Criminal Division)
EWHC/(Admin)	Neutral case citation for High Court case (Administrative Court)
QB/KB	Queen's Bench/King's Bench
UKHL	Neutral case citation for House of Lords case
UKPC	Neutral case citation for Privy Council case
WLR	Weekly Law Reports
[ ]	Indicates para/section of some judgments

Key statute references

BA 1976	Bail Act 1976
CAA (year)	Criminal Appeal Act (various years as indicated)
CCA 2013	Crime and Courts Act 2013
CDA 1998	Crime and Disorder Act 1998
CEA (year)	Criminal Evidence Act (various years, as indicated)
CJA 2003	Criminal Justice Act 2003 (and other years as indicated)
CJCA 2015	Criminal Justice and Courts Act 2015
CJPOA 1994	Criminal Justice and Public Order Act 1994
CPIA 1996	Criminal Procedure and Investigations Act 1996
CYPA 1933/1969	Children and Young Persons Act 1933/1969
HRA 1998	Human Rights Act 1998
JA 1974	Juries Act 1974
LASPO Act 2012	Legal Aid, Sentencing and Punishment of Offenders Act 2012
MCA 1980	Magistrates' Courts Act 1980
PACE 1984	Police and Criminal Evidence Act 1984
PCC(S)A 2000	Powers of Criminal Courts (Sentencing) Act 2000
POA 1985	Prosecution of Offences Act 1985
YJCEA 1999	Youth Justice and Criminal Evidence Act 1999

Contents

PART II CRIMINAL EVIDENCE

IT'S CRIMINAL!

Introduction

This book covers a range of related topics: criminal procedure, evidence and sentencing in the courts of England and Wales. It is written primarily for students on the Bar Professional Training Course ('BPTC'), but will also be of use to solicitors and other practitioners. It can be used both as an overview, as your course progresses, and as a revision guide, as you prepare for your professional examinations or experience early practice. What it is not, is a substitute for your own learning: this book can do a lot for you, but it cannot do it all.

So there are some ground rules. *The first is that you must learn your way around the accepted practitioner texts.* If you are on the BPTC, then you will have been given a copy of *Blackstone's Criminal Practice.*[1] This is a companion work of sorts to *Blackstone's Civil Practice*, but has an older pedigree. It covers a broader canvas and so is sub-divided into 'parts' rather than 'chapters'. It also contains more academic law, and (of necessity) more statutory source material, which is usefully integrated with the explanatory text to which it relates. Pertinent guidelines and codes of practice are left to the Appendices. Otherwise, if you have used *Blackstone's Civil Practice*, you will recognise the lay-out and the thin and crinkly (but surprisingly durable) paper.

There are other practitioner texts (with even longer pedigrees), most notably the redoubtable Archbold[2] which specialises in practice and procedure in the Crown

1 Oxford University Press, Oxford.

2 Archbold, *Criminal Pleading, Evidence & Practice* Sweet & Maxwell, London. It now has a separate companion volume for the magistrates' court.

Court, and *Stones' Justices Manual*,[3] which focuses on the magistrates' courts. One of the benefits of *Blackstone's Criminal Practice*, however, is that it covers, in one volume and in equal measure, procedure applicable to all criminal courts and so best caters for a wide curriculum. Most importantly, the BPTC exam syllabus is now set by reference to topics and paragraphs contained in it. For these reasons, it is the one which I will most often cite (as BCrP).[4]

All such practitioner works usefully combine secondary and primary source material. All are published annually and produce (cumulative) supplements when between editions. And they all work in much the same way, and are available (usually on-line and in hard copy) in any decent law library, if you have not actually been given one on your course. So it does not matter which practitioner text you prefer in the long run (much may depend on what is preferred by judges you usually appear in front of). In the short-term, however, focus on the text which allows you to best prepare for the task in hand. The important thing is to know how to navigate such works efficiently and access the information you need to know.

Let's be honest - no one reads these books for pleasure. They are reference works for practitioners who understand the subject and need to keep up-to-date. Their primary purpose is to inform, not teach. You do not have to love them, but you do have to know how to use them.

There are also some excellent textbooks written for the student as well as professional audience, which your course may suggest to you. Unless the text is 'set' by your tutors, I always advise test-driving such books, certainly before buying (they are expensive, and again are in law libraries) - you may get on better with some styles than others. It is also important to ensure the information is as up-to-date as possible. Criminal procedure, in particular, can change with the year's fashions (or politicians). Throughout this book you'll find reference to John Sprack's regularly

3 Butterworths & Co, London.

4 2017 edition, including supplement. And note that since August 2016 this is the standard text in the Crown Court.

updated *A Practical Approach to Criminal Procedure* ('*Practical Approach*'),[5] which is detailed and accessible. So far as criminal evidence is concerned, everyone has their favourite. The highly regarded *Modern Law of Evidence*[6] by Adrian Keane & Paul McKeown ('*Modern Law*') is comprehensive and thoughtful. I still appreciate the insights in Chris Allen's *Practical Guide to Evidence* (*Practical Guide*). Others have since updated the book; as a result, it has lost some of its charm, but still contains some useful information.[7]

The second ground rule is that you yourself must engage directly with some of the primary and other relevant source material. And there is a ton of it! Statutes, rules, practice directions, codes of practice, guidelines galore: criminal litigation makes civil litigation look positively minimalist. You do not want to let yourself be overwhelmed by it all, but don't be frightened of it either. At the end of the day, do not just rely on what someone else tells you the law is - go that one step further, and have a look for yourself. Constantly amended legislation can be a struggle (even I avoid parts of the Bail Act if I can), but much of the source material is surprisingly accessible. They are all available on-line.[8] The Sentencing Council's Guidelines, for example, are both readable and comprehensible. You could learn most of what you need to know about criminal evidence just by reading the Judicial College's Crown Court Compendium Part 1.[9] The Criminal Procedure Rules (CrimPR) and Practice Directions (CrimPD) are written in clear, straightforward language. And by the time you finish this book you should know several statutes intimately, including PACE 1984, CJA 2003, CPIA 1996. I will refer you to all of these, and more, in the pages which follow and you should make a point of acquainting yourself with them. But take it slow and easy - you do not need to go all the way on the first date!

Reading primary source material, of course, includes *reading some cases.* And by cases I do not mean the headnotes or summaries or a précis or an analysis in a textbook (although read those too if you wish): I mean *actual judgments given by actual*

5 Oxford University Press, Oxford, 15th Edn, 2015. Peter Hungerford-Welch has produced a slimmed down version of his *Criminal Procedure and Sentencing* (Routledge, 8th Edn, 2014) which has a companion website for updating.

6 Oxford University Press, Oxford, 11th Edn, 2016

7 If I refer to Chris Allen's *Practical Guide*, I am referring to the 2008 (4th) edition by him. References merely to *Practical Guide* refer to the joint effort, 5th Edn, 2016.

8 See generally list in Sprack, *Practical Approach*, 29.12

9 And its Companion (Part II on Sentencing) is also very helpful. My references are to the February 2017 version.

judges! For some reason, students tend to come to their professional training courses, if not with an aversion to reading cases, then with a very strong desire to find a way to avoid doing so. This is a short-sighted attitude and utterly counter-productive. There is no better way to learn about the law than to see it in operation, and that is just what the cases do. A well-written judgment, which sets out the facts and relevant law clearly, and explains why the case has been decided the way that it has, will teach you a whole lot more about the rules and principles involved than any secondary source. And it is usually much more interesting to read.

To encourage you in this endeavour, at the end of most chapters I have made some suggestions for (a little) additional reading. Sometimes this will be a relevant practice form or a part of the rules, but usually I will suggest that you read a judgment[10] in a case (or two). They are all available on-line. The cases I suggest will not necessarily be the leading case in the subject, nor the most recent, nor the most talked-about.[11] I have tried to choose cases which are particularly well-written, or fun to read, or even a bit quirky, so that you can see how useful they are and to show you that, contrary to the popular belief of many students, *cases are your friends*!

The third ground rule is that you must learn how to keep yourself up-to-date. Civil procedure modernised itself in one fell swoop[12] - one day we all woke up to find the old edifice has been torn down and something entirely new put in its place. Reforms in criminal procedure have been more piecemeal - a little like someone who is always doing DIY and either adding to, extending or renovating the original house. Criminal evidence invites judicial interpretation, sentencing policy can fall prey to policy initiatives, and trying to pin down criminal procedure can sometimes seem like trying to pin the tail on a hyperactive donkey. Which is not to say the law is an ass: it is just that some aspects of it are very changeable.

Indeed it is evolving as I write. So you must take responsibility for learning

10 And I mean the judgment: you can skip all the preliminaries and go straight there. Some reports set out the legal argument as well, which can be interesting too, but I want you to focus on what the judge says.

11 These will be referred to in the relevant chapters themselves, so feel free to read them too.

12 See *Be Civil!: A Guide to learning civil litigation and evidence* (Worth Publishing, 3rd Edn, 2015) by the author.

to keep yourself up-to-date, for example by keeping your eyes and ears open and always checking the most recent supplements to (the most recent) practitioner texts. For examination purposes, your course leaders will help you, so watch out for any updates and information regarding the law (or the exam syllabus) which they give you. There are also many websites that can assist, including venables.co.uk and crimeline.info/updater. And pay attention to the 'news'. You may be surprised how much of what goes on impinges on this subject. Soon you will be finding the mistakes in TV dramas and other fictional accounts of criminal trials.

So if you do your part, I will do mine. This book ranges over several topics. It is really three subjects in one, criminal litigation, evidence and sentencing, which we have kept together to make it easier to cross-refer, especially from evidential to procedural points. The intention is to assist your learning by making clear the connections between, the reasons for, and the essential ingredients of the various rules and principles governing criminal cases. This will help you both to learn and apply them. If the bigger picture is clear, the smaller details should more easily fall into place. There are some study tips at the end of each chapter, and I close the book with a brief guide to how to approach revision and the types of examination questions you will encounter on the BPTC.

1. FIRST THINGS FIRST

If you have any experience of (or are also learning about) civil litigation, the first thing you will notice is that the criminal courts have taken 'cuttings' from the Civil Procedure Rules and transplanted them onto their own turf, and for much the same purpose: to rationalise the rules and practice across all of the criminal courts. The

Criminal Procedure Rules were first published in 2005, and periodically revised, until completely overhauled and restructured in 2015. They now follow a similar pattern to the Civil Procedure Rules, in that the rules and accompanying practice directions are now more clearly linked to each other. The rules are updated periodically, and you will find them in BCrP's supplement (which helpfully puts the allied practice directions in shaded grey boxes).

They begin with that now familiar litigation concept: the *overriding objective*, which is that 'criminal cases be dealt with justly'.[13] Rule 1.1 goes on to set out a number of aspects of criminal litigation which are part of achieving this objective, and which attempt (so far as words can) to capture, recognise and accommodate some of the in-built and inescapable tensions in a system which essentially pits the state against the individual. Thus one wants to 'acquit the innocent and convict the guilty': 'deal with the prosecution and the defence fairly': 'respect' witnesses and victims but 'recognise the rights' of the defendant: deal with cases according to their 'gravity' and 'complexity', and so on.[14]

However it is expressed, this overriding objective permeates the conduct of criminal litigation. The courts must play their part by active case management, both leading up to and during trial, and are given extensive power to do so. This includes early identification of the real issues in, and the needs of, the case, as well as its participants; setting a procedural timetable; monitoring the progress of the case; discouraging delay; encouraging cooperation and compliance and ensuring that evidence is given in the most efficient and clear way. Where pertinent, standard forms and/or technology should be used so as to avoid unnecessary hearings (for example by dealing with applications and giving directions by telephone, live link or email). Appropriate sanctions should follow a failure to comply with time-limits and other court orders or rules.[15]

13 CrPR, r 1.1(1)

14 *Ibid*, r 1.1(2). Note the word 'includes' - the list is not exhaustive.

15 CrPR, r 3.2 - r 3.5

As part of this process an initiative called Better Case Management was rolled out nationally in January 2016 (with a Crown Court Digital Case System).[16] The main aim is to facilitate robust case management, reduce the number of hearings and maximise engagement and compliance with the system. All 'participants' in a case are under a duty to 'prepare and conduct' criminal cases in accordance with the procedural rules, directions and court orders, and so as to further the overriding objective. This even includes a 'grassing' provision requiring one party to report the failures of another! At the commencement of proceedings, each party (and the court) must appoint a case progression officer to assist with the process.[17]

Note, however, that the point of effective case management is to avoid unnecessary postponement and surprises. So, it must always be tempered by the requirements of justice, which at times may need to be delayed to avoid its being denied.[18]

2. KEY CONCEPTS

Criminal jurisdiction in England and Wales is essentially shared between the magistrates' courts and Crown Court. The latter, along with the High Court and the Court of Appeal, make up the Senior Courts.[19]

Criminal trials essentially take one of two forms: *summary trial* or *trial on indictment.* Summary trials are conducted in local magistrates' courts, and are presided over by lay magistrates (also known as lay justices of the peace), who determine both issues of law and fact. Lay magistrates are not professional judges, but men and women who are willing and able to take time to sit regularly at least two or three times a month. A small minority of magistrates are full-time professional judges (district judges).

16 See *ibid*, r 1.2(c) and also gov.uk/government/news/crime-news-better-case-management-rollout-in-england-and-wales

17 These objectives and requirements find resonance in CrimPR Pt 3 and allied Practice Directions.

18 See comments of Judge LJ in *R v Jisl* [2004] All ER (D) 31, at para 114-118

19 They were once known as the Supreme Courts but when the Appellate Division of the House of Lords was re-branded the Supreme Court, the others became the Senior Courts. And the Supreme Courts Act 1981 became the Senior Courts Act 1981

Trials on indictment are conducted in the Crown Court (a single court which sits in various locations around the country). The trial is presided over by a professional judge,[20] who controls the course of the trial and determines all issues of law. Matters of fact (including the ultimate question of guilt or innocence) are determined solely by the jury, who are randomly drawn from a wider cross-section of the community than lay magistrates, and sit for a very short, defined period. Only in very exceptional cases would a trial be conducted in the Crown Court without a jury.

Similarly, criminal offences are divided into two types: *summary offences* and *indictable offences*. The latter category sub-divides again into those which *must* be tried on indictment ('indictable only) and those which *may* be tried on indictment' (triable 'either way'). As we shall see, where adult defendants are concerned, an 'either-way' offence can be tried summarily if both the magistrates' court and the defendant concerned agree to this. As you might expect, the least serious offences are summary offences and the most serious offences are triable only on indictment - the rest fall somewhere in the middle. Special rules apply to juveniles.

So off we go. But before we start, there is one *final ground rule*, and that is: *you must have some fun* reading this book. And if, by the end of it, you have *understood* what you have read, both in principle and in application (as opposed to merely memorising or 'learning' rules and so on), and if you have also abided by my ground rules, then you should be well able to meet the challenges that await you.

20 A circuit judge for most cases, but a full or part-time (Recorder) High Court judge for the more complex or high profile. See BCrP D 3.4f

It is worth reading ...

Have a careful read of CrPR, r 1.1 - 1.3 and r 3.2 - 3.5, 3.9 and 3.11

The judgment of Thomas LJ in *R (on application of the DPP) v Chorley Magistrate's Court* [2006] EWHC 1795 (Admin), about a prosecution which turned on the technicalities of service of the results of a blood alcohol analysis. You could usefully revisit this case later on, but for now focus on paras 24-30 on the importance of what were then new Criminal Procedure Rules.

PART ONE

criminal procedure and sentencing

CHAPTER 2

Preliminaries to prosecution

Before we can begin talking about what goes on during the criminal trial process, it is necessary to consider how cases get before the courts. You may not be studying to be police officers but you need to know something about the extent of their powers - it could affect what goes on later in court. Individuals need to know their rights, police officers need to know the law - and you need to know about both. Due process starts on the streets.

The main source of the law governing police powers is the Police and Criminal Evidence Act 1984 - so well known to the world of lawyers and law enforcement that it is only referred to as PACE. You don't really even need to remember the year - it has no rivals. But who could forget 1984 anyway!

PACE 1984 is a piece of primary legislation which governs the exercise of police powers - from stop and search, to arrest, through to detention and charge. Much of the fine detail, however, is left to the Codes of Practice covering the various aspects of police procedure, starting with Code A (stop and search) up to Code H (terrorism suspects). These Codes are, in effect, a guide to the proper conduct of criminal investigations. PACE 1984 sets out the framework; the Codes put the flesh on the statutory bones.

It is worth noting that a breach of the Codes does not (in itself) amount to an offence or civil wrong - but it can affect the fairness of the proceedings and the admissibility of evidence. This is one reason why you need to be familiar with them,[1] and their function. The Codes which most often impact on criminal litigation are aspects of Code C (which deals with the treatment, detention and interviewing of suspects) and Code D (which deals with the identification of suspects by witnesses).

You also need to know how criminal cases get to court. There are essentially three routes. One is a private prosecution. This is one brought by an individual or entity (for example, the RSPCA), not the state. It is a rarity for various reasons. They often have poorer prospects of success: one of the more famous examples was the (failed) private prosecution brought by the family of Stephen Lawrence in 1994.[2]

Public prosecutions are usually commenced in one of two ways. Relatively minor criminal matters (for example, many motoring offences which do not give police a power of arrest) are commenced by 'written requisition and charge'. This is a way of instigating proceedings without having to involve the court beforehand. The written charge sets out the nature and particulars of the offence (for example speeding - when, where and to what extent) and is issued with the requisition, which 'requires' (hence, the name) the person concerned to appear before the magistrates' court to answer the charge. The court does not get involved until the case comes up before it,[3] and if the defendant is able to (and does) plead guilty by post, the magistrates might never see him at all![4]

Most serious prosecutions, however, begin with a suspect who is arrested by the police and ultimately charged with the offence(s). This 'arrest and charge' procedure is the focus of this chapter. There are several aspects to consider about this third route to court.

---

1 You do not need to learn all the detail - check your exam syllabus for examinable material. PACE 1984 and the accompanying Codes are set out in Appendix 1 of BCrP or on-line at the gov.uk website.

2 See timeline of the trials and tribulations of achieving some justice in this case at bbc.co.uk/news/uk-16283806. Private prosecutions are brought by the old process of 'information and summons' (the relevant information is laid in front of the magistrates, who then issue the summons). See BCrP D 5.7ff

3 This procedure is available to a range of 'relevant' prosecutors (e.g. Dept of Work and Pensions, TV Licensing Authority). See BCrP D 5.4ff

1. THE ARREST

Most arrests are made without a warrant. Of course, the court has the power, in certain circumstances, to grant arrest warrants, but it would be very tiresome if every time the police observed criminal activity, they had to go to court if an arrest was necessary. Where an arrest without warrant is concerned, there are two questions to consider: was there a power to arrest and, if so, was the arrest executed properly?

A. POWER OF ARREST WITHOUT WARRANT

The power to arrest without warrant has *two* aspects to it: the police must have *reasonable grounds* both for (i) suspecting the person has committed, is committing or is about to commit an offence *and* for (ii) believing the arrest is *necessary* to achieve a legitimate objective, namely one or more of the following:

(a) to enable the person's (real) name or address to be obtained,
(b) to prevent physical injury or damage to property,
(c) to protect a child or other vulnerable person,
(d) to allow the prompt and effective investigation of the offence or conduct in question *or*
(e) to prevent the person disappearing (when this would hinder the investigation of the crime).[5]

To be reasonable, the basis for suspecting the commission of an offence must be honestly held and objectively rational, not emotional. It need not necessarily be the result of evidence admissible in court - it could be based on a tip-off or logical surmise, but not on a 'hunch'. Arrests are often effected before sufficient evidence to charge a

4 See below Ch. 8. In 2015 this process was further streamlined (for intended guilty pleas to the least serious summary offences) with a Single Justice Notice Procedure: see BCrP D 5.6

5 s 24 PACE 1984

suspect has been gathered.

In limited circumstances, a private citizen has power to effect an arrest (the so-called 'citizen's arrest'). For an example of how *not* to do it, see *R v Pearce*.[6]

B. PROPERLY EXECUTED ARREST

Arrest is essentially a lawful restraint on the arrested person's liberty. A person 'helping police with their inquiries' is (at that moment anyway) free to go home. An arrested person is not. It is important that the individual concerned knows where he stands.

Thus, an arrest is properly effected *either* by informing the arrested person in words (and a language) he can understand that he is under arrest *or* by physically seizing him and telling him as soon as practicable thereafter that he is under arrest. Reasonable force may be used, but not handcuffs unless really needed.[7]

The arrested person must be told of the reasons for the arrest, even where this is obvious. And this should be recorded in the police officer's notebook.[8] If the arrest was lawfully executed, it does not matter that it was motivated, for example, by the desire to investigate some other crime. But the arrest will not be proper if there were in fact no reasonable grounds for suspecting that an offence had been committed.

C. ARRESTING ISSUES

Once arrested, two things should happen: the 'caution' should be administered and the individual should either be bailed or taken to a designated police station.

(i) The caution

Once the police officer moves from curiosity to 'reasonable suspicion', he ought to 'caution' the suspect.[9] If an arrest follows, then again (unless it had just been

6 [2013] EWCA Crim 808

7 PACE 1984 s 117, and BCrP D 1.7/8

8 Officially called an 'Evidence and Action Book' (EAB)

9 Code C, para 10.1. Do not confuse, as well you might, this 'caution' with that which is an alternative to prosecution (discussed below).

administered) the caution must be given.[10] The usual form of words is (as you are no doubt aware): *You do not have to say anything. But it may harm your defence if you do not mention when questioned something which you later rely on in court. Anything you do say may be given in evidence.* This lets the suspect know that in certain circumstances the trial court may be allowed to draw 'adverse inferences' from his silence under questioning. In circumstances where no such adverse inferences may be drawn (such as a detainee at a police station who has been denied access to legal advice), then the old style caution should be given.[11]

(ii) Custody or street bail

Once arrested, the person should normally be taken to a designated police station straightaway, where proper procedures can continue in the proper environment. There are two exceptions to this: one is where the suspect is taken somewhere else consensually, for example, to check out his alibi.[12] The other is when he is given so-called 'street bail'.[13] This means that instead of being taken immediately to the police station, the arrested person is released under an obligation to attend there at a future time and day. Conditions may be attached, for example, to ensure that the suspect does not interfere with witnesses. The purpose of 'street bail' is to give the police officer the ability to stay on the streets, rather than have to go back to the police station, either because he has more pressing things to do at that moment or it would otherwise suit the investigation of the offence in question. In any case, the bailed suspect must be given a written notice setting out all relevant detail, and if he fails to attend the police station as required, he will be subject to arrest. Pre-charge police bail should not last more than 28 days, unless the circumstances are exceptional, and any change in bail conditions would normally be sought from the relevant police station.[14]

10 Unless the arrested person's behaviour makes this impracticable: Code C, para 10.3/4

11 This is *"You do not have to say anything, but anything you do say may be given in evidence"*. See BCrP D 1.83 and Annex C to Code C. As to adverse inferences, see Ch. 23

12 *Dallison v Caffery* [1965] 1 QB 348

13 s 30A PACE 1984

14 The 28 day limit was added by the Police and Crime Act 2017, in response to high profile personalities lingering for months on police bail. See generally Ch. 3 on bail.

(iii) Powers of search

Even before an arrest, the police have powers to stop and search members of the public. Usually they need to have 'reasonable grounds' to suspect the commission of an offence, but in some serious cases (for example those involving dangerous weapons) all that is really required is reasonable grounds for suspecting that the stolen or prohibited item will be found. These powers are to be employed 'fairly, responsibly and without unlawful discrimination',[15] but are open to abuse. So far as the power to search premises *before* an arrest is concerned, a magistrates' court may issue a warrant authorising such a search if the offence is (a) serious enough, (b) the evidence likely to be cogent enough (and not protected by legal privilege) and (c) there is no other alternative. Once a suspect is arrested, however, there are powers to search both the suspect himself (for example if he has anything on him which might aid his escape or provide evidence of an offence) and relevant premises (if there are reasonable grounds for believing that relevant evidence will be found there). The detail of these extensive powers is beyond the scope of this book,[16] but it is worth noting that breaches can have serious implications, both for the admissibility of evidence at trial as well as the suspect's civil rights.[17]

2. AT THE POLICE STATION FOLLOWING ARREST

Once at the police station, the basic idea is that the case is investigated further to see whether any charges should be brought against the (now arrested) suspect. This all has to be done fairly and properly, which again is what the Codes of Practice are directed at ensuring (in this case, Code C).

What essentially happens is this. The suspect is put under the control of the

15 Code A, para 1.1

16 For useful summary, see Sprack, *Practical Approach,* 3.71ff

17 Evidence obtained in circumstances rendering the proceedings unfair could be excluded at trial under s 78 PACE 1984. See Ch. 14

custody officer, who should be an officer of at least the rank of sergeant and have no connection to the investigation. This last requirement is important - it ensures that the custody officer has no direct stake in the outcome of the investigation and can be objective about the suspect's treatment. The custody officer must create and maintain a custody record.[18]

An important part of the custody officer's duties is to review the suspect's detention and consider the evidence against him. There are basically three options: order the suspect's immediate release, charge the suspect or sanction further detention without charge.[19]

The first two options are not particularly controversial, but the third one is. How long should the police be able to keep hold of an arrested person while they try to gather evidence against him? The first thing to note is that in order to further detain him without charge at this stage, the custody officer must have *reasonable grounds* for believing that such detention is necessary:

- to secure or preserve evidence in the case, *or*
- to obtain such evidence by means of further questioning.

If the suspect is so detained, this sets up what you might think of as a *detention timetable*, requiring a close review of the situation at set intervals. There have to be severe limits to how long a suspect can be detained without charge, which nevertheless give the police some scope for questioning the suspect on their home turf. All throughout the process, the suspect and/or his solicitor may make representations about continued detention, and appropriate risk assessments (for example for vulnerable or ill suspects)[20] must be made by the police.

18 As to what to include see Code C, para 11.7

19 If there was not yet enough evidence to charge the suspect, another possibility might be to release him on police bail, subject to recall as it were. This leaves open the possibility of asking him further questions, since once charged, no more questioning of the accused can take place. BCrP D 1.47

20 Appropriate advice may be necessary. See Code C, paras 3.6-3.10 and BCrP D 1.63ff

A. DETENTION WITHOUT CHARGE TIMETABLE

The timetable is complex, so just get to grips with the basics.

(i) There must be a review within *six* hours after a detention was first authorised

(ii) A second review must be held within *nine* hours of the first

(iii) After a further nine hours, we get to the first major crunch point. *24* hours will have passed and at this point, the suspect *must* either be *charged or released* (unconditionally or on police bail) *unless*:

  (a) the suspect is under arrest for an indictable offence, *and*

  (b) an officer of at least the rank of superintendent has reasonable grounds for believing that further detention is necessary to secure or preserve evidence or to obtain such evidence by further questioning, *and*

  (c) the investigation so far has been carried out diligently

The power to detain without charge beyond 24 hours ought to be used sparingly.

(iv) If detention continues, although reviews will take place every nine hours, if the suspect is not charged or released, the next crunch point comes at 36 hours. The suspect *must* be released or charged after *36 hours* unless a *magistrates' court* has issued a warrant of further detention. The matter is heard in private, with at least two magistrates, and the suspect is entitled to free representation. The magistrates basically need to be satisfied that what the superintendent believed 12 hours previously still holds true. If a warrant is granted, it may be for a period not exceeding another 36 hours.

(v) After a maximum of *72 hours*, the court may authorise detention for a further 36 hours (and on the same basis and for the same maximum of 36 hours).

(vi) After *96 hours*, the game is up. The suspect must be[21] either charged or released.

B. INTERVIEW AND IDENTIFICATION

Two important avenues to securing relevant evidence are through (i) police interview and (ii) witness identification. The rules governing these aspects of police investigation and conduct are Codes C and D, which are intended to ensure that the integrity and fairness of the process is maintained, while at the same time allowing the police to go about their business of catching criminals. We all know that the police aren't perfect, but neither are some of the people they have to interview. These rules help keep the authorities on the right side of the line, without unnecessarily tying their hands.

(i) Interview

The relevant part of the Code is C.11. In brief, note the following, which are mostly a matter of common sense really:

(a) The suspect must be *fit* to be interviewed. If, for example, he is ill or drunk, it may not be appropriate to conduct an interview; indeed an interview could in some cases be actively harmful.[22]

(b) The suspect must be interviewed under *caution*. If there has been a significant break in the interview, the suspect should be reminded of the words/import of the caution.

21 Unless the Terrorism Act 2000 applies.

22 See especially Code C, Annex G ('Fitness to be Interviewed')

(c) Anything of substance which might have been said by the suspect before interview (for example, a nervous chat in the police car on the way to the station) - or indeed any significant silences - should be addressed as soon as the interview is underway. In effect the interviewer should ask the suspect whether he confirms or denies the earlier statement or silence and/or wants to add anything.[23]

(d) The interview should *normally* be carried out at the *police station* (unless waiting until the police get the suspect there would likely lead to harm to others, destruction of evidence and so forth).

(e) Interviews need to be carried out in properly lit and ventilated rooms, and the suspect given adequate bathroom and refreshment breaks and so on.

(f) Interviews should normally be contemporaneously recorded. If the suspected offence is indictable, the interview should normally be an audio recording (if not audio-visual).[24]

(g) For obvious reasons, vulnerable suspects (for example, the very young, mentally ill people, or adults with learning difficulties) require special care.

Finally, one vexed issue can be when an interview should *cease*. Once it has been ascertained that there is (or is not) sufficient evidence to charge the suspect, the risk is that further questioning may only serve an improper function (for example, to 'break down' the suspect to get a confession). Sometimes, however, it is hard to know where the line is drawn between a continuing investigation and improper questioning. Getting the suspect's version of events is obviously an important part of the process of deciding whether there is enough evidence to charge. The Code makes clear that this not only includes allowing the suspect to give any innocent explanation, but also

23 Code C para 11.4 and note 11A

24 Recording protocol is contained in Codes E (audio) and F (audio-visual). And see generally interviewing suspects BCrP D 1.81ff

any relevant follow-up questioning in order 'to test' that the 'explanation is accurate and reliable, eg to clear up any ambiguities or clarify what the suspect said'.[25] The important point is that when the police know (reviewing all the evidence in the case) that they have enough to charge, the interview must cease.

(ii) Identification

If a suspect has been identified as the perpetrator of a crime, then this can be very strong evidence against him. But when and how a suspect has been identified are important considerations in deciding how probative such evidence actually is. An essential part of this equation is whether, and in what circumstances, a previous identification was carried out during the police investigation. Generally if a witness has not previously identified the accused before testifying, the court will be unimpressed when that witness points at the prisoner in the dock and 'fingers' him for the first time. It is too easy in such cases for witnesses to identify a defendant not because of what they saw him do, but because of where he is then sitting.

The rules relating to the reception of identification evidence at trial come from the common law. These are discussed in Chapter 24. The police procedure relating to identification of suspects, including the holding of 'parades' and so forth, is contained in Code D. In brief, note the following.

(a) If there is any possibility that the perpetrator's identity will be *contested* at any future trial, then the police ought to give the suspect the opportunity of an 'identification procedure' at which witnesses can try and pick him out. In the absence of such a procedure, the witness's identification evidence could be ruled inadmissible under PACE 1984, s 78.

25 Code C, para 11.6

(b) A distinction is made between eye-witnesses who know or recognise suspects (for example, the victim of a known assailant) and those who do not (for example, a bystander to an altercation), and are later asked if they can recognise the perpetrator. Identification is much more apt to be controversial in the second situation than in the first.

(c) Before any ID procedure is carried out, a written record of the description of the suspect first given by the witness ought to be made.[26] This is just common sense: to see if the suspect in fact looks anything like the person the witness says he saw. It is especially important if the police show the witness a photo array.[27] This record should be made available to the suspect and/or his solicitor as soon as practicable (so they can note any discrepancies between the description and the suspect's actual appearance).

(d) If a witness has identified (or purported to, or may be able to identify) the accused as the perpetrator and the identification is disputed, then an appropriate identification procedure *must* be held (by an officer of the rank of superintendent or above, not otherwise involved with the investigation), *unless* it is *not practicable* to do so (where, for example, the appearance of the suspect or, in the case of a voice identification, his accent, is very unusual) or it *would serve no useful purpose* (for example when the suspect is well known to the identifying eye-witness).[28]

(e) Where the suspect is 'known' to police and 'available', there is a choice of identification procedures, namely[29]

- Identification parade (when the witness sees the suspect lined up with others who resemble him). This used to be the procedure of choice, assuming the suspect was willing to take part. The preferred procedure is now a video identification.

---

26 Code D, para 3.1

27 Only one witness at a time should be shown photos: see *ibid*, Annex E

28 *Ibid*, para 3.12

29 *Ibid*, para 3.4

- Video identification is a sort of 'movie' version of the ID parade, where the witness is shown moving images of a known suspect as well as others who resemble him. This might be the only possibility if the (known) suspect is *un*available.[30]
- Group identification (when the witness sees the suspect in an informal group). In *R v Jamel*, for example, a group identification was arranged on the basis that a parade was impracticable. The suspect was of mixed-race and the procedure took place in the street where it was expected a wide variety of people from various races would be found.[31]

A fourth possibility is confrontation of the suspect by the witness, but this is a method of last resort. It is not really much better than a 'dock identification', but defendants have been known to insist on it, in the hopes (often misguided) of getting a blank look back from the witness.

(f) Where the suspect's identity is *not* known to the police the witness may be taken to a particular neighbourhood or place to see whether an identification can be made. This process (because it happens pre-arrest and not in the police station) has its own safeguards built into it (like not pointing at a known offender and saying: *"Is that the one?"*!).[32]

C. RIGHTS OF SUSPECT UNDER ARREST

A suspect under arrest has important rights while at the police station. These include:

(i) The right to have someone informed

A suspect has the right (as you might expect) to have a friend, relative or other such person told, as soon as practicable, of his arrest.[33] The suspect may be allowed to

30 See generally discussion of possibilities in BCrP D 1.127ff

31 [1993] Crim LR 52. The accused was identified, but as it happened no-one else of mixed race appeared. The procedure was not faulted on appeal, but the situation might well have been different had the accused been paraded around in an overwhelmingly white neighbourhood.

32 Code D, para 3.2

33 PACE 1984, s 56(1)

make a phone call or be given writing materials for the purpose. If there are legitimate concerns that informing the person the suspect has chosen may undermine the investigation or cause harm to others and so on, then the police may delay this.

(ii) Vulnerable suspects

Suspects who are either under 18 or mentally disabled (or otherwise vulnerable), are entitled to the assistance of an 'appropriate adult'. Usually no interview should take place in the absence of such a person.[34]

(iii) The right to see a solicitor

This is a crucial right. If the police delay the suspect access to a solicitor, they better have a good reason! Thus, by virtue of PACE 1984 itself, a person who has been arrested and is being held in custody is entitled, upon request, to consult privately with a solicitor at any time. The suspect must be informed of this right, and if he declines legal advice, he should be asked why (and the reason recorded). The Codes go on to make clear that:

(a) police should not say anything to try and 'dissuade' the suspect from exercising this right.
(b) A detained suspect has the right to have a solicitor present during interview.
(c) The right to legal advice must never be denied, and may only be delayed (for up to 36 hours) if:
    - The suspect has been arrested (but not yet charged) with an indictable offence, and an officer of not less than the rank of superintendent authorises the delay because he has *reasonable grounds* for believing that the exercise of the right to legal advice at that

34 See BCrP D 1.63ff

time will lead to interference with evidence or cause harm to others or alert others implicated in the crime that the police are on to them or hinder the recovery of property, *or*

- awaiting the arrival of the named solicitor would cause undue delay, *or*
- the suspect changes his mind about wanting legal advice or his choice of lawyer, *or*
- the solicitor of the suspect's choice is not available and he declines the assistance of the duty solicitor.[35]

So, if legal advice has been requested, then an interview must await the arrival of the solicitor (or the legal advice). If a suspect decides half-way through an interview that he wants legal advice or a solicitor present, there should be a break to await the arrival of the solicitor or taking of legal advice. This is just common sense. The only exceptions are those circumstances set out above.

The solicitor's role at the police station is an important one: to 'protect and advance the legal rights of their client'.[36] If access is *delayed*, the suspect must be told why, and the reason should be entered in the custody record. Wrongful *denial* of access to legal advice may well render otherwise admissible evidence (for example a confession) inadmissible.[37]

Access to legal advice is fundamental to fairness and is taken very seriously by the courts. Concerns in the profession have been expressed both about how well (and how often) legal help is getting to suspects in the police station, both because of the marginalisation of legal advisors from the pre-charge process, and the extent to which the police act as 'gatekeepers' of police station legal advice.[38] The latest threat to this basic right comes not from the police or the courts, but from politicians. Unless the suspect is a privately paying client, continued constraints on legal aid

35 See s 58 PACE 1984 and Code C, para 6.6

36 See full text of Code C, Pt 6 and note 6 D

37 See Ch. 21

38 See Report of Legal Services Research Centre, summarised in *Counsel Magazine*, June 2013, p. 31. Assistance at the police station is provided under The Police Station Advice and Assistance Scheme.

may mean less choice both about who gives them advice, and by what means. At the police station, free advice is available, but a suspect may well find that it comes from down the end of a telephone. The Defence Solicitors Call Centre[39] will decide whether a solicitor needs to make a 'station call' - rather like NHS 111, except the individual concerned can't be told to go to casualty!

3. CHARGE

There was a time when it was the police who generally decided whether to charge a suspect. Then there was a period when the primary responsibility for this went to the Crown Prosecution Service (CPS). Now[40] the job is more or less divided between them so that:

- For less serious offences (for example, summary only, low level criminal damage, shoplifting, and either-way offences suitable for being dealt with by the magistrates), the police decide whether to charge.
- In respect of other (more serious) offences, the decision is made by the Director of Public Prosecutions (DPP), via the CPS (or other prosecutor, where relevant).

In either case, the test is basically the same, namely:

- Is there *sufficient* evidence to provide a *realistic prospect* of conviction (sometimes called the 'evidential sufficiency' rule) *and*
- If so, is it in the *public interest* to charge the suspect, or can the matter be dealt with some other way? For example, some family members who 'help' their loved ones to die (by getting them to a country where

39 See Ch. 12

40 See BCrP D 2.7

assisted suicide is legal, and so on) may avoid prosecution on this basis (depending on the circumstances).

ALTERNATIVES TO CHARGE

It is as well to remember that there are alternatives to charging a suspect, as Charles Saatchi publicly learned.[41] I imagine we all know about Fixed Penalty Notices, and of course an informal warning is always possible, but for adults the main alternatives to prosecution are a *simple caution* and a *conditional caution*.

A simple caution is not a conviction, but it is more than a telling-off. It can be referred to in criminal proceedings and might well be revealed in future criminal record checks. The idea is to offer a proportionate (and cost-effective) response to low-level and/or one-off and/or first time offending. Where appropriate, a simple caution can only be given where there is sufficient evidence to justify a prosecution (it being an alternative to prosecution); the offender admits his guilt; and the offender agrees to the caution, knowing that it could be referred to in court in the event of a future conviction.[42]

A conditional caution is a 'caution plus', in other words a caution which has conditions attached to it with which the offender must comply. Typically such conditions would be an apology to the victim or participating in some act of restorative justice or compensation.[43]

4. NEXT STOP, THE MAGISTRATES' COURT

Once a suspect has been charged, the matter will be put before the court. No matter how serious the charge, *the first stop is always the magistrates' court.*

41 After being caught on camera not having a quiet word with his wife, Nigella Lawson: bbc.co.uk/news/uk-22947383

42 If convicted of a very different offence, the fact of a caution on some other matter would rarely be very relevant. The simple caution scheme was updated in 2015. See the very readable guidance, *Simple Cautions for Adult Offenders* (2015) which is available on the gov.uk website.

43 The conditional caution was introduced by the CJA 2003. There is a special, non-statutory scheme for possession of cannabis. For more detail of the caution schemes see BCrP D 2.24ff.

One decision remains to be made by the custody officer, and that is whether the accused should be brought to court from custody or released to attend on bail, and abide by any other conditions imposed. With some restrictions,[44] the police have the same power to grant bail as the courts. These are discussed in detail in the next chapter.

revision tips

- Distinguish the 'steps' of arrest and charge procedure: a mere suspect may become an arrested suspect, who may become an accused charged with a criminal offence. In particular, do not confuse the arrest stage with a later decision to prosecute or charge the individual (or not).
- 'Reasonable grounds' is an important concept - remember it!
- Know the detention timetable. Time usually starts to run when the arrested person first arrives at the police station or (if earlier) 24 hours after arrest ('the relevant time').

It is worth reading ...

Dip your toe into the Codes of Conduct under discussion in this chapter.

The judgment of Waller LJ in *R v James (Albert George)* [2004] EWCA Crim 1433. A man, a dog and a sawn-off shotgun. This is a murder conviction which came back for reconsideration many years later. It provides a useful history lesson, and confirms the importance of PACE 1984 in protecting a suspect's rights, especially the right to legal advice. Don't worry if you do not understand all the procedural references at this point - come back to the judgment when you have got to the end of the book, when you will get even more out of it.

Charles v CPS [2009] EWHC (Admin) - a short judgment on the rationale for and importance of administering the (correct!) caution to suspects. See especially para 10, particularly if you watch a lot of TV.

44 For example, the courts can, but the police cannot make it a condition of bail that the accused reside in a bail hostel. See generally BCrP D 2.45

CHAPTER 3

To bail or not to bail
(that is the question)

1. ADJOURNMENTS AND REMANDS

Aside from very simple matters like TV licence or uncontested road traffic prosecutions, criminal cases rarely start and finish in one sitting. Therefore, at any stage before a case is sent to the Crown Court for trial, or at any time before or during a summary trial, a magistrates' court may need to adjourn proceedings. As you might expect, the discretion to adjourn should be exercised judiciously. Defendants may need legal representation, evidence may need to be gathered or mistakes may need to be rectified. Cases should proceed expeditiously, and without unnecessary delay, but if a break is needed in order for justice to be done, then as a matter of common sense an adjournment should be granted.[1]

In most situations, when a criminal court adjourns a case, it will usually fix the next hearing and then decide whether the accused should spend the intervening time in custody or out on bail.[2] This is known as *remanding* the defendant. Although magistrates have some discretion simply to adjourn a case, they are always entitled, and in the more serious cases are required, to remand the defendant when they do so.[3]

A remand thus occurs when the court adjourns a case and either bails the

1 See, *DPP v Petrie* [2015] EWHC 48 (Admin), and BCrP D 5.27

2 A person released on bail will be free to leave but obliged to come back! The granting of bail in criminal cases is governed by the Bail Act 1976 (BA 1976).

3 See BCrP D 5.30 and Magistrates' Courts Act 1980 (MCA 1980), s 5,10,18. In practice, magistrates would only adjourn without remanding in the most trivial of cases or where the defendant is a business (as in food health prosecutions).

accused or commits him to custody for the period of the adjournment[4] - 'adjournment plus' as it were. Remember too that there are important differences between a simple adjournment and a remand on bail, even though the accused may walk out the same door in either case. First, when a case is simply adjourned, there is no requirement to set the date for the next hearing (although it often will be fixed). If there is a remand, the date to which the accused is remanded *must* be fixed. Secondly, a defendant who is not remanded on bail and fails to appear when the matter resumes in court suffers no consequence except that the case could very well continue in his absence (or a warrant be issued for his arrest). By contrast, an accused who has been bailed is under a *duty* to appear at the appointed day, time and place and *commits an offence* if he fails to do so without reasonable cause.[5]

A. REMAND ON BAIL

A decision about whether or not to grant bail to the accused (or to renew his bail) can arise at almost any stage of proceedings, from the detention and charge procedure at the police station[6] to the appellate courts - and many points in between. Typical junctures are during adjournments prior to the magistrates trying a case or sending it to the Crown Court for trial; upon sending cases to the Crown Court for trial or sentence; while awaiting pre-sentencing reports and in the Crown Court either in its appellate or trial capacities. In effect, whenever there needs to be a break or 'time out' in the process or proceedings, the question of bail can arise.[7] The longer the break, the more important the decision becomes for the accused.

It is important to have a firm grasp of the principles surrounding bail, not only for your examinations (or pupillage interviews!), but because a bail application may well be one of the first assignments of the fledgling criminal advocate. It is important to know what you are doing.

4 MCA 1980, s 128(1)

5 BA 1976, s 6. And see below.

6 See Ch. 2

7 But see below as to the limit on the number of bail applications which may be made. The occasions when bail may be granted (and by which courts) are usefully set out in Sprack, *Practical Approach*, 7.09

B. GENERAL 'RIGHT TO BAIL'

The first thing to remember is that, *subject* to the considerations set out below, and special rules for especially serious offences, s 4 of the Bail Act 1976 gives to an accused adult appearing in front of a magistrates' or the Crown court, a so-called 'right' to bail. More accurately, it creates a *rebuttable presumption in favour of bail*, so that it is for the prosecution to show good reason why bail should be withheld (or withdrawn) and not for the defence to show why it should be granted (or renewed).[8] This makes sense, since as a matter of general principle it is not usually appropriate to imprison someone who has not yet been convicted of any offence. Following conviction, this presumption persists only if the defendant's case is adjourned for reports prior to sentencing.[9] Otherwise, once convicted, bail may still be granted, but the presumption in favour of this outcome, logically enough, disappears. At that stage, any interest the defendant may have had in returning to court to face the music may well have dissipated somewhat.

The situation is different, however, where a defendant is accused, in effect, of being a dangerous recidivist. Here, the need to protect the public provides an effective counterweight to an unconvicted person's right to liberty. In these cases there is something approaching a presumption *against* bail.[10] Thus, a defendant charged with one of the most serious offences against the person (for example, murder, manslaughter, rape[11]), who has previously been convicted of such an offence (or culpable homicide), will only be granted bail if there are 'exceptional circumstances which justify it'.[12] The European Court of Human Rights recently declared this approach to be compatible with Art 5 of the European Convention on Human Rights (the right to liberty), confirming that where someone had been convicted of such a serious offence and was now charged with a similar offence, this was good reason to require exceptional circumstances before granting bail.[13]

8 So far as bail at the police station is concerned, s 38(1) of PACE 1984 gives the accused something very like s 4's 'right' to bail. See Ch. 2

9 See Ch. 10 for (adult) sentencing.

10 Casting no more than an evidential burden on an accused: *R(O) v Harrow Crown Court* [2007] 1 AC 247. As to presumptions generally, see Ch.15.

11 See Criminal Justice and Public Order Act 1994 (CJPOA 1994), s 25(2) for a complete list.

12 *Ibid*. If the previous conviction was manslaughter or culpable homicide, this provision only applies if the circumstances of its commission were serious enough to justify a sentence of imprisonment or long-term detention.

13 *O'Dowd v United Kingdom* [2011] Crim LR 148

Furthermore, those accused of murder merit an additional element of caution. Only a Crown Court Judge may grant bail to a person charged with murder,[14] and bail *may not* be granted to such a defendant *unless* the court thinks there is 'no significant risk' that while on bail the accused will commit an offence likely to cause injury (physical or mental) to another person.[15] Not every alleged murderer will be denied bail on this basis, of course - but most will.[16]

2. BAIL ACT 1973, SCHEDULE I, PT I: REASONS FOR REFUSING BAIL

Pt I of Sch I of the Bail Act 1976 sets out various situations when the court may refuse bail, because any presumption in favour of bail has effectively been rebutted. Some are purely practical provisions and others reflect the potential dangers of releasing some suspects. Because one such obvious risk, that of absconding, is greatest when the accused is facing a custodial sentence, the focus is explicitly on defendants charged with (or facing sentencing for) at least one *imprisonable* offence.[17] In addition, recent amendments by the Legal Aid, Sentencing and Punishment of Offenders Act 2012 (LASPO Act 2012) make clear that, where sentence is relevant to the reason for refusing bail, there must be a 'real prospect' that the defendant will *in fact* receive a prison term if convicted of the offence to which the bail application relates.[18]

A. THE 'BIG THREE' REASONS FOR REFUSING BAIL

Assuming then that there is a real prospect of the defendant receiving a custodial sentence, the first set of circumstances listed in Schedule I enumerates the three

14 Coroners and Justice Act 2009, s 115(1)

15 BA 1976, s 6ZA (as inserted by the Coroners and Justice Act 2009, s 114(2)

16 This additional element of caution may have been prompted by the case of Gary Weddell, a policeman who was charged with his wife's murder. While on bail pending trial, he killed his mother-in-law: telegraph.co.uk/news/uknews/1575553/Policeman-bailed-for-murder-kills-mother-in-law.html

17 Parts I (indictable offences) and IA (summary offences) of Schedule I, BA 1976. Part II applies to non-imprisonable offences, but it is very rare for a court to refuse bail in such cases.

18 S 90 and Sch 11 LASPO 2012 and BCrP D 7.15

main risks of releasing an accused on bail and so are most often relied upon by prosecutors. You might think of them as the 'Big 3'. Thus bail *may*, but need not be granted if the court is satisfied that there are *substantial grounds* for believing that the defendant, if released on bail (whether subject to conditions or not) would:

(i) fail to *surrender* to custody *or*
(ii) *commit* an offence while on bail *or*
(iii) *interfere* with witnesses or otherwise *obstruct* the course of justice whether in relation to himself or some other person.[19]

Note the choice of wording. The court's 'belief' is directed to the *grounds* which give rise to the risk of absconding and so forth, not to the likelihood, as such, of the event itself happening. There is no burden of proof and the inquiry is informal and essentially speculative, although the court's decision must not be based on irrational or flimsy grounds.[20] There must be some evidence to justify the refusal of bail.

B. PREVIOUS BAD BEHAVIOUR WHILE ON BAIL

In addition, there are other circumstances where bail may be refused. Two of these are also covered by the LASPO Act 2012 amendment, and so require a real prospect that the defendant will receive a custodial sentence. So, assuming this to be the case, the court *may*, but need not grant bail if (i) the accused has already absconded once in the proceedings,[21] or (ii) he is alleged to have committed the offence with which he is now charged (being indictable) whilst on bail - neither of which situation, of course, would bode particularly well for his good behaviour out on the streets. Furthermore, if, in either case, the offence for which bail is being

19 BA 1976, Sch 1, Pt 1, para 2 (my emphasis)

20 *Mansfield Justices ex parte Sharkey* [1985] QB 613. See BCrP D 7.13

21 Strictly, the accused must have been arrested for absconding in the proceedings: BA 1976, Sch 1, Pt 1, para 6

considered is so serious as to carry a maximum punishment of life imprisonment (for example, rape or robbery), then, if the accused is over 18, bail may not be granted unless there is 'no significant risk' of his re-offending or absconding (as the case may be). If he is under 18, then the court will 'give due weight' to his previous behaviour when deciding about bail.[22] Clearly, if it appears that an accused has already misbehaved once whilst on bail, and the offence with which he is now charged is so serious that a significant prison sentence is on the cards, then it would rarely be appropriate to grant bail.

C. DOMESTIC VIOLENCE RISK

Finally, an additional basis for refusing bail added by LASPO Act 2012 is geared to offences of domestic violence. Thus, an accused need not be granted bail if the court is satisfied that there are substantial grounds for believing that while on bail he would injure or threaten a member of his family or some other person with whom he is closely associated domestically.[23]

D. RELEVANT CONSIDERATIONS WHEN ASSESSING RISK

To assist the court, para 9 of Sch 1 gives guidance on how to assess the sorts of risks described above. It says the court should have regard to common sense considerations, as relevant, such as:

(i) the nature and seriousness of the offence (the more serious the offence, the more likely that a conviction will result in a lengthy prison sentence)

(ii) the character and antecedents[24] of the defendant (previous convictions can increase the term of imprisonment; hardened criminals may be less likely to return to court than the upstanding citizen)

---

22 This latter requirement was introduced by the Criminal Justice Act 2003 (CJA 2003), s 14 and 15

23 So-called 'associated persons' as defined in the Family Law Act 1996.

24 These are relevant to sentence. See Ch. 10

(iii) the associations and community ties of the defendant (someone lacking local roots or a reason to stay in one place may be more apt to 'jump' bail)

(iv) the defendant's past record for answering bail (even if a defendant has a criminal record, a history of always answering bail can be very useful to him in this context)

(v) the defendant's past record for committing offences on bail

(vi) the strength of the prosecution case (the weaker the evidence, the stronger the argument for bail) … and so on.

E. OTHER PRACTICAL REASONS FOR REFUSING BAIL

Other purely *practical* reasons for refusing bail are also set out in Schedule 1.[25] Most of them speak for themselves. Thus bail *may*, but need not be granted if:

(i) the court is satisfied that the defendant should be kept in custody for his own protection (the infamous case of the killers of Jamie Bulger comes to mind) or welfare (if a juvenile - a homeless teen perhaps); *or*

(ii) the defendant is already in custody for another crime (in which case there is not much point in bail); *or*

(iii) the court needs more time to make a proper decision on bail (it may be the defendant's first appearance and he may not have legal representation); *or*

(iv) the case is adjourned for reports and it is not practicable to complete this unless the defendant is in custody, *or*

(v) the accused has tested positive for the presence of a Class A drug in his body, the offence for which bail is sought involves or is connected with Class A drugs, and the accused (being an adult) refuses to commence

25 BA 1976, Sch 1, Pt 1, paras 3-5, 6A and 7

or continue with a drug programme geared to countering drug misuse and dependency.

For obvious reasons, the sentence which the accused might receive is irrelevant to these particular reasons for refusing bail, because they are not essentially geared to the risk of absconding, and so on.

3. BAIL CONDITIONS

Bail may be granted unconditionally, which means there are 'no strings attached' except for the overarching obligation to surrender to custody at the appointed date, time and place. Sometimes, however, the court requires additional conditions. Not surprisingly, this is known as granting 'conditional bail'.[26]

Conditions are often the quid pro quo to the defendant getting bail at all, and so it is important to know the sorts of requirements which are commonly attached to the grant of bail, and the purpose they serve. It is no good suggesting a condition which does not address the concerns of the prosecution or the court. Essentially, conditions are either financial or behavioural in nature.

A. FINANCIAL CONDITIONS

The most common financial condition is the provision of one or more *sureties*. A 'surety' is the term used for a person who promises to pay the court a sum of money if the defendant fails to surrender to custody as required. The undertaking into which a surety enters is called a 'recognizance', and can be given in court or, in certain circumstances, outside, for example, at the police station after an accused has been

26 BA 1976, s 3. Like s 2, there are so many amendments to this section of the Bail Act that attempting to read it is rather like wading through alphabet soup. Better initially to get the detail from BCrP or other secondary sources.

charged.[27] If the defendant 'skips' bail, the surety may be ordered to pay some or all of the amount in which he stood surety.[28] This is known as 'forfeiting' (or 'estreating') the recognizance. The sum required to be paid in that case is treated like a fine, and so the implications of a surety's failure to pay up can be very serious indeed.[29]

Therefore, it is vital that no-one should be put forward (by defence counsel, for example) as a surety who does not clearly understand the implications of, accept responsibility for and have the means to meet the obligation if necessary. The whole point of this kind of condition is that the surety will be both motivated and capable of doing all he or she can to ensure that the accused surrenders to custody, so it is important that the surety has some influence over (and ideally some means of monitoring) the accused's behaviour. Knowledge that the surety would be disappointed (to say the least) were the defendant to abscond should, so far as possible, act as a deterrent to his doing so.[30]

A defendant must remain in custody until any sureties required by a court have 'entered into their recognizances', and so it is useful if such people are standing by if this is a condition which is either to be advocated or anticipated. Note too that a surety for an adult[31] has only the *one* obligation - to ensure that the accused does not abscond - and is not responsible for seeing to it that the accused complies with any other conditions of bail (for example, not to commit further offences on bail). Examiners like to test this last point.

A surety is not required to pay over any money unless and until the accused fails to answer his bail. Contrast this situation to that where, as a condition of the grant of bail, the *accused himself* is required to give security for his surrender into custody. This means that a defendant (who cannot be his own surety[32]) deposits money or other valuables into court, which will be forfeit if he absconds. In other words, an accused who gives security parts with the money up front and, to motivate

27 BA 1976, s 8(4)

28 As those who stood surety for Wikepedia's Julian Assange found to their considerable cost (£140,000): bbc.co.uk/news/world-19868355. Instead of attending an extradition hearing, he fled the jurisdiction (courtesy of the Ecuadorian Embassy).

29 This could include imprisonment

30 It is standard practice for police to check whether a surety has previous convictions. See BCrP D 7.56/57

31 A person agreeing to be a surety for a juvenile may well be expected to act 'parentally' and ensure the minor's good behaviour. See BCrP D 7.55

32 BA 1976, s.3(2)

his reappearance, only gets it back when he does so. A third party can assist a defendant to give security (by providing the money),[33] but the obligation remains personal to the accused.

B. BEHAVIOURAL CONDITIONS

Instead of, or in addition to a financial condition as described above, the court can also require the defendant to comply with any number of other conditions 'as appear necessary' to ensure that he does not abscond, commit offences on bail and so on, or for his own protection.[34] Such conditions focus on the defendant's behaviour and typically include things like requiring him to report to the police at designated intervals, surrender his passport, reside at a certain address, and can extend to more intrusive requirements like keeping a curfew and/or wearing electronic tags or (with consent) attending a drug rehabilitation programme. More negative conditions can include orders not to contact potential witnesses (for example, for the prosecution) or to keep away from specified people or places (for example, the home of the victim).

When deciding whether or not to impose these sorts of conditions, the court must perceive a real (as opposed to a fanciful) risk that the requirement is necessary to prevent some objectionable behaviour (further offences being committed and so on). However, it need not have the 'substantial grounds' for its belief which it has to have in order to refuse bail altogether for the same sorts of reasons.[35]

4. BAIL APPLICATIONS

Most bail applications are made at the magistrates' courts, although if made in the Crown Court the procedure is essentially the same. The court will usually ask

33 As also happened in the Julian Assange case (see fn 28). Jemima Khan was among those who deposited money as bail security: guardian.co.uk/media/2012/sep/04/julian-assange-backers-lose-bail. Thus it is possible to have a combination of both forms of financial guarantee.

34 BA 1976, s 3(6). A convicted defendant remanded on bail pending reports prior to sentencing must be required to make himself available for relevant medical examinations. *Ibid* and s 30(2) MCA 1980

35 *Ex parte Sharkey*, op. cit. and see BCrP D 7.47

the defence whether there is an application for bail and (if so) ask the prosecutor whether there are any objections. Sometimes the court's decision will be a forgone conclusion, so that if bail is unopposed, a court is unlikely to withhold it; and if no application for bail is made, a court is unlikely to think it appropriate to grant it (although it helps if the objection is stated for the record).

Assuming, however, that there is an opposed bail application, then what happens is essentially as follows. The prosecution first briefly outlines its case and puts forward its objections to bail. In early applications, these will usually be based on information from the police, which is typically given by way of a completed CPS form.[36] It must be made clear which exception to the general right to bail is being relied upon, and which factors (for example, previous convictions, no fixed abode) are considered relevant. The defence then answers the prosecutor's objections as best it can - either by arguing that the objections raised are themselves insufficient or unfounded (for example that previous convictions were the result of immaturity, the defendant has family in the area) and/or by arguing that the objections can be met by appropriate conditions (for example the accused could be required to live with his grandmother).[37] If sureties are to be suggested to the court, ideally they should be on hand and it may be helpful to call them into the witness box so that the court can judge the quality of the person willing to act in this capacity.

It is important, as a defence representative making the bail application, that you meet the opposing arguments head-on and realistically. It is no good pretending that legitimate objections do not exist. But neither should it be a cursory exercise - you must do all you can to argue the case for bail as effectively as possible. It can be useful to think creatively about conditions which will meet prosecution fears in the particular situation (and not limit yourself necessarily to off-the-peg solutions), and it is vital that you get the defendant's consent to any condition before you propose it. It

36 CrimPR, r 14.5(1)-(3)

37 It is thus the defence which usually suggest conditions. If the prosecutor does so, he should be specific about what condition is proposed and what purpose it would serve: CrimPR r 14.5(4)

is no good if he is not willing or able to abide by the condition.

The prosecutor will not normally reply to defence submissions, but can do so, for example, to correct any errors or misconceptions. Having heard arguments for and against bail, the court will then make a decision. There are essentially three choices: unconditional bail, conditional bail and no bail (that is, remand in custody). Whenever the court refuses bail to an accused with a 'right' to bail, reasons must be given.[38]

A. LIMITS ON THE NUMBER OF BAIL APPLICATIONS

It is important to make the most of any bail application, because there are *strict limits* on how many applications can be made based on the *same* information or facts. However tempting it may be to rehearse and repeat an application for bail at every remand, hoping for a better result each time, it becomes a pointless exercise when there is nothing new to say. For this reason (if there is nothing new to say) an accused is allowed only *two fully argued* bail applications, one (typically) on his first appearance before the court and (assuming he was remanded in custody on that occasion) the second at the next hearing, when a fully instructed legal representative can effectively marshal all sensible arguments to meet, so far as possible, any prosecution objections.[39]

After those two attempts have been exhausted, any further submission is at the court's discretion *unless* the defence can point to some fresh argument (whether factual or legal)[40] that has not previously been aired. The new fact or fresh argument does not need to be major, but it should be some 'new consideration' which might (not necessarily will) make a difference.[41] Once the accused has used up his two argued applications (and there is nothing else to add), further remand hearings can become a meaningless exercise in foregone conclusions. For this reason, successive remands in custody can sometimes take place in the absence of the defendant, as discussed later.

38 This is also the case if the court grants bail in those cases where the impetus is against bail (for example murder cases). See Sprack, *Practical Approach*, 7.45 for a run down of the requirements for recording and giving reasons for bail decisions.

39 The route to this result is a little tortuous, but the case law is now reflected in Part IIA, paras 2 & 3 of Sch 1 BA 1976 (inserted by CJA 1988, s 154). The court must consider at each remand point whether the accused should remain in custody or be given bail, and a defendant has a right to support an application with any argument of fact or law, 'even if it has been advanced previously'. But the court 'need not' hear argument 'which it has heard previously'. Interpreted generously, this translates into only two fully

B. CHALLENGING THE BAIL DECISIONS OF THE MAGISTRATES' COURT

Both prosecution and defence may challenge bail decisions, depending on the circumstances. To summarise:

(i) Concerns about conditions (or lack of them)

Where a court has granted unconditional bail, the *prosecution* may apply to it for conditions to be imposed.[42] Where a court has granted conditional bail, *either prosecution or defence* may apply for a variation in (or removal of) the conditions. Cases sent to the Crown Court can be dealt with there.[43]

(ii) Reviews or appeals by prosecution

Where the court has granted bail in respect of an indictable offence, the prosecution may apply for a *reconsideration* of that bail decision if new information later becomes available which casts new light on the correctness of that decision.[44]

The prosecution also has a right to *appeal* a magistrates' decision to grant bail in limited cases, that is, where the offence is imprisonable and the prosecution was conducted by the CPS (or equivalent). The prosecution must (logically enough) have made representations against bail before it was granted - otherwise they may have no-one to blame but themselves! Oral notice of appeal should be given to the magistrates at the end of the hearing when bail was granted (and before the defendant gets out the door!), followed up immediately (within two hours) by written confirmation. Such an appeal, which should really only be brought if bail poses a serious risk of harm,[45] is made to the Crown Court[46] and takes the form of a rehearing, which should be held within 48 hours.[47] *The point is that the matter should be resolved very quickly.*

---

argued applications as of right. Courts must issue certificates confirming if/when full argument was heard: BCrP D 7.78

40 Sometimes referred to, rather loosely, as a 'change in circumstance'. See generally BCrP D 7.70ff

41 See, e.g., *R(b) v Brent Youth Court* [2010] EWHC 1893 (Admin)

42 BA 1976, s 3(8)

43 *Ibid*

44 BA 1976, s 5B

45 The prosecution right of appeal should only be used in cases of 'grave concern': *see* BCrP D 7.95

46 Unless the case is an extradition case (or the appeal is from a Crown Court decision to grant bail): CrimPR, r 14.9(1)(b)

47 Not counting weekends or holidays: *ibid*, r 14.9(8)

Do not confuse this right of appeal (which arises immediately following the decision in relevant cases) with the review procedure described above. The power to review will be triggered some time *after* the decision to grant bail. Moreover, the defendant will typically be at large while a review is conducted, whereas he is kept in custody pending an appeal.[48]

(iii) Defendant's appeals to the Crown Court

A defendant refused bail by magistrates following a fully argued bail application is usually[49] able to make a further application to the Crown Court - even if he has not yet exhausted his quota of applications in the lower court.[50] In most cases the magistrates will have issued a certificate stating that they refused bail following full argument and giving reasons for the decision.[51] At least 24 hours before the application, written notice should be served on the prosecutor, who will either oppose the application (in person or on paper) or not.[52] The Crown Court hearing will usually be conducted in chambers, in essentially the same way as in the magistrates' court. The defendant has no right to be produced from prison, but may appear by video link.

(iv) Judicial review

Bail decisions may be judicially reviewed in the High Court (typically after bail has been refused by both magistrates and Crown Court), but such applications are rare, and rarely successful. The decision would have to be perverse or wrong in law for it to be quashed.[53]

48 CrimPR, r 14.9(3). But the accused should be present at the appeal hearing if he wishes. See *Allen v United Kingdom* [2011] Crim LR 147 and BCrP D 7.94

49 Senior Courts Act 1981, s 81 (as amended) and BCrP D 7.81

50 In such circumstances an application to the Crown Court would be an alternative to a second application to the magistrates.

51 Unless sending the defendant to the Crown Court for trial or sentence or pending appeal.

52 CrimPR, r 14.8, and BCrP D 7.83-7.85

53 See BCrP D 7.89

5. CONSEQUENCES OF BREACHING BAIL OBLIGATIONS

An accused can fail to comply with bail in one of two ways - either by absconding or by breaching other conditions of bail.

A. ABSCONDING

The principal obligation required of a defendant released on bail is to surrender to custody at the appointed date, time and place. A failure to meet this obligation without good reason is known as 'absconding'. If a defendant does not turn up at court when required, four questions may arise for the court's consideration:

(i) Can the court proceed with the case in the defendant's absence?

Defendants are routinely warned that if they fail to attend at trial, the court may well proceed with the case in their absence. If an accused was alerted to this possibility, and no good reason for his failure to attend is given,[54] then more often than not the court will go ahead without him - even if the charge is serious.[55] But every case is different and what the court does will depend on the circumstances. For example, a defendant's presence would normally be required at a mode of trial hearing,[56] and so proceeding in his absence might not be possible. And the court should always be alert to the interests of justice. The discretion to proceed in the absence of the defendant should be 'exercised with caution and with close regard to the overall fairness of the proceedings'.[57]

(ii) How can the defendant's attendance be secured?

Depending on how seriously the court views the failure to attend, the court has three options:

54 MCA 1980, s 11(2A). There is no obligation on the court to inquire into the reasons for the defendant's absence: MCA 1980, s 11(6)

55 *R v O'Hare* [2006] EWCA Crim 471

56 See Ch. 4

57 *R v Jones* [2002] UKHL 5, at [13] per Lord Bingham, cited in *Drinkwater v Solihull Magistrates' Court* [2012] EWHC 765 (Admin)

(a) issue a warrant for the defendant's arrest (called a 'bench' warrant, since it comes from the judicial bench). The usual form of warrant simply orders the arrest of the accused and that he be brought before the court. There is a discretion to issue a warrant 'backed for bail', but this is not usually appropriate given that the warrant is being issued because the defendant has already failed to meet his bail; *or*

(b) send a warning letter to the defendant's last known address; *or*

(c) adjourn and extend bail. This is the option the court would choose if it felt there was a good excuse for non-attendance.

Guidance issued in 2006 by the Senior Presiding Judge, Thomas LJ, encourages the use of warning letters rather than warrants backed for bail (which are something of a contradiction in terms); calls for proper evidence to be submitted if a defendant claims to be too unfit to attend court (as in a medical certificate); and makes the point that if the defendant is to be re-bailed, it would be unusual (given his failure to attend) to extend bail on exactly the same conditions as before.[58]

(iii) How shall the defendant be punished for his failure to attend?

A person released on bail in criminal proceedings who fails to surrender to custody without reasonable cause, will be *guilty of an offence*.[59] This is so even if he is ultimately acquitted of the offence in respect of which he was remanded on bail. The only contentious issue is usually the reason for the defendant's absence, and it is for him to prove, on the balance of probabilities, that he had *reasonable cause* for non-attendance. The offence of absconding is entirely separate to the offence in respect of which the defendant was bailed and this should be reflected in any sentence for absconding. The magistrates should try cases of failure to attend in

58 See judiciary.gov.uk/docs/judgments_guidance/protocols/bails_trials_absence.pdf and CrimPD III 14B.2

59 s 6(1) BA 1976

their own court, although they may commit the defendant to the Crown Court to be sentenced (for example, if they feel their sentencing powers are inadequate).[60] In the Crown Court, absconding is essentially treated as criminal contempt.[61]

In addition, there will be other negative consequences for a defendant who has been found guilty of absconding. So far as the case in respect of which the absconding took place, any presumption in favour of bail may be lost.[62] Furthermore, so far as cases in the future are concerned, a defendant who has absconded once will be less likely to get bail in future, since his record in answering bail will have been blighted.

(iv) How shall a surety be dealt with if the defendant absconds?

Where bail was granted subject to sureties, and the defendant absconds, the court before which he was due to appear must order that the surety be forfeit and issue a summons to the surety requiring him to appear and show cause as to why he should not be ordered to pay up. This is all pretty much a formality since the defendant's absconding itself triggers the obligation to pay. It is unusual (but not unheard of[63]) for the surety to be relieved of his obligation to pay the whole of the amount promised.[64]

B. ANTICIPATED ABSCONDING/BREACH OF BAIL CONDITIONS

Where a person has been bailed to attend court, a police officer, by virtue of s 7 of the Bail Act 1976, may *arrest him* without warrant prior to the bail date if:

(i) the officer has reasonable grounds for believing that he is not likely to surrender to custody; *or*

(ii) the officer has reasonable grounds for believing that he has broken or is likely to break a condition of his bail; *or*

60 See procedure at CrimPD III 14C and relevant sentencing guidelines, both in BCrP supplement. Sentencing is discussed in Ch. 10

61 See *ibid* and summary in *Practical Approach* at 7.64ff

62 See above and BCrP D 7.29

63 See, e.g., *York Crown Court ex parte Coleman and How* [1987] Crim LR 761

64 For the orders made in the Assange case, see reference at fn 28

(iii) a surety has given written notice to the police that the person bailed is unlikely to surrender to custody and for that reason the surety wishes to be relieved of his obligations.[65]

If arrested under these provisions, the defendant must be brought before the court to be dealt with as soon as practicable and in any event within 24 hours.[66]

It is important to appreciate that s 7 does no more than give police a power to arrest without warrant. Unlike absconding, breach of any other bail condition *does not, of itself, constitute an offence*,[67] although once brought back before the court under these provisions, the consequences for the accused can be serious - more onerous conditions may well be imposed or bail may be withdrawn altogether.

6. REMANDS IN CUSTODY

A remand in custody is clearly a serious matter for an unconvicted defendant. It may, in the circumstances, be a justified intrusion on his liberty, but it still necessitates the oversight of the justice system. For this reason, defendants remanded in custody must be brought back before the courts regularly and have their cases adjudicated as expeditiously as possible. There are time limits governing both of these aspects of pre-conviction incarceration, known as custody time limits.

A. PERIODS OF REMAND IN CUSTODY BY THE MAGISTRATES' COURT

Subject to some important exceptions, when magistrates remand an accused in custody prior to summary trial (or sending the case to the Crown Court for trial), the period of the remand must not exceed eight clear days.[68] This need for a weekly

65 BA 1976, s 7(3)
66 See BCrP D 7.102
67 See, e.g., *R (Grangar) v Leicester Crown Court* [2008] EWCA Crim 2987
68 The defence and prosecution can agree a longer period of remand. MCA 1980, s 128(6) and BCrP D 5.31/36

appearance, however, may well be at odds with the natural pace of a case, which could take some weeks or even months before a summary trial or other pre-trial matters can take place. The result could well be that all the defendant achieves by being brought back to court each week (aside from a day out) is to be told that he will be remanded in custody for another week. Certainly, if the defence have used up their quota of bail applications,[69] and there is no other progress to be made in the case, then returning the defendant to the court so often becomes a costly exercise in futility.

In recognition of this fact, it is possible to remand in custody for up to 28 days. An accused, if he is an adult and legally represented in court, *can agree* to let the court conduct the next *three* remands in his absence.[70] The case will still be listed every week, but the remand is simply a formality. On the fourth occasion, the accused must attend court again (whether he wants to or not). The process could then be repeated.

Easier still, the magistrates can simply remand the accused in custody for a period not exceeding 28 days. This is possible if:

(a) the accused has already been remanded in custody in the case, *and*

(b) he is present in court when the extended remand is ordered, *and*

(c) the court has fixed a date when the next stage of the proceedings will take place.

In such cases, the accused's consent is *not* required[71] and the remand will last until the next hearing date or 28 days, whichever is the sooner. This nowadays is the usual method for avoiding unproductive weekly remands. It is also worth noting that in any event communicating with defendants from prison by television link is

69 See discussion above

70 s 128(1A)-(1C)/(3A) MCA 1980 (added by the CJA 1982)

71 s 128A(3) MCA 1980 (added later by the CJA 1988). A bail application could be made during this remand if it were appropriate to make it.

now increasingly common pre-trial - bringing the court to the defendant, as it were, rather than the defendant to court.[72]

Where magistrates remand an accused in custody after conviction (for example, while reports are prepared prior to sentencing), the period must not exceed three weeks at any one time.[73]

B. TOTAL PRE-TRIAL CUSTODY TIME LIMITS

Not surprisingly, there are also limits on how long *in total* an accused can be kept in custody before trial. These are set out in s 22 of the Prosecution of Offences Act 1985.[74] For example, 56 days is the maximum period between an accused's first appearance in the magistrate's court and his trial for a summary offence; 70 days is the maximum period between first appearance in the magistrates' court and sending the case to the Crown Court; 182 days is the maximum period between the date when an indictable offence is sent for trial[75] and the start of the trial. And so on. Clearly the more complex or serious the case, the longer the period. These limits are important in two respects; first, they ensure that cases proceed with some expedition, although extensions may, for good reason (and assuming the prosecution has not been dilatory up to that point) be given. Applications to extend *must* be made *before* the custody time limit has expired.[76] Secondly, once a time limit has expired (and assuming no extension was granted), the accused is given an absolute right to bail.[77]

72 An accused is treated as present in court when attending by 'live link'. See generally BCrP D 5.38

73 MCA 1980, s 10(3). The maximum is four weeks if remanded on bail: s 30(1)

74 And the Regulations made thereunder (as amended): see BCrP D 15.15

75 Under s 51 CDA 1998. See generally Ch. 4

76 See POA 1985, s 22(3) and BCrP D 15.23

77 And only post-release conditions (for example a residence condition) can be imposed. For a useful summary of time limits and discussion, see Sprack, *Practical Approach*, 7.23-25

revision tips

- Have a clear grasp of bail procedure, not only the *how* but also the *how many* (remember, only two fully argued applications are allowed without some new information).
- Distinguish between the principal obligation of bail itself (to return to court) and other conditions which may be attached (for example, to reside in a particular place). Absconding is itself a criminal offence; breach of *other* conditions only gives the police a power of arrest. Examiners like to test you on this difference.
- Distinguish between a *surety* and the *giving of security.* The *only* obligation of a surety for an adult accused is to ensure the latter's attendance at court.
- Be aware of (and distinguish between) options open to defendants and prosecutors if the decision on bail does not go their way.

It is worth reading ...

The judgment of Gage J in *R (Vickers) v West London Magistrates' Court* [2003] EWHC 1809 (admin), which makes clear the difference between s 6 of the Bail Act (which makes absconding an offence) and s 7 (which gives only a power of arrest in respect of breach, or threatened breach, of other bail conditions or *threatened* absconding). The facts are simple; the court was pretty patient, and the eventual decision to remand into custody was really a practical one in the circumstances. It is also a good little example of a judicial review, so come back to it after studying appeals. The fact that the defendant's lawyer was named Mr Fiddler is just an added bonus.

CHAPTER 4

Plea and venue procedure:
trial allocation for either-way offences

Every case starts in the magistrates' court, but not all cases stay there very long (although most do). One of the first decisions for that court is trial venue. For adults,[1] the question will be: should the case be tried summarily in the magistrates' court, or should it be sent to the Crown Court for jury trial? Sometimes the answer to this question will be obvious, but even so it is for the magistrates to ensure the case gets to the correct place.

Some destinations are pre-ordained. As discussed in Chapter 1, offences are classified as either *summary* or *indictable*. Summary offences must normally[2] be tried in the magistrates' court - this is what is meant by cases being 'tried summarily'. Summary offences are all statutory and include a vast array of minor (and not so minor) offences, from littering to assaulting a police officer in the execution of his duty.

Indictable offences sub-divide into those which *must* be tried on indictment and those which *may* be tried on indictment. As you would expect, offences which can *only* be tried on indictment (hence the expression 'indictable only') are the most serious, whatever the circumstances (for example, murder, robbery, rape). Adult defendants accused of such offences must always be sent, forthwith, to the Crown Court to be tried.[3]

---

1 For juvenile offenders, see Ch. 11

2 Sometimes summary offences accompany related indictable offences up to the Crown Court: see Ch. 5

3 Under s 51 Crime and Disorder Act 1998 (CDA 1998)

But a very large number of offences fall somewhere in the middle. They are indictable, but can be tried summarily if both the magistrates and defendant agree - and so they are known as being 'triable either way'. Certain indictable offences are put into this hybrid category either because, although serious, they are not in their nature the very worst of crimes (taking a motor vehicle without consent, for example) or because the enormity of the offence will vary depending on the circumstances of its commission (an example is theft, which can range from shoplifting a bit of extra food for hungry children, to stealing an elderly person's pension money, to city traders stealing millions of pounds).[4] *Such offences thus need a dedicated system for deciding which way, in any given case, the 'either-way' offence should go - to be tried in the magistrates' court or in the Crown Court.* This is commonly known as the 'mode of trial' (or allocation) procedure.[5] However it is described, it is important to understand how the magistrates' courts determine where an 'either-way' offence is to be tried - both procedurally and because of the possible implications for the accused, who may well play a crucial role in the decision. The essential thing to remember is that at this stage, an offence triable either way will *only* be allocated for summary trial if:

(i) the defendant indicates that he will plead not guilty (thus necessitating a trial) *and*

(ii) *both* the magistrates *and* the defendant agree to summary trial.

Assuming the need for a trial, it will be for the magistrates[6] to decide first whether they think the case is suitable for summary trial or not. If they feel the case is better suited for the Crown Court, then the magistrates will 'decline jurisdiction'. If they are willing to hear the case, however, then it will be for the defendant to decide whether or not he should exercise his right to trial by jury.[7] Juries might

4 See, e.g., useful list in Sprack, *Practical Approach*, at 8.07

5 Mode of trial is more a description of type (summary trial or trial on indictment); allocation refers more to destination (magistrates' or crown court). They really amount to the same thing.

6 Hearings to determine mode of trial may take place before one magistrate, but almost always take place before a lay bench of at least two. A different bench would try the case.

7 There is a right to trial by jury of indictable offences. If defendants are jointly charged with an either-way offence, each has an individual right to make an election as to mode of trial. It can make life a little tricky if they make different choices. See BCrP D 6.18

8 The rule thus applies to any case which may be tried

(statistically) be more apt to acquit, but on conviction, the sentence in the Crown Court could (not necessarily will) be more severe than that capable of imposition by the magistrates. It is an important decision all round, and it follows that the accused (and the court) should, so far as possible, have sufficient information about the case at hand to make informed choices. There are thus three aspects or stages to the process of determining where an *either-way offence is to be tried*. As a matter of logic, they occur in the following order.

(1) The defence is given initial details of the prosecution case,
(2) an indication of the defendant's plea is taken and, if the need for a trial is indicated,
(3) the trial venue is decided. The whole process is sometimes referred to globally as the 'plea and venue' procedure.

1. INITIAL DETAILS OF PROSECUTION CASE

The prosecution must provide the defence with a certain amount of advance information, what the rules call 'initial details', about the case against the accused. It does not matter if the information is requested or not - the point is to equip defendants to make sensible decisions for both plea[8] and venue purposes. The prosecution can choose whether to provide this information by means of a case summary or witness statements (with supporting documents), or a combination of the two, but in any event the defendant's previous convictions should be included.[9]

If not requesteed by the defence, these initial details can be provided as late as the beginning of the day of the first hearing. If requested, they should be provided

in the magistrates' court, whether summary only or triable either way: CrimPR r 8.2 and accompanying Practice Direction. It also applies to the trials of juveniles, as to which see Ch.11

9 CrimPR, r 8.3(a)(ii), CrimPD II 8A. The rules provide that these details should be served both on the defence and the 'court officer' (r 8.2(1)). It used to be thought that the magistrates making the mode of trial determination should not be told of a defendant's previous convictions, but this was a rather strange prohibition given its relevance to the decision and the fact that a differently constituted bench could try the case. It disappears with the reforms brought about by the CJA 2003.

as soon as practicable.[10] The defendant's representative would be expected to go through the information with the accused, advising on plea and venue and related matters before they are determined at that hearing. An adjournment is possible if justice (and effective case management) demands it, but this should be considered the exception, not the rule.

Do not confuse this obligation on the part of the prosecution, to give advanced information about its case, with the rules regarding disclosure by the prosecution of 'unused information', discussed further in Chapter Seven. The former is all about giving initial details of the nature of the evidence which the prosecution intends to *use* at trial. The latter is all about alerting the defence to evidence which the prosecution has but *does not* intend to use.

2. PLEA BEFORE VENUE (PBV)

It is an important part of the decision on trial venue to know whether the accused intends to plead guilty or not - only if the plea is not guilty is it necessary to have a trial at all. Before any venue determination, therefore, the accused is asked to 'indicate'[11] his plea were the case to go to trial (which is why this part of the process is known as 'plea before venue'). The court clerk will read the charge to the accused and ask him to say whether he intends to plead guilty or not guilty. They will explain[12] to him the implications of the answer he gives, namely:

(i) if he indicates a guilty plea, he will be treated as having been convicted, (just as he would have been had he tendered a guilty plea at a summary trial). The magistrates will then proceed directly to the

10 And in any event no later than the beginning of the day of the first hearing: CrimPR r 8.2(1) and (2). A failure to provide adequate information could result in an adjournment and an order that the information be provided (possibly with a costs sanction). See BCrP D 5.20

11 The accused can change his mind, as former MP Chris Huhne did just before his trial in 2013 for perverting the course of justice (for lying about who was driving his car when it was caught speeding on camera): bbc.co.uk/news/uk-21320992. A defendant can change his plea (or 'indication') from 'not guilty' to 'guilty' even after the trial has started. A change from 'guilty' to 'not guilty' is a little more difficult beyond a certain point.

12 MCA 1980, s 17A(4) and useful summary in BCrP D 6.7

sentencing stage. Having heard relevant information about the offence, the defendant's antecedents, mitigation and so on, the magistrates will *either* sentence the defendant themselves (possibly adjourning for reports first) *or*, if they regard their powers of punishment to be inadequate, commit the defendant to the Crown Court for sentencing.[13] In either event, the accused should get maximum credit for his early guilty plea when it comes to sentencing.[14]

(ii) If, however, the defendant indicates a not guilty plea,[15] it will be necessary to have a trial, and so the court will then go on to decide where the case should be allocated for that purpose.[16]

3. MODE OF TRIAL (MOT) DETERMINATION: STANDARD PROCEDURE

Both sides are given an opportunity to make representations on the appropriate venue for trial.[17] The prosecution will go first, followed by the defendant. This process is often very brief. If the prosecution is content with summary trial, and so too is the defendant, than the magistrates will often not need much convincing to consent to jurisdiction. If the magistrates consider a summary trial appropriate, but the defendant wants trial by jury, he only needs to say so when he is 'put to his election' - at this point, the choice of venue is entirely in his hands. The only situation where the defence submissions assume real importance is where the prosecution ask for jury trial, but the defence are eager that the case stays in the magistrates' court. Only rarely can the Crown insist on trial on indictment,[18] but lay justices are apt to give great weight to the views of the prosecution. If the latter object to summary

13 *Ibid*, s 17A(6). And see Ch. 5 for committal to the Crown Court for sentence.
14 See Ch. 10
15 Or if he fails to indicate how he would plead: MCA 1980, s 17B(3) as amended.
16 *Ibid*, s 18
17 *Ibid*, s 19(2)(b)
18 MCA 1980, s 19(4),(5)

trial, it will be next to impossible for the defence to convince the magistrates to accept jurisdiction and try the case summarily.

As you might expect, factors relevant to the mode of trial decision (to which representations would be directed) will be the nature of the offence, any aggravating or mitigating circumstances surrounding its commission, and any other matters making one or other venue the more suitable. The main focus of the court's attention, of course, will be on whether the magistrates' powers of sentencing are sufficiently great to punish the offender appropriately if he is convicted.[19] Logically, it helps the court to gauge this accurately if it knows of any previous convictions of the defendant (which very much affects sentence) and the court should give the prosecution the opportunity to provide this information.[20] Where the accused is charged with more than one offence, the magistrates must look at the *totality* of the allegations and not consider each offence in isolation.

This venue procedure often takes only a few moments to complete, yet can have important ramifications, for the defendant as well as the criminal justice system. It is worth noting the following points.

A. VENUE CHOICE WHEN ADVISING DEFENDANTS

Before a defendant is put to his election, it is important that he is well advised about the possible pros and cons of each destination. The magistrates' court is less formal (no wigs and gowns, for example) and so less daunting than trial on indictment. This can be an advantage for the nervous newcomer. In addition, summary trial is swifter and cheaper - cases will not necessarily be listed more quickly, but they are very likely to take less time, and so be less expensive, than jury trials. This would obviously be relevant both to the question of the affordability of the defendant's own costs of representation, especially if he is not legally aided,

19 See Sentencing Council definitive guideline, Pt 24 (Allocation), SG-596, (updated in 2016).

20 MCA 1980, s 19(2)(a) and (3), as amended by CJA 2003, Sch 3. The bench which tries the case would not normally know about these until after a conviction.

and on the amount of any prosecution costs he might be ordered to pay should he be convicted.[21] Appeals from the magistrates' court are also more straightforward than appeals from the Crown Court.[22]

Most importantly, perhaps, the sentence handed down after summary trial is *likely to be less severe* than that following trial on indictment. This is because of the limits on the magistrates' sentencing powers.[23] This will be particularly relevant where the defendant wants to plead not guilty, but the risk of being convicted seems high. Bear in mind, however, that magistrates do have the power to commit a person convicted of an either-way offence to the Crown Court for sentence if they believe their powers are insufficient. Obviously if this were clearly apparent to them from the outset, they should probably have refused jurisdiction to try the case in the first place, but it sometimes happens that during or after trial serious aspects of the offence (or offender) are revealed which require a greater capacity to punish than the magistrates have. It is obviously very important that a legal advisor considers, and the defendant knows of this power to commit for sentence before the latter makes his election.[24]

Indeed, when putting the accused to his election, the court itself must explain this to him. Moreover, the magistrates must be careful not to raise what is known as a 'legitimate expectation' about a specific sentencing outcome, if they want to keep all their sentencing options open (including committal to the Crown Court for sentence). According to the case law, if such an expectation is raised and it is a reasonable one, then it should not be dashed by a change of heart.[25] This aspect of the mode of trial procedure has been put on a more formal statutory footing by CJA 2003 amendments, in that once the magistrates have decided the case is appropriate for summary trial, the defendant, before being put to his election, will be told that he may seek an indication from the magistrates as to 'whether a custodial or non-

21 Indeed the greater costs of jury trial has resulted in special rules for criminal damage and shoplifting cases, discussed below. And see generally Ch. 12

22 For example, no leave is usually required to appeal from the magistrates' court' to the Crown Court. See generally Ch. 13

23 See Ch. 10

24 See advice checklist in *Practical Approach, N.08*

25 Usually after a pre-sentencing report reveals something unsavoury.

custodial sentence would more likely be imposed if he were to be tried summarily and pleaded guilty'.[26] The magistrates *need not give* such an indication, but if they do, the defendant will then be given a chance to reconsider his original indication of plea. Were he then to indicate a guilty plea, the magistrates will proceed to sentence, but a custodial sentence will only be available if it were indicated.[27]

Having said all of that, the Crown Court is still considered the venue with the better chance of securing an acquittal (for some accused, at all events[28]). One reason for this may be the strict division of labour there between judge and jury. For example, it is not easy to feel entirely confident about evidence which is excluded during[29] a summary trial. This is because the magistrates, who are judges of both law and fact, hear the disputed evidence before ruling on its admissibility. It is impossible to 'unhear' the information and it is difficult for lay magistrates not to be influenced by it (even when they rule it legally inadmissible) when deciding on a defendant's guilt. The contrast with the Crown Court is stark. There the judge rules on such legal questions in the absence of the jury, who can then go on to decide the facts without having heard the excluded (sometimes highly prejudicial) evidence. One may also feel that judges sitting in the higher court are better equipped (certainly than lay justices) to handle complex questions of law. Both these aspects of trial on indictment are considered advantageous when legal argument is going to play an important role in the proceedings.

Finally, of course, there is always the sense that jurors - whether because they are less case-hardened, more open-minded or just more gullible - are willing to entertain a healthier scepticism about police and other prosecution evidence than the magistrates and so more readily give defendants the benefit of the doubt. In any event, this remains, for many a defendant, a compelling reason to elect trial by jury.

---

26 S 20(3) MCA 1980 as amended by CJA 2003

27 MCA 1980, s 20(4)-(7) and s 20A(1) and BCrP D 6.12

28 Vicky Pryce (ex-wife of Chris Huhne, who was similarly charged, and tried for perverting the course of justice) did not, ultimately, fare so well, which goes to show that statistical odds will not assist an individual with a weak defence: bbc.co.uk/news/uk-21496566. And see fn 11, above.

29 Sometimes matters of admissibility can be determined pre-trial, but not always.

B. VENUE DECISION FROM COURT'S PERSPECTIVE

From the court's point of view, it is important to get the allocation decision right, thus ensuring that cases are tried at the appropriate level. If magistrates are overly cautious and refuse jurisdiction too often, then Crown Court lists will get clogged with cases which could perfectly well have been dealt with summarily. Equally, there is little point keeping a case in the magistrates' court which really ought to go to the Crown Court, especially if it is obvious that the defendant would have to be committed there for sentencing. This merely gives him the biggest drawback of the Crown Court, without any of its benefits.

The Allocation Guidelines (which are written from the court's and not the defendant's perspective) put it this way: in general, either-way offences *should* be tried summarily unless the outcome would *clearly* be a sentence in excess of the court's powers or for reasons of *unusual* legal, factual or procedural *complexity*. Logically enough, the court should assess this in light of current sentencing guidelines for the offence(s) in question and in view of any aggravating or mitigating factors put forward, which will help it plot where in the sentencing range this particular offender might fall.[30] It is worth remembering that there is no longer a maximum amount which the magistrates can fine on conviction for either-way offences. Further (assuming the case is not too complex), the magistrates are also told (in bold!) to bear in mind their power to commit offenders to the Crown Court to be sentenced. The impetus is thus very much in favour of the magistrates accepting jurisdiction, unless the case is obviously out of their league.

C. PRESENCE OF ACCUSED

Given the extent of the defendant's participation in the mode of trial decision, it is obviously crucial that he be present, even if only 'virtually'.[31] Rarely would

30 Sentencing Guidelines, op. cit., SG-596. It used to be that the magistrates assessed the case at its worst from the defendant's point of view (thus ignoring any mitigation). Not surprisingly, this did not assist in accurately predicting sentence any more than being kept in the dark about an accused's previous convictions. For allocation purposes, the magistrates need to know the good and the bad. And see Ch. 10 for sentencing powers.

31 If the facilities exist, a defendant in custody may participate using live video link: s 51 CDA 1998. It is not such a diversion for the accused but it saves money. CrimPR r 3.2(4) *strongly* encourages use of live links.

allocation take place if he were not there. One such occasion would be where the accused is legally represented, there is a good reason for his absence (through illness, for example) and he consents to the matter going ahead without him. Otherwise, the only reason for proceeding without the defendant's consent is where his behaviour is so disruptive that it warrants his exclusion and he has legal representation who can attend and articulate his choice of venue for him. This latter is the *only* reason for proceeding without him at the PBV stage.[32]

D. CHOICE OF CHARGE AND MODE OF TRIAL

The prosecution can sometimes exert control over whether a defendant will be tried summarily or on indictment by its choice of charge. A defendant's behaviour might give prosecutors an option: to allege a very serious summary offence or a less serious either-way offence. If the facts could fit either, so that the sentencing outcome would not be much affected by where the case was tried, then a defendant might hope to be charged with an either-way offence, so he can elect trial by jury; but the prosecution can avoid this outcome by deliberately choosing to charge the summary offence, thus ensuring that the case is tried in the magistrates' court. A defendant charged only with a summary offence cannot ask to be charged with an either-way offence just so he can elect trial by jury!

There was a time when prosecutors sometimes tried to hedge their bets by first charging an either-way offence and then, if the accused elected trial by jury, attempting to replace that original charge with one that is summary only.[33] This tactic has been frowned upon judicially unless the change is in keeping with the overriding objective,[34] and the CPS Code for Crown Prosecutors now specifically warns that prosecutors 'should not change the charge simply because of the decision by the court or the defendant about where the case will be heard'.[35]

32 See BCrP D 6.9

33 Sometimes it can work the other way. Prosecutors, aggrieved that both the magistrates and the accused agreed to summary trial of an either-way offence, substituted or added one which was indictable only to force the case up into the Crown Court. The Court of Appeal liked this ploy even less: *R v Brooks* [1985] Crim LR 385

34 See *DPP v Hammerton* [2010] QB 79

35 CPS Code, para 6.4

E. CHANGE OF HEART

There may be occasions when either the defendant or magistrates may wish they had made a different choice about mode of trial. As the allocation procedure becomes more informed and more procedural, the court's ability to switch from accepting or refusing jurisdiction diminishes.

The situation is different for a *defendant*. A typical scenario is an unrepresented accused who opts for summary trial and then, having later received legal advice, wishes to elect jury trial. He needs the magistrates' permission to change his election, but this is usually forthcoming if there is any doubt about his having understood the implications of his choice, and there seems to be no ulterior motive in his making the application.[36] After all, the defendant has a right to be tried on indictment if the offence is indictable. The usual test is: did the accused 'properly understand the nature and significance of the choice to which he was put'?[37]

It is also possible for the *prosecution* to apply for an either-way offence to be tried on indictment instead of summarily, so long as they do so before the start of the summary trial.[38] Presumably prosecutors will only use this procedure if something has transpired since mode of trial was determined which makes trial on indictment more appropriate - otherwise they would have mentioned it on that earlier occasion. Not surprisingly, the magistrates should only accede to the application if it is satisfied that the magistrates' sentencing powers would be 'inadequate'.[39] If the magistrates agree, they will send the case to the Crown Court for trial in the usual way.

36 A very late application in a case going very badly could betray an attempt to get a better bite of the cherry in the Crown Court.

37 *Birmingham Justices ex parte Hodgson* [1985] QB 1131

38 S 25(2A) MCA 1980 (as amended by CJA 2003)

39 s 25(2B) *ibid*. The maximum aggregate sentence will be the relevant threshold when considering more than one charge arising out of a single or series of offence(s): s 25(2C)

4. CRIMINAL DAMAGE AND LOW VALUE SHOPLIFTING

Criminal damage is an offence which occurs with some frequency, but which varies widely in its severity. It is triable either way, but if every defendant elected trial by jury, the Crown Court lists would get congested with some relatively minor cases. *Special rules* thus apply to criminal damage charges to ensure that only the most serious are tried on indictment. These provisions are found in s 22 MCA 1980 and provide that where the defendant is charged with criminal damage (*other than* damage, or attempted damage, by *fire*) and the value of the damage does not exceed £5,000, then the magistrates *must* proceed as if the offence were summary only. Note that these provisions do not make such offences summary, but only treat them as summary for the purposes of deciding where they should be tried. An accused has to work pretty hard to do more than £5,000 worth of damage, so the result of this special procedure is that most criminal damage cases have been barred from trial by jury.[40]

Thus when an offence of criminal damage comes before the magistrates for a venue decision, the court *adapts* the normal mode of trial procedure as follows.

(i) The magistrates must first consider (having regard to representations made by prosecution and defence) *the value* of the thing which has allegedly been criminally damaged. 'Value' for these purposes effectively means the market value - any consequential loss is irrelevant for allocation purposes.[41]

(ii) If the value is clearly £5,000 or less, then the magistrates proceed as if the offence were only triable summarily. The accused has no right to trial on indictment but nor can he be committed to the Crown Court

40 See generally BCrP D 6.22ff

41 See, e.g., *R v Colchester Justices, ex parte Abbot* [2001] Crim LR 564

for sentencing.[42] Moreover, the maximum sentence the magistrates can impose is *three* months imprisonment or a £2,500 fine. No doubt these restrictions represent a quid pro quo for losing the right to elect trial by jury in such cases.

(iii) If the value involved is clearly over £5,000, the charge is treated like any other offence which is triable either way and the court follows the standard procedure. If the offence is tried summarily, the normal maximum sentences in the magistrates' court apply and the defendant can be committed to the Crown Court for sentencing.

(iv) If the value is uncertain, the accused is told that he has a choice of venue, but *if* he elects summary trial the lower maximum penalties will apply if he is convicted and again he cannot be committed to the Crown Court for sentencing. In a sense he is offered a one-off 'special deal' summary trial. If he does not take it, then the court reverts to the standard procedure for determining mode of trial of either-way offences.

(v) Where the defendant is charged on the same occasion with two or more offences of criminal damage which appear to form a series of the same or similar character (as part of a spree, for example), the court should look at the *aggregate* value of the things damaged when determining mode of trial. Thus, if the total value of all the items damaged does not exceed £5,000, then the magistrates must proceed as if the offences were all summary, regardless of the number of offences.[43]

Since 2015, similar provisions apply to 'low value' shoplifting[44] (which falls under the general remit of theft). Statute now provides that where the value of the goods

42 Unless some other basis for doing so applies (e.g., breach of suspended sentence). See Ch. 10

43 MCA 1980, s 22(11). For sentencing generally see Ch. 10 (Adults).

44 As in theft (or aiding and abetting theft) from a shop while posing as a customer. See s 22A MCA 1980 (added by Criminal Justice and Courts Act 2015, s 52).

stolen does *not exceed £200*, the offence is no longer to be treated as triable either way - rather it is to be tried and sentenced as a *summary offence* (so magistrates must do both). *However* (unlike the criminal damage procedure), the defendant's right to elect Crown Court trial is *preserved*, so he can still elect trial by jury.[45]

revision tips

- Make yourself a basic flow chart setting out the steps to determining mode of trial. Be aware of the perceived advantages/disadvantages to defendants of each venue.
- Be alert to the special rules about criminal damage and low level shoplifting. Keep the thresholds and sentencing implications in mind. This is good exam fodder.

It is worth reading...

R (on application of Abbott) v Colchester Justices [2001] All ER 178. This is an interesting case involving damage to experimental crops of genetically modified maize. The protesters presumably wanted the case to go to jury trial (where they felt they had a better chance of succeeding), but the prosecution was determined to keep it in the magistrates' court. It is a good reminder of the special rules for criminal damage cases. (If you have trouble finding it online use search words 'criminal damage + crops + value' if you find the case citation does not work).

45 *Ibid*, s 22A(2). Note that a person convicted by magistrates under these provisions may not appeal against conviction solely on the basis that the offence should not have been treated as low value shoplifting.

CHAPTER 5

Kicking the case upstairs

1. GETTING CASES TO THE CROWN COURT FOR *TRIAL*

Once it is clear that a case needs to get out of the magistrates' jurisdiction and go up to the Crown Court for trial, the next procedural issue is, how does it get there?

Historically, this occurred as part of what were known as 'committal proceedings', which at one time always involved the magistrates in a detailed and time-consuming consideration of the evidence in order to ensure that there was a prima facie case to be made against the defendant. Eventually, concerns were raised about the duplication of time and effort involved in committal proceedings when the case went to trial, and so in the 1980's, there began a slow procedural trend away from a complex judicial process and towards a more sterile, if efficient means of dispatching cases quickly to the Crown Court.[1]

The pace of change has picked up steadily in recent years. A major stride came with the enactment of s 51 of the Crime and Disorder Act 1998 (CDA 1998) which abolished committal proceedings for indictable-only offences and substituted an administrative exercise in the form of 'sending' cases to the Crown Court. Either-way offences followed. By the end of 2013 committal proceedings had been abolished in England and Wales.[2] Thus an accused will never be 'committed' to

1 See, e.g., brief overview in Sprack, *Practical Approach*, 13.01ff.

2 The relevant rules are now found in CrimPR Pt 9

the Crown Court for trial, but 'sent' there. What follows sets out the position, so far as adults are concerned.[3]

It is worth distinguishing between the following three ways[4] in which cases get to the Crown Court for trial, bearing in mind that in any event the exercise is essentially *procedural*, not judicial, and can be discharged by a single magistrate.

A. SENDING CASES UNDER S 51 CDA 1998

Once the magistrates establish that the case before them either must (indictable only) or should (if allocated there after a mode of trial hearing) be tried in the Crown Court, then they *must* send the defendant there 'forthwith'.[5]

This is effectively an administrative exercise. The magistrates' court issues a notice under s 51(7) specifying the location of the Crown Court where the defendant is to be tried, which will be chosen by reference to the needs of the case (for example, Class A offences require High Court and equivalent judges[6]), the desire to expedite the trial (waiting times at different Crown Courts can play a part here) and convenience to the participants (in terms of travel and so on).[7]

In an attempt to prevent prejudicial information being made public, reporting restrictions apply so that only superficial details may be reported about the case at this stage (the name and age of defendant, the charge(s), the Court where the case will be tried and so on). These may be lifted when and if it is in the interest of justice to do so.[8]

The court will make any ancillary orders as appear necessary (having asked both prosecution and defence for views), especially as to bail and case management. The magistrates must set a date for a Plea and Trial Preparation hearing, to take place within 28 days of the case being sent for trial, unless the defendant has indicated a guilty plea in which case it should be as soon as possible.[9]

When a case has been sent to the Crown Court under s 51, it is to be regarded

3 Juveniles will be considered in Ch. 11

4 Check your examination syllabus for the detail/process which will be tested.

5 Subject only to their power to adjourn (for example if the accused needs time to mount a bail application) or stay proceedings as an abuse of process (this would be rare): s 51(1), (2) and s 51(5) CDA 1998

6 CrimPD XIII E.1

7 CrimPR, r 9.3(3)

8 CDA 1998, s 52A. A newsworthy example was the case of Lib Dem MP Chris Huhne. Restrictions were lifted after he pleaded guilty to perverting the course of justice: see Guido Fawkes' blog: 29/01/2013

9 See BCrP D 10.22 and CrimPD I 3A.10

as having been adjourned by the magistrates *sine die* (Latin, meaning 'forever and a day'). In other words, that should be the last they hear of it.

B. PROSECUTION NOTICES IN CASES OF SERIOUS FRAUD OR INVOLVING CHILD WITNESSES

The trend for quickly sending cases to the Crown Court which are destined to be tried there pre-dates the CDA 1998. It began with the cases discussed below. The wholesale sending of cases under s 51, has now rendered this transfer procedure, if not obsolete, then of limited importance. But it survives as a separate means of getting certain cases to the Crown Court, and you should know what it is.

The prosecution notice procedure applies to two very different, but obvious sorts of indictable offences which need not linger in the magistrates' court: cases involving serious fraud[10] and those involving child witnesses.[11] The procedure has essentially been replicated in the CDA 1998 (as amended) to cater for the post-committal world.[12]

(i) Complex fraud cases

A designated prosecuting authority (the DPP, Serious Fraud Office or similar) may give notice to the relevant magistrates' court (that is, the one which at the time has jurisdiction over the case) whenever it thinks there is (i) sufficient evidence to try the accused, and (ii) that evidence reveals a fraud of 'such seriousness or complexity that it is appropriate that the management of the case should without delay be taken over by the Crown Court'.[13]

10 CJA 1987, s 4

11 CJA 1991, s 53

12 As ss 51B and 51C CDA 1998 (as amended). See generally, BCrP D 10.34ff. Older rules refer to this as a 'transfer' procedure, but the 2015 rules now include it under the general 'sending' provisions: CrimPR, r 96

13 Wording in CDA 1998 s 51B(1)(b)

(ii) Serious cases involving child witnesses

Similarly with cases of sexual or other violence involving child witnesses. The idea originally was to spare the children involved the additional ordeal of having to give evidence more than once.[14] The procedure was created before the days of sophisticated special measures for vulnerable witnesses, but has been up-dated to live side-by-side with them.[15]

A child, for these purposes, is a person under the age of 17.[16] It is the DPP who may give notice if he is satisfied that (i) there is sufficient evidence for a trial, (ii) that a child will be called as a witness at the trial, and that (iii) to avoid 'any prejudice to the welfare of the child, the case should be taken over and proceeded with without delay by the Crown Court'.[17] The procedure applies to the whole range of cases of violence, kidnap and sexual abuse likely to traumatise children either as victims and/or witnesses.

The important thing to remember is this transfer procedure effectively involves the magistrates' court *responding to instructions* from prosecuting authorities, rather than acting on its own initiative, as it does when it sends cases to the Crown Court. Thus, the magistrates' court will always deal first with any transfer requests, although these will become increasingly infrequent.

The prosecution notice must specify to which Crown Court the case is to be transferred, and once given, the magistrate's role in the matter ceases, save for questions of bail, witness orders and legal representation. Once the transfer has been requested, there is really no room for discussion or complaint, which is not surprising, since the point is to save time, not generate argument. After all, the chances of such cases being appropriate for summary trial (assuming the defendant is not also a child) must be infinitesimal. Any challenge to the cogency of the case to answer can be made in the Crown Court.

14 Which no longer happens of course with the sending of cases under s 51 but it just seemed easy to bring this notice procedure into an amended CDA 1998.

15 For special measures for vulnerable and other witnesses, see Ch. 17

16 Or who was under 17 when a recording to be used as evidence in court was made: CDA 1998 s 51C(7)

17 *Ibid*, s 51C(1)(c)

C. VOLUNTARY BILLS OF INDICTMENT

This is another route to the Crown Court, but it is very rarely taken. It has nothing to do with the magistrates' court, but it is useful to mention it here. In exceptional circumstances, a High Court Judge has the power to order that a defendant be tried on indictment.[18] This is known as 'preferring' a voluntary bill of indictment. This procedure should only be used where there is 'good reason to depart from normal practice':[19] for example, as a means of jointly trying two defendants when only one had been sent for trial (and so only he appears on the indictment), but the second has just been traced (or arrested). 'Preferring' (or submitting for consideration) a new indictment naming both defendants would be a neat and simple solution.[20]

You are unlikely to be examined in any depth about this rather archaic procedure, but you should know what it is - if only to eliminate a wrong answer (or less good option) in a single best answer/multiple choice question.

D. UPSTAIRS/DOWNSTAIRS

Sometimes an accused is charged with a range of offences arising out of the same scenario or set of circumstances. What if some of these are summary offences, and so ought to be tried in the magistrates' court, but others need to be sent to the Crown Court? If the offences are related factually, they should probably be dealt with together. But the accused cannot be in two different places at once. So what happens?

Where it makes sense that they do so, a lesser offence can 'go along for the ride' with the more serious offence (let's call this the lead case) up to the Crown Court - sometimes simply to be conveniently adjudicated in the same *place*, but on occasion to be included on the same indictment and so adjudicated at the same *time*. Beginners love to hate these provisions, and they can be confusing, but in truth they

18 Administration of Justice (Miscellaneous Provisions) Act 1933, s 2 (as amended by the CJA 2003). See BCrP D 10.44 for procedural details as necessary.

19 CrimPD II 10B.4

20 Alternatively magistrates may send up related defendants/cases to catch up with one already on the way (discussed below) or the prosecution could apply to amend an existing indictment against D1 to add D2. Sometimes preferment of a voluntary bill is the *only* option. See BCrP D 10.49

merely represent a sensible solution to a logistical problem. There are two different situations which must be clearly distinguished.

(i) *Magistrates* sending *related offences* with the lead offence: s 51 CDA 1998

If an assortment of charges arises out of a criminal incident or series of incidents, it makes sense to deal with them all in one place. If the lead offence is sent to the Crown Court, then it will effectively act as a 'magnet' for the others.

Thus, if magistrates are sending an adult defendant[21] for trial in the Crown Court under s 51 then at the same time they *must* also send that defendant there in respect of:

(a) any *related* either-way offences *or*

(b) any *related* summary offences (if punishable with imprisonment or disqualification) with which he is also charged.[22]

And if a *second* adult *defendant* appears on the same occasion charged with an either-way offence which is *related* to the lead case, then that co-defendant must *also* be sent by the magistrates to the Crown Court for trial.[23] Essentially, cases are 'related' if they arise out of circumstances which are the *same as or connected to* those giving rise to the lead case[24] - it is this connection which makes it sensible to send them all to the same place to be dealt with.

Sometimes related cases (or a co-accused) as described above appear for allocation *after* the lead case has already departed for the Crown Court. In such cases, the magistrates *may*, but are not compelled to, send those related charges to the Crown Court. An important consideration would be how far ahead of the others

21 See Ch. 11 for juvenile defendants.

22 CDA 1998, s 51(3). So it has to be a relatively serious summary offence.

23 *Ibid*, s 51(5). And if there are related charges against that co-accused, then they must be sent up too!

24 CDA 1998, s 51E(c) & (d) and see BCrP D 10.6. Strictly speaking, an either-way offence is only related to an indictable-only offence if it could have been included on the same indictment. See Ch. 6

the lead case is, and whether those following could realistically (and procedurally) catch up with it.

The Crown Court will then deal with all these related charges as seems appropriate, and in keeping with the overriding objective. Even if triable either way, indictable offences are obviously quite at home being tried in the Crown Court (with the lead case). Insofar as dealing with the related *summary* offences, much may depend on how well the accused fared in the trial on indictment. Once the trial on indictment has *finished*, the court will usually take a plea from the accused on the summary charge(s). Crown Court judges have the power to act as District Judges and so can carry out the functions of the magistrates' court as required. Thus, if the plea to the summary offence is guilty, then the accused must be dealt with as if he were in the magistrates' court. If he pleads not guilty to the summary charge (which he may well do if he was acquitted of the indictable offence) then the case against him will either be dismissed (if the prosecution says it wishes to offer no evidence), or sent back ('remitted') to the magistrates' court for them to deal with it,[25] or the Crown Court judge could try the case as if he were a magistrate.[26] Whatever seems most just and sensible should rule the day.

Note that it is the *magistrates* who send related cases with the lead case to be dealt with by the Crown Court under s 51 CDA 1998. It is important to distinguish this procedure from the following:

(ii) *Prosecutors* including *linked* summary offences *on the indictment*: s 40 CJA 1988[27]

There are a handful of summary offences which may be included by prosecutors on an indictment, to be tried jointly with the indictable offence(s) to which they are factually related in some way. This provision pre-dates the s 51 procedure discussed

25 See generally, CDA 1998, para 6, Sch 3
26 Courts Act 2003, s 66
27 See generally BCrP D 11.17

above, and operates quite differently from it, although both provisions require sufficient connection between the summary and indictable offences.

Thus, the first requirement of s 40 is that the summary charge must either be founded on the *same facts* as an offence on the indictment or else form part of a series of offences of the *same or similar nature* as an offence on the indictment. Secondly, *only* specified summary offences can qualify, including:[28]

(a) common assault
(b) assault on a custody (for example, prison) officer
(c) taking a motor vehicle without consent
(d) driving whilst disqualified *or*
(e) criminal damage which must be tried summarily under the s 22 procedure.

What you will notice about these offences is that they very typically occur in the process of the commission of more serious (thus indictable) offences. Robbers escape in get-away cars; people who should not be driving are often at the wheel and so on. If you appreciate why these particular summary offences have been chosen for this particular procedure, then you will more easily recognise when your knowledge of it is being tested. Curiously, you might think assaulting a police officer in the execution of his duty is *not* one of the named summary offences which can be linked under this provision - examiners sometimes try and catch you out on that one.

The final requirement is that some evidence of the linked summary offence having occurred should appear in the information which forms the basis on which the indictable offence is sent to the Crown Court for trial. Other than this, the magistrates are not involved with the inclusion on the indictment of these summary

28 As set out in s 41(3) CJA 1988. The Home Secretary can add to this list, so long as the offence is punishable by imprisonment: s 41(4)

offences. Their role is limited to getting the indictable offence to the Crown Court; it is for the *prosecutor* to choose whether a linked summary offence goes onto the same Crown Court indictment.

Linked summary offences are tried in exactly the same way as the other charges on the indictment.[29] However, given that this procedure is essentially an exercise in efficiency, it is important that the defendant is not prejudiced by its operation. It follows, therefore, that if convicted of the linked summary offence, the sentencing powers of the Crown Court are limited to those of the magistrates' court.[30]

2. COMMITTING TO THE CROWN COURT FOR *SENTENCE*

The magistrates will no longer 'commit' for trial, but their powers to commit for sentencing are alive and well![31] When defendants are convicted or plead guilty in the magistrates' court, they will usually be sentenced there. In certain circumstances, however, the magistrates can commit convicted defendants to the Crown Court for sentencing. A lot depends on the nature of the offence. A defendant is *only* exposed to the enhanced sentencing powers of the Crown Court when he has been convicted of an *either-way offence* in the magistrates' court. The main[32] powers of committal for sentence are found in the Powers of Criminal Courts (Sentencing) Act 2000 (PCC(S) A 2000) and can be deployed in the following situations.

A. AFTER CONVICTION OF AN EITHER-WAY OFFENCE: S 3 PCC(S)A 2000[33]

This is the most straightforward scenario. If the defendant is over 18 and has been convicted of an either-way offence (after trial or pleading guilty), he may be

29 Crown Court procedure is discussed in Ch. 9

30 MCA 1980, s 40(2)

31 Committing for sentence was never a time-consuming operation so there was no need to change it. Now you can use the vocabulary to help you keep the two functions separate: 'send' for trial; 'commit' for sentence.

32 For other possibilities see list at BCrP D 23.29

33 The new s 3A provides for committal to the Crown Court for sentence following summary conviction of a specified 'dangerous offenders' offence. This is discussed in Ch. 10

committed to the Crown Court for sentence if the magistrates feel their sentencing powers are inadequate.[34] Defendants must always be warned of this possibility when asked to make a trial venue choice.

We have seen that when determining mode of trial, and deciding whether or not to accept jurisdiction to try an either-way offence, the magistrates should determine as accurately as possible whether their sentencing powers are up to the task. The court should now be told of the accused's previous convictions, so that they can be factored into the equation at that stage. It is still possible for the court to become aware of something after the mode of trial has been decided which then prompts them to commit for sentence (for example, the accused has asked for other offences to be taken into consideration[35] or some distasteful details about the commission of the offence only came to light during the trial). But generally speaking, an accused should have some confidence in concluding that if the magistrates are willing to try the either-way case summarily, they are also willing to sentence upon conviction. Otherwise, there is not much to be gained from electing summary trial.[36] Certainly, if the magistrates have raised in the accused's mind a legitimate expectation (or otherwise indicated) that his case will *not* be committed to the Crown Court for sentencing, they should not go back on their word.[37]

A committal for sentence under s 3 will be either in custody or on bail. In sentencing, the Crown Court may deal with the accused just as they would have done had he been convicted of the offence on indictment.[38] This might create some disincentive for appearing to face the music, but if an accused was on bail before committal for sentence, the usual practice would be that bail should continue, unless there are good reasons for remanding in custody.[39]

---

34 For punishment purposes or in order to protect the public. PCC(S)A 2000, s 3(2)

35 As to which see Ch. 10

36 See *North Sefton Magistrates' Court, ex parte Marsh* (1995) 16 Cr App R (S) 401 and BCrP D 23.33

37 See BCrP D 23.35ff

38 PCC(S)A 2000, s 5

39 BCrP D 23.39

B. AFTER PLEAS OF GUILTY AND NOT GUILTY OF RELATED EITHER-WAY OFFENCES: S 4 PCC(S)A 2000

Just as with sending cases for trial, a logistical problem can arise when an accused is charged with a variety of offences arising out of the same incident or series of incidents, and he pleads guilty to some offences, but not guilty to others. As a matter of principle, sentencing should be based on the totality of the offending in question, and so if the not guilty plea is to be tried in the Crown Court, then it makes sense for the others to be committed to that court for sentence, once the outcome of the trial on indictment is known. Thus a defendant who has been sent for trial on an indictable offence may also be committed for *sentence* on other, *related*, either-way offences ('the related offences') to which a guilty plea has been indicated.

What happens as regards sentencing depends partly on the outcome of the trial on indictment and partly on whether the magistrates would have committed the related offences for sentencing in any event (under s 3). If the accused is found guilty in the Crown Court trial, then that court may sentence in respect of the related offences as if the defendant had also been convicted of them on indictment; in other words, all sentencing options are open to the court.[40] If, however, the defendant is *acquitted* following the trial on indictment, then the Crown Court, in sentencing in respect of the *related* offences, is limited to the powers of the magistrates' court, unless the latter had indicated that they would, in any event, have committed the accused to the Crown Court for sentence.[41] This is to ensure that a defendant is only being exposed to the greater sentencing powers of the higher court when the circumstances warrant, and not as a result of an efficiency measure.

40 PCC(S)A 2000, s 5

41 Under s 3 PCC(S)A 2000 discussed above and see BCrP D 23.42ff

C. ANY OTHER SUMMARY STRAGGLERS: S 6 PCC(S)A 2000

If there are any *related* offences left behind after the operation of s 3 and s 4 PCC(S)A 2000 described above,[42] then s 6 allows the magistrates to commit the defendant for sentence in respect of any of these so long as he has been found (or pleaded) guilty to them. This effectively allows magistrates to commit defendants to the Crown Court for sentence in respect of summary offences, which is otherwise not possible.[43] It allows the Crown Court to deal with everything in one place, and ensures that no related offences get inconveniently left behind in the magistrates' court. Given that the purpose is again purely one of *efficiency* (and ensuring a proper sentence for the totality of offending), it will not come as a great surprise that in sentencing in respect of any of these tail-end summary offences, the Crown Court is limited to the powers of the magistrates.

revision tips

- Remember that cases are 'sent' to the Crown Court for trial; defendants are 'committed' there for sentence. Use the vocabulary to help you make distinctions.
- Understand the reason for the provisions which result in summary offences going up to be dealt with in the Crown Court with related indictable offences.
- Focus on the purpose and logic behind the various provisions discussed in this chapter. This will help you remember the detail. Invent some little case studies to help trigger your memory.

It is worth reading ...

The judgment in *R (Harrington) v Bromley Magistrates' Court* [2007] EWHC 2896 (Admin). Serious injuries, a remorseful accused, and a generous (but not irrational) indication by the magistrates only to commit for sentence if the pre-sentence report showed the offender to be a danger to the public. It didn't, he wasn't and so his legitimate expectation should have been realised. The defendant obviously had some dosh - let's hope he did something nice for the taxi driver!

42 Or other powers to commit, see footnote 32

43 See examples at BCrP D 23.55

CHAPTER 6

Indictments

The indictment is the name for the formal document which sets out the charges to be tried in the Crown Court, to which the accused pleads guilty or not guilty at the beginning of his trial: this is where the reference to being 'tried on indictment' comes from. Each charge against a defendant is contained in a separate 'count' on the indictment. A jury can only try one indictment at a time, but an indictment can contain more than one count, and charge more than one defendant.

Like Particulars of Claim in civil cases, indictments have headings (including a unique reference number) and conform to certain formal requirements.[1] At the top is the word '**INDICTMENT**', followed by the place of trial (for example, '**THE CROWN COURT** at **READING**') and the name of the case. Public prosecutions are always brought in the name of the Queen (or King, as the case might one day be): for example, '**THE QUEEN** v **JOSEPH BLOGS**'. After this comes a standard preamble before setting out the specific counts (that is, '**JOSEPH BLOGS** is charged as follows:-')

Indictments are normally drafted by the Crown Prosecution Service (CPS), although counsel may occasionally be asked to do this in complex cases. A draft 'bill' of indictment becomes an 'indictment' once it is served on the Crown Court (this is known as 'preferring the indictment'). A draft indictment

1 The law governing the form and content of indictments is principally contained in the Indictments Act 1915 (1A) and the CrimPR Pt 10, as supplemented by accompanying Practice Directions (CrimPD II). See also, useful example scenario in *Practical Approach*, 15.02 ff

may be generated electronically *when* the case is sent to trial,[2] or served on the defence and the court by the prosecution *afterwards*. If the latter, this should happen within 28 days from the date the prosecution served the evidence on which their case is based, but there is scope for extending this deadline.[3] In any event the indictment should be served at least 7 days before the Plea and Trial Preparation Hearing (PTPH).[4]

1. COUNTS ON THE INDICTMENT

When drafting the indictment, the essential question that arises is this: what count or counts should be contained in it, and against whom? Usually the indictment will contain the same charges as those sent by the magistrates for trial in the Crown Court. But the indictment may contain, as well as or instead of the original charges,[5] any indictable offences supported by the previously disclosed evidence of the prosecution case.[6] So, for example, if the defendant was sent for trial on a charge of theft, the indictment could include alternative counts of both theft and handling stolen goods to cover the possibility that the accused might say that he did not steal the items, but merely received them.

The most important rules you need to get to grips with focus on the counts of an indictment - either how they are to be worded, or how many counts and/ or defendants may be included in the one document. These are set out below. Examiners are particularly fond of testing the rule against duplicity, if only to throw it into a multiple choice question as a tempting wrong answer.

2 See CrimPR, r 10.3ff. The paper copy must ultimately be officially endorsed so as to identify the date the draft became a true indictment: r 10.2(7).

3 *Ibid*, r 10.4. The Crown Court can grant extensions, even after the period has expired.

4 CrimPD II 10A.9

5 S2(2) Administration of Justice (Miscellaneous Provisions)Act 1933

6 CrimPR, r 10.2(4)

A. FORMAT OF COUNTS ON AN INDICTMENT

A count is essentially divided into two parts. The first is the 'Statement of Offence', which should describe the offence 'in ordinary language', identifying any legislation (if any) which creates it (for example, 'Theft contrary to s 1(1) of the Theft Act 1968'). The second is the 'Particulars of Offence', which should give sufficient factual information so as to 'make clear what the prosecution alleges against the defendant' (for example, 'JOSEPH BLOGGS on 1st day of January 2017 stole an iPhone 6S mobile phone belonging to JOHN SMITH').[7] The point is that the defendant should know what he is accused of having done, so where specifics are relevant and known (as to whose or what property was stolen or what place was burgled, for example), then these details should be included. It is not, however, always necessary to write out fully all of the elements of an offence.[8]

B. THE RULE AGAINST DUPLICITY

An indictment may contain several counts, but each count must only allege *one* offence. This is know as the rule against duplicity: if a count alleges more than one offence, then it is said to be 'bad for duplicity' (in the sense of double[9] rather than deceptive). At the heart of this rule is the need for prosecutors to be clear and precise, for the sake of the jury as well as the defence, and to pin their colours to the mast in each individual count. So, for example, one count alleging that the accused 'stole or handled' certain items would be bad for duplicity because two different offences (theft and handling) are alleged in the same count. The prosecution needs to make up its mind - it may be perfectly appropriate to allege both *on the same indictment*, but *not in the same count.*

Sounds simple, but the rule is not always as easy to apply as you might think. This is because it is sometimes possible for several acts to constitute one offence. It has

7 *Ibid*, r 10.2(1). BCrP usefully sets out specimen counts for most of the common indictable offences.

8 As you can see from the theft example above, where 'stole' is used to encapsulate the nature of the crime. But offences can vary in this regard. Compare, for example, the specimen counts for theft and handling: BCrP B 4.3 and B 4.161

9 'Duple', an expression also used sometimes, is an old-fashioned word for 'double'.

been said that the rule against duplicity should be 'applied in a practical rather than a strictly analytical way' so that a number of acts of a similar nature may be said to constitute a single offence if they form one activity or 'transaction'.[10] If, for example, a burglar broke into your flat and stole a TV from the sitting room, a microwave from the kitchen and a watch from the bedroom, you probably would not think of yourself as having been burgled three times, even though three different items were lifted individually from three separate rooms. Or as CrimPR, r 10.2(2) now puts it: 'more than one incident of the commission of the offence may be included in a count if those incidents taken together amount to a *course of conduct* having regard to the time, place or purpose of commission'.[11]

In thinking about and applying this idea, it is useful to consider different factual permutations, which might help you identify whether, and to what extent, the rule against duplicity is (or is not) being infringed.[12] These include the following.

(i) Several items of property (from same victim)

As in the burglary example above, one count for an offence against property may allege that several items were stolen, damaged and so forth, where logic says that the several acts amounted to a *single spree*. *R v Wilson*[13] is a good example. In that case, it was argued on appeal (perhaps rather desperately) that a count alleging that the accused stole a number of items from Debenhams (three jumpers, a pair of shorts, two pairs of trousers, four dimmer switches and a cassette tape) was bad for duplicity because the goods came from different departments of the store and so there should have been different counts relating to each department. The Court of Appeal dismissed this argument saying that the various acts of theft had amounted to a single course of conduct and so could legitimately be regarded as amounting to a single offence.

10 *DPP v Merriman* [1973] AC 584, per Lord Diplock at 607C

11 My emphasis. This is probably a modern articulation of the decision in *Merriman*, *ibid*.

12 See also guidance on 'multiple offending counts' in CrimPD, II 10A.11 and BCrP D 11.50ff

13 (1979) 69 Cr App R 83

When you go to the supermarket, you do not think of yourself as doing five 'shops' just because you buy something from the vegetable section, something else from housewares, cakes from the bread aisle and so on. It is really no different if you steal the stuff.

In each of these examples, you will notice that the victim is the same in respect of the various things stolen and there is a marked repetition of methodology. Different victims usually require different counts, as discussed below. Equally, if a jury were to be asked to make value judgments about the various items or individual incidents concerned, this too may be a reason for separate counts.[14]

(ii) Several dates

Generally speaking, the rule against duplicity requires that criminal acts occurring on different dates should be charged as individual offences in separate counts.[15] In essence, offences committed on different occasions tend not to form a single transaction or activity. However, it is sometimes possible for one count to allege a 'continuing offence' - that is, one which took place continually or intermittently[16] *over a period of time*. The difference is usually between the *same sort of offence committed repeatedly* but separately on a number of dates (which normally requires separate counts) and an offence being committed *once between a start and an end date*. The most obvious example of a continuing offence is conspiracy,[17] because it is on-going in its nature - it begins when the parties first conceive their unlawful plan and continues until that plan comes to an end. But even more mundane activities can be viewed as a continuing offence. In *DPP v McCabe*,[18] a charge alleging that the accused stole 76 library books from South Glamorgan Library between two specified dates was held not to be duplicitous. Where there is an appropriation of a number of articles (note the similarity both of item and victim), but no evidence as to exactly when

14 As in *Bristol Crown Court, ex parte Willetts* (1985) 149 JP 416, where the accused was charged with possession of five obscene videos. The Divisional Court said five separate counts was preferable because the jury needed to decide in each case whether the video in question was, in fact, obscene.

15 As, e.g., in *R v Thompson* [1914] 2 KB 99 where it was said that a count alleging the commission of incest on *"divers days between the month of January 1909, and the 4th of October, 1910"* was 'irregular' because it clearly alleged more than one offence.

16 See, e.g., *Hodgetts v Chiltern District Council* [1983] 2 AC 120, per Lord Roskill at p. 128

17 See BCrP D 11.32-11.34

18 [1992] CrimLR 885

the individual thefts took place, then the prosecution is entitled to charge, in effect, the accumulated grand total over a specific period of time - a so-called 'multiple incidents' count.[19]

(iii) Several victims

It is unusual for a count to name more than one victim, even where one criminal act has several identifiable victims. Thus, in *R v Mansfield*[20] the defendant was charged with seven counts of murder in respect of a single act of arson which resulted in the deaths of seven people in a hotel. The same would have applied to indictments in respect of the serial activities of people like Fred West and Harold Shipman. *R v Wilson*, discussed above, is another good example. Before his spree at Debenhams, Mr Wilson had helped himself to various items from Boots, but the allegation in respect of the latter was charged in a separate (single) count.

(iv) Statutory offences and alternative methods of commission

If a statute creates a single offence, albeit one which can be committed in several different ways, then in theory the alternatives may be charged in a single count without its being duplicitous (whether this would be good drafting is another matter). If, however, an enactment creates more than one offence, each offence for the jury's consideration must be alleged in a separate count. Again, this principle is rather easier to articulate than it is to apply. The cases show that determining the number of offences a statute may be said to create, whether one or several, can turn on 'fine analysis and a degree of pragmatism'.[21]

One situation to look out for is Sec 22 Theft Act 1968, which provides a good example of how this rule works, without actually following it to the letter. Strictly speaking, s 22 creates the one offence of handling stolen goods (which can be

19 Another example might be an employee who steals small amounts from petty cash over a period, but this is not discovered until the shortfall is later noticed. Such cases are sometimes referred to as 'general deficiency' cases, because the deficit occurs little by little over time. For a good example, see *R v Lunn* [2017] EWCA Crim 34

20 [1977] 1 WLR 1102

21 In other words, the judge's grasp of statutory interpretation: see examples at BCrP D 11.56

committed in some 18 different ways!), but over the years it has come to be viewed as effectively creating two offences: (a) dishonestly receiving stolen goods and (b) the other 17 ways of handling stolen goods (undertaking or assisting in the retention or removal of stolen goods, and so on). The various possible ways of committing this second form of handling can, and usually will, all be charged in a single count in order to cover all the possibilities. But one count charging both receiving and the other forms of handling would be regarded as defective. If the prosecution really do not know whether the accused received the stolen goods or committed some other form of handling, then there should be two alternative counts to this effect on the indictment. The jury can then choose whether to convict on the receiving count (usually considered the more serious form of handling) or on the alternative count.[22]

2. MULTIPLE DEFENDANTS AND COUNTS

What happens when there is more than one offence committed by one defendant, or offences committed by more than one defendant? How does one determine how many and which counts to include on an indictment, and against how many accused? Like civil actions, there are rules about this (known colloquially as the 'joinder' rules) which are largely a matter of common sense. Unlike civil cases, ensuring the defendant (in particular) gets a fair trial also plays a significant part.

A. JOINDER OF COUNTS ON ONE INDICTMENT

This is all about how many counts can properly be included in one indictment. Two or more counts may be joined on the same indictment but only if all the charges are founded on the *same facts*, or form or are part of a series of offences of the *same*

22 See *R v Nicklin* [1977] 1 WLR 403. Nothing on the face of the indictment indicates the counts are alternatives, so this will need explaining to the jury. See Crown Court Compendium Pt 1 6-3

or similar character. If this test is not met, the court must exercise its power to order separate trials.[23] This is really a way of recognising that where charges are sufficiently connected to each other, it probably makes sense that they are tried together in front of the same judge and jury (but never makes sense if they are not so connected). Note however that, as we shall see, even if counts are properly joined there is a discretion to order separate trials where justice demands it.

It is useful to look at the two 'limbs' of this rule.

(i) Limb 1: 'Charges founded on the same facts'

The simplest application of this limb of the rule is a case like *R v Mansfield*, referred to above, where the accused was alleged to have set fire to the Worsley Hotel in Bayswater on 12 December 1974, as a result of which seven people died. Three arson counts and seven murder counts were all included on the indictment since they were all caused by the single act of setting the blaze. It would be odd if it were otherwise.

The same would apply to a continuous chain of criminal conduct. For example, the bank robber who flees at high speed through town in the 'get-away' car, crashes into a shop window and struggles to avoid capture by the police, could be charged in one indictment with counts of robbery, dangerous driving, criminal damage and assault with intent to resist arrest.[24]

But offences need not necessarily have been committed closely in time to be included on the same indictment. They could be said to 'arise from the same facts' if offence B would not have occurred but for offence A having been committed. The leading case on this is *R v Barrell and Wilson*[25] where W was charged in counts 1 and 2 (jointly with B) for assault and affray arising out of a fight at a discotheque, and in count 3 with attempting (much later) to pervert the course of justice by seeking to persuade witnesses to the brawl to 'modify' their evidence. The Court of Appeal

23 See CrimPR, r 3.21(4) and CrimPD II 10A. This is a slightly different way of articulating this requirement, but the test remains basically the same.

24 This example is given in Sprack, *Practical Approach*, 15.19

25 (1979) 69 Cr App R 250

held that the counts were properly joined because they had a 'common factual origin': had the appellants not been accused of acting as alleged in counts 1 and 2, there would have been no reason for the behaviour which resulted in count 3. The time lag did not negate the factual connection.[26]

A factual link can also be established by a 'coincidence of time and place'. In *R v Roberts*[27] during a police search of the accused's home, both illegal drugs and illegal firearms were found. The Court of Appeal held that the firearm and drug charges had been properly joined on the same indictment - the factual connection had been established by the drugs and firearms having been found at the same place at the same time.

Even if the counts are 'mutually destructive' in the sense that the accused can only be found guilty of one or the other, but not both, they may still be legitimately joined on the indictment if they are 'founded on the same facts' as discussed below.[28] Indeed it is common practice to include in an indictment counts for stealing and handling the same property, even though a conviction for theft would preclude a conviction for handling, and vice versa.[29]

Similarly the jury can be offered a menu of alternative possibilities, from which they will choose only one, depending on how they find the facts. Let's say, for example,[30] that a defendant broke the victim's nose and jaw (without breaking the skin). He might be charged on the same indictment with assault occasioning actual bodily harm (ABH) contrary to s 47 of the Offences Against the Person Act 1861; unlawfully and maliciously inflicting grievous bodily harm (GBH) contrary to s 20; and causing GBH with intent, contrary to s 18. The judge would direct the jury to go through the counts in descending order, and if they decided the accused had intended and did cause really serious harm, they would convict of the s 18 offence; if they were sure about the gravity of the injuries but not the accused's intentions, they

26 Similarly if an accused used a stolen contactless card to purchase goods. He could be charged with (1) theft or handling of the card and (2) obtaining property by deception in respect of each transaction, no matter how much time had elapsed between his acquiring the card and his dishonest use of it: as illustrated in *Practical Approach*, 15.19

27 [2008] EWCA Crim 1304

28 *R v Bellman* [1989] AC 836

29 Although prosecutors may need to take care in some cases that both counts do not mutually destruct in the sense of leaving a jury unable to decide on either count. BCrP D11.69

30 *Practical Approach*, D15.31

would convict of the s 20 offence; if satisfied merely that the defendant had caused some harm, they would convict of the s 47 offence; and if in doubt of all of the above, they should acquit.

(ii) Limb 2: Series of 'same or similar character'

The first limb of the rule covers factual links between charges. This second limb brings legal connections into the equation. For two or more offences to belong to a series of the same or similar character there must be a *legal as well as factual* 'nexus' between them: *Ludlow v Metropolitan Police Commissioner.*[31] Mind you, if the legal nexus is strong enough, the factual similarity can sometimes be relatively slight (as in Ludlow itself, since the fact that both offences occurred at pubs was coincidental). In *R v Marsh,*[32] for example, an indictment containing counts for criminal damage and reckless driving were said to be improperly joined with a count for assault which related to an entirely separate incident. Because there was no legal connection between the assault charge and the others, the Court of Appeal said that the common factual element of violence was insufficient of itself to provide a nexus.

It is also worth mentioning that a mere evidential connection may not be enough to satisfy the requirement. Compare, for example, two cases decided on appeal in 1993. In *R v C,*[33] the accused was charged with rape and attempted rape. Although the counts were in respect of incidents occurring 11 years apart from each other, the victim in both cases was the defendant's daughter. It was held that the counts were properly joined. In *R v Williams,*[34] on the other hand, it was alleged that the defendant had falsely imprisoned a 13 year old girl, having indecently assaulted her five days earlier. The Court of Appeal held that these were two separate incidents and the two offences were not of a similar character, despite an evidential nexus. Clearly every case is different, but given the degree of subjectivity involved in

31 [1971] AC 29. In that case the accused had been charged with (1) attempted theft at a pub in Acton on 20 August and (2) robbery at a different pub in Acton in September. The prosecution argued on appeal that 'similar character' meant exclusively a legal similarity and the defence argued that it meant exclusively a factual similarity. The House of Lords rejected both submissions, saying that both legal and factual similarity must be considered.

32 (1985) 83 Cr App R 282

33 The Times, 4 February 1993

34 [1993] CrimLR 533

applying this limb of the rule,[35] prosecutors ought to err on the side of caution when drafting indictments.

B. SPECIMEN OR SAMPLE COUNTS

Where a person is accused of a continuous or systematic course of criminal conduct, it may be preferable to proceed by way of a 'sample' or 'specimen' count instead of charging multiple counts of offending. This may be the case where a particular form of abuse or dishonesty over a long period of time is being alleged. To keep the indictment to a manageable length, a limited number of (representative) sample counts can be put on the indictment. The prosecution should provide the defence with a list of all of the offending of which it is alleged the specimen counts are samples. It is of course important that defendants know what they are being accused of, and have the opportunity to respond according. The fact that a defendant pleads guilty or has been found guilty of what prosecutors describe as a 'specimen' offence does *not* entitle the judge to sentence him as if he had been found guilty of other offences which were not on the indictment, unless the accused clearly admits such offending or asks the court to take such other offences 'into consideration' ('TICs').[36] As a matter of principle an accused cannot be deprived of his day in court through the prosecution expedient of sample counts.

C. JOINDER OF DEFENDANTS ON ONE INDICTMENT

More than one defendant may be included on a single indictment in one or other of two ways: (i) two or more defendants may be accused of committing the same offence(s) together (a joint count), and/or (ii) an indictment may charge different defendants with different offending (separate counts). It is useful to look at both of these possibilities separately, but bear in mind that in respect of

35 See useful illustrations set out in BCrP D 11.71

36 *R v Canavan* [1998] 1 Cr App R 79. And see Ch.10. There is now an alternative approach set out in the Domestic Violence, Crime and Victims Act 2004 where in effect a jury tries the sample count and a judge alone then tries the other offences which that sample count was said to represent. See BCrP D 11.36ff and guidance in *R v A* [2015] EWCA Crim 177

any one indictment, both may be applicable.

(i) Joint counts

One count in an indictment can name more than one defendant if it is alleged that all of those named participated in committing the alleged offence. This is merely a convenient way of accusing more than one person of committing a single crime together.[37] If three persons were accused of the same offence, it would be very tedious to have to write this out three different times in three different counts, merely changing the name each time. It is so much easier to accuse Tom, Dick and Harry in the same breath.

Moreover, this common sense principle applies even if some of the defendants named in the one count are accused of playing a 'secondary' role in the 'principal' activity.[38] So, for example if B (a bank employee) gives information to C and D which enables them to enter the bank as trespassers to steal money, and A stays outside in the get-away car to drive them off afterwards, then clearly there have been different levels of participation in the crime. A and B are what are known as secondary offenders since they aided and abetted the burglary, but did not physically carry out the deed themselves. They could be charged specifically as accessories, but there is no requirement to do so, and in fact it would typically happen that all four would be charged with the principal offence.[39]

The prosecution in its opening speech would make clear what the extent of each defendant's role is alleged to have been, and if one of the accessories were to plead guilty, his lesser participation will be made clear as mitigation before sentencing.[40] The jury are, of course, entitled to convict some (or even just one) of those jointly charged in the one count, and acquit the others.

In exceptional circumstances, as discussed below, where trying defendants

37 And so there is no problem with duplicity here. The rule against duplicity prevents accusing one person of more than one offence in a single count. Here we are talking about charging more than one person with one offence.

38 Accessories and Abettors Act 1861, s 8 which provides that all secondary offenders are liable to be 'tried, indicted and punished as a principal offender'.

39 Unless a jury would be confused by this, as they might be, for example, if the charge was rape. In such cases, prosecutors might feel it is better to charge an accessory with 'aiding and abetting'. And see BCrP D 11.73/74

40 See Ch. 10

jointly charged would cause unfair prejudice to an accused, separate trials can be ordered.

(ii) Separate counts

It is also possible to join defendants in the same indictment, but charge them in separate counts, so long as the *various counts themselves are all properly joined* according to the rules.[41] Clearly there must be some factor linking the offences and the perpetrators. A typical example is a theft and subsequent handling of the stolen property: if A breaks into a jewellers and steals several watches, rings and bracelets, and B, C, and D separately 'fence' the various items stolen, then charges against all of them may go on the same indictment. A will be charged with burglary; the rest will be charged with whatever form of handling is appropriate in each individual case.[42] In the leading case of *R v Assim*, there were two defendants, a receptionist and a doorman at the same nightclub, who were charged with injuring two separate customers during one altercation. The receptionist (D1) was charged with wounding V1 as he attempted to leave the premises without paying his bill; another guest, V2, tried to intervene and was allegedly assaulted by the doorman (D2). Since the defendants' respective acts of violence had two separate victims, they could not be charged in a single count. But joining the separate counts on the same indictment was justified (and sensible) because of the proximity of time and place, and apparent cause, of the events of that evening.

Again, as discussed below, the court has a discretion to split the indictment and order separate trials if a defendant is unfairly prejudiced by a joint trial. Such orders are not common, but it is perhaps slightly easier to split an indictment where the defendants are charged in separate counts, than when they are jointly charged in one.

41 As discussed above. For a recent horrific example of multiple incidents and multiple defendants, see *R v A*, op. cit., fn 36 where a husband and his father were both charged with counts of rape of the complainant wife. The husband's mother was charged with interfering with witnesses.

42 s 27(1) Theft Act 1968 provides for the various handlers of stolen property to be charged together in the same indictment. But see BCrP D 11.75

Remember too that the rules about joining defendants in the same or separate counts can and often do operate simultaneously. *R v Barrell and Wilson*, discussed above, is a good example. The defendants were both charged with affray (joint count), but only Wilson was alleged to have perverted the course of justice, and this separate count was properly joined to the same indictment because of its factual link to the others.

D. OVERLOADING THE INDICTMENT

The joinder rules are not particularly strict, but however inter-connected the charges or the criminal activities of co-accused might be, it is possible to have too much of a good thing. For this reason, those drafting indictments (or hearing applications to sever) must both appreciate and guard against the perils of an 'overloaded' indictment. Too many counts and/or too many defendants, especially if the case is a complex one, can make the lives of judge and jury a misery, and bring no benefit to criminal justice. The appeal courts may be reluctant to quash convictions on this basis, but they often warn of the dangers. The case of *R v Thorne*[43] is a prime example. The indictment covered three separate armed robberies and included counts for related conspiracy to rob, handling some of the proceeds and conspiracy to pervert the court of justice by threatening potential witnesses. In all there were ten counts and 14 accused. The trial involved ten firms of solicitors, 27 counsel, lasted seven months and included a 12 day summing-up from the judge (it makes me tired just thinking about it!). None of the appeals were allowed simply because the trial had been too long, but the Court of Appeal said the indictment was clearly overloaded and had placed an intolerable burden on both judge and jury.

Justice is not served by throwing everything at the defendant, and so indictments should contain only what is needed to fairly try and punish criminal

43 (1977) 66 Cr App R 6

behaviour, and no more. As their Code puts it, Crown Prosecutors should 'select charges which (a) reflect the *seriousness* of the offending; (b) give the court *ample* sentencing powers; and (c) enable the case to be presented in a *clear and simple* way'.[44] If there is genuine uncertainty, then alternative counts may be necessary, but they should not be included as a matter of course. In particular, counts should not be included for tactical reasons, for example to scare or cajole the accused into pleading to some (or some lesser) offences.[45]

3. SEVERANCE, MISJOINDER AND AMENDMENT

'Severance' is an expression which, historically, has referred to ordering separate trials of offences which were properly joined in one indictment. If counts had not been properly joined - if there had been a 'misjoinder' - it was thought that this invalidated the entire indictment and could not be rectified by severance. Over time this (rather technical) distinction fell out of favour, so that if counts have been improperly joined, the situation now is that the court must sever the indictment and order a separate trial of the properly joined counts. Courts may also order separate trials if fairness demands it, but this is rarely exercised.

A. SEVERANCE: DISCRETION TO ORDER SEPARATE TRIALS

Even if the counts or defendants have been properly joined, the court has a discretion to 'sever' the indictment and order separate trials if it feels that an accused may be 'prejudiced or embarrassed'[46] in his defence, either by reason of being charged with more than one offence in the same indictment, or because for some other reason it is desirable that he be tried separately (for example, from other

44 Code for Crown Prosecution, para 6.1 (my emphasis). In a 'course of conduct' case, the prosecution 'needs to ensure that there are one or more sufficiently broad course of conduct counts, or a mix of individual counts and course of conduct counts, such that the judge will be able to sentence the defendant appropriately on the basis of his criminality as revealed by the counts on which he is convicted' per Fulford LJ in *R v A*, para 47, op. cit., fn 36

45 *Ibid*, Para 6.3

46 'Embarrassed' is an archaic description which refers not to the accused blushing self-consciously, but to being hindered or compromised in his ability to defend himself.

defendants) for any one or more offences charged in the indictment.[47] It is important to appreciate that this power to sever, important as it is, will only be exercised in *exceptional* circumstances. The joinder rules are themselves geared to identifying when a single trial would be sensible, and so more often than not the rationale for there being one trial will outweigh any arguments for split trials. In the case of *R v Ludlow*[48] it was made clear that where counts are properly joined, the judge should only sever the indictment if there is a 'special feature' justifying separate trials. So far as joint counts against the same defendant, examples given in that case include:

(i) where evidence in respect of one offence would be difficult to 'disentangle' from evidence relevant to the other counts; *or*
(ii) where evidence against the accused on one count would so prejudice him in the eyes of the jury that they would be unable to approach the other counts with an open mind; *or*
(iii) where the evidence on all counts is weak but the jury might view the case by reference to the sum of its parts; *or*
(iv) where the evidence in respect of the counts varies disproportionately and the jury might assume that if guilty of some of the offences the defendant must be guilty of the others.

In any event, the *burden rests on the defence* to show exceptional circumstances justifying split trials. This may be easier to do in some cases than in others. Where, for example, defendants are charged with committing an offence jointly, the benefits of a single trial are usually overwhelming. A single trial saves the time and the expense of the same witnesses having to tell their stories twice. It is more

---

47 Indictments Act 1915, s 5(3): CrimPR, r 3.21(4)(b)
48 Op. cit., and see generally BCrP D 11.86-11.88

likely to give a jury a full and accurate picture of what actually happened, and eliminates the risk of two juries coming to inconsistent conclusions on essentially the same evidence. To convince a judge to order split trials in such cases, one defendant would have to show that a fair trial could not be achieved unless the indictment is severed.

The usual defence anxiety is that a jury would be prejudiced by hearing evidence which is inadmissible against the accused seeking separate trials, but in the vast majority of cases this risk (which is particularly keenly felt when defendants are blaming each other) is mitigated by means of proper and clear instructions to a jury about how to approach the evidence in the case. As the Court of Appeal put it in *R v Miah*,[49] 'the fact that a co-defendant is running a 'cut-throat' defence is common and is very seldom a successful ground, standing alone, for severance'.

The presumption in favour of one trial may be a little more easily offset where a defendant is charged with multiple counts (particularly if the indictment is seen as overloaded), or where the co-defendant is charged in a separate count (especially if the evidence in respect of that count does not significantly overlap with the evidence relevant to the others). But the circumstances still need to be exceptional. In *R v Laycock*,[50] for example, one of several counts against the defendant alleged possession of a firearm when he was a 'prohibited person', having been sentenced to imprisonment for more than three years. The Court of Appeal was very critical, both because the indictment was overloaded and because the firearms offence contributed little to the catalogue of other allegations, beyond pure prejudice - it did not add to the judge's sentencing power, for example, but made it obvious on its face that the accused had previous (serious) convictions. It struck the court that there was no real need to secure a conviction on the firearm offence in particular, and even if there were, a separate trial would have been fairer.

49 [2011] EWCA Crim 945
50 [2003] EWCA Crim 1477

At all events, it is as well to remember that the discretion to sever is used sparingly. Rather obviously, such applications (usually made by defendants) should be heard before trial, but a judge can order separate trials at any stage of the proceedings.

B. MISJOINDER

If counts are improperly joined to an indictment then (as we have seen) the court must exercise its power to order separate trials so that the case proceeds only in respect of those counts which were properly included.[51] This may not solve the problem, (what about the misjoined count?) from the prosecution's perspective however, and indictments can suffer from other defects (eg a duplicitous count). There may be other solutions to bear in mind.

(i) General power of amendment

Once an indictment has been served, if it is defective, the judge must order that it be amended, unless such amendment would cause injustice.[52] When an amendment appears necessary, the prosecution should apply for it (preferably with an amended version for the judge to see). Failing this, judges may raise the matter themselves. Where necessary, the defence (who may or may not have brought the defect to the prosecution or court's attention) should be given time to consider how its position might be affected by the proposed amendment.

So long as not unjust, *any* defect in an indictment (however trivial or serious) may be cured by amendment. A misjoinder can be cured in this way too, by deleting the offending count, so that what is left is a properly constituted indictment.

Moreover, new counts may be inserted into the indictment either in substitution for or in addition to those originally drafted. This sort of amendment is not curing

51 CrimPR, r 3.21(4)(a)

52 Indictments Act, s 5(1). Injustice should not be too narrowly construed for these purposes: *R v Booker* [2012] 3 All ER 905

a defect, as such, but merely adding counts which could be (but were not earlier) perfectly properly joined onto the indictment.

Amendments may be ordered at any stage of proceedings, although the later the amendment, the greater the risk of injustice. Having said that, technical amendments can be made surprisingly late in the day provided no harm has been done.[53]

(ii) Stay the indictment

Another solution to misjoinder is to stay (in other words, effectively ignore) the initial indictment, and allow the prosecution to serve one or more fresh indictment(s), with properly joined counts. If the initial indictment was enough of a mess, this can be a neat and simple answer. An indictment can be partially stayed, so that proceedings simply continue only against the remaining count or defendant.[54]

(iii) Motion to quash the indictment

Either party may apply to quash an indictment, although this will usually be a defence application. If such a motion succeeds, the result is that the accused may not be tried on that (or that part of the) indictment. Sounds promising for an accused, but the problem with such motions is that prosecutors have all manner of means of dealing with the potential or actual fall-out of such applications. First of all, the grounds for a motion to quash are very limited.[55] Secondly, even if the motion succeeds, the defendant is not thereby acquitted - the prosecution is entitled to commence fresh proceedings (and to try not to make the same mistake twice). Finally, a suitable application by the prosecution to amend can often fend off a successful application. Motions to quash have their place, but they are of limited value to defendants.

53 See BCrP D 11.100ff

54 *R v Munro* [1993] CrimLR 393

55 See BCrP D 11.110 ff

revision tips

- Make sure you understand the rule against duplicity. Do not confuse it with the rules about when it is proper to have more than one count and/or more than one defendant charged in the same indictment.
- Think in terms of different factual scenarios regarding joinder of counts and joinder of defendants etc. You may well be asked to identify the best answer regarding counts on an indictment.

It is worth reading ...

R v Barrell & Wilson (1979) 69 Cr App R 250. Shaw LJ's judgment is short, but the case demonstrates both joinder of defendants and joinder of counts. It is a straightforward application of the principles.

Judgment in *R v Lunn* [2017] EWCA Crim 34. Don't let the accountancy double-speak put you off. This is a relatively straightfoward case of tax fraud. It references the 2015 criminal procedure rules and you will hear the clang of the prison gates.

If you have the stomach for it, the judgment in *R v A* [2015] EWCA Crim 177. It is (painfully) easy to follow and there are an awful lot of procedural points about indictments here.

CHAPTER 7

Pre-trial disclosure

There once was a time when it was almost exclusively prosecutors who were under any obligation to make pre-trial disclosure of relevant information which came into their possession while preparing a criminal case. This was the common law's way of compensating for the 'resource gap' between the individual and the state. The former, whose liberty was often on the line, usually has far fewer facilities at his disposal. Meanwhile, the prosecution service enjoyed the benefit of a range of staff and services, not least of which are the police and various forensic scientists. If you've ever seen *Law and Order*, you will know what I mean! It was thought that a more level playing field was achieved by requiring the prosecution to disclose the nature of most of the relevant evidence to which it had access - both that which assisted its case, and that which undermined it (or assisted the defence case).[1] The first of these gave a defendant *notice* of the case he had to answer; the second might give him *ammunition* with which to do so.

The prosecution's duty to disclose has not changed all that much over the years,[2] although the obligation to reveal information adverse to its case (known, rather prosaically, and with classic English understatement, as 'unused' material because the prosecution will not use it at trial) is now subject to a statutory regime. This is the Criminal Procedure and Investigations Act 1996 (CPIA 1996), as

1 But not sensitive material covered by public interest immunity - see below and Ch. 16

2 But the vocabulary can be confusing. The obligation to give details of the prosecution case is often known as the duty to provide 'advance information' or 'initial details'. The prosecution's 'duty to disclose' usually refers specifically to the obligation to reveal to the defence information which undermines that case or assists the defendant's case.

amended by the CJA 2003 and as supplemented by various guidance, protocols and rules.[3]

Historically defendants were not required to disclose much of anything about their case pre-trial, as was consistent with the presumption of innocence and the prosecution's burden of proof. But this changed radically with CPIA 1996. Now they must disclose the nature of their case in considerable detail. Several reasons are typically given for this, effective case management and avoiding 'trial by ambush' among them. In addition, it is said that knowing the accused's case makes it possible for prosecutors to ensure that they have disclosed all relevant unused material to him.[4] These are all sensible aims, although in some respects defendants are now required to reveal rather more tactical information about their case than are prosecutors, and can be punished more severely for their failure to do so. Perhaps this is unavoidable given their respective positions. At any rate, in the Crown Court, juries may need to be given careful directions about this to ensure fairness.[5]

In the front line, of course, are the police (and others in the role of investigators). These are the people who will first see relevant evidence in a case. In order to ensure that the prosecutors know of, and have access to, all the material it is obliged to disclose to the defence, those investigating a case have a duty to record and retain it.

These various duties are summarised below, in the order in which they normally occur initially, bearing in mind that in *all* cases the obligation is a *continuing* one, so that even if additional disclosable information later comes to light (after the first round of disclosure, for example), it should still be disclosed (and asap).

---

3 CrimPR Pt 15, and see especially A-G Guidelines on Disclosure ('A-G Disclosure Guidelines') and Judicial Disclosure Protocol, both at App 4, BCrP. Don't get distracted by the range of sources (summarised at BCrP D 9.5). Just concentrate on the disclosure obligations of the parties.

4 A-G Disclosure Guidelines, paras 19, 39

5 See Crown Court Compendium Pt 1 17-4

1. DUTY OF INVESTIGATORS

It is no good imposing a duty on prosecutors to disclose information to defendants, if there is no way of ensuring that the relevant material survives the investigation stage intact. For this reason there is an obligation on those whose job is investigating crime, like the police,[6] to '*record and retain*' (in a 'durable or retrievable' form) relevant (or potentially relevant) material which is *gathered* in the course of an investigation (for example, evidence found on the accused), or *generated* by it (for example, in interview with the accused). Material is relevant if it 'has some bearing' on the offence or person under investigation;[7] it is important to note that the requirement is to retain material which *either helps or hinders* the prosecution case, because one way or another this is precisely what the prosecution must reveal to the defence. Thus the sorts of items covered by this duty not only include[8] things like crime and expert's reports, witness statements, custody and interview records, but also material casting doubt on the reliability of a witness (for example, previous convictions of that witness) or of a confession. It also includes 'negative' information, such as the fact that nothing unusual was observed by anybody at a particular place at a particular time, if this is relevant.

Every investigation should have an investigator and a disclosure officer.[9] The latter's job is to ensure and certify compliance with the obligation to record and retain - both are required to be 'fair and objective', and to 'work together with prosecutors' on disclosure issues. If there is doubt about an item's relevance, investigators should always err on the side of caution and they are specifically required to draw adverse material to the attention of the prosecutor.

Once it is clear that there is to be a trial, then a disclosure schedule of unused material should be prepared. This sets out the relevant material which does not

6 See CPIA 1996, s 23 (police) and s 26 (others, like customs officers, charged with investigating crime).

7 So purely ancillary items or duplicate copies need not be recorded or retained.

8 See non-exhaustive list set out in CPIA Code of Practice (2015), para 5.4. This is easy on the eye and is on the gov.uk website.

9 In small cases these might be one and the same person. In complex cases there may be a disclosure team, but there should always be a 'lead' disclosure officer. These roles are important, but doubts are sometimes expressed on whether funding for them is adequate to the task. See BCrP D 9.8-9.10

form part of the case against the accused, and will not therefore be used by the prosecution at trial, but which may be of some assistance to the defence, on whom this schedule will ultimately be served. As you might expect, if relevant material is considered 'sensitive' (and so, arguably, not in the public interest to disclose) it should be recorded on a separate (confidential) schedule.[10]

The disclosure officer's duty is a 'continuing one', and so as new or newly relevant material comes to light, it must also be recorded and retained. In particular, the situation should be *reviewed* once the nature of the defence becomes known, because (for example) this information may well point to the relevance or value to the defence of existing, but previously undisclosed material.[11]

Relevant material must be retained at least until criminal proceedings are concluded. This is logical enough. So too is the fact that where an accused has been convicted, the material should be retained for at least another six months or until the defendant is released from custody, whichever is longer. There might be an appeal![12]

2. DUTY OF PROSECUTORS

Prosecutors must make appropriate disclosure from the outset of a case. Preliminary information about the case against the accused should be given early on so as to assist defendants to make plea, mode of trial and other decisions. The duty to disclose unused material principally arises under the CPIA and applies equally to the magistrates' and Crown Court.[13] At all events the prosecution should be proactive so far as disclosure is concerned.[14]

10 See generally BCrP D 9.12

11 Prosecutors share this duty to 'review' and (where appropriate) 'reveal'. See BCrP D 9.13 and 9.24. And A-G's Disclosure Guidelines, para 15.

12 See BCrP D 9.11

13 See Judicial Disclosure Protocol, para 30

14 See *R* [2016] 1 WLR 1872, set out at BCrP D 9.13. This case involved a complex fraud and a mountain of material, but the principles are of general application.

A. PROSECUTION CASE *AGAINST* DEFENDANT

Before the first hearing in the magistrates' court, the prosecution must serve on the court and (if he requests) on the accused, 'initial details' of the case against the accused.[15] The usual practice is to send a standard information package, including the charge sheet, summary of the prosecution case, key witness statements and a print-out of any previous convictions.[16]

B. PRE-TRIAL DISCLOSURE OF 'UNUSED' MATERIAL: CPIA 1996

It is obviously necessary for defendants to know in advance about the case against them - even better to find out what material the prosecution has come across which is detrimental to that case, and which might help them get acquitted! Thus the obligation on the prosecution to disclose relevant material it won't use, but the accused might, is a particularly crucial one. By its operation, an accused in effect gets the benefit of anything the Crown's vast investigative service turns up which might help his case.[17]

CPIA 1996 thus requires the prosecutor to provide the defence with copies of, or access to, any material (not previously disclosed[18]) which 'might reasonably be considered capable of *undermining* the prosecution case against, or *assisting* the case for, the accused'.[19] This test, which is an objective one, is very widely drawn, and would seem to include anything which shows a defect, discrepancy or inconsistency in the prosecution case. The A-G Disclosure Guidelines set out various matters[20] which should be considered when deciding whether the test is satisfied, including the capacity of the information to suggest an *alternative theory* of the case or other explanation for the accused's actions than that put forward by the prosecution; the use which might be made of it in *cross-examination* (whether as to credibility or a matter in issue in the case); its ability *to support a defence argument* for the exclusion of an item

15 If the accused does not request the information, it must be 'made available' to him. See also Ch. 4

16 Even if strictly the rules do not require all of this information being provided if the accused is in custody at the time. See BCrP D 21.25

17 A-G Disclosure Guideline, para 4-8 and BCrP D 9.15ff

18 At common law, unused material may be disclosable at an earlier stage, for example, to assist the defence with a bail application. This is said to be part and parcel of being a 'reasonable prosecutor'. See discussion at BCrP D 9.14

19 CPIA 1996, s 3, A-G Disclosure Guideline, para 8 (my emphasis).

20 A-G Disclosure Guidelines, para 12

of evidence or a stay in proceedings (information about the accused's mental state or capacity while being interviewed may well be relevant to this).[21] The guidelines also emphasise that the value of unused material needs to be judged by reference to what is known at the time, but at the same time it should be considered holistically - something viewed in isolation may look very different when looked at together with other information.[22]

One category of material which might undermine the prosecution case, for example, and so qualify for disclosure is a prosecution witness's previous convictions. In *R v Vasilious*,[23] the accused's conviction was quashed and a new trial ordered because the prosecution failed to disclose the previous convictions of one of their own witnesses. The Court of Appeal said that the guilty verdict was unsafe because, without the information, the defence had been deprived of a means of attacking the credibility of the prosecution witness and forced to pursue a different strategy. Of course, one always has to look carefully at the *relevance* of such information, especially if its revelation might do positive harm to the relationship of the witness with others or breach his right to private life, but if it has a bearing on the testimony of the witness (and is not otherwise 'sensitive' material) then it should be disclosed.[24]

If no disclosable unused material exists, then the prosecutor must serve a written notice to this effect on the defence.[25] If the prosecution are not using otherwise disclosable material because it is 'sensitive' (and for that reason they do not want it disclosed to the defence either) then permission to withhold the material on the basis of an overriding public interest should be sought from the court. The basis for such a claim is called public interest immunity, which in a criminal context is typically raised to protect the identity of police informers and/or to keep secret locations secret. The A-G Disclosure Guidelines make clear that before making such an application,[26] 'prosecutors should aim to disclose as much of the material as they possibly can'

21 See *ibid*, para 8
22 *Ibid*, para 10
23 [2000] Crim LR 845
24 If such evidence of bad character is or may be admissible under s 100 CJA 2003 (which limits the ability to put previous convictions to a witness other than the accused) then presumably it is disclosable. See, e.g., *HM Advocate v Murtagh* [2011] 1 AC 731 as discussed in BCrP D 9.19 and Ch. 19
25 CPIA 1996, s 1(b)
26 Para 65. See also *R v H*[2004] 2AC 134 and BCrP D 9.50ff. The procedure is found at CrimPR r 15.3. Public interest immunity is discussed in Ch. 16

(for example by giving the defence redacted or edited copies or summaries).

Having said all of that, it is important to appreciate that it is not the prosecution's role actively to do the defence's work for it. In particular, material which is *neutral or damaging to the defence case need not be disclosed*.[27] Prosecutors only have to disclose unused material which undermines their own case or which supports the defence case.

Prosecution disclosure of unused material should take place 'as soon as practicable'.[28] In the Crown Court, this would normally occur in time for the defence to prepare a defence statement prior to any Plea and Trial Preparation Hearing.[29] In the magistrates' court, the obligations under CPIA only arise after a not-guilty plea (when a 'streamlined' disclosure certificate[30] is required), but the prosecution should also be 'alert' to the possibility that such material might assist a defendant who pleads guilty, for example, in a bail application or for sentencing.[31] Thus any relevant disclosure should occur in the magistrates' court before the hearing at which a plea is taken. If no such material exists, then an assurance to this effect must be given.

Unused material is disclosed either by giving copies to the defence or allowing the defence to inspect the material at a reasonable time and place. At the same time, the (non-sensitive) disclosure schedule itself must be served[32], so the defence can cross-check that they have actually seen all the items listed.

If the prosecution fail to make proper disclosure, then the defence can apply for an order that it do so, but only after a defence statement has been served.[33] This is the usual sanction. Only in extreme cases would a prosecution's failure to disclose result in the case being halted or stayed on grounds of abuse of process. But it happens.[34] In the face of such applications, the key question for the court will always be the extent to which the behaviour of the prosecution has prejudiced the accused and/or undermined the proper administration of justice. Any fault on the part of

27 See, e.g., *R v Khan* [2007] EWCA Crim 822 cited at BCrP D 9.16

28 CPIA 1996, s 13

29 See Ch. 9

30 See BCrP D 9.22

31 CPIA Code of Conduct, para 6.3-6.5 and *DPP ex parte Lee* [1999] 1 WLR 1950

32 CPIA 1996, s 4

33 *Ibid*, s 8 and see below

34 See, e.g., *R(L)* [2011] 1WLR 359

the defence may also be relevant. The defence should play its part in ensuring that attention is not 'diverted' from the real issues.[35]

Prosecutors remain under a *continuing* duty to review the question of disclosure - even as the trial progresses.[36] Whenever such material comes to light, it must be disclosed as soon as reasonably practicable. In particular, once a defence statement is served, the investigator must review the file and draw the prosecutor's attention to any new or newly relevant material which might qualify for disclosure to the defence.[37]

2. DUTY OF DEFENDANTS

Some defendants may feel that what CPIA giveth with the one hand, it taketh away with the other. Certainly, it places an obligation on the accused (at least in the Crown Court) to disclose extensive information about his defence which the common law had not been willing to impose.[38] The justification for this rests primarily with effective case management and the need to alert prosecutors to the evidential value of any unused material. As the A-G Disclosure Guidelines put it, 'defence engagement must be early and meaningful for the CPIA regime to function as intended'.[39]

Therefore, once a case has been sent to the Crown Court for trial[40] and initial prosecution disclosure has taken place, the accused must give a *defence statement* to the court and the prosecution.[41] A defence statement is a written statement which sets out:

(i) the *nature* of the defence, including any particular defences on which he *intends to rely* and the *facts he relies on* in support of that defence;
(ii) the matters of fact on which he *takes issue with* the prosecution, with reasons *why*; *and*

35 See below, *Prosecution Appeal*: *R v O* [2011] EWCA Crim 2854 and A-G Disclosure Guidelines, paras 2 and 3
36 CPIA 1996, s 7A
37 See example at BCrP D 9.24
38 Requiring extensive defence disclosure was thought to interfere with the burden of proof.
39 A-G Disclosure Guidelines, para 39
40 See Ch. 5
41 CPIA 1996, s 5

(iii) any *points of law* which he wishes to take (and any *authority* on which he wants to rely).[42]

Everything about their case, it would seem, except the kitchen sink!

If the defence statement discloses an *alibi*, relevant particulars should be given - name, age, address and so on of any alibi witnesses to be called or (if such detail is not known) as much information as possible to assist in identifying the person(s).[43] Any other witnesses which the defence intends calling should be also be disclosed (with pertinent details) to the court and the prosecutor, but on a *separate* sheet.[44]

The defence of course needs to see the prosecution case and any relevant unused material before it can complete and serve a defence statement and witness list, and so the time for doing so only starts to run, as it were, on the day the prosecution complies (or purports to comply) with its primary disclosure obligation. Once the latter has happened, defendants have 28 days in the Crown Court to comply with their disclosure obligations. In the magistrates' court (where *only* the alibi notice and witness lists are *obligatory*) they have 14 days. Defendants can apply for an extension of time, but must do so before the time for disclosure has expired. Extensions will not be granted lightly.[45]

According to the Judicial Protocol, judges will 'expect to see defence case statements that contain a clear and detailed exposition of the issues of fact and law in the case'.[46] This is in part to focus court time on the real issues in dispute, but also to stop defendants 'making general and unspecified allegations and then seeking far-reaching prosecution disclosure in the hopes that material may turn up to make them good'.[47] The question then arises: what happens if the defendant fails to disclose adequately? What happens if no statement is served? Or an inadequate statement is served? Or a defendant gives testimony inconsistent with

42 *Ibid*, s 6A(1)

43 *Ibid*, s 6A(2). S 21A(2) also requires that police officers and others take care in conducting interviews of witnesses notified to them by the defence (so as not to scare them off!). BCrP D9.35

44 In time this may also include names of experts which defendants have instructed: CPIA s 6D (not yet in force)

45 CPIA 1996 (Defence Disclosure Time Limits) Regulations 2011 (SI 2011/209), regs 2 and 3

46 Para 35 (in BCrP Appendix 4)

47 As articulated at para 15 of the predecessor to the current A-G Disclosure Guidelines

that previewed in the statement?[48]

In terms of sanctions, a defendant runs two main risks from inadequate disclosure. One is that the court and other parties may be able to comment on the failure[49] and the other is that the court or jury may be able to hold that failure against the defendant when deciding on guilt.[50] Much will depend on the nature of the inadequacy, the reason for it, and what adverse inferences might properly be drawn from it. The question will be: what, if anything, does the procedural failure say about the credibility of the defence which the accused ultimately relied upon at trial? If, for example, the accused serves no statement at all (or serves it very late) it might (not necessarily will) follow from this that his defence at trial is a late invention.[51] Other failings may be more justifiable, or not the accused's fault, or so minimal as to be disregarded. Every case is different and in the Crown Court it will be for the judge to decide whether, and if so what, to tell the jury about it. The judge may allow the jury to see the defence statement.[52] One thing is pretty clear: failure to disclose defence evidence does not render it inadmissible as such, and courts should think carefully about excluding defence evidence altogether, even that which appears at the 11th hour.[53]

Finally, it is worth noting the following points about defence disclosure.

(i) Continuing nature of the obligation to disclose

I have made the point that it is disclosure by the prosecution which triggers the timetable for defence disclosure. Equally, defence disclosure triggers a review by the investigator, who (in light of the information on the defence statement) must draw the prosecutor's attention to any relevant unused material which has not yet been disclosed. The obligation to disclose is a continuing one, as and when new or newly relevant material or information comes to light.[54]

48 CPIA, s 11 sets out the various ways the defendant can go wrong in serving his case statement. See BCrP D 9.42

49 Comment by other parties will require the leave of the court in some circumstances, for example, failure to mention an admissibility point or properly identify a witness. See BCrP D 9.43 and 9.45

50 s 11(5) CPIA 1996

51 And so the posititition is analogous to s 34 CJPO 1994, as to which see Ch. 23

52 See Crown Court Compendium Pt 1 17-4 for a useful summary.

53 See, e.g., *R v Mamun Ullah* [2011] EWCA Crim 3275, and examples of possible directions to the jury.

54 A-G Disclosure Guidelines, paras 28, 42

(ii) Nature of the disclosure from the accused

You will notice that the scope of disclosure required of an accused is different from, and rather broader than that required of the prosecution. However note that (unlike prosecution disclosure) *there is no duty on defendants to disclose material they do not intend using.* Nevertheless, defendants are obliged to go beyond disclosing their defence or names of witnesses and are required to reveal a lot about how their case will be presented at trial.

In part this is the inevitable consequence of the different functions of the protagonists. It is not the role of the accused to assert and establish his innocence; it is the prosecution's job to prove guilt. All the defence lawyer needs to do to succeed is cast reasonable doubt on the prosecution case. But this is often the more subtle or pervasive role, involving challenges to the prosecution evidence on a variety of levels (admissibility, fairness, veracity). It can therefore be difficult for defence lawyers to know precisely what and how much to say on the defence case statement. An appropriate degree of detail can result in the release of further unused prosecution material which might assist the defence.

But there are dangers in both too little information (which might look like the accused is still deciding what the defence is) and too much (which might limit room for manoeuvre at trial) - both of which could result in adverse inferences being drawn if the discrepancy between the defence statement and the defence at trial looks suspiciously large. As to the accuracy of what is disclosed, presumably this is to be judged by reference to what, at that particular time, the defence knows about the case against him. One thing that is certain, however, is that defendants cannot be asked and so are not required to disclose information protected by privilege.[55]

55 See Ch. 16 and BCrP D 9.30

(iii) Statements drafted by solicitors

It is solicitors who usually draft defence statements. To remove any doubt as to who in fact is making (or updating) the statement, where a solicitor purports to do this on behalf of the accused, the statement is treated as having been given with the authority of the accused, unless the contrary is proved.[56] This is essentially to avoid a defendant later distancing himself from its contents. It is probably best practice if the accused himself does actually sign the statement (having been advised of the implications and so forth), but this is not a strict requirement. As a matter of professional conduct, barristers should not draft such statements unless they are properly familiar with the case and confident that the guidelines and other requirements are being followed.[57]

(iv) Voluntary nature of defence case statement in the magistrates' court

It is important to remember that, unlike the Crown Court (where they are mandatory), defence case statements *are voluntary in the magistrates' court.* There are no juries in summary trials, of course, but the justices can still draw adverse inferences if there is a suspicious discrepancy between the defence on the day and what was advertised. The only real advantage in serving a defence statement in the magistrates' court, therefore, is that it triggers a review of the prosecution evidence to see if there is any previously undisclosed material which would assist the defence as set out in that defence statement. If the latter would not add anything to what the prosecution already knows (for example, because the accused said the same thing in a police interview), there is little to be gained by defendants in serving a case statement in the magistrates' court.[58]

What is normally required in the magistrates' court is the completion of a Preparation for Effective Trial form. This is not a disclosure document, as such,

56 See Ch. 15 and BCrP D 9.32

57 Solicitors are perhaps more apt to draft these than counsel.

58 See BCrP D 21.26

but where an accused plans to plead not guilty he will normally be required to complete the relevant parts of the form before the first hearing, which in fact asks for a significant amount of detail. Only if the defendant makes formal admissions in the relevant section of that document, however, will any of the information be admissible against him as such.[59]

(v) Disclosure between co-defendants

So far as disclosure between co-defendants, this is not yet covered by the statutory scheme, but this may soon change.[60] At common law, if disclosure between defendants does not occur voluntarily, then the court should normally make an appropriate order to ensure that it does. Logically, what should happen is that a defendant serves copies of his defence statement on all other defendants, as well as the prosecution and the court. It would be a little odd if everyone else but the co-defendants got to see this!

(vi) Disclosure from third parties

Sometimes material which will assist the defence case will be in the hands of a third party,[61] that is, someone other than the prosecutor. For example, in a child abuse allegation, the relevant local authority may have evidence showing that the alleged victim has made false allegations in the past.[62] This would be helpful for the defence to see, so how does this happen? There are essentially three routes to disclosure in such cases:

(a) Investigators cannot turn a blind eye to lines of inquiry which may result in evidence which undermines the case against an accused. Therefore, if the material is something which the investigation has (or

59 *R v Newell* [2012] EWCA Crim 650

60 BCrP D 9.31

61 No relation to civil litigation's third parties!

62 As in *R v Bushell* [2001] Crim LR 471

could have) turned up, then this should be disclosable as a normal part of the CPIA disclosure regime discussed above.

(b) The third party may be willing to disclose the information to the defence voluntarily.

(c) The accused succeeds in an application compelling the third party to disclose the evidence.[63] The application (which is like seeking a witness summons) is made on notice (so the third party can argue against disclosure), supported by written evidence to satisfy the court that the third party is likely to be able to give or produce evidence which is likely to be material to the case, but which they are not willing to disclose voluntarily. If public interest immunity is claimed by the third party as a reason for not making voluntary disclosure, the court will in effect be asked to weigh this against the competing public interest of the proper administration of justice.[64]

revision tips

- Be clear about who has to disclose what - and in what order.
- Be clear about the extent and nature of disclosure required by both prosecution and defence. Note similarities and differences.
- Remember that a defence statement is obligatory in the Crown Court, but voluntary in the magistrates' court (but the standard forms used there disclose some similar information).

It is worth reading...

The judgment of Hughes JSC (you can skip the preliminaries) in *Nunn v Chief Constable of Suffolk Constabulary* [2015] AC 255, a judicial review case which went all the way to the Supreme Court on the prosecution's disclosure duties *after* conviction of the accused. The police tried to be helpful, but the requests began to get rather speculative. The case reads like a particularly gruesome episode of CSI!

63 The power to make such orders differs depending on whether made in the magistrates' or Crown Court, but the procedure is now the same (CrPR r 17.3). For more detail see BCrP D 9.74

64 See generally BCrP D 9.71ff

CHAPTER 8

Summary trial of adults

As you know by now, all cases start in the magistrates' court. The vast majority are tried there as well. The course of a summary trial follows a predictable pattern, and is the same whether the charge is a summary offence or triable either way. In the latter case, as we have seen, the trial venue will have been determined previously at a mode of trial hearing.[1] Summary offences (subject to very limited exceptions[2]) are always tried in the magistrates' courts.

This chapter will outline the trial procedure for adults. The procedure for young people and children is covered in Chapter 11.

1. PRE-TRIAL CONSIDERATIONS

Efficient preparation is important. The requirement that the parties co-operate with active case management applies in the magistrates' court just as in the Crown Court. This cooperation basically boils down to assisting with the early identification of the issues, through the use of standard forms and directions, and keeping to a procedural timetable which is geared to the complexities and justice of any given case.[3] Matters which may arise to be dealt with pre-trial in the

1 See Ch. 4
2 E.g., where the summary offence is linked to an indictable offence to be tried in the Crown Court: see Ch. 5
3 See CrimPD I 3A.3 and BCrP D 21.39ff

magistrates' court include the following.

A. THE CHARGE

Public prosecutions in the magistrates' court are brought by written charge.[4] The content of a written charge is very similar to the contents of a count in an indictment[5] and so, for example, should give reasonable particulars of the offence charged and refer to relevant legislation. The main difference between the two is the format: unlike counts on an indictment, a written charge is not split into the 'statement' of offence and 'particulars' of offence. But the same basic information is there.

Note that the court may not try an accused for a *summary* offence unless the charge was issued[6] within six months of the offence having been committed.[7] This is an intentionally short limitation period for the most minor of infractions, but it does *not* apply to either-way offences tried summarily - presumably because the latter are apt to be both more memorable (so witnesses should remember the detail for longer) and more serious (and so more important to prosecute).

The rule against duplicity, and similar principles about joinder, discussed in Chapter 6 also apply to the magistrates' court. Thus a charge should allege only one offence, but two or more accused may be jointly charged with having committed that one offence together. Similarly, more than one incident may be included in one charge if the allegation is that the various incidents amounted to a single 'course of conduct'.[8] Where there are two or more charges against one defendant (or two or more defendants accused in separate charges), the magistrates may try the charges together if no party objects. If there is an objection, separate trials must be ordered unless the interests of justice (looked at in the round) are best served by a single trial. Making this determination essentially involves balancing factors such as the clear presentation of the prosecution case against minimising risk of unfair prejudice to the accused.[9]

4 Private prosecutions are still brought by information and summons: see Ch. 2

5 See Ch. 6

6 By analogy to when the old-style 'information' was 'laid', which is how the provision is worded: BCrP D 21.18

7 MCA 1980, s 127

8 CrimPR, r 7.3(2)

9 See *Chief Constable of Norfolk v Clayton* [1983] 2 AC 473. The bench deciding on separate trials will have to consider (in light of what it has heard about the case) what role it plays in either trial.

Where defects in the charges are discovered, the magistrates have very wide powers of amendment.[10] They also have an important discretion (albeit to be exercised in exceptional circumstances) to dismiss the charge, without hearing the evidence, on grounds that the prosecution constitutes an abuse of process - for example because of undue delay. Even where proceedings have been commenced in time, a delay in the prosecution of the case thereafter can sometimes be unfair to an accused. Memories relating to relatively minor incidents can fade pretty quickly and it may be unjust to ask witnesses to remember them one or two years down the line.[11]

B. DISCLOSURE

The rules about disclosure are discussed in detail in Chapter 7. The prosecution's duty to give details of its case against the accused, and to disclose 'unused material' to the defence, is essentially the same in the magistrates' court as it is in the Crown court. What is very different is that service of a 'defence statement' in the magistrates' court is voluntary, not obligatory.[12] Examiners like to find out whether students know this! In any event, case management forms required in the magistrates' court are able to extract much the same information.

C. SECURING THE ATTENDANCE OF WITNESSES

If a witness will not attend court voluntarily, the magistrates have the power to issue a witness summons if satisfied that the witness will be able to give or produce material evidence. The procedure, which applies in both the magistrates' and Crown Court, is set out in Pt 17 CrimPR and discussed at Chapter 17.

10 MCA 1980, s 123. If necessary an adjournment may be granted if an accused has been misled by the error and needs time to consider his position. See generally BCrP D 21.11ff

11 See e.g., *R(CPS) v City of London Magistrates' Court* [2006] EWHC 1153, BCrP D 21.23 and specific examples discussed at Sprack, *Practical Approach*, 10.26-10.31

12 CPIA 1996, s 6. See Ch. 7

D. PRE-TRIAL HEARINGS AND RULINGS

Pre-trial hearings are now common, both for case-management reasons and to hear argument about exclusion of evidence or some other point of law or procedure. An accused who has been charged at the police station may well find himself appearing for the first time in front of a single justice, who is able to exercise the court's powers sitting alone and will deal with certain typical (and predictable) preliminary matters, including legal representation and eligibility for legal aid.[13] If the accused is in custody, charged with an either-way offence, the court should proceed 'at once' with allocating the case for trial. If the case is triable only in the magistrates' court, then the court should 'forthwith' give such directions as are necessary, either for trial (if a not guilty plea) or sentencing (if a guilty plea). The Preparation for Effective Trial form must be used for all cases to be tried in the magistrates' court to ensure efficient case management.[14]

Legal rulings may also be necessary, for example on the admissibility of evidence. The court may make such rulings (on application or its own initiative) if the parties have (logically enough) been given the opportunity to be heard and if it is in the interests of justice to do so. An unrepresented accused must be given the chance to apply for legal aid.[15] Such rulings will bind the court which eventually tries the case (even if it is differently constituted), unless there is some 'compelling reason' for that court to vary or discharge the pre-trial ruling.[16] If, for example, prosecution evidence is excluded following a pre-trial hearing, then the obvious advantage to the accused is that the trial court was not exposed to the evidence, which would have been the case had the argument taken place there.

13 Crime and Disorder Act 1998 (CDA 1998), s 49/50. In this context, the justices clerk/legal adviser is also empowered to make early administrative, but not really judicial decisions, and so could, for example, adjourn and list another hearing but not remand the accused in custody. See BCrP D 21.34

14 An accused in custody can attend a pre-trial hearing by live TV link if appropriate. See CrimPR, r 3.2(4) and CrimPD I 3A.3-3A.6

15 See MCA 1980, s 8A and generally BCrP D 21.35

16 MCA 1980, s 8B

2. SUMMARY TRIAL PROCEDURE

Summary trials follow a similar basic pattern to trial on indictment. The major differences are the constitution of the court itself (especially the absence of a jury) and the extent to which what goes on there can be, and often is, conducted in the absence of the accused. The conduct of summary trials is governed by the MCA 1980, and the CrimPR Pt 24.

A. ROLE OF CLERK (LEGAL ADVISER)

In the absence of a District Judge (who himself is legally qualified to try cases sitting alone), lay magistrates must always be accompanied by a legally qualified 'clerk', known these days by the more accurate and modern description of 'justices' legal adviser'.[17] His or her most important function is to give the court legal advice, both in court (for example, when a point of law is raised during trial) or out-of-court (for example, while the justices are deliberating).[18] In a sense, the justices' clerk is their 'legal brain', informing them on questions of law, matters of procedure, and the effect of legal precedent; reminding them of the evidence; and helping them to formulate and properly record reasons for their decisions.[19] He or she also has a duty to ensure that proceedings are conducted fairly, and this can include assisting an unrepresented defendant or asking questions of witnesses to clarify the evidence. What the legal advisor must *not* do, however, is play any part in *making findings of fact* - that is the magistrates' job.[20]

B. PROCEEDING IN THE ABSENCE OF THE DEFENDANT

In a trial on indictment, the accused must be present in court to plead to the indictment and should normally[21] be in court throughout his trial. Cases in the

17 CrimPR, r 24.15(1)

18 See generally *ibid* 24.15(2)-(4)

19 See CrimPD, V1 24A

20 Although he or she can help the magistrates to be in a position to do so: *ibid* 24A.12. The legal advisor can help with questions of *mixed* law and fact: 24A.5

21 See Ch 9. A defendant who is represented is deemed to be present, unless their presence is expressly required by statute (for example, in response to bail), so that if such an accused wanted/needed to be absent, he could. Only if an accused is so disruptive that proceedings cannot continue, could he be ordered to be excluded from the actual trial.

magistrates' court, on the other hand, *can and often do* proceed in the absence of the defendant[22] - either because he was able to plead guilty by post, or the accused (who would otherwise have been expected to attend) simply fails to show up at his trial, and there is no particular reason not to continue without him.

(i) Pleading guilty by post and the single justice procedure

If the offence is minor enough, the evidence clear enough and liability strict enough, it makes sense (and saves time and money) to allow defendants to plead guilty by post. If the prosecutor chooses, s 12 MCA 1980 makes this procedurally possible. Thus, if the offence is summary (and so sentencing must remain with the magistrates) and the proceedings have been commenced by written charge and requisition (that is, not following arrest by the police), then an accused of at least 16 years of age may be given the opportunity to plead guilty by sending a letter to this effect to the relevant court. This procedure is well suited for simple road traffic and similar sorts of offences, where appearing in court is not apt to make any difference to the outcome.[23]

The accused is served with sufficient information about the alleged offence and the evidence against him and told that he can plead guilty by post if he wishes and what will happen if he does. A person who chooses to do this would then notify the court of this fact, and may include any relevant information in mitigation. In such cases, neither prosecution nor defence need be present in court, which simply proceeds on the basis of the written statements of both parties. If content to accept the plea,[24] the magistrates proceed to sentence. They cannot, however, impose a custodial sentence or disqualification from driving in the defendant's absence, and if so minded would have to adjourn for the latter to attend.

If the accused, having indicated he was pleading guilty by post, were actually to appear on the day, the court can proceed to deal with the case as if he were absent

22 If the *prosecution* fails to attend, then magistrates may adjourn or dismiss the case, or (if the case is part heard) complete the trial and treat what has gone before as the entirety of the case against the accused. This could mean that the defendant would not face cross-examination by the prosecution. See BCrP D 22.23

23 See *ibid* D 22.28. Fixed penalty notices are to an extent a modern version of, or alternative to, this procedure, which the police will use when that penalty seems appropriate. Recipients are 'tempted' to plead guilty by a 'reduction' in the fixed penalty - but can contest the case if they wish.

24 If the magistrates felt the 'mitigation' amounted to a defence, they would refuse to accept the guilty plea.

(so long as he consents), although he should be given the chance to make any oral submissions in mitigation if he wants to. If such a person wanted to change his plea to 'not guilty', he can do so by giving written notice to the court, and the case will proceed in the normal way.[25]

In 2015, a 'single justice procedure' was introduced which serves similar purposes. This enables a single justice to deal with a summary offence, *not punishable by imprisonment*, allegedly committed by someone of at least 18 years old who seems to want to plead guilty and does not object to having the case dealt with by the single justice. The case is dealt with entirely 'on the papers'. Sentencing powers are (by definition) limited to non-custodial sentences (but can include disqualification and other ancillary orders). If the single justice procedure is being used, then the s 12 procedure will not be necessary and so will not apply.[26]

(ii) Failure to attend when expected: s 11 MCA 1980

Sometimes defendants, who are expected to attend for trial, just don't turn up. In the magistrates' court the impetus *is very much in favour of going ahead regardless*. Otherwise, many cases would never get started, much less completed. Indeed, if the accused is an adult, there is essentially a statutory presumption in favour of the court doing so. According to s 11(1) MCA 1980, the magistrates *must*, if the defendant is over the age of 18, hear the case in the defendant's absence if he or she fails to attend (they *may* do so, if the defendant is under 18), *unless* it appears to the court to be contrary to the interests of justice to do so. If the offence is triable either way, then a trial in the magistrates' court could only proceed if it was clear that the accused had, at a previous hearing, consented to summary trial.

Obviously, it is important for the court to be satisfied both that the accused had sufficient notice of the proceedings *and* was made fully aware that the court

25 MCA 1980 s 12(6), s 12A(1) and 12A(5)(c). A change of plea will, of course, add to the costs of losing, if this is the inevitable outcome.

26 See s 16A MCA 1980 and BCrP D 22.33

could proceed in his absence - either because he was present (and told as much) at a previous hearing or was served with the relevant documentation (and warning) within a reasonable time of the court date.[27] As to the latter, the magistrates only need be satisfied that the relevant documents were properly served - for example, that they were sent to the correct place by first class post. As in civil cases, it is not necessary to prove that they were actually received, although if it later transpires that the defendant had no knowledge of the proceedings, these can effectively be unravelled (to be started again, if the prosecution choose) by the accused making a 'statutory declaration'[28] to that effect.

The ability to proceed in the defendant's absence should in any event be exercised with some caution. If the defendant had been knocked down by a bus on his way to court, it would obviously be harsh to start without him (unless perhaps he was represented and actively wanted the trial to begin).[29] Thus, the court should not proceed in the defendant's absence, if it appears that there is an acceptable reason for his failure to appear. Having said that, it is not the magistrates' responsibility to investigate the reasons for a defendant's absence,[30] so if no sensible explanation is forthcoming, they are under some compulsion to proceed without him (if he is an adult), unless of course they nevertheless feel it is contrary to the interests of justice to do so. The court must always keep its finger on the fairness pulse. A custodial sentence cannot take effect, however, without bringing the offender before the court.[31]

C. TAKING A PLEA

The first thing that happens in a summary trial is the taking of the defendant's plea. The clerk/legal advisor will read the charge out and ask the defendant if he pleads 'guilty' or 'not guilty', having first explained the implications of his choice.[32] If the

27 CrimPR, r 24.12(3)(c)

28 Effectively a formal statement: see BCrP D 22.21

29 See Lord Bingham's examples in *R v Jones* [2002] UKHL 5 at [6] and principles in *R(Killick) v West London Magistrates' Court* [2012] EWHC 3864 (Admin), discussed in BCrP D 22.18

30 MCA 1980, s 11(6) and s 11(2A)

31 *Ibid*, s 11(3)

32 Some other options (such as pleading not guilty to the offence charged, but guilty to some lesser offence) which are available in the Crown Court, are not available in the magistrates' court, although the latter have their own ways of achieving similar results (such as inviting the prosecution to charge the lesser offence, to which the accused can plead guilty). See generally BCrP D22.3

accused had already indicated a plea of not guilty at an early administrative or mode of trial hearing, then he will confirm this (although he could still change his plea to guilty, if he wishes). If the accused says nothing (or when the case is proceeding in his absence), then a not guilty plea will be entered on his behalf.

D. EQUIVOCAL PLEAS

Sometimes the accused says something, but it is not entirely clear what he is saying - is he really pleading guilty or not guilty? This is known in the trade (at least in the magistrates' court[33]) as an 'equivocal plea'. The most obvious instance of an equivocal plea occurs when the accused says he is guilty, but then immediately qualifies this with words which amount to a defence (for example: *"I plead guilty. I hit him but I was just defending myself"*). When this happens, the magistrates should try to resolve the ambiguity, by giving appropriate explanations and so forth, and take the plea again.[34] If it remains equivocal, then a not guilty plea should be entered.

An equivocal plea can also reveal itself *after* pleas have been taken. This can occur, for example, during sentencing, when something said in mitigation reveals a possible defence. At this point, the magistrates should consider whether to exercise their discretion to allow a change of plea at this late stage (see below).

It can also happen that nothing is said at either the plea or sentencing stage to cast doubt on the guilty plea, but the defendant later alleges, as a ground of appeal, that he pleaded guilty under duress or otherwise involuntarily. If it is decided on appeal that, *in retrospect*, the plea was equivocal because of this, then the case should be remitted back to the magistrates with an order that they enter a not guilty plea and proceed to try the case.[35]

You will notice that when in doubt, the default position is always to enter a not guilty plea, in which case the court will proceed to trial (or adjourn to a later date).

33 In the Crown Court such is referred to as an ambiguous plea. Same difference!

34 If there is no attempt to clarify the plea, its validity can be challenged on appeal.

35 *R v Plymouth Justices, ex parte Hart* [1986] QB 950

Only if the accused *unequivocally* pleads guilty, may the court convict him without hearing any evidence.

E. CHANGE OF PLEA

It is also possible, within reason, for a defendant to change his mind about his plea. At any time before sentence is passed, the magistrates have a discretion to permit a change of plea from 'guilty' to 'not guilty'. Whether they exercise this discretion in the defendant's favour will depend on what has motivated the defendant's request. Going in the other direction is, as you might imagine, even easier. A defendant who has pleaded not guilty may, with the court's permission, change his plea to guilty at any time *before the justices retire*[36] to consider their verdict.

F. CONDUCT OF THE TRIAL

Before trial, the clerk should (by reference to the Preparation for Trial forms) summarise the allegations and matters in dispute. Thereafter, the running order of events in a summary trial is as follows:

(i) Prosecution case

On a not guilty plea, the prosecution must prove the charge(s). It follows therefore that they present their case first. The prosecution are entitled to make an opening speech, which (if given at all) tends to be kept short and sweet. Unlike jurors, magistrates are well (perhaps overly) familiar with the sorts of cases which come before them, and do not need or want a long introduction.

After the opening (if there is one), and if it would assist the court to understand the case (and where its focus of attention should be), the defence may be asked to identify briefly what issues are in dispute. The prosecution will then present the

36 Compare this with jury trial, when the change of plea (from 'not guilty' to 'guilty') can be made any time up to the jury returning their verdict. This is because jurors, who may otherwise consider a verdict for some days, can be recalled by the judge mid-deliberation (effectively to be told 'never mind'), which is not the case with magistrates.

evidence on which it relies. Some of it will take the form of written statements; some of it will be in the form of 'live' witnesses.

Written witness statements

Where evidence is uncontroversial, then the parties may make use of s 9 Criminal Justice Act 1967 (CJA 1967), which allows a written witness statement to be read into evidence in criminal proceedings so long as it contains a declaration of truth; copies have been served on all parties; and none has objected to this course of action. This is a sensible, if formal requirement, when evidence does not need to be tested or challenged.[37]

Sometimes more controversial evidence has been ruled admissible in written form (for example, hearsay statements under s 116).[38] In either case, the written statements should be read out or summarised aloud by the party adducing the evidence.[39]

The fact that such evidence is admissible in the form of a witness statement does not mean it necessarily has to be believed - even if it cannot be challenged in cross-examination, it could, for example, be contradicted by other evidence. Note, too, that any formal admissions made at trial should be recorded in writing.[40]

Oral evidence

Otherwise, evidence will be given, and tested, orally. Any special measures directions[41] should be complied with. The sequence of events for oral evidence is, of course, evidence-in-chief, cross-examination and re-examination. The prosecution must be prepared to call (if only to tender for cross-examination by the defence) all of their witnesses who are in court and whose statements had been served (as notice of the evidence they intended to call). If necessary the magistrates

37 Such statements should be in prescribed form: CrimPR r 16.2. S 9 statements may be edited and adapted as necessary (e.g. statements on two occasions can become a 'composite statement'. See generally CrimPD V 16.A

38 See Ch. 20

39 CrimPR, r 24.5

40 *Ibid*, r 24.6 and see Ch. 14

41 This could include evidence given by video-link. See Ch. 17

can call a witness not called by any party. Remember too that the court has the power to limit the length and nature of any party's line of questioning, especially if it reveals a novel line of attack or seeks to raise surprising new issues.[42] Witnesses who will give evidence should wait outside the courtroom until they are called (to ensure their evidence is not tainted by what they might hear), unless that person is the defendant or an expert witness.

(ii) Defence objections to prosecution evidence

Defence objections to prosecution evidence which are raised at summary trial can pose a quandary. This is because the magistrates are judges of both law and fact, and so cannot avoid hearing evidence which they may ultimately rule as inadmissible. Over the years, questions have arisen as to how and when such decisions are to be taken (for example, should the magistrates mimic the Crown Court and always hold a 'trial within a trial'?), and whether a bench which has ruled evidence to be inadmissible should then be prevented from sitting in ultimate judgment in the case.[43] The short answer is that the court has complete discretion as to how and when best to deal with such submissions, and whether to continue trying the case if evidence has been heard but then excluded. The guiding principle is justice - would a fair-minded and informed observer conclude there was a real risk of prejudice? Most such rulings would not prevent the justices from continuing with the trial, but there may well be exceptional cases, where the evidence is so prejudicial that, in order for justice both to be done (and to be seen to be done), it is best that a differently constituted bench conduct the trial. This, of course, is the context in which the benefit of effective case management and pre-trial rulings are most keenly felt.[44]

42 See BCrP D 22.39 and CrimPD VI 24B

43 See, e.g., case of *R (on the application of Ratra) v DPP* [2004] EWHC 87

44 See the magistrates' court Effective Preparation for Trial Form, which is intended to identify such issues and deal with them before trial.

(iii) Half time: possible submission of no case to answer

Once the prosecution has presented all of its evidence and closed its case, consideration must be given to the question of whether there actually is a case for the defence to answer. Usually a submission of 'no case' is made by the defence, but, if not, the court should itself consider whether the prosecution evidence is 'sufficient for any reasonable court to convict'.[45] The prosecution should always be given the opportunity to argue the point before a decision is made.[46]

A submission of no case to answer in the magistrates' court should succeed in one of two situations. The first is where the prosecution has failed to adduce evidence of an *essential ingredient* of the charge (which would make a conviction an impossibility). In such a case, the magistrates have a discretion to let the prosecution re-open their case to fill in the gap, but this should be the exception, not the rule - otherwise prosecutors would always be able to make up for poor planning and presentation after the event. An example of when this discretion would be properly exercised might be where the prosecution had been led by the defence to believe that an aspect of the case was not being contested, and the misconception could and should have been corrected by the defence earlier. It is the prosecution's job to prove the case but, even so, it is not appropriate for an accused to 'sit tight' and let the prosecution proceed under a misapprehension merely as a way of acquiring ammunition for a later submission of no case to answer.[47]

The second situation where a submission of no case to answer can succeed is where the prosecution evidence has been so discredited in cross-examination or is otherwise so manifestly unreliable that *no reasonable tribunal could safely convict on it.* As the magistrates are judges of both law and fact,[48] if it is clear at half-time that they could not convict on the basis of what they have already heard, then it would be pointless and (since the burden of proof is on the prosecution) wrong to carry

45 CrimPR, r 24.3(3)(d)

46 *Barking and Dagenham Justices, ex parte DPP* (1995) 159 JP 373

47 *R(CPS) v Norwich Magistrates' Court* [2011] EWHC 82 (Admin), per Richards LJ at [22]

48 The position is different in the Crown Court, where the judge's own view of the credibility of a witness is not generally considered relevant to a decision on a submission of no case to answer, since this is a matter for the jury. See discussion at BCrP D 22.53 and 22.54

on any further.

If a submission of no case is rejected, there is no obligation on the justices to give reasons.[49] If the submission is upheld, then the accused is found not guilty and discharged.

(iv) Defence case

Assuming there is a case to answer, it will then be for the defence to present its case. The rules do not provide for a defence opening, but in any event, the nature of the defence should by this time have become clear through the cross-examination of the prosecution witnesses. Thus, the defence will usually begin by calling its evidence, which again can be in the form of s 9 statements (or other admissible written hearsay) and/or oral evidence. It is important to note that if the defendant is to give evidence, he should do so *before* other defence witnesses are called.[50] This is because he is in the courtroom throughout the trial, and might otherwise be tempted to trim his evidence in light of what others before him have said. If the defendant is not to give evidence, he must be well aware of the risks and possible negative implications of his not doing so. This is discussed in detail in Chapter 23.

At the end of the defence case, if the prosecution want to introduce evidence to rebut an allegation made during the defence case, then the magistrates may allow them do so.[51] Note, however, that this is not an invitation to present a party's case out of order or compensate for omissions in the presentation of one's case - only evidence which is admissible at that point should be allowed in. This suggests that if the need for rebuttal could have been foreseen, then it would normally be too late to seek to do so now. In deciding whether to permit such new evidence being adduced at this stage, the magistrates should take care to be fair to the defendant, but without losing sight of the overriding objective of ensuring that cases are dealt with justly.[52]

49 *Moran v DPP* [2002] EWHC 89

50 PACE 1984, s 79

51 Either party may 'introduce further evidence if it is then admissible (for example, because it is in rebuttal of evidence already introduced)'. CrimPR r 24.3(3)(g). It will usually be prosecutors who seek to take advantage of this provision.

52 See cases discussed at BCrP D 22.61ff

(v) Closing speeches[53]

The prosecution may only make a closing speech if the defendant is legally represented or the defence have called evidence other than that given by the defendant. The defence may, and practically speaking will always make a closing speech - he who has the most to lose should have the last word!

3. POST-TRIAL CONSIDERATIONS

A. VERDICT

A district judge sitting alone will normally announce his decision immediately after the defence closing. Lay justices will almost always retire to consider their verdict, and the clerk should be very careful not to (or appear to) interfere with this aspect of the process. The verdict need not be unanimous; a majority decision will do.[54]

In reaching their decision, the justices may rely on local knowledge, so long as both parties have an opportunity to speak to the issue to which that knowledge relates. It is also possible, although only exceptionally necessary, for the justices to allow further evidence after they have retired to consider their verdict.[55]

With some statutory exceptions,[56] one thing magistrates cannot do (which juries can) is acquit on the offence charged and substitute a conviction for what is known as a 'lesser included offence'. But something they can do (which the Crown Court cannot) is direct that a case be re-heard by a differently constituted bench if they have second thoughts about the correctness of their verdict or procedures (assuming the case has not already been appealed, discussed in Chapter 13). This is a useful ability of the magistrates' court to rectify its own mistakes.

Finally, justices need not give reasons if they acquit the defendant, but if they

53 CrimPR, r 24.3(3)(h)

54 On the rare occasion a case is heard by an even-numbered and evenly divided bench, the case will have to be reheard by a different bench. For obvious reasons, such an outcome is to be avoided if at all possible.

55 See, e.g., *Malcolm v DPP* [2007] 1 WLR 1230

56 See examples at BCrP D 22.71

convict, they are required to give 'sufficient' explanation for their decision.[57] This is so the accused can make a sensible decision about a possible appeal.

B. SENTENCING AND COSTS

If the accused is found guilty, then the court will proceed to sentence (after an adjournment, if this is necessary). This aspect of procedure is dealt with in detail in Chapter 10. Costs are briefly discussed in Chapter 12.

revision tips

- Be clear about circumstances in which magistrates' courts can proceed in the absence of an accused.
- Note differences between trial procedure in magistrates' courts and that in the Crown Court. But remember that there are also lots of similarities.
- In an examination, always note carefully the details of any scenario you are given, especially which court is involved.

It is worth reading ...

CrimPR, r 24.3, which in one page clearly sets out the running order in summary trial.

Magistrates' Courts Preparation for Effective Trial Form, which illustrates the issues which effective case management in the magistrates' courts should have identified (and dealt with) pre-trial. This can be found at the gov.uk website.

57 CrimPR, r 24.3(5) and (6)

CHAPTER 9

Crown court trials

A trial on indictment in the Crown Court trial is like summary trial, but with bells and whistles, wigs and gowns! The most pronounced differences derive from the division of labour between the judge, who deals with all questions of law, and the jury, which decides the facts of the case and determines guilt or innocence. Crown Court trial procedure is 'topped and tailed' more elaborately than that in the magistrates' court, but much of what goes on in the middle is the same.

1. PRE-TRIAL ISSUES AND PROCEEDINGS

The court is under a duty to be proactive about managing its cases, and the parties are required to engage fully in the process.[1] Pre-trial preparation is especially important in the Crown Court, where cases are apt to be more complex, involve more witnesses, raise more legal questions and generally take more time. If a case is destined for a guilty plea, the sooner this happens the better; and the more effectively a contested case is managed before the trial actually starts, the more efficient the conduct of that trial is apt to be.

1 This includes early and effective communication between prosecution and defence, and between them and the court. See CrimPR, Pt 3 and accompanying CrimPD I which gives effect to the Leveson initiatives for 'Better Case Management (BCM).' See also BCM Newsletter, 5 January 2016, Issue 5 and BCrP D 15.39

A. PLEA AND TRIAL PREPARATION HEARING

Once a case is sent to the Crown Court for trial, there must be at least one (and in many cases only one) pre-trial hearing, called the Plea and Trial Preparation Hearing (PTPH). If a 'guilty' plea has been indicated, the purpose of the PTPH is to pass sentence if possible. Otherwise, it is to ensure that all steps required to prepare the case for trial have been taken (or properly timetabled) and necessary directions given.[2] The PTPH will usually be held within 28 days of the case being sent to the Crown Court. The indictment should be lodged at least 7 days before the hearing itself.[3]

In the Crown Court, the standard Plea and Trial Preparation Hearing Form is used for case management.[4] It both sets an agenda of sorts for the PTPH, and acts as a record of pre-trial case progression. The form requires prosecution and defence to provide relevant information, which must be made available to the court for the PTPH and which they should have discussed together beforehand. Each party is required to nominate a person responsible for progressing the case and with whom others can communicate.[5] Ultimately, the intention is to create a fully digital system for case management.

The PTPH should give time to 'allow the court to make, record and distribute clear orders timetabling the preparation of the case for trial'.[6] Issues needing to be dealt with at this point range from the number of witnesses and the nature of the evidence a party wishes to call (for example, special measures for live witnesses,[7] directions for expert evidence[8]) to questions of admissibility of certain kinds of evidence (bad character,[9] a disputed confession[10] or other hearsay evidence,[11] for instance). An accused can attend the PTPH by live TV link (unless the court feels that he would not be able to participate effectively in this way).[12] In a straightforward case a trial date should be set.

Ideally the PTPH should be the *only* pre-trial Crown Court hearing, and

2 If the PTPH is to be used for sentencing, there should be sufficient notice of and time allowed for this. The defence should be prepared to mitigate and a pre-sentencing report should be available if required (even if only a verbal report). See CrimPD I, 3A.17/18

3 This period could, exceptionally, be extended - one reason for doing so might be to ensure that the trial advocate is able to attend the PTPH. Continuity is important.

4 CrimPD I 3A.3. And see generally BCrP D 15.47ff

5 CrimPR, r 3.4

6 See revised guidance for cases sent to the Crown Court after January 2016, p. 6, which can be found at justice.gov.uk/courts/procedure-rules/criminal/docs/october-2015/cm007-eng.pdf).

7 See Ch. 17

8 See Ch. 22

further progression of the case can be managed using telephone or other electronic communication.[13] Some cases, however, *may* require further hearings because of their seriousness, special needs or just because this is necessary to achieve the overriding objective. Examples in the rules include trials of Class I offences, cases involving unrepresented defendants, and cases involving vulnerable witnesses. A defendant is not required to attend such further case-management hearings, unless the court so orders.[14]

To assist in giving 'teeth', any rulings which the judge (having heard representations from all parties) chooses to make on the admissibility of evidence or other questions of law will *bind* the trial court, *unless* there has been a material change of circumstances since the order was made and the trial judge is satisfied that it is in the interest of justice to vary or discharge it.[15] There is also *no general ability* to appeal such rulings (although a defendant who is convicted may base any subsequent appeal against convictions on such rulings, just as if they had been made at trial; and there is a limited scope for the prosecution to appeal rulings which are fatal, or nearly fatal, to their case[16]). The point of pre-trial case management is to *expedite* the trial process, and this would not be achieved if constant appeals could be made from them or if the advocates always had a clear run at a better outcome at the trial itself. Having said that, pre-trial rulings should not tread on matters which should properly be dealt with at trial.

B. ARRAIGNMENT AND PLEA ISSUES

At the arraignment (now usually conducted at the PTPH), the accused formally pleads to the indictment. If there is more than one count, a plea should be taken on each separate count, unless one of these is an alternative to another[17] to which the accused has already pleaded guilty. If there is more than one defendant, pleas should

9 See Ch. 19

10 See Ch. 21

11 See Ch. 20

12 CrimPR r 3.2(4)(b)

13 CrimPD I 3A.20/21

14 Do not confuse further or follow-up case management hearings with so-called 'preparatory' hearings, which are in something of a league of their own and only deployed in limited circumstances (eg complex fraud). BCrP D 15.51

15 Criminal Procedure and Investigations Act 1996 (CPIA 1996), s 40

16 E.g. so called 'terminating' rulings. For more information see Ch. 13

17 Where a defendant can be guilty of one or other alternative counts (for example, theft of or handling the same goods), but not both.

be taken from them individually. The rules set general parameters of between 2 and 16 weeks of sending cases to the Crown Court for pleas to be taken, but the PTPH (where this usually happens) should generally occur within 28 days of sending.[18]

The two usual pleas, of course, are 'guilty' or 'not guilty' and defendants usually enter one or other of these. There are, however, some other possibilities or applications which can arise at the arraignment stage. We have come across a few of these when discussing summary trial. Some possibilities, however, are peculiar to the Crown Court.

(i) Ambiguous/equivocal plea

What the magistrates typically refer to as an 'equivocal' plea,[19] the Crown Court calls an 'ambiguous' plea. They are effectively the same thing. So, if an accused purports to plead guilty, but qualifies this by saying something which suggests he might have a defence (for example, *"Guilty, but it was an accident"*), then the court must resolve the ambiguity before proceeding. In particular, the court should explain (or ensure the defendant understands) the relevant law, and seek to ascertain his true plea.

If an ambiguous plea cannot be clarified, then as always the default position is that a not guilty plea be entered. If the court were to proceed on a guilty plea which was ambiguous or unclarified, this could be a ground of appeal, so always better to play safe (by entering a not guilty plea) than sorry.

Sometimes, an accused will tell his counsel that he is innocent but wants to plead guilty 'just to get things over with'. Such a person should always be dissuaded from pleading guilty to an offence he denies, and have the implications of a guilty plea in such circumstances explained. In particular, both logic and honesty would make a plea in mitigation of sentence difficult, since the advocate could neither suggest innocence (which would render the plea ambiguous) nor even

18 Unless a guilty plea is indicated, in which case the sooner it happens the better: CrimPD I 3A.10/11. For arraignment procedure see CrimPR r 3.24 (take care with some editions of BCrP's supplement which contains a 'typo' at r 3.24(5)(b), where an important 'not' is missing!)

19 See Ch. 8

remorse (since a person cannot feel remorse about something they have not done). The accused may also need to be reassured about the judicial process following a not guilty plea.[20]

(ii) Special pleas

In the Crown Court, there are a few special questions which can arise about a defendant's plea. Rather old fashioned language is sometimes used, but once you have been introduced to these expressions, you will remember what they mean.

(a) Failure/Unfitness to plead

An accused may fail to enter a plea for one of three reasons:

- because he is physically unable to do so, sometimes referred to (archaically) as 'mute by visitation of God'. This is now rare, given the various ways which can be used these days to assist the disabled to communicate.[21]
- because he remains silent out of choice (known as 'mute by malice'). In such cases, the court will enter a plea of 'not guilty' on the defendant's behalf.[22]
- because he is mentally incapable of doing so, also known as being 'unfit to plead'. In 2016 the Law Commission made recommendations to reform this area of law 'radically' (including a draft bill), but it remains to be seen when and if these will make it on to the statute books.[23]

(b) Double jeopardy

It is a mainstay of the constitution that a person cannot not be prosecuted twice,

20 If, notwithstanding, the accused still insists on pleading guilty, counsel may continue to represent him but should make a note (on the brief, for example) of the circumstances and advice given. This could arise in the magistrates' court too, of course.

21 See BCrP D 12.18

22 CLR 1967, s 6(1)(c)

23 So watch this space for future developments. See e.g. discussion in criminallawandjustice.co.uk/features/Reform-Unfitness-Plead) and as appropriate BCrP D.12.2ff

either to acquittal or conviction, for the same offence. This principle, which is known as the *rule against double jeopardy*, is intended to protect the individual from the arbitrary power of the state and prevent prosecutorial harassment. Where a defendant contends that he has, on a previous occasion, been acquitted or convicted of an offence contained on an indictment, he may invoke the rule by raising a plea of 'autrefois acquit' ('previously acquitted') or 'autrefois convict' ('previously convicted'), as the case may be. These are known as 'pleas in bar' since, if upheld, they act as a bar to any further proceedings on the charges to which they relate.[24]

Over the years, *two important inroads* have been made into the application of the double jeopardy rule. The *first* relates to the so-called 'tainted acquittal'. If a person has been acquitted of an offence[25] there is scope for that acquittal to be quashed if:

- it appears that it was achieved through proven witness tampering or other interference with a potential/actual witness or a juror *and*
- it is not contrary to interests of justice to re-try the acquitted person.

Application is made to the High Court by the prosecution for an order to quash the acquittal and order a new trial.[26]

The *second* major exception, created by ss 75-97 of the CJA 2003, relates to the emergence of new and compelling evidence of the commission of a very serious criminal offence (for example, murder, rape, terrorism charges and so on). In effect, these provisions permit an accused to be retried for such an offence, of which he has earlier been acquitted, where there is 'new and compelling evidence' against the defendant and it is in the 'interests of justice' to do so. This application is made to the Court of Appeal.[27]

24 The same applies to the plea of pardon. The double jeopardy rule is highly technical in its operation. For further detail see *R v Beedie* [1997] 2 Cr App R 167 and BCrP D12.20ff

25 Committed on or after 5 April 1997

26 See ss 54 to 57 CPIA 1996 and BCrP D12.38

27 For more detail see BCrP D 12.40ff. There is also a useful diagram of these provisions in Sprack, *Practical Approach*, Figure 17.1

(c) Application to dismiss

Having received initials details of the prosecution case, but before pleading to the indictment, the accused may apply (in writing or orally) for some or all of the charges to be dismissed. If the application is to be made orally, then written notice of intention to do this must be given (the PTPH form is the usual vehicle for this). Although the context is slightly different (since no trial has yet begun), the test for dismissal is similar to that for a submission of 'no case to answer'.[28]

(iii) Mixed pleas

The term 'mixed pleas' refers to an accused pleading guilty to some charges but not others, or to multiple defendants pleading differently to counts on an indictment, as in the examples below.

(a) Different pleas from different defendants

Where there are co-accused, and one pleads guilty and others not guilty (to offences properly joined on the same indictment[29]) the normal practice is to adjourn sentencing the former until after the trial of the latter. If the jury convicts, the co-accused can then all be sentenced *together* when the extent of each person's participation in the criminal activity should be clearer. To do this also reduces the risk of a disparity between sentencing outcomes for the commission of similar offences.

If a co-accused who pleads guilty also intends to 'turn Queen's evidence' (in other words, give evidence for the prosecution against some or other of the remaining accused[30]), this raises the concern that the evidence which that witness may give will be motivated less by the truth and more by the hope or expectation of a lighter sentence as a reward for his co-operation.[31] Sentencing that accused before he gives his evidence would be one answer, but it is not a perfect solution and it is generally

28 CrimPR r 9.16 and BCrP D 10.23ff. And see below for submission of 'no case to answer'.

29 See Ch. 6

30 As to such a person's competence to give such evidence, see Ch. 17

31 See generally Ch. 10

thought that even in this situation, sentencing should normally be postponed until the end of the trial of the other defendants.[32] This, of course, exposes him to attack under cross-examination that he is giving evidence for the prosecution in the hope of a reduced sentence.

More importantly, however, whether to sentence a co-accused who pleads guilty before or after the trial of his co-accused, must in the last resort remain *a question for the judge.*[33]

(b) Different pleas from an accused

On a multi-count indictment against a single defendant, the latter might plead guilty to some offences, not guilty to others. If the prosecution intend to proceed to trial in respect of the not guilty pleas, then sentencing in respect of the counts to which the defendant pleaded guilty should normally await the outcome of that trial. This is only common sense. Sometimes, however, the prosecution is content that the accused be dealt with solely on the basis of the counts to which he has pleaded guilty. The question then arises as to what is to be done in respect of counts to which the defendant pleads not guilty. The prosecution can (as a form of so-called plea bargaining) agree not to proceed with prosecuting those counts and has two options, either:

- *to offer no evidence* in respect of the remaining count(s) on the indictment, in which case the accused will be formally acquitted[34] of them, *or*
- to ask that those remaining counts *be 'left' on the court file.* This does not result in an acquittal, but the prosecution may not proceed against the accused in respect of those counts without the leave of the court (or the Court of Appeal) and the file will be marked accordingly.

---

32 *R v Weeks* (1980) 74 Cr App R 161

33 *R v Palmer* (1994) 158 JP 138 and see BCrP D 12.78

34 CLA 1977, s 17. Prosecuting counsel would normally explain his decision to the court, but even were the judge to disapprove, the prosecution cannot ultimately be forced to call evidence. The situation would be different if judicial approval were actively sought. See BCrP D 12.82.

The first of these is appropriate when the prosecution believes that the evidence, on closer inspection, does not really support a conviction on the remaining count(s). Leaving counts 'on the file' will be the better choice when the evidence may be there, but the time and money to secure a conviction is not justified in view of the guilty pleas which have been entered. Defendants obviously prefer it if no evidence is offered on the remaining counts, because there is no threat of resurrection, but it is pretty rare that a count left on the file is later prosecuted. It can happen, however,[35] and so it is important to be able to *distinguish between these two outcomes.* Examiners also like to know you know the difference! Just remember that counts left on the file can still (albeit in very limited circumstances) be given the kiss of life; but once the prosecution offers no evidence on a count, it is a dead duck (and no one wants to kiss one of these!).

(iv) Other influences, decisions and bargains

An accused who pleads guilty must do so voluntarily. If his choice is not a genuine one, or the plea freely made, then it may be quashed on appeal. Equally, it is important that the defendant is fully aware of all of his options and their implications. Relevant information or input into a defendant's plea decision might come from three perspectives: the judge, the defendant's own legal advisors, and even the prosecution.

(a) Judicial indication of sentence on guilty plea

There may be occasions when the judge will give the defendant an indication of the sentence to be passed on a guilty plea. We have looked at this in the context of the magistrates' court and plea before venue decisions.[36] A similar process applies in the Crown Court, about which it is important to note the following.

35 For example, in the unlikely event that a conviction on one of the other counts is set aside on appeal. Similar outcomes are also possible where there are mixed pleas as between co-defendants: See *Ibid*, D12.81

36 See Ch. 4

- Although the judge may remind the defendant's advocate that his client is entitled to an indication of sentence, it is for the *accused* to seek such an indication (and not for the judge to proffer it).
- If asked by the accused for an indication, the judge then decides whether or not to give it, or postpone doing so, and is *not* required to justify this decision (although most are willing to say in what circumstances an indication might be given). The important point is that the judge is *not obliged* to give an indication of sentence.
- However, once *given*, an indication is *binding* on the judge who gave it (and any other judge in the case) for a reasonable amount of time (unless sentencing guidelines change). A defendant should think of it as a 'time-limited' offer. He has a reasonable amount of time to consider his position, but once that time has passed, the indication ceases to have effect. This is only common sense, since the idea of the judicial indication of sentence is to encourage guilty defendants to plead guilty early,[37] not to lock judges into a sentence guarantee (nor to encourage innocent people to plead guilty). Thus, any advance indication of sentence given by a judge should normally be confined to the maximum sentence if a guilty plea were entered *at the stage* at which the indication is sought.[38] This is not the same thing as the maximum which might be handed down following conviction by a jury!
- Indications of sentence should not be sought if (as between prosecution and defence) there is uncertainty about whether the guilty plea is acceptable to both sides or about its factual basis. Any agreed basis negotiated between defence and prosecution should be reduced into writing ('written basis of plea') and a copy provided to the judge.[39]

37 The later the guilty plea, the smaller the possible discount for doing so becomes. See Ch. 10

38 A judge should not be asked to indicate ranges of sentences depending on pleas to different offences: *R v Omale* [2011] Crim LR 804

39 See CrimPD VII C1.3 and A-G Guidelines on accepting such pleas, discussed at BCrP D 12.64, 12.87 and Appendix 2.

- Indications of sentence are usually sought at the PTPH, and in open court (but without a jury). Only rarely would it be appropriate to have such a discussion privately in judge's chambers.[40]
- To give an indication of sentence, the judge must be in possession of all relevant information (for example, an impact statement from the victim, if any; defendant's antecedents and so on). A judge who wishes to give an indication of sentence, subject to a piece of the sentencing puzzle later falling into place (for example, an assessment of risk for the purposes of the dangerous offenders provisions), may do so.[41]
- What a judge must not do (or seem to do) is pressurise or bully a defendant into a guilty plea, in particular by describing, by reference to a trial, 'the much longer sentence which he would impose compared to the sentence which he proposes if the defendant pleads guilty'.[42] Such could render any resulting guilty plea involuntary and vulnerable to being set aside on appeal. This is especially important for judges dealing with unrepresented defendants.

The leading case on this subject is *R v Goodyear*[43] where the Court of Appeal gave comprehensive guidance on judicial indication of sentence in the Crown Court. It is a case you should know by name (remembering it won't make you tired!).

(b) Counsel's advice

The role of the advocate is to give clear, accurate and professional advice so that the accused can make informed decisions and choices in his own best interests. Thus, in the context of judicial indication of sentence, discussed above, it is the advocate's job to ensure that his client knows the following:

40 When such discussions should be properly recorded. See *Attorney-General's Reference* (No 80 of 2005) [2005] EWCA Crim 3367 cited at BCrP D 12.62

41 See, e.g., *R v Kulah* [2007] EWCA Crim 1701 and see Ch. 10

42 Per Rose LJ in *R v Wedlock-Ward* [2005] EWCA Crim 3367, at para 29

43 [2005] 3 All ER 117 and summarised at BCrP D 12.61ff

- that he should not plead guilty unless he is guilty, *and*
- that unduly lenient sentences can be referred to the Court of Appeal[44] *and*
- that the judge's indication of plea reflects the situation at the time it is given and is a limited offer only. It is then for the defendant to make the decision about his plea.

There is a line to be drawn between giving the accused a 'reality check' and effectively telling him he has no choice but to plead guilty, and it is important that advocates do not cross it.[45] Advocates must be free to perform their duty, namely to give the accused the best advice possible and, if need be, in strong terms. It will often include advice that, in accordance with the relevant authorities and sentencing guidelines, a court will normally reduce a sentence as a result of a guilty plea and that the level of reduction will reflect the stage in the proceedings at which the willingness to plead guilty is indicated. But it should always be emphasised that the defendant must not plead guilty unless he or she is guilty of the offence(s) charged.[46]

(c) Plea of guilty to a 'lesser offence'

It is sometimes open to a jury to find a defendant not guilty of the offence alleged in a count on the indictment, but guilty of some other 'lesser' offence.[47] Where a jury is able to do this, then so too can the accused in terms of his choice of plea - in other words, he may plead not guilty to the offence charged, but guilty of a lesser offence of which the jury could have convicted him.[48]

In a sense, pleading guilty to a lesser offence is a half-way house between a guilty and not-guilty plea. If such a plea is accepted, the defendant is treated as having been acquitted of the offence actually charged and the court will proceed to

44 See Ch. 13

45 Contracting legal aid remuneration does not assist in this. See Ch. 12

46 Having sought an indication of plea can sometimes pose ethical dilemmas if counsel then goes on to represent the defendant at trial.

47 A 'lesser' offence is one which is 'included' within a more serious offence (for example, the crime of robbery is essentially theft plus violence) or is a less culpable version of the offence charged (for example, manslaughter is a less culpable version of homicide than murder). Verdicts are discussed below.

48 Criminal Law Act 1967 (CLA 1967), s 6(1)(b)

sentence him for the lesser offence.[49] Whether the prosecution accepts this plea from a defendant will depend,[50] essentially, on the strength of the evidence and whether the guilty plea offered (and the court's ability to sentence on it) adequately reflects the wrong which was done. Remember too that in this context, the 'lesser offence' to which the accused may plead guilty is *not* on the indictment. Do not confuse this situation with that, discussed above, where an accused pleads to alternatives (not necessarily hierarchical) which *are* on the same indictment.[51] You could get to a similar sort of result in terms of so-called plea 'bargaining',[52] but by a different procedural route.

(d) Pleading guilty personally

Finally, defendants must plead guilty or not guilty *personally*, although a failure to do the latter may be less problematic than a failure to do the former.[53] This is because a guilty plea is followed by the imposition of a sentence, and a certain criminal record, whereas what follows a not guilty plea is (one hopes) a fair trial.

C. ABUSE OF PROCESS

The right to a fair trial is a fundamental right of any accused, enshrined both in domestic and ECHR law, and Crown Court judges (like magistrates) have the power to stop a trial if it is considered grossly unfair to the defendant to continue. The defendant would apply in the Crown Court[54] to 'stay' the indictment on grounds of abuse of process; such an application should be made by written notice to the court no later than 14 days before the date set for trial.[55] Notice should be served not only on the prosecution, but also all co-defendants (who may well want to join in on the application). The Court should exercise the power to stay proceedings as an abuse of process where either (i) the accused cannot receive a fair trial or (ii) it would be unfair for

49 *Ibid*, s 6(5)

50 What influence the judge may have in this decision is debatable: see BCrP D 12.79

51 So, for example, only counts which were actually *on* the indictment can be left on the file.

52 Note that plea bargains in the wider American sense of prosecutors refraining from bringing certain charges or asking for lighter sentences from a judge do not happen here. Indictments are drawn up independently of defendant's wishes and prosecutors do not suggest sentences. See discussion in Sprack, *Practical Approach*, 17.29ff

53 A guilty plea which is not entered in person by a defendant is a nullity: *R v Ellis* (1973) 57 Cr App R

54 A similar power exists in the magistrates' court. See Ch. 8

55 Once notice is given,

the accused to be tried at all (however fair the process).[56] This is a neat, but very broad articulation of the principle, and has been held to include failings like a protracted delay in proceedings which was prejudicial to the defendant; the prosecution's losing (or destroying) evidence which could be helpful to the defence; or abuse of executive power. Both Art 6 of the ECHR and the overriding objective to deal with cases 'justly' are apt to be used to underpin any such argument on behalf of the accused.[57]

2. THE TRIAL

A. JUDGE ONLY TRIALS

Trial by jury is a central feature of trial on indictment. Defendants who have a choice and elect trial on indictment, do so precisely because a jury 'of their peers', and not a professional judge will be the ones deciding whether they are guilty or innocent. Juries both epitomise and dispense, at least theoretically, criminal justice in a democracy. However, there are rare occasions when judge-only trials are thought to be justified. There are essentially two main situations.[58]

(i) Jury tampering

Where the court is satisfied that that there is evidence of a 'real and present' danger of jury tampering[59] which (despite attempts to minimise it) is so substantial that it is in the interests of justice to conduct the trial without a jury, then a judge-only trial may be ordered.[60]

(ii) Sample counts

This possibility[61] is not brought about by anxieties about the proper functioning of the jury, but in an attempt to save time where the sheer number of counts might be

certain automatic directions apply. See generally CrimPD, I 3C.1ff

56 See e.g., *R v Maxwell* [2011] 4 All ER 941 per Lord Dyson at [13] and cases cited at BCrP D 3.67/68

57 For detailed discussion see generally BCrP D 3.66

58 A third option for judge-only trials in complex fraud cases was never brought into force: BCrP D 13.76

59 This includes threatened or actual harm to, intimidation or bribery of, jurors, their family or friends: CJA 2003, s 44

60 *Ibid*

61 Created by s 17 DVCVA 2004

more than one jury should have to cope with. In essence the procedure allows the jury to try sample counts, leaving the remaining counts on the indictment able to be tried by a judge sitting alone. The latter should try the remaining counts in light of the jury's verdict on the sample counts, and thereafter sentence in accordance with overall culpability of the accused.

B. JURY TRIAL

In the ordinary course of events, trial on indictment is heard by judge and jury. If the defendant pleads not guilty, then (unless the prosecution choose to offer no evidence) a trial must be held, and the first order of business will be to 'empanel', or swear in a jury.

Juries are to be drawn from a broad cross-section of society. Serving as a juror is considered a civic duty and, with some exceptions,[62] everyone aged 18 to 75, who is on the electoral register, has lived in the United Kingdom for at least five years and is not otherwise excluded (e.g. those with certain criminal convictions) is eligible for jury service.[63] Lawyers, judges and police officers were once excluded (as knowing too much about the system). This exemption was removed in 2004, although it will always be necessary to keep an eye on the composition of any particular jury, to ensure that there is no scope for apparent conflict of interest or bias. Problems can arise with any juror (for example, if he or she knows a participant in the trial), but police officers and CPS employees can pose obvious risks in some circumstances.[64]

Jurors are summoned, at random, to attend for jury service; the names and addresses are taken from the electoral register.[65] The usual procedure is to summon many more jurors for service than are likely to be required, so that at the end of the day there are sufficient numbers to make up a jury. It is a criminal offence not to answer a jury summons without reasonable cause (for example, sudden hospitalisation) and no-one is entitled to refuse to do jury duty. But some of those

62 See Schedule 1 of the Juries Act 1974 (JA 1974)

63 JA 1974, s 1. The maximum age was raised to 75 by the Criminal Justice and Courts Act 2015

64 See *Armstrong v UK* [2014] ECHR 1368 and discussion at BCrP D 13.27, particularly as to apparent bias

65 The use of the electoral register as the jury pool has its obvious drawbacks, not least of which is the exclusion from jury service of the disenfranchised, thus producing pockets of under-representation by those who may be most able to identify with the circumstances of some of those in the dock.

summoned will inevitably have their service deferred or be excused from service. It's a bit like overbooking a plane; the airlines prefer too many passengers on the day, not too few, even if some of them do not get to fly!

The next stage is to 'empanel' a jury from amongst those summoned. About 15 potential jurors come into the courtroom. The clerk[66] reads out 12 names and these people go into the jury box. The clerk will explain to the defendant that the list of names to be called out will form the jury in his case, subject to his right to challenge jurors before they take the juror's oath. There are two main challenges which can be made in this jurisdiction.[67]

(i) Stand-by

This sort of challenge is confined to the *prosecution*. Just as the juror begins to take the oath, the prosecution may call out *"Stand by"*. The judge will then explain to the juror that he or she will not sit on this jury, but should remain available for another. The prosecution does not need to give any reasons for this challenge, although the motivation will usually be some information about the individual gleaned, for example, from the Police National Computer, which makes that person unsuitable, in the prosecution's eyes, to try the case. It might also be used if the prosecution (with the defence's agreement) think that a juror seems inadequate to the task: for example if that individual had difficulty as he began to read the jury oath from the card, and the case involves lots of documentation. There is no limit on the number of people the prosecution can stand by, but the power must be used responsibly.[68] Judges have the power to stand jurors down, but this is rarely exercised, and when attempted (for example to correct some perceived imbalance) is usually disapproved.[69]

66 This is an administrative clerk. Do not confuse the clerk in the Crown Court with the legal adviser/clerk in the magistrates' courts.

67 The system is very different in most American states, where impartiality is thought to be best achieved through careful (and painstaking) vetting of jurors. In England and Wales, impartiality is thought to be secured through a process which is essentially random, and where there is only limited scope for challenging jurors. Certainly you wouldn't make a film about it!

68 See Code for Crown Prosecutors, in Appendix 3 of BCrP

69 See BCrP D 13.36ff

(ii) Challenge for cause

This form of challenge is open to *both* prosecution and defence. It is used to challenge potential jurors either on the basis that they are disqualified or otherwise ineligible for jury service or because they may reasonably be suspected of bias. Again, the challenge is made before the juror completes taking the oath. As the prosecution have the right to stand by jurors without giving a reason, it will be the defence who are most apt to use the challenge for cause procedure,[70] although it is very limited in its scope. For example, only exceptionally is one entitled to ask questions of jurors to establish whether they may be biased or not, and only after prima facie evidence of the juror's unsuitability has been given. A defendant making a challenge has to satisfy the judge (on the balance of probabilities) that the objection is justified, and this is difficult to do on what is usually very little information. Because of these procedural hurdles and limitations, defence challenges for cause are a relatively rare event.

When a juror is stood down or successfully challenged, he or she is replaced by another from the pool, until 12 jurors have been sworn in, and the jury thus 'empanelled'. All Crown Court trials begin with these 12, but if a couple are lost along the way, the case can still continue. *Up to three jurors* may be excused or discharged during the course of a trial because of illness or other necessity. If more than three jurors can no longer serve, then the trial must be abandoned (to be started afresh at a later date with a completely new jury).

Once the jurors have all been empanelled, the trial will begin with the clerk reading out the indictment, confirming to the jury that the defendant has pleaded not guilty and effectively telling them that it is their job, having heard the evidence, to 'say whether he/she be guilty or not'.

70 The defence no longer have a right of peremptory challenge.

C. PROCEEDING IN THE ABSENCE OF THE ACCUSED

An accused has a general right to be present at his trial and a right to be legally represented. We have seen that a defendant can attend a pre-trial hearing via live link, but when it comes to entering a plea and the actual trial, the accused should be there in the flesh (and have the benefit of such special measures - for example, an interpreter - as may be required to ensure he can follow what is going on). The court has a *discretion* to proceed with the trial without the defendant, but should *not* do so *unless* satisfied both that the defendant has knowingly waived his right to attend *and* that it would be fair to proceed in his absence.[71] The case law and the rules emphasise the need for *great caution* in exercising this discretion, and in so doing the court should consider things like: the reason for the defendant's absence (his fault or not?); whether an adjournment would allow the case to continue later with the accused present; how is the public interest best served; and the disadvantage to the defendant of continuing without him (what is the likely outcome if he is convicted?). Only rarely would the court carry on in the absence of a defendant who is unrepresented.[72]

D. UNREPRESENTED DEFENDANTS

Entitlement to legal aid for representation in Crown Court trials is now subject to a means test. As a result, many defendants no longer qualify for 100% public funding and choose to represent themselves rather than pay expensive lawyer's fees. This poses challenges, not only for them but also the court, who will seek to give the accused such assistance in conducting his defence as seems appropriate.[73] There are some things, of course, which a litigant in person may not do (for example cross-examine a complainant in a sexual offence case).[74] Unrepresented defendants will thus need to have explained to them what can and cannot be

71 See BCrP D 15.82 and 15.83. Note that the death of the defendant brings any criminal proceedings to an end: see *Guardian* newspaper report, Fri 7 April 2017, p. 14

72 See Crown Court Compendium Pt 1 Ch. 3-3 for general principles and what the jury should be told.

73 If an accused dismisses his legal team, but remains eligible for legal aid, the court should adjourn for him to find new representation. BCrP D 17.17. Concerns have been expressed about how well unrepresented accused are supported.

74 See Ch. 17

done, and the implications of some of their choices (especially as to whether to give evidence or not). The jury too may well need to have some guidance about how to deal with the situation - what the judge will say will vary depending on whether the defendant has been unrepresented from the outset, or 'lost' his representation mid-way through the trial.[75]

E. CHANGE OF PLEA

As in the magistrates' courts, there is scope in the Crown Court for a defendant to change his mind about his plea. Suppose a defendant pleaded guilty to some counts on the indictment, but not guilty to others. He may be awaiting sentence on the guilty pleas pending the outcome of the trial of the counts to which he pleaded not guilty. If during the trial, he wants to change any one of those 'guilty' pleas to 'not guilty', can he? The court has discretion to allow an accused to change his plea from 'guilty' to 'not guilty' at any stage before sentence is passed. But to give permission the judge will want a *very* good explanation for the change of heart. Permission to withdraw the guilty plea is unlikely to be given unless the defendant had not been properly advised or otherwise did not realise that he had a defence when he pleaded guilty.[76]

Going the other direction is, as always, much easier. A defendant who has pleaded not guilty may change his plea to guilty at any time before the jury has *returned* a verdict. Thus the jury could be mid-deliberation when the guilty plea is entered. This is rather different than the magistrates' court (where the cut off point is when the justices retire to consider their decision), presumably because a jury might spend days deliberating and the judge remains available to tell them to stop (and ask them to return a formal verdict of guilty). If the change of plea comes before the matter has been put in the jury's hands, then typically defence counsel would just ask that the indictment be put again to the accused, who will then plead 'guilty.'

75 See BCrP D 17.18 and Crown Court Compendium Pt 1 Ch.3-5

76 See, e.g., Lord Lane CJ's comments in *R v Drew* [1985] 1 WLR 914, at p. 923. The relevant procedure is in CrimPR r 25.5

F. CONDUCT OF THE TRIAL

The judge at the trial on indictment is usually a circuit judge (or equivalent), unless the case is a serious one, in which case it will be a High Court judge (or equivalent). The prosecution must be legally represented; the accused is entitled to be represented, although unrepresented defendants have become more common since entitlement to legal aid in the Crown Court became subject to a means test. Some solicitors will have rights of audience in the Crown Court, although most instruct counsel.

It is important to note that prosecuting counsel have important duties and obligations[77] in conducting cases and enjoy greater independence from those instructing them than do defence counsel. In particular, where there is a dispute between the CPS and counsel as to the presentation and general conduct of the prosecution, it is the latter's view which must prevail.

At the start of the trial, the judge should ensure that the jury understands the charge(s) and give some general guidance on how jury members should discharge their duties (for example, by avoiding the internet, ignoring media reports, trying the case only on the evidence and so on). Thereafter, the running order of events is as follows:[78]

(i) Prosecution case

When the defendant pleads not guilty, the burden is on the prosecution to prove the case against him. It follows therefore that the prosecution presents its case first. Counsel will begin with the opening speech, the purpose of which is to identify the issues in dispute as well as briefly outline the prosecution case - the idea is to help the jury understand what the case is about. If there is any dispute about the admissibility of any prosecution evidence (and no ruling about this was given previously), then no mention of that evidence should be made at this point. The opening should

77 These, and especially the all important Farquharson guidelines, are usefully summarised in BCrP D16.2

78 For preliminary instructions see CrimPD VI 26.G.3. See also CrimPR r 25.9(2) which clearly sets out the running order. See also BCrP D 16.9ff as required.

essentially be factual, explain that the burden is on the prosecution to prove its case so that the jury are 'sure' of guilt, and that the jury should ultimately take the law from the judge. The usual advice for the beginner is to avoid histrionics and to 'open low' - if the jury's expectations about the evidence are raised too high, a few evidential bumps in the road might undermine their confidence in the entire prosecution case. Emotive language should be avoided.

After the prosecution opening, the defence may be asked to set out its position on the issues, if this would assist the jury's understanding of the case. If the defence were to decline, the judge can order that the jury be given the defence statement (edited as necessary). The prosecution will then present the evidence on which it relies. Some of it will take the form of written statements; but most of it will be in the form of 'live' witnesses. Each party is responsible for ensuring the attendance of its own witnesses.

Oral evidence: the general rule

The general rule is that the prosecution must call to give *oral* evidence all the witnesses whose evidence was included in the bundle of disclosed statements[79] when the case was sent to the Crown Court for trial from the magistrates' court or has otherwise been served on the defence. This is to ensure that all such witnesses will be made available for cross-examination. It is important that the defence has an opportunity to test (or otherwise make the most of) the prosecution evidence, and so there are very *few* exceptions to this rule. They are where:

(a) the defence consents to the witness's evidence being read to the court. Where evidence is uncontroversial from start to finish, then s 9 Criminal Justice Act 1967 (CJA 1967) permits a written witness statement to be read into evidence in criminal proceedings so long

79 Sometimes referred to as 'witnesses whose names appear on the back of the indictment' because at one time they did, literally, appear on the back of the indictment. And see BCrP D 16.17

as it contains a declaration of truth and copies have been served on all parties, and none has objected to this course of action. This is a sensible provision when evidence does not need to be tested by cross-examination or challenged in any respect. The judge will explain to the jury that this evidence is as good as the evidence given 'live', and is being presented in written form to save time and money. Such evidence may be edited as necessary (eg by creating one 'composite' statement out of several other statements, or redacting an original witness statement) to meet any defence objections or to ensure fairness:[80]

(b) The evidence is disputed but has been ruled[81] admissible in written form (for example, hearsay statements under s 114(d) or 116 CJA 2003[82]), and so may be read out to the jury without the consent of the defence. In such cases the jury must be warned of the need to take particular care because the maker of the statement is not there to have his or her evidence challenged in cross-examination. Remember, too, that the fact that such controversial evidence is admissible in the form of a witness statement does not mean it necessarily has to be believed. It could, for example, be contradicted by other evidence just as the evidence of a live witness could be:

(c) The prosecution takes the view that their evidence is no longer credible (but they must still have the witness attend court so the defence can call him if they wish); *or*

(d) the witness would so contradict the prosecution case that it would make more sense for that person to be called as a witness for the defence (thus rendering it 'unused' material which should have been disclosed as soon as its value for the defence was revealed).[83]

---

80 s 9 statements should be in prescribed form: CrimPR Pt 16 and see CrimPD V 16A and examples in BCrP D 16.52

81 Usually at the PTPH or other case management hearing.

82 See generally BCrP D 16.35ff. Hearsay evidence is discussed in Ch. 20

83 *R v Russell-Jones* [1995] 1 Cr App R 538, at 544

Equally, the prosecution may only call such witnesses whose evidence was available when the case was sent or transferred to the Crown Court for trial, unless the defence was alerted to additional witnesses by way of a notice of additional evidence. This is achieved by serving a copy of the witness's statement on the defence along with a notice that the prosecution intends to call the evidence at trial. Such evidence can be read out in court unless the defence objects (within seven days of service of the notice), in which case either the live witness is called or the evidence abandoned. This procedure is to ensure that the defence is not taken by surprise; there is no time limit for serving a notice of additional evidence, but if it is at or so close to trial that the defence is unable to deal with it adequately, then the judge should either grant an adjournment or exclude it under s 78 PACE 1984.

Each witness called for the prosecution will take the oath or affirm. The usual sequence is then followed:

- evidence-in-chief (unless the witness is only being tendered for cross-examination) including identification of any items of real evidence, which become exhibits in the case,
- followed by cross-examination,
- followed by re-examination, if necessary.[84]

If there is some duplication of prosecution evidence,[85] it is possible for the prosecution merely to 'tender' the second and subsequent witnesses for cross-examination (and not bother with their evidence-in-chief).

Special measures may have been directed for a distressed or vulnerable witness[86] and these should be complied with. Witnesses who will give evidence should wait outside the courtroom until they are called (to ensure their evidence is

---

84 See generally Ch. 18

85 For example, where several police officers attended the crime scene.

86 See generally Ch. 17

not tainted by what they might hear) unless (by way of exception) that person is the defendant (who attends throughtout) or an expert witness. It is through the giving and testing of oral evidence, that the jury can best hear, see and assess for themselves the credibility of any witness's evidence.

Formal admissions

Formal admissions are not common, but unless made orally in court (when everyone is watching and listening) must be in writing signed by the person making it and will be read out to the jury.[87] The rules apply to both sides; either prosecution or defence can make formal admissions. The matter can be dealt with on one of the pre-trial standard forms or arise at trial (possibly once evidence for the prosecution has been heard). A formal admission only binds the party making it in respect of the criminal proceedings in which it was made, but including any subsequent appeal or retrial.

(ii) Defence objections to prosecution evidence

Many defence objections to prosecution evidence can be dealt with effectively before trial, either at the PTPH (if it can be determined purely on legal argument) or, if evidence needs to be heard, as a preliminary issue to be dealt with at the start of the trial (but before a jury has been empanelled). Written statements to be read out at trial can (by agreement) be edited to omit inadmissible evidence. Sometimes, however, the matter needs to be dealt with at trial. It is a fundamental feature of trials on indictment that questions of law (which includes the admissibility of evidence) are decided by the judge alone, and in the absence of the jurors, so that their objectivity will not have been adversely affected if the evidence is ruled inadmissible. We tend, by and large, not to employ the American custom of constantly telling (or depending on) jurors to ignore what they have heard; we try

87 CJA 1967, s 10 and see Ch. 14

to make sure they do not hear it in the first place.[88]

If there are evidential or legal issues which do arise at trial, defence counsel should firstly alert his opponent, who in turn should adapt his presentation accordingly. The prosecution will proceed as normal until the point at which the disputed evidence would be adduced, when (usually defence) counsel will invite the judge to ask the jury to leave (often under the guise of having 'a much needed cup of tea' in the jury room while legal issues which 'need not concern' them are discussed).

Once the jury have left, there may just be pure legal argument; defence counsel raises his objections, prosecuting counsel replies and the judge makes a ruling. The jury can be brought back in and the trial continues. If the evidence was ruled admissible, the jury will hear it; if not, they won't.

Sometimes, however, the arguments for exclusion are dependent on the circumstances in which evidence was obtained, and those may be disputed. This requires the judge to determine the facts before making a legal ruling (based on those findings). This requires what is called a 'trial within a trial' because the judge hears evidence from witnesses (on the 'voir dire', as it is called, named for the special oath witnesses take for this procedure), before making his decision. There is a useful summary of the standard procedure set out at BCrP D 16.41.

Let's look at the example of the admissibility of a confession statement, which the defence seeks to exclude under s 76 and/or s 78 PACE 1984.[89] This should be dealt with before trial, wherever possible, but if the matter were to arise at trial, then once the jury has left the courtroom, the police officer who took the confession statement would testify as to its making, no doubt highlighting the proper procedures which were followed, and then be cross-examined by the defence, who will suggest deficiencies in the process (for example, threats or promises which were made, no access to a solicitor and so on). Other police officers who can give relevant evidence

88 Occasionally a judge may have to tell jurors to disregard some aspect of a witness's evidence, but usually this is the result of the answer given (which may have strayed into inadmissible territory), not the question asked.

89 See generally Ch. 21

may be similarly questioned. The accused himself may[90] then give evidence, and could also call any witness who can back up his version of events.

All evidence given on the voir dire (in this example) is related solely to the admissibility (or not) of the confession. The judge then hears submissions from both sides and makes a ruling. The jury returns to the courtroom. If the confession has been ruled inadmissible, they will hear nothing of it. If it has been ruled admissible, the same evidence advanced on the voir dire will often be repeated before the jury as part of the parties' respective cases. So far as the defence is concerned, the objective is no longer to convince the judge to rule the confession inadmissible, but to convince the jury, on the same facts, that the confession is not credible[91] because of the circumstances in which it was made.[92] There are three important things to notice about all of this:

(a) A 'trial within a trial' is only necessary when a decision on the admissibility of evidence really cannot be made without making findings of *fact*.

(b) A 'trial within a trial' is a prime example of one of those times when a Crown Court judge, who is the sole arbiter of the law at a trial, must also make a factual determination. *Juries* are the principal fact finders so far as issues of guilt or innocence are concerned (and of course never make legal rulings). But the judge does, from time to time, have to make findings of fact in order to make his or her legal rulings, and this is one of those times.

(c) The circumstances in which a confession (or other evidence) is obtained may be relevant both to whether the evidence is admissible or not (a legal question) and the weight which, if admissible, it will carry.

90 Depending on the evidence so far. Remember that the burden of proof is on the prosecution.

91 As to the important difference between admissibility of evidence (a legal question for the judge) and the weight of evidence (a factual question for the jury), see Ch.14

92 Some defence advocates would prefer to do things the other way around, in other words, first impugn the credibility of the evidence in front of the jury and then seek a ruling on admissibility (and, with luck, an instruction to the jury to ignore the evidence

(iii) Half time: possible submission of no case to answer?

Once the prosecution has presented its evidence, oral and written, it will conclude by saying something like 'that is the case for the Crown'. Consideration must then be given to the question of whether this case is really worthy of answering by the defence. A submission of 'no case to answer' is usually made by the defence, but if the accused is unrepresented, or it appears that defence counsel is not going to make the submission, the judge can raise the matter on his own initiative. The submission is made (and the matter considered) in the absence of the jury and the prosecution, of course, is given an opportunity to respond. The application may be made in respect of some or all of the counts on the indictment, and to the extent that it is successful the judge will instruct the jury to acquit, on that count, the accused on whose behalf the submission was made.

The test is very similar to that in the magistrates' court, adapted for the division of labour between judge and jury. In a nutshell, there is no case to answer if the prosecution have failed to adduce evidence on which a jury, properly directed by the judge, could properly convict.[93] This envisages a number of possible scenarios, some more straightforward than others. If, for example, the prosecution have failed to adduce evidence of an essential ingredient of the offence charged, the submission would clearly have to succeed, although omissions caused by correctible procedural errors or misconceptions about the issues in dispute should be raised at an early stage and not left until the end of the prosecution case.[94] Note too the power of the court to allow the prosecution to re-open their case.

Equally, if a crucial aspect of the prosecution case rests on circumstantial evidence from which no reasonable person could draw the required inferences, the submission should also succeed. The difficulty arises, as Lord Lane himself put it in the leading case of *R v Galbraith:*[95]

---

completely). They think this order of events deprives prosecutors of having had a 'dry run' on a voir dire. See discussion at BCrP F16.45ff

93 *R v Galbraith* [1981] 1 WLR 1039, discussed in detail at BCrP D 16.54ff

94 See, e.g., Thomas LJ's comments in *R v Penner* [2010] EWCA Crim 1155, at [16]-[19]. The danger, of course, is that this can interfere with the burden of proof (insofar as it puts some onus on defence counsel to do the prosecution's job for it).

95 Op. cit., at p. 1042, B-D

> Where there is some evidence but it is of a tenuous character, for example because of inherent weakness or vagueness or because it is inconsistent with other evidence … Where the judge comes to the conclusion that the prosecution evidence, taken at its highest, is such that the jury properly directed could not properly convict upon it, it is his duty, upon the submission being made, to stop the case … Where however the prosecution evidence is such that its strength or weakness depends on the view to be taken of a witness's reliability, or other matters which are generally speaking within the province of the jury and where on one possible view of the facts there is evidence upon which a jury could properly come to the conclusion that the defendant is guilty, then the judge should allow the matter to be tried by the jury.

This distinction is sometimes easier to understand than to apply. The important thing to remember is that issues of credibility are quintessentially matters for the jury, and the judge should not step on the latter's toes by effectively second guessing what they would (or should) decide. But a case based on evidence which is incapable of performing the task asked of it by the prosecution,[96] should not be left to the jury. It is sometimes difficult to know where the line is drawn, but the 'proper approach' is neatly set out in BCrP.[97] In summary:

(a) If there is no evidence to prove an essential element of the offence, then clearly a submission of no case to answer must succeed;
(b) But if there is some evidence which, on the face of it, goes some way towards proving each essential element, the case should normally be left to the jury; unless the evidence is so weak that no reasonable jury (properly directed by the judge) could convict on it, in which case a

96 As to occasions when the 'silence' of the accused can (and cannot) be used to assist a prosecution to mount a case to answer, see Ch. 23

97 See BCrP D 16.59 and discussion of particular cases which follow.

98 *Ibid*, and see Ch. 24 regarding identification evidence.

99 See, e.g., *R v Shippey* [1988] Crim LR 767

100 There is no obligation to do this, but it would be a brave (or desperate) advocate who risked calling no evidence and merely

submission should be upheld;

(c) Evidence may be weak by virtue of the 'sheer improbability of what the witness is saying, from internal inconsistencies in the evidence or from its type, which the accumulated wisdom of the courts has shown to be of doubtful value (especially in identification evidence cases)';[98]

(d) The question of whether a witness is lying is nearly always one for the jury, but there may, exceptionally, be cases[99] where the lack of credibility is so apparent that any reasonable tribunal would be forced to conclude that the witness is untruthful, and so it would not be proper for the case to proceed.

(iv) Defence case

Assuming there is a case to answer, it will then be for the defence to present its case.[100] Only if the defence intends to call at least one witness of fact *other than, or in addition to*, the evidence of the accused, is it entitled to make an opening speech.[101] In fact, defence counsel rarely feel the need to make an opening speech (unless the case is very complex) since the nature of its case should already be apparent from the cross-examination of the prosecution witnesses.

In the vast majority of cases these days, the accused will be called to give evidence. This is because if he does not go into the witness box to tell his side of the story, the jury may be entitled to conclude that he has no story to tell.[102] If the accused decides *not* to testify, despite counsel's advice to the contrary, the latter should ensure that the defendant confirms this in writing (usually endorsed on counsel's brief). The judge should always make sure a defendant is aware of the possible consequences of not testifying.[103]

If the accused is to give evidence, he must always be the *first* witness.[104] This

addressing the jury on the basis that the prosecution had not proved its case beyond reasonable doubt.

101 Even where not entitled to an opening speech, the defence may be asked (after the prosecution opening) to identify the issues in dispute. See BCrP D 17.7

102 See generally the discussion of adverse inferences in Ch. 23

103 See BCrP D 17.12 and Ch. 23

104 Unless the judge gives leave to the contrary: PACE 1984, s 79. But a character witness must *always* be called *after* the accused gives evidence. See *ibid*, D 17.9

is because he is in the courtroom throughout the trial, and might otherwise be tempted to trim his evidence in light of what others before him have said. The nature of his defence should, of course, have been disclosed in the defence statement, which is obligatory in the Crown Court,[105] so his evidence should not come as any great surprise to the prosecution. If it does, he will have some explaining to do as to why he did not mention material details sooner.[106]

Names and addresses of defence witnesses and any expert evidence will also have been disclosed pre-trial. Only with the permission of the judge could previously undisclosed expert (or other) evidence be called at this stage.[107]

Just as with prosecution evidence, some of the defence case may be presented in written form, either by agreement or because of a court ruling. Note that if further (admissible) evidence becomes relevant (for example, to rebut evidence given previously) it may also be introduced (by any party).

Co-defendants: who goes first?

If there is more than one defendant, and they are separately represented, each must present their entire case in *the order their names appear on the indictment* (but leaving the closing speeches until everyone's evidence has been given). Examiners sometimes like to test this proposition in conjunction with the rule that the defendant himself (if giving evidence) is always the first witness for his own defence case. Counsel for a co-defendant also typically cross-examine other co-defendants before the prosecution does so.

So, if the indictment is against D1 and D2, who are separately represented[108] and both want to give evidence and both have other witnesses to call, then the order in which the oral evidence is given would be:

105 See Ch. 7

106 See adverse inference directions discussed at Ch. 23

107 See generally Ch. 22 for expert evidence.

108 If two or more accused are jointly represented by the same legal team they are treated as presenting a joint defence. Counsel would give an opening on behalf of them both, and then call their evidence in turn.

(a) D1's case goes first (he is first on the indictment)
- Opening speech (if desired)
- D1 himself must give evidence first. He is cross-examined on behalf of D2 and then by prosecution, re-examined if necessary
- D1's other witnesses give evidence and are cross-/re-examined as above

(b) D2's case follows
- Opening speech (if desired)
- D2 himself must give evidence first. He is cross-examined on
- behalf of D1 and by prosecution, re-examined if necessary
- D2's other witnesses give evidence and are cross-/re-examined as above

(c) At the end, closing speeches would be in the order: Prosecution, D1, D2

(v) Pre-summing up discussions

Where complex directions need to be given to juries, the judge will often discuss with counsel what he or she should say. This should happen in the absence of the jury (obviously), and before the closing speeches. Counsel are under a duty to assist the court to deliver a fair trial (whether it assists their own case or not).[109]

(vi) Closing speeches

The prosecution may only make a closing speech if the defendant is legally represented and has called witnesses of fact apart from giving his own testimony (or the court gives permission). In any event, it may not be thought necessary. Any closing speech given by the prosecution should, as in all things, be professional and measured.

The last word (save for the judge's summing up) *always goes to the defence* in a

109 See BCrP D 18.13

criminal trial, for he has the most to lose. It is an important piece of advocacy, which would never be waived. It is the last chance to convince the jury (by reference to the evidence, not wishful thinking) why it should have a reasonable doubt about the defendant's guilt, and so acquit him.[110]

(vii) Summing up to jury

Typically, after prosecution and defence have made their closing speeches, the judge will 'sum up' the case to the jury, having conferred with counsel as appropriate. This is the final stage of the trial, and a very critical one. The summing up need not be long, if the case is straightforward, but it must always be done. If it is not, or if it is not done fairly and properly, this can form a ground of appeal. But note that these days a judge's summing up won't necessarily all come at the very end.

For example, given that a judge's summing up conveniently divides into directions on the law and directions on the evidence, it may be sensible to *split* the summing up so as to give the first of these before the closing speeches, and then comment on the evidence after those speeches have been made.[111] Similarly, the rules now require judges to 'give direction about the relevant law *at any time* at which to do so will assist jurors to evaluate the evidence.' Thus it might be sensible for the judge to give certain directions (for example, about specific types of evidence) much earlier, when the evidence in question is about to be heard.[112]

These days, too, it is common for judges to give jurors a '*written route*' to a verdict (unless the case is very simple). This involves setting out a series of questions, the answers to which will lead the jury to their verdict. Before doing this, the judge ought to submit a copy to counsel for their comments.[113] It is counsel's job, in any event, to draw any potential errors in a summing up (oral or written) to the court's attention.

110 See comments regarding proper content of prosecution and defence speeches at *ibid*, D 18.18ff

111 See *ibid* D 18.21

112 CrimPR r 25.14(2)

113 *Ibid* r 23.14 and CrimPD VI 26K

Cases vary, but every summing up will include the following aspects:[114]

(a) The respective functions of the judge and jury

Questions of fact are for the jury, who must take their law from the judge. If the judge expresses a view on the facts, he must make it clear to the jury that they are free to disregard that view.

(b) Directions on the burden and standard of proof

This is discussed in more detail in Chapter 15.

(c) Directions on the relevant law and the evidence

The judge should explain the relevant law involved in the case and its relationship to the facts of the case. In the process the judge should explain the main features of both the prosecution and defence case. It is particularly important that the defence case is put fairly and fully to the jury.

(d) Give any special evidential directions

There are various circumstances when judges are required to give certain instructions to a jury: for example, a *Turnbull* direction (disputed identification), *Vye* direction (defendant's good character), *Lucas* direction (defendant's established lies). They will also need guidance on how to deal with such things as bad character evidence, hearsay evidence, alibi evidence and also the implications of a defendant's failure to answer police questions or give evidence in court. These aspects of a case (and what judges should tell the jury) are all discussed in detail[115] in the evidence section of this book.

114 For more detail, see BCrP D 18.25ff

115 With many references to the Crown Court Compendium.

(e) More than one defendant and/or count

Very careful directions need to be given about how the jury treats evidence against co-defendants, in particular when evidence is admissible against one but not the other. It is important that the jury knows they must consider the case against each defendant and on each count separately.

3. POST-TRIAL CONSIDERATIONS

A. JURY RETIRES TO CONSIDER THEIR VERDICT

When the jury retire they are put in the charge of the jury bailiff, who promises to take the jurors to a private place (the jury room) where they can discuss the case without interference. Jurors will be reminded about trying the case on the evidence alone (and so on), and only discussing the case with fellow jurors during deliberations. They will be told their verdict should be unanimous. The jury will have written guidance (and relevant evidence) with them for the task ahead. If necessary, they may ask the judge for further explanation of the law arising in the case, although too many of the same questions can result in the judge discharging the jury if this betrays an inability to reach a verdict.[116]

B. THE VERDICT

There are two aspects of the jury's verdict that examiners especially like to test: one is the jury's ability to return a verdict of guilty of a lesser offence, and the other is majority verdicts.

116 As happened with the jury in the first Vicky Pryce prosecution, although the judge could perhaps have masked his disapproval a bit better: telegraph.co.uk/news/politics/liberaldemocrats/9883130/Jury-discharged-in-Vicky-Pryce-trial-after-failing-to-reach-verdict.html. See BCrP D 19.18

(i) Guilty of a lesser offence

Generally speaking a jury has the choice, in respect of each count on the indictment, of finding the defendant guilty or not guilty. Sometimes, however, they have another alternative - that of finding the defendant not guilty of the offence charged, but guilty of a 'lesser' (indictable) offence which was not on the indictment. This is only permitted if s 6(2)-(4) and s 4(2) of the Criminal Law Act 1967 (CLA 1967) applies, which we have looked at briefly above when considering the related topic of accepting a plea of guilty to a lesser offence.

According to s 6(3), if an allegation in a count on an indictment 'amounts to or includes' (either expressly or by implication) an allegation of another (indictable) offence, the jury may find the accused not guilty of the offence charged but guilty of that other offence. The notion of the 'lesser included offence' is a common law principle, which has been supplemented by s 6(3) CLA 1967 itself. Typical examples of offences which give the jury the option of returning a verdict of guilty of what is usually described as a 'lesser' offence are:

(a) on a count of murder the jury can convict of manslaughter;
(b) on a count of robbery the jury can convict of theft,
(c) on a count of s 18 wounding with intent,[117] the jury can convict of unlawful wounding under s 20.[118]

And so forth. *Do not confuse* this with the jury having to return verdicts on alternative counts, both of which appear on the indictment. If the two are strict alternatives (for example, when both theft and handling of the same goods is included on the indictment), in law an accused can do one or the other, but not both. If the jury finds the defendant guilty of one of these two, they are

117 s 18 Offences Against the Person Act 1861 (OAPA 1861)

118 *Ibid*, s 20. And see BCrP D 19.58 on the judge's discretion to give directions on returning such verdicts.

discharged from returning a verdict on the other. Where more hierarchical alternatives are included, the jury will always be asked about the more serious first. For example, assuming two alternatives (for example, s 18 and s 20 OAPA 1861), then if the jury returns a verdict of guilty to the more serious of the two, they will be discharged from returning a verdict on the less serious. If they return a verdict of not guilty on the more serious offence, they will then be asked for their verdict on the less serious.[119] Otherwise, juries must return verdicts on all counts of the indictment individually.

(ii) Majority verdicts

There are two issues regarding majority verdicts: how big a majority is required and how long does the court wait before accepting such a verdict?

Ideally the jurors should return a unanimous verdict of 12, and they are given at least two hours (plus ten minutes settling in time) to achieve this.[120] How much longer beyond this they should be given to achieve unanimity is up to the judge. The more complex the case, the longer the judge will give the jury to get to grips with it. But the minimum figure to keep in mind is *two hours, ten minutes.*

Once the judge decides that (subject to the two hour, ten minute minimum) a majority verdict is permissible, the jury will be given a direction to this effect and sent out again, still urged to seek unanimity. Where this proves impossible, the question then arises as to what is an acceptable majority. Given that up to three individual jurors may be discharged during the course of the trial (for example for misconduct[121] or illness), the permissible majorities are:

With 12 jurors: 11-1 or 10-2

With 11 jurors: 10-1

With 10 jurors: 9-1

119 If the jury cannot agree on the more serious count, but find the defendant guilty of the less serious count, then the judge will have to decide whether to give them more time in respect of the former or not.

120 Juries Act 1974, s 17 and see CrimPD VI 26Q

121 As in the case where the juror contacted a defendant on Facebook! See bbc.co.uk/news/uk-13751454

Note that if there are less than 12 jurors, there can be only one dissenter. If the jury has been reduced to nine, then only a unanimous verdict is permissible. If and *only if* the verdict is guilty, the size of the majority must be stated in open court.

C. DISCHARGE OF JURY

If a verdict is not reached within what the judge considers a reasonable time, the jury will be discharged. This does not result in an acquittal and if the prosecution still believe that the evidence is there for a conviction and it remains in the public interest to prosecute, then there is very likely to be a re-trial.[122] The position gets to be a little more tenuous if a second jury also cannot reach a verdict. At that point the prosecution is more likely to (but will not inevitably) offer no evidence, from which of course an acquittal will follow.

D. SENTENCING AND COSTS

If the accused is found guilty, then the court will proceed to sentence, often after an adjournment for reports (if relevant, bail may need to be reconsidered depending on issues such as the gravity of the offence and likely sentence). Sentencing is discussed in the next chapter: costs are discussed (briefly) in Chapter 12. Bail was covered in Chapter 3.

122 As happened to Vicky Pryce, who was convicted second time around. bbc.co.uk/news/uk-21496566

revision tips

- Be aware of the various issues which can be raised so far as pleas and 'plea bargaining' are concerned.
- Know the latest case management requirements and initiatives.
- Understand how the division of labour between judge and jury impinges on Crown Court procedure. Know the majority verdict rules.
- Check your exam syllabus for areas of focus.

It is worth reading ...

Neill LJ's judgment in *R v Beckford* [1996] 1 Cr App R. It is easy to follow and restates some important principles.

The judgment in *R v Ullah (Mamun)* [2011] EWCA Crim 3275 is easy to follow. The defence had closed its case and then suddenly produced a witness. The trial judge was neither amused nor interested, but the Court of Appeal felt he had gone too far in not allowing the evidence to be heard. There is a reference to another noteworthy case and also an interesting discussion about a possible re-trial.

Have a look at the PTPH form, available online.

CHAPTER 10

Sentencing of adults

The end of a trial is not the end of the story, by any means. For some, it might be the beginning of a stretch in prison. Whether an offender has pleaded guilty, or been found guilty, the court's next job is to sentence him. This is a critical, and at times complex, Pt of the procedural equation. It is important to understand sentencing from various angles: the purpose, the process, the possibilities. You must have a clear grasp of the methodology - judges do not just pluck sentences out of thin air. This knowledge will be necessary, not only for your exams but for your practice. Defendants need to be advised from the outset what might be on the cards for them and at the sentencing stage you may need to deploy your most effective advocacy, as well as your common sense. Your client's future could depend on it.

Sentencing is a *vast* and complex topic - even the edited version of the sentencing guidelines runs to hundreds of pages.[1] Like any practitioner source, you must learn to navigate this (and other documents), but for the moment, concentrate on the essential principles and basic rules of sentencing. You have to walk before you can run!

1 In supplement to BCrP - Sentencing Guidelines (SG) - SG 1ff. Note that sentencing law and procedure is in the process of being rationalised and codified. Draft legislation is not expected before 2018, but pay attention when it happens!

1. PRE-SENTENCE PROCEDURE

Before the court can pass sentence, it needs quite a lot of information, both about the offence and the offender. Some of this will come from the prosecution, some from the defence, and some usually comes from an independent source in the form of reports of one kind or another. Without it, those passing sentence cannot do their jobs properly.

Whether the court embarks on the procedure described below immediately after conviction, or not, will depend on the circumstances and needs of the individual case.[2] An adjournment may well be necessary for any number of reasons: for example, to obtain reports[3] on the offender ('to adjourn for reports' is a common expression); to await the outcome of a co-accused's trial;[4] or even to see the result of the offender's trial on other related charges. If meantime the Crown Court wishes to keep all sentencing options open to it, it should have made this clear to the accused.[5]

In the magistrates' court, sentencing decisions are taken by the majority of the magistrates, unless a district judge is sitting alone. In the Crown Court the decision is taken by the judge alone;[6] in particular, he or she is not bound by any suggestion or view of the facts held, or expressed, by the jury. The pre-sentence process is otherwise very similar in both the Crown Court and the magistrates' court (if less elaborate and less formal in the latter) and, in outline, can be divided up as follows.

A. THE OFFENCE: FACTS AND IMPACT

(i) Role of prosecutor

If the conviction follows a trial, then the facts of the case should be pretty clear to all concerned. If the accused pleaded guilty, however, prosecuting counsel's first task will be to inform the court about what happened by summarising the facts

2 If there is an adjournment, the offender may be remanded in custody or on bail and may be required to assist as appropriate (for example, by making himself available for interview so a report can be compiled): BA 1976, s 3(6)(d). This could include remand to hospital for a report on his mental health, if a hospital order is being considered: Mental Health Act 1983, s 35–36.

3 If adjourned for reports, the presumption in favour of bail still applies. See generally Ch. 3

4 See BCrP D 12.77 about the general desirability of sentencing co-accused together, even where one pleaded guilty and then gave evidence against the remaining defendant(s).

5 The judge could still be held to an indication of sentence at this stage,

surrounding the commission of the offence. There are guidelines on how to do this.[7] Suffice to say that prosecutors, who are there to represent the public interest as well as to inform the court, should present a fair and balanced picture, including any known mitigating facts if the accused is unrepresented, as well as the aggravating features of the crime; the impact, if any, which it has had on the community or any individual victims; and any other matters pertinent to sentencing, such as any statutory requirements. If needed or requested, prosecutors may give assistance on sentencing parameters, but it is *not* their role to advocate for a particular, or particularly punitive, outcome.[8] Their job is to assist, not dispense justice.

(ii) Victim's impact statement

Care should be taken if a 'Victim's Personal Statement' (VPS) forms part of this picture being presented to the court (most often in the Crown Court). Such a statement must be set out in a proper form (as a witness statement, and available in advance to the defence like any other statement admissible under s 9 CJA 1967[9]) and when referring to it, prosecuting counsel should avoid emotionally charged language. It is particularly important to appreciate the *limits* of such statements. Their sole function is to make clear the effect of the crime on the victim (or close relatives if appropriate), not to proffer an (inadmissible) opinion on an appropriate sentence.[10] Judges must approach such statements with a degree of caution.

(iii) *Newton* hearing

And what happens if an accused pleads guilty, but his version of how (not whether) the offence occurred, is different than the prosecution's (usually his is less serious, to reduce the sentence)? If the divergence is not significant, and would not in any event affect the sentence, then both sides are often able to agree on a scenario they can each

---

if the offender tendered a timely guilty plea on the basis of such an indication.

6 Unless sitting with lay magistrates as an appeal court.

7 See, e.g., Attorney-General's Guidelines on Acceptance of Pleas in BCrP Appendix 2

8 One exception to this is a specialist ancillary order, such as compensation or confiscation, which it is prosecuting counsel's duty to apply for specifically. See BCrP D 20.3

9 See Ch. 8 and 9 on trial procedure.

10 See *R v Perkins, Bennett, Hall* [2013] EWCA Crim 323 and CrimPD V11, F 1-3, summarised at BCrP E 1.30

(truthfully[11]) accept. But where the difference is 'substantial' (and incapable of being glossed over), then the court must be told. Having heard submissions from both sides so it is clear where the discrepancy lies, a Crown Court would have three choices:

(a) accept the defence version 'as far as possible' (at least for the purposes of sentencing). This is likely when the factual differences are minimal and unlikely to much affect the judge's sentencing options and decision; *or*

(b) conduct a '*Newton* hearing'[12] to resolve the matter, which means the judge will hear whatever evidence the parties wish to call on the disputed issue, and then come down in favour of one version or the other; *or*

(c) let a jury decide (in effect, try both alternatives). This is appropriate where the two versions are effectively describing offences which could be separately charged. For example, if an accused denies using a firearm in the course of a robbery, then the indictment could be amended to include counts both for robbery and carrying a firearm with intent. At trial, if the jury acquit of the latter offence, but convict on the former, the defendant will be sentenced on the basis that he committed the robbery unarmed.[13]

The principles are essentially the same in the magistrates' court, although if they are feeling like passing the buck, the justices can commit the defendant to the Crown Court for sentence and leave it to the judge there to sort out.[14]

What the sentencer *must never do* is simply assume the prosecution version is correct without hearing further evidence, *unless* the defence version is manifestly absurd and incapable of belief (in which case a hearing would presumably serve no

11 The prosecution should not agree to accept a plea on the basis of false facts. Agreed facts should be set out in writing and signed by both counsel: *R v Underwood* [2005] 1 Cr App R (S) 478

12 So called after the leading case, *R v Newton* (1982) 77 Cr App R 13

13 Example given in *Underwood,* op.cit., per Judge LJ at para 10

14 See BCrP D 23.38

useful purpose). Even in such a case, however, the judge should make clear to the defendant that he finds his story incredible and give him an opportunity to convince the court that a *Newton* hearing is warranted.[15] Essentially, defendants ought (as always) to be given the benefit of any real doubt.

It is the defence who should alert the court and the prosecution (if they do not know already) that a guilty plea is to be put forward, but on contested facts. This allows the prosecution to line up its witnesses, so that a *Newton* hearing can go ahead if the court orders.

Such hearings must be conducted properly, so that strict rules of evidence apply and the burden of proof is on the prosecution to prove their version to the criminal standard. The court must direct itself properly on the law. The procedure is effectively the same in both the magistrates' court and the Crown Court (since no jury is involved), although if the defendant is to be committed to the Crown Court for sentence, then it makes sense that the *Newton* hearing should be conducted there.[16]

A defendant who gives no evidence (in person, or through other witnesses) as to his version of events runs the usual risk that the judge will infer that he does not have a (credible) story to tell. This is especially so when the defendant's version of events is peculiarly within his own knowledge and so is difficult to challenge evidentially (for example, *"I did not know it was cocaine, I thought it was cannabis"*).

Believe it or not, *Newton* hearings may also be necessary if the defendant pleaded not guilty. For example, having heard some or all of the prosecution case, the defendant may want to change his plea to guilty. If there remains a factual dispute which needs resolving for sentencing purposes, the court would normally hear the relevant defence evidence and treat the entire proceedings as a *Newton* hearing. And where one co-accused has pleaded guilty, and the other has been found guilty, it is usually best when sentencing the former to give him the chance of a

15 If the prosecution do not dispute the facts as such, but rather the accused's interpretation of them, it should still assist the court in making relevant findings for sentencing purposes: *R v Tolera* [1998] Crim LR 425

16 If the magistrates conduct a *Newton* hearing, find against the defendant, and then commit for sentence, the Crown Court may (but need not necessarily) hold a second hearing: *R v Gillan* [2007] EWCA 380

Newton hearing, if necessary, rather than relying on the evidence revealed at the trial of his co-accused which the accused was unable to challenge.[17]

Finally, given that defendants get a reduction in sentence for pleading guilty, how does a *Newton* hearing affect this calculation? The whole point of the guilty plea is to save the time and expense of a trial. A guilty plea requiring a *Newton* hearing gives us a bit of both worlds. As you might expect, where the offender's version of events is accepted following such a hearing, it will have no effect on the reduction; but where the prosecution version is accepted, this means the offender will receive rather less credit for the guilty plea than he otherwise would.[18] Finally, if sentence is appealed against, and the Court of Appeal decides that a *Newton* hearing ought to have taken place, it will pass sentence on the defendant's version of events.[19]

B. THE OFFENDER: ANTECEDENTS AND CHARACTER

Once the facts of the offence are clear, the next step is to give the court information about the 'antecedents' and 'character' of the offender. In the magistrates' courts this information will be prepared by the police and contained in the CPS file. In the Crown Court, it should be made available to prosecutors once the case is sent for trial. The detail should be checked carefully to ensure it is accurate and up-to-date.

'Antecedents' typically refer to details of the offender's age, education, employment, domestic circumstances, income and so on. 'Character' is principally concerned with his criminal record (if any), which can have a drastic effect on sentence. The court will usually focus on the last three convictions which are similar or otherwise relevant to penalty.[20] Spent convictions should be marked as such, but not referred to unless absolutely necessary (for example, by the judge to explain his sentence).[21]

17 *R v Dudley* [2012] Crim R 230

18 See Sentencing Guidelines, Pt 1, para 4.3(iv)(SG-4)

19 See generally summary of guidance in *R v Underwood*, op. cit., at BCrP D 20.9

20 See BCrP D 20.45-20.47 and CrimPD II 8A.6

21 When convictions are officially spent, the offender's slate is wiped clean for most purposes - unless the person keeps offending. In criminal proceedings spent convictions may be referred to, but only with permission of the judge. See generally BCrP D 20.49

If the defence wish to challenge the prosecution information, it would be usual for the latter to call the police officer in the case. The burden of proof remains on the prosecution to prove contested detail. Insofar as previous convictions are concerned, this is easily done in most cases by producing the certificate of conviction and proof that the person being sentenced is the person who was previously convicted.

C. REPORTS

After the prosecution has presented its information about the offence and the offender, the judge reads any pre-sentence reports (PSR). These are reports prepared to assist the court in determining the most appropriate method of dealing with the offender.[22] If he is an adult, the report is usually prepared by a probation officer; a younger offender may have a report about him compiled by a social worker, probation officer or member of the Youth Offending Team.

The point of the report is to give *independent professional perspective* on the offence and the offender, including his attitude to what happened, any explanation as to how he has got to this point in his criminality, the likelihood of his reoffending and so forth. In particular the report should consider what form of sentence might best assist in his rehabilitation and make relevant sentencing proposals. The reporter will take information from many sources - the offender himself, his family, his employer (with permission) and so on. If the offence in question was committed shortly after his release from prison, the reporter may also consult the prison authorities to see what insight they can provide, given that the effect of the previous custodial sentence on the offender was not apparently a very positive one! If necessary, medical and psychiatric reports may be sought.

It may be possible at times (if the accused is an adult) for such information to be given orally as a sort of 'fast delivery' report. Usually, however, the report

22 CJA 2003, s 158

is produced in writing and a copy given to the defence advocate, who will be very keen to see what it says (and hopeful that it may be useful in framing submissions regarding sentence). If the defence wish to challenge any aspect of the report, then its maker may need to be called for questioning.

It is important to note, for practical as well as examination purposes, that when a court is considering either a custodial sentence, or community order (both of which restrict the offender's liberty to greater or lesser degree), then the court *must* obtain and consider a pre-sentence report, *unless* (in the case of an adult) this is considered 'unnecessary' (perhaps because the appropriate sentence is clear and will be unaffected by a, or a new, report).[23]

D. MITIGATION

This is where the skills of the defence advocate really come into the equation. Once all the other information and evidence discussed above is before the court, defence counsel will present mitigation on behalf of the offender. Defence counsel might call a character witnesses, but this is comparatively rare. It is rarer still to call the defendant himself.

The purpose of the 'plea in mitigation' is to put the offending into context, ensure that all relevant matters are before the court, especially those which might go to lessen the gravity of the crime and so reduce the severity of any sentence - and to persuade the court, wherever possible, to keep the defendant out of prison. It is a vital piece of advocacy, which requires powers of persuasion as well as common sense. It is no good pretending your client is an angel, if he is not; but prison should always be considered a sentence of last resort, and there may well be scope to convince the court to make some other order. Pleas in mitigation tend to divide into two (sometimes overlapping) aspects:

23 *Ibid*, s 156. And see e.g. *R v Jamous* [2015] EWCA Crim 1720, cited at BCrP E 1.27. If the offender is under 18, a report must be obtained unless there is an existing report which the court has considered. See Ch. 11

(i) mitigation relating to the commission of the *offence* (for example, a spontaneous act, crime motivated by desperation not greed, defendant led astray by others) *and*

(ii) mitigation relevant to the *offender* (for example, the defendant has no previous convictions, he assisted the police, he showed remorse, he attempted to compensate victim).

If the defendant pleaded guilty (depending on when the guilty plea was entered), this should earn the offender a 'discount' - either in the form of a reduction in the time served in custody (or doing unpaid work), the amount payable by fine, or in the form of a more lenient type of sentence altogether. There is a sliding scale of discount, ranging from a one-third (earliest opportunity) to one-tenth discount (last minute plea).[24]

E. SENTENCE

Last, but certainly not least - the court pronounces sentence. It will do so in open court, with reasons, and the offender will have its effects (and the implications, where relevant, of any non-compliance) explained to him.[25] A Crown Court judge (or district judge) will normally do this immediately after mitigation (they have probably been mulling it over for a while); lay justices in the magistrates' court may need to retire, and if necessary consult their clerk/legal advisor as to their sentencing powers.

What follows is an outline of the process which the court goes through in determining sentence. It will set out the powers of the various courts, including the kinds of issues that can arise which examiners like you to know.

24 See below.
25 CJA 2003, s 174

2. SENTENCING PRINCIPLES AND PROCESS

The act of sentencing is a highly regulated exercise in common sense and doing one's best in difficult circumstances. The court has an offence and an offender in front of it, and a sentencing framework at its disposal, and all of these aspects need to go into the mix to produce fair and consistent outcomes.

A. PURPOSES OF SENTENCING

The purposes of sentencing (where the judge has a choice) are many and varied. Insofar as the sentencing of adults is concerned, the objectives are (in no particular order of importance): punishment, reduction in crime (including by deterrence), reform and rehabilitation, protection of the public and the making of reparation. This applies also to corporate offenders.[26] Where juveniles are concerned,[27] their welfare and the public interest in their not becoming adult offenders is added to the list.

Often these objectives conflict: the best way to protect the public may be by incarcerating the offender, but this may be the least effective way to rehabilitate him. Be that as it may, these functions must be at the back of the sentencing judge's mind at all times.

B. HIERARCHY OF SENTENCE

The mainstream[28] judicial toolkit for sentencing ranges from the non-punitive at one end (absolute and conditional discharge) all the way to immediate incarceration at the other. In between (from better to worse) are fines, community orders and suspended sentences. You might think of these options as rungs on a ladder, with the more forgiving at the bottom, and the most punitive at the top, some of which can be combined. In certain cases, the sentencing outcome will be determined by

26 *Ibid* s 142(1) and *R v Sellafield* [2014] EWCA Crim 49

27 *Ibid* s 142A(2), and see Ch. 11

28 Ancillary and specialist sentences are discussed below.

the offence itself (for example, mandatory life sentence for murder), or by the status of the offender (for example if he is a juvenile, where special rules and vocabulary apply[29]). Generally speaking, however, where on this ladder the court's attention will be focused will be dictated by the seriousness of the offence and the culpability of the offender. It's no good asking the court to fine a violent armed robber.

C. THRESHOLDS

Two rungs on this ladder are especially important. They are the community sentence and the custodial sentence rungs - or 'thresholds' as they are called. In order to pass either sort of sentence, which to a greater or lesser degree involves imposition on the liberty of the offender, the relevant threshold must be crossed. Thus before passing either sentence, the court must always consider whether the offender has 'crossed' the community sentence threshold[30] or, as the case may be, the custodial threshold.[31] Obviously one will cross the community sentence threshold before (and perhaps on the way to crossing) the custodial sentence threshold, although one can of course get to the custodial threshold in one leap. In any event, the notion of crossing the relevant threshold is a convenient way of describing a situation which, all things considered, is so serious that some lesser sentence *cannot* in the circumstances be justified.

Thus, seriousness is (unsurprisingly) a key component in sentencing. It determines whether relevant thresholds have been crossed, the nature and length of any sentence, the extent of any community sentence requirement, the level of any fine. In short, any sentence must be 'commensurate' with the *seriousness* of the offence. It is a fairly broad concept, determined by two main 'parameters: the *culpability* of the offender and the *harm* caused (or risk of harm caused) by the offence.[32] In simple terms, the nastier the consequences intended and/or achieved by the perpetrator,

29 See Ch. 11

30 'A court must not pass a community sentence on an offender unless it is of the opinion that the offence, or the combination of the offence and one or more offences associated with it, was so serious as to warrant such a sentence': CJA 2003, s 148(1)

31 'The court must not pass a custodial sentence unless it is of the opinion that the offence, or the combination of the offence and one or more offences associated with it, was so serious that neither a fine alone nor a community sentence can be justified': CJA 2003, s 152(2). And see BCrP E 2.7/8

32 Sentencing Guidelines, Pt 3, para A1.4(SG-22)

the worse his crime. Any number of factors can add to or detract from seriousness; these are known as *mitigating* and *aggravating circumstances.* Some may relate to the offence itself (but not, generally, its prevalence); others, to the offender. The sorts of things which might mitigate an offence are: provocation, minor role in crime, co-operating with police, remorse. Aggravating features include operating in gangs, racist motives, repeat offending and abusing a position of trust. The list is almost endless,[33] but you will be able to recognise such features when you see them. They can be critical to sentence - such factors can put an offender across, or pull him back from, a relevant threshold.[34]

Thus, in sentencing an offender, the court needs to choose from sentencing options available to it, bearing in mind: (i) the seriousness of the crime itself, including the circumstances of its commission and the number of victims, (ii) the achievable purpose of sentencing in the case at hand and (iii) any other legitimate reasons for dealing with the offender more leniently or more harshly than might otherwise be the case. In a sense, any sentencer must ask: what *can* I do, and what *should* I do in this situation?

If each individual judge used his or her own personal system to answer these questions, there would be a real risk of uncertainty and inconsistency in sentencing. To assist judges, therefore, official guidance comes in the form of Sentencing Guidelines issued by the Sentencing Council, which bring together the concepts we have been discussing in a methodical format. You should have a look at these[35] - not to learn them all (they are for reference, not memorising!) but to see how they are laid out and the information they include. You must certainly know what they are and how to use them. There is a section of the guidelines adapted for sentencing in the magistrates' court.[36]

It might assist to set out what happens as a step-by-step guide.

33 Some are statutory: others are not. See, e.g., *ibid*, para 1.20ff and SG-22-SG-27

34 CJA 2003, s 166(2)

35 Available on-line (sentencing-guidelines.gov.uk/docs) and in BCrP supplement (margin reference in brackets). Note that in future this may one day be replaced with a newly codified regime.

36 Sentencing Guidelines, Part 12

(i) The court first determines appropriate range and 'starting' point

This is what the sentencing guidelines are for. These subdivide offences into categories by reference to broad levels of seriousness, and set out various factors to assist in determining into which category a particular case would fall. Within those categories, they provide a sentencing range by reference to levels of culpability and harm and identify a 'starting' point within each sentencing range, based on a first time offender, convicted following a not guilty plea.

For example, the robbery section[37] is broken down into five broad variations of the offence (two of which relate to young offenders). Let's assume a 'dwelling robbery' committed by an adult. Three levels of both culpability and harm in the commission of the offence are determined by reference only to factors listed there (giving nine possible outcomes). Thus, use of a weapon and serious harm caused to a victim would place the offence in the most serious 1A sentencing range (10-16 years custody range; starting point of 13 years), whereas lesser culpability and little or no harm would put it into the least serious 3C range (custody range of one - three years; starting point of 18 months).

Or, to take a less serious example, look at failure to surrender to bail in the magistrates court,[38] which sub-divides into 'deliberate failure' (sentencing range: community order (low) to ten weeks custody, with a starting point of 14 days), 'negligent' failure/failure causing delay (sentencing range of fine to community order (medium), with a starting point of a fine) and 'surrenders late but case proceeds as planned' (sentencing range and starting point are both a fine).

(ii) Consideration of aggravating or mitigating factors

Next, the court will consider factors which aggravate or mitigate sentence in the particular case. These may relate to the offence or the offender. Aside from the

37 See Pt 5 (SG-34), updated in April 2016.

38 See Pt 9 (SG-217) Guidelines are given for the Crown Court as well.

generic possibilities,[39] each offence listed in the guidelines will normally set out a list of features which typically occur in the commission of that sort of crime. The sentencer should decide whether any combination of relevant factors should result in an upward or downward adjustment from the starting point. So, going back to our robbery example, wearing a disguise or targeting a vulnerable victim will incline the judge to adjust upward to a harsher sentence; voluntarily returning the property to the victim, downward to greater lenience.

(iii) The consideration of additional factors

In completing steps (i) and (ii), and having formed a preliminary view on sentence, the court may also need to consider some additional, more extraneous factors, and in any event bear in mind certain overarching principles.

(a) Offences taken into consideration / sample offences

The rule, logically enough, is that a court can only sentence in respect of those offences of which the accused has, on the occasion in question, been convicted (either by pleading or being found guilty). Having said that, when being sentenced for such offences, the offender sometimes asks that other offences (usually linked in some way) be 'taken into consideration'. These are known colloquially as 'TICs'.

TICs are offences which the offender admits and asks the court to take into account in sentencing, but in respect of which he is not formally convicted (nor sentenced, as such). Sounds strange, but the point is that the offender no longer has such offences 'hanging over his head', because once taken into consideration in this way, he would never (by convention) be prosecuted for them. The advantage for law enforcement, of course, is that it increases police crime clear-up rates, because TIC offences are considered as 'solved', and a costly investigation and trial is avoided.

39 See lists in Pt 3 D of the Sentencing Guidelines (SG-25) and BCrP E 1.14-1.20

Typically, what happens is that a person is arrested, charged and admits to one or more of a certain kind of offence. The police believe that he may be responsible for other (similar) offences, and invite his response to their suspicions about these other crimes. If he is amenable to having these other offences 'TIC'd', a 'schedule' is drawn up for the suspect to sign. The offences he is formally charged with are prosecuted in the normal way and he pleads guilty. When the relevant time comes, and before sentence is passed, prosecuting counsel inform the court that the accused wants 'other matters to be considered'. The offender himself will have to confirm that he does admit the offences on the TIC list and wants them treated in this way.

If the court agrees to take the offences into consideration, then these are generally treated as an aggravating feature, since they reveal other offending.[40] But this is offset, at least in part, by the benefit of assisting the police to solve crime, saving court time and money and demonstrating a desire to 'wipe the slate clean'. In some cases, the overall effect may be quite neutral, but every case is different and should be considered on its own merits.[41]

(b) Additional personal factors

If the offender's previous convictions have not been taken into account yet, then this is the time to do so. Such are a typical (and all too common) aggravating feature, but should not lead to disproportionate severity in sentence. They may also indicate that a type of sentence attempted in the past (for example, a community sentence) is not achieving its purpose, and so cause the court to impose a different sort of punishment.

If it has not been already, other personal mitigation (such as good character or ill health) may also need to be considered at this point. Credit will be given for time already spent in custody on remand, or on bail with qualifying electronically

40 If there are enough of them it could justify going up to a more serious sentencing range. The same effect is sometimes achieved with sample offences. See BCrP D 20.53

41 See *R v Miles* [2006] EWCA Crim 256 and generally SG-578ff

monitored curfew, if appropriate.[42] In any event, care must always be taken not to 'double-count' aggravating or mitigating factors, so that the overall result is fair.

(c) Deferral of sentence

Sometimes, the judge will be told in mitigation that since committing the crime in question, the offender has turned a corner in his life (for example, by getting a new job or marrying his very reliable girlfriend), and in order to give him time to show that he is as good as his (or his counsel's) word, the court may be persuaded to defer sentence. The court can defer sentencing for up to six months, at which time it should have regard both to the offender's conduct during this period and any relevant change of circumstances (perhaps his girlfriend turns out not to be so reliable), when eventually passing sentence. The offender must consent to the deferral and understand the basis for it (and it should not happen more than once per case). In general the courts should not defer sentence when the desired improvement in behaviour can be catered for in sentencing the offender (by attaching a relevant requirement to a community sentence, for instance). When sentence is deferred, the offender is not bailed, but simply told when to return for sentence to be passed.[43]

(d) Totality principle

One way fairness is achieved is by keeping a firm eye on the so-called 'totality' principle. This is particular important where a court is dealing with an accused convicted of several offences. It is a common sense notion, which ensures that an overall sentencing result is a just and proportionate reflection of the totality of offending - nothing more and nothing less.

The totality principle means that, when sentencing for more than one offence, a court should pass an overall sentence which 'reflects all the offending behaviour

42 For example, where a custodial sentence is passed. The time already spent in custody/ under severe curfew ('time served') should be in connection with the same (or related) offence. Unless the time served is the justification for a much shorter sentence, then the credit will generally happen administratively and does not require a judicial direction, although one will normally be given: *R v Bhayani* [2015] EWCA Crim 352 [56]. Credit for the onerous bail condition is calculated at roughly half the rate of time served on remand. For detail see BCrP E 2.12-2.16, and the Crown Court Compendium Pt 2 S4-9

43 See generally Sentencing Guidelines, Pt 2, Section 1 (SG-12)

44 See Sentencing Guidelines, Pt 23 (SG-585)

before it and is just and proportionate'.[44] This can be achieved by various mechanisms, including individual sentences to run concurrently and keeping an eye on aggregate fines. It is usually impossible to achieve fairness by sentencing for individual offences and then simply adding these all up for a grand total. It is necessary to address both the offender and the offending more holistically.

(iv) Apply appropriate reduction for early indication of guilty plea

This aspect is left until the very last, because it results in a reduction in the (punitive elements of the) total sentence. The process has become very formalised over the years, and so is fairly predictable. There is even a very handy sliding scale represented in the Guidelines,[45] ranging from a third reduction for a plea at the 'first reasonable opportunity'[46] to a tenth reduction for a plea at the door of the trial court (or during trial). A reduction could change a custodial to a community sentence. The virtues of an early guilty plea are obvious - it avoids the time and expense of a trial, saves victims and witnesses the ordeal of giving evidence, and it generally assists in the administration of justice if guilty people plead guilty.[47] The later the plea, the less time, expense and aggravation is saved, and so the lower the reduction. If the offender was caught 'red handed', however, and the prosecution case is so overwhelming that it could be said the accused really did no-one but himself any favours, then a guilty plea (however early) will likely attract no more than a 20% reduction.[48]

(v) Court decides final sentence and gives reasons

The decision on sentence should be stated and explained in open court – in ordinary language so its implications can be understood. This is required, for example, if the sentence has been increased due to racial or similar aggravation, and is especially important if the sentence has come outside an existing guideline.[49]

45 Sentencing Guidelines, Pt 1, D SG-4

46 For most offenders appearing in the Crown Court, the 'first reasonable opportunity' will be at the magistrates' court or immediately on arrival at the Crown Court, but this is a matter for the sentencing judge and will always depend on the circumstances in each individual case: *R v Caley* [2013] 2 Cr App R (S) 305. And see Annex 1 to SG 4 (at SG-8) and BCrP E 1.8/9

47 This is the principal motivation for reducing sentence. See Sentencing Guidelines, Pt 1B SG-2

48 See SG-5. I heard of a case of theft of a mobile phone equipped with an 'app' which took a photo of the thief as he tried to use it - and sent the photo to the owner's email address. The owner took the photo to

Much of this is common sense, but the importance of the Sentencing Guidelines is that they offer a means of ensuring consistency and fairness in sentencing across the board, while at the same time allowing individual circumstance (in the form of aggravating and mitigating features, both in terms of the offence and the offender in question) to be factored into the equation. There is a duty on the courts to follow relevant Sentencing Guidelines unless satisfied that it would be contrary to the interests of justice to do so.[50]

Court of Appeal decisions also provide a source of guidance about how judges arrive (or should arrive) at their sentencing decisions, especially where the Sentencing Guidelines are silent on an aspect of sentencing. The Court of Appeal will be loath to interfere with the sentencing judge's broad discretion, but is there to do so if the legislative framework or Sentencing Guidelines have not been correctly applied. But you must be careful to regard most sentencing appeals as very 'case specific', and not as setting precedent.

3. HIERARCHY OF SENTENCING OPTIONS

Armed with the background information set out above, what follows is a basic outline of various sentencing possibilities,[51] starting with the least punitive.

A. ABSOLUTE/CONDITIONAL DISCHARGE[52]

An *absolute* discharge is really no punishment. Its imposition may reflect the triviality of the offence or special factors associated with its commission. It is, in effect, the sentence for the blameless offender, as in *R v O'Toole*,[53] where an ambulance driver collided with another vehicle while responding to an emergency call.

the police, the defendant was arrested, charged, pleaded guilty but was given *no* discount. Welcome to the digital age! Going this far was disapproved in *R v Caley* op.cit.

49 See CJA 2003, s 174 and BCrP E 1.23

50 Coroners & Justice Act 2009, s 125

51 Some sentences are beyond the scope of this book (for example, deportation, hospital orders and civil orders, e.g., ASBO). For detail on these, consult BCrP

52 Powers of Criminal Courts (Sentencing) Act 2000 (PCC(S)A 2000), s 12-15

53 (1971) 55 Cr App R 206

A *conditional* discharge has one string attached. The court may discharge an offender on condition that, during a specified period of time, he commits no offence. The specified period runs from the date of the order, but must not exceed three years. If during that time he commits an offence, he may be sentenced both for the original offence and the new offence - or the court could let the conditional discharge stand, and simply sentence for the later offence. The implications of breach need to be explained to an offender who is made the subject of a conditional discharge.

When a court re-sentences an offender for the original offence, it may impose any sentence which could have been passed first time around. If a Crown Court judge proposes to re-sentence an offender in respect of a conditional discharge imposed by the magistrates' court, then the former is limited (in that task) to the sentencing powers of the magistrates. If it happens the other way around, then the magistrates would have to commit the offender to the Crown Court to be dealt with. This is because Crown Court judges can act as magistrates as necessary, but not vice versa. If one magistrates' court granted the conditional discharge, another can re-sentence in respect of it with the former's consent.[54]

Any court may discharge an offender, absolutely or conditionally, whatever his age and whatever his offence (provided, of course, the sentence is not fixed by law). A discharge cannot generally be combined with a more punitive measure when sentencing in respect of the *same* offence, but it is not uncommon when sentencing in respect of two or more offences, to discharge in respect of one (the least serious, naturally) and deal more punitively with the other(s). Discharge can often be combined with an ancillary order, including confiscation orders.[55]

B. FINES

This is the most common form of sentence used in the magistrates' court, whether the

54 See generally BCrP E 12
55 See below and *R v Varma* [2012] 3 WLR 776 in BCrP E 12.1-4

offence is summary or triable either-way. Maximum fines imposable for summary offences are fixed (usually by the statute creating the offence) by reference to a standard scale whose maximum is £5,000. Since March 2015, *either-way* offences dealt with summarily can be punishable by a fine of *any* amount,[56] although of course sentencing guidelines should be followed and the totality principle applied. The same is true of the Crown Court, which has never had a statutory maximum, although some sentences there (e.g. hospital order) cannot be combined with a fine.

(i) Fixing the fine

Fixing an appropriate fine is similar to any sentencing process. First the court begins by deciding what fine is appropriate in view of the seriousness of the offence, to include any relevant aggravating or mitigating circumstances. Next, it considers whether that figure should be reduced due to any additional personal mitigation, including an early guilty plea. Finally, it takes account of the offender's financial circumstances.[57]

The Magistrates' Courts Sentencing Guidelines gives relevant guidance in respect of some commonly prosecuted offences, which work just like the examples described earlier. Note that indicative fines there are based on the offender's weekly disposable income, and described by bands; for example, A (half weekly income), B (weekly income) and C (one and a half times weekly income). The process is virtually the same when setting fines in the Crown Court.

(ii) Enforcement of fines

A court imposing a fine usually should, or will, give the offender time to pay if necessary (although they could see if he has any money on him to put towards it![58]). If a court gives an offender time to pay a fine, it will either set the time by which the

56 With no maximum aggregrate. The £5,000 ceiling for either-way offences was removed by s 85 Legal Aid, Sentencing, and Punishment of Offenders Act 2012 (LASPO Act 2012). See BCrP E 15.8

57 The court can make a 'financial circumstances order' requiring the offender to provide a statement of means. See generally CJA 2003, s 162 and SG-352/BCrP E 15.14ff

58 PCC(S)A 2000, s 80(1)

whole amount should be paid, or order payment by fixed installments. In the Crown Court, where the fines tend to be bigger, a longer period of time for payment is often allowed (for example, two to three years) than is given in the magistrates' courts (usually about 12 months[59]).

(iii) Consequences of default

When imposing a fine, the Crown Court *must* fix a term of imprisonment to be served in default of payment (the smaller the fine, the shorter the term in default). This can only happen in the magistrates' courts if the offence was punishable with imprisonment and it seems appropriate to do this (for example because it appears the offender has the means to pay immediately).

Either way, a failure to pay a fine ordered to be paid by the court is effectively a contempt of court, and so can ultimately be punished by a term of imprisonment. But this should be viewed as an absolute last resort. Enforcement of fines is essentially the job of magistrates' courts, who will investigate the reason for non-payment (wilful refusal or lack of funds?) and alternative ways of getting the money (for example, by making an attachment of earnings order so a little money is regularly deducted from the offender's wages).[60] A fine should not really turn into a custodial sentence!

However, fines can be, and often are, combined with other orders - even a custodial sentence, although this combination might make paying the fine difficult (if it is to be paid from income rather than the offender's savings). It is more common to combine a fine with a community order, discussed below.

(iv) Surcharge

The victim surcharge was first introduced in 2007. Since April 2016, when a court passes sentence (other than an absolute discharge or a mental health order) it must

59 Magistrates' sentencing guidelines indicate that fines which cannot be paid within 12 months should not normally be imposed. Defendants should always be asked for immediate payment, but in exceptional circumstances an offender might be given 3 years to pay a fine. See SG-367, paras 43 and 44 and BCrP E 15.21

60 For more detail see brief discussion in *Practical Approach*, 25.31-25.37

also order that the relevant surcharge is paid. The amounts depend (in part) on the severity of the sentence. The idea is that the money should go to help victim support groups, courtesy (however unwillingly) of perpetrators.

C. COMMUNITY SENTENCES

The community sentence is a non-custodial order, but imposes some restrictions on the offender's freedom in the form of one or more obligations imposed by the sentencing court. It is important to remember that the community order is a *single generic sentence*, which is then adapted as appropriate for the particular offender by choosing requirements from something resembling a 'drop down menu' of possibilities.[61] The list is a long one, but typical (and in some cases stereotypical) requirements are:

(a) An unpaid work requirement, of between 40 and 300 hours, to be completed within 12 months;

(b) A programme requirement, which states that the offender must take part in an accredited programme (for example, an anger management course), at a particular place for a set period of time;

(c) A prohibited activity requirement, which prohibits the offender from taking part in certain activities (for example, attending football matches) for a specified period;

(d) A residence requirement, which dictates where the offender will live for a stated period;

(e) A curfew requirement, which requires the offender to stay in a particular place for certain periods of the day (between 2 and 16 hours). This is commonly linked to a residence requirement and/or electronic monitoring requirement, and must not last for more than six months.

61 CJA 2003, s 177, for adult offenders. Juveniles are considered in Ch. 11

And so on.[62] There are certain requirements which require the consent of the offender, for example the mental health, alcohol treatment, and drug rehabilitation requirements.[63] This is only logical, for if the offender is not willing or able to participate in such programmes, there is little point in sending him on one.

Electronic monitoring is not (at the time of writing) a free-standing requirement, and so can *only* be used to ensure *compliance* with certain other community sentence requirements. It is generally necessary when curfew and exclusion requirements are concerned.[64]

(i) Threshold requirement

Community sentences (not exceeding three years) are only available for imprisonable offences. Remember that to be ordered, the relevant threshold *must* be passed.[65] Other options should have been considered (possibly tried and failed) and the offending be so serious as to justify the sentence. The court will often be guided by the pre-sentence report, which is mandatory whenever the court is considering a community order, unless the court (in the case of an adult offender) considers it unnecessary. Requirements should be compatible with one another.

(ii) Purpose of community orders

In choosing community sentence requirements, the court should be guided by principles of *suitability* and *proportionality*, restricting an offender's liberty only to a degree 'commensurate' with the seriousness of his offending. If the offender is not also fined, *at least one* of the community sentence requirements should be punitive in nature (unless there are exceptional circumstances). The impact on others of a particular requirement should also be considered.

---

62 For complete list see BCrP E 8.9ff. The most recent additions are the rehabilitation activity requirement, foreign travel prohibition order requirement and the alcohol abstinence and monitoring requirement.

63 CJA 2003, s 153(2)

64 This could change. See BCrP E 8.29

65 See s 1501 CJA 2003. Powers to give the court discretion to impose a community order (instead of a fine) whenever dealing with a 'persistent' offender who has been fined on at least 3 previous occasions, have not yet been brought into force. See BCrP E 8.6

(iii) Failure to comply

If an (adult) offender fails, without reasonable excuse, to comply with his community sentence requirements, then he is entitled to *one* warning about the implications of another such failure. Thereafter, failing to comply should result in his being brought back to court which (once breach is admitted or proved) *must* deal with him in one of a number of specified ways. One option is to amend the order so as to impose more onerous requirements. Another is to revoke the order altogether and re-sentence, always ensuring that the offender is dealt with in any way in which (but no more harshly than) the court which originally sentenced him could have done. Aditionally, the court now also has the option of fining an offender (up to a maximum of £2,500).[66]

Whenever a court is dealing with an offender for such a failure, it must take into account the extent to which he has already complied with the requirements of the community order. This is only common sense. If, for example, an offender completed several hours of unpaid work, any new sentence should give credit for this.

(iv) Revocation

On application by the offender, a community sentence may be revoked if, because of a change of circumstances, it is in the interests of justice to do so.

Equally, the court may revoke a community order where an offender who is the subject of a community sentence commits a further offence. If the community sentence was made by magistrates, then either they (or the Crown Court acting as magistrates if the offender finds himself there) may revoke the original order and (if appropriate) deal with the offender for the original offence in any way which was available at the time the community sentence was ordered. If the Crown Court

66 This last was added by LASPO Act 2012, s 67. Option 9(1)(c) in Schedule 8 (referred to in BCrP E 8.32) cannot logically apply unless and until s 151 CJA 2003 comes into force.

made the original order, then if the subsequent offence is in front of magistrates they may send the offender to the Crown Court for them to deal with revocation. In either case, the court should take account of the extent to which the offender complied with the requirements of the community sentence.[67]

D. CUSTODY

Before a custodial sentence is passed, certain sensible requirements must first be met. For example, a first sentence of imprisonment may not be passed on an offender who is not legally represented, without first giving him a chance to be so represented.[68] Secondly, as discussed above, pre-sentence reports must normally be obtained and considered by the court before imposing a term of imprisonment. Reasons for and the effect of such a sentence must be given in open court and, of course, the custody threshold must have been crossed.

Remember, however, that the fact that the custody threshold has been crossed, does not mean that custody should inevitably follow. A term of imprisonment should be viewed as a sentence of *last resort*, and be as *short as the seriousness of the crime allows*. If, for example, the point is to introduce someone who has never been in custody to the 'clang of the prison gate', the exposure should be comparatively short. Prison is not well known for turning people away from crime.

Cases on the borderline (in other words, those hovering between community sentence and imprisonment) should be considered especially carefully, although if consent is required for a community sentence and the offender is unwilling to give it, a custodial sentence may be the only alternative.

(i) Custody for those aged 18 to 20

Note that in England and Wales, defendants aged between 18 and 20 are

67 See CJA 2003, s 151 and BCrP E 8.34
68 PCC(S)A 2000, s 83(1)

considered to be adults,[69] but they are only just adults, and if a custodial sentence is appropriate for such a person, the applicable sentence is not imprisonment, as such, but 'detention in a young offenders institution'.[70] The minimum term is 21 days, but the maximum could never exceed that which could be imposed were the offender 21 years or older. This is another attempt to keep younger offenders away from more hardened adult criminals, but such institutions themselves are not particularly conducive to 'going straight'. The ten year old killers of toddler Jamie Bulger[71] were both famously released on licence at the age of 18 just so they would not end up in such a place.

(ii) Concurrent and consecutive custodial sentences

Where an offender is given custodial sentences in respect of more than one offence these may be made to run *concurrently* (that is, all served simultaneously) or *consecutively* (one after the other).[72] The judge should expressly state which is to be the case,[73] failing which it will be presumed that the sentences are to be concurrent. The ability to run custodial sentences either consecutively or concurrently gives the court flexibility, although the power must be used sensibly. Concurrent sentences tend to be appropriate, for example, where the offences were all committed in one escapade or as a related series of criminal events; unrelated offences (or offences committed at different times) would be more amenable to sentences running consecutively. Furthermore, one has to be careful with consecutive sentences, to keep on the right side of the totality principle, so that the total sentence (when you add them all together) is commensurate with the seriousness of the overall conduct of the offending.[74] It is sometimes easiest for the sentencer to work backwards, having first decided on a proper overall aggregate. Remember too that the court can mix and match concurrent and consecutive sentences.

---

69 And so cannot be tried in the youth court - see Ch. 11

70 PCC(S)A, s 96

71 See further, Ch.11

72 This is also possible if the court is sentencing someone already serving a prison term to another custodial sentence. See generally BCrP E 2.19ff

73 CrimPD, VII E 1

74 CJA 2003, s 116(3)(b) and see above.

A good illustration of such sentencing is found in the case of *R v Hussain*.[75] In that case the defendant had tried to smuggle Indian hemp through customs at Heathrow. He was sentenced to three years for possessing a dangerous drug and two years to run consecutively for unloading prohibited goods from an aircraft. The Court of Appeal held that since both offences resulted from the very same act (leaving the plane in possession of the hemp), it was wrong in principle to impose consecutive sentences. The joy of the successful appeal was short-lived for Mr Hussain, however, because the sentence was varied to one of five years' imprisonment for each offence, to run concurrently.

(iii) Suspended sentences

Suspended sentences are custodial sentences, without the pain of prison. If a custodial sentence is suspended, it will be suspended for a certain period of time, during which the offender may be ordered to comply with one or more of the same sorts of requirements included in a community sentence. The period of suspension is known as the 'operational period' and any time to be spent complying with the community sentence requirements is known as the 'supervision period'. Both must last between six months and two years. They need not be, but often are co-extensive, but in any event the supervision period may not outlast the operational period.[76]

In effect, a suspended sentence is something of a half-way house between a sentence of immediate imprisonment and a community sentence. Generally speaking, the longer the sentence which is suspended, the longer will be the operational period, but requirements during the supervision period will tend to be less onerous than had a community sentence itself been imposed.[77]

Only relatively short prison sentences are amendable to suspension, that is,

75 [1962] CrimLR 712
76 CJA 2003, s 189(3),(4)
77 See Sentencing Guidelines, Section 2 (Pt 2) para 2.2.14 (SG-17) and BCrP E 6.1ff

those which do not exceed two years in the Crown Court, or the relevant maximum in the magistrates' court.[78] This means that the custodial sentence does not take effect *unless either* during the supervision period, the offender fails to comply with the requirements named in the order, *or* during the operational period the offender commits another offence (whether or not punishable with prison).[79]

Warnings may be given in respect of the community requirements, but if the court is satisfied that the offender has either failed, without reasonable excuse, to comply with any of the supervision period requirements or has been convicted of an offence during the operational period, then it has the following choices. It can

(a) activate the suspended sentence (in other words, order that the offender serve the original sentence which was suspended), *or*
(b) activate the suspended sentence, but shorten the period of custody (perhaps to reflect the amount of time the person did do as required), *or*
(c) amend the order, for example by extending either the operational or supervision periods or imposing more onerous community orders, *or*
(d) impose a fine not exceeding £2,500.[80]

There is a presumption that a court would do the first of these, unless in all the circumstances it seems unjust. Obviously, in making this decision, the court would take account of how long and how well the offender complied with the requirements of the suspended sentence, and also the circumstances of any new offence. For example, if the new offence occurred very late in the operational period, it may be more appropriate to amend the order than activate the suspended sentence.[81]

78 In both cases the term must exceed 14 days.
79 CJA 2003, s 189(1)(b)
80 See BCrP E 6.12
81 See Sentencing Guidelines, Pt 2, Section 2, (Pt 2B) para 2.2.15 (SG-18)

(iv) Length of sentences

Any custodial sentence imposed must be within the permitted maximum. Sometimes this is set by the common law (for example, manslaughter, murder); more often these days it is set by statute.

(a) In the magistrates' courts

In the magistrates' courts, there is a natural limit on length of custodial sentence. This is often why those charged with either-way offences elect summary trial. In a nutshell, the maximum custodial sentence the magistrates can pass in respect of an offence, whether summary or triable either way, is six months (or the maximum prescribed by the statute which creates the offence, whichever is less).[82] Where the magistrates are dealing with more than one offence, it is important to note that sentences can be made to run consecutively, but the maximum aggregate is six months, no matter how many offences there are, *unless* the court is dealing with *two or more either-way offences*, in which case the maximum aggregate is 12 months. Examiners love to test students on this, so always check the factual matrix of the question. If there is only one either-way offence in the story, the maximum aggregate will be six months, no matter how many other summary offences there are.[83]

(b) In the Crown Court

Maximum sentences are usually set by statute and tend to correlate to the gravity of the offence. Most sentences imposed, of course, are well below the maximum. In our robbery example above, the maximum permitted sentence is life in prison, but even the most serious starting point is nowhere near this. What would tend to happen nowadays is that recidivists and dangerous offenders would come out of

82 Unless this natural ceiling is expressly overridden in the statute: see generally BCrP E 2.5 and D 23.14ff. If provisions of the CJA 2003 come into force, these limits may increase to various unmemorable periods (for example. maximum sentence for an imprisonable summary offence would be 51 weeks). The entire sentencing edifice may be overhauled before this happens, so watch this space!

83 There may be various ways of getting to this aggregate. Sentences for various summary offences can run consecutively so long as (when added together) they do not exceed a total of six months (so three+three, or five+one and so on).

the normal sentencing scheme and be subject to a more heavily punitive approach.

Most prisoners serving sentences of 12 months or more,[84] must be released 'on licence' after serving half their sentence (to last for the remainder of the sentence). Standard conditions attached include the prisoner keeping in touch with his probation (or other responsible) officer, being of good behaviour and not committing further offences. More specific conditions may be prescribed. Generally speaking, early release is *not* to be taken into account when sentencing.

Again, special rules apply to the most dangerous offenders, who come under a special regime, described below.

(v) Special sentence for dangerous and persistent offenders

In recent years there has been something of a growth industry in more mandated (if not mandatory) sentences - and in particular specific 'routes' to life sentences, which 'guide' judges to the imposition of a life sentence, without ultimately forcing them to do so. Some discretion (tiny though it is) remains. These and other sentences mandated by law, are:

(a) Murder: mandatory life sentence

If convicted of murder, an adult offender must be sentenced to life imprisonment. As we all know, however, 'life does not (necessarily) mean life' behind bars, because when judges order a life sentence for murder, they must set a mimimum period of detention. The worse the crime, the longer this 'minimum term' will be.[85] At the end of the minimum term, the prisoner will be eligible to be *considered* for parole, but it does not follow by any means that he will be released, and if he is, he will be 'on licence' for the rest of his life. Much will depend on the circumstances. Very rarely, such sentences attract a 'whole life' minimum term (as, for example, in the case of the Moors murderer, Ian Brady).[86]

---

84 And see now the new extended supervision requirements for offenders released following sentences of less than two years: BCrP E 2.25/26

85 This used to be known as the 'tariff'. See Sch 21 CJA 2003 and generally BCrP E 3

86 Such would be subject to the Secretary of State's power to release any life sentence prisoner exceptionally on compassionate grounds. This was said to make whole life tariffs compatible with Art 3 of the Human Rights Convention. See *Hutchinson v UK* [2015] 61 ECHR 393 and BCrP E 3.3

When such a sentence (again only for murder) is handed down in respect of an offender aged 18 to 20, it is referred to as 'custody for life'. Such cannot be subject to a 'whole life term', as it can with older adults, but otherwise minimum terms are given and operate in much the same way.[87]

(b) Dangerous offenders: special route to life sentences

Until 2003, there was no specially mandated sentencing regime for dangerous people other than those convicted of murder; normal sentencing principles (which after all focus on culpability, harm and the need to protect the public) could cope, but the level of discretion involved in the process bothered some politicians, who needed to be seen to be doing something about crime and, more particularly, criminals. In 2001, the *Halliday Report on Sentencing* proposed a more coherent framework for dealing with those convicted of the most dangerous offences of sex and violence.[88] The result was a special regime for such offenders, first created by the CJA 2003, which essentially operates to steer the judicial discretion more proactively to passing life sentences in certain circumstances. The provisions set out below apply to adults.[89]

i. Dangerous Offender Provisions: s 225 CJA 2003

If certain conditions apply, judges must impose life imprisonment. Some of the prerequisites relate to the offence, some to the offender. Therefore, if:

- the offence for which the person has been convicted is a serious offence of a *violent or sexual nature*[90] for which the maximum punishment is life imprisonment (these are the very worst such offences: think rape, attempted murder, terrorism, child abuse and so on), *and*
- The court considers that the public is at risk of serious harm from the offender committing further offences of a violent or sexual nature *and that* the seriousness

87 See BCrP E 3.11

88 *Making Punishment Work: Report of a Review of the Sentencing Framework for England & Wales*

89 For discussion of dangerousness; see BCrP E 4.19ff; for juveniles, see Ch. 11

90 In Sch 15 to CJA 2003 a large number of violent and sexual offences are 'specified' as covered by the scheme. 'Serious' specified offences are those attracting maximum sentences of ten years or more.

of the offending in question justifies a sentence of life imprisonment,
- then in those circumstances the court must impose a life sentence.

Obviously a lot of the information about the culpability and risk of harm from future offending will come from pre-sentence reports and other such information. Of particular interest will be the offender's personal circumstances, attitude to offending, emotional state and so on.[91] Such reports will contain 'an assessment of risk', which tends to be graded on a scale of Low to Very High. It will be for the sentencer to take the information and decide whether all of the criteria are met for the imposition of a life sentence. Just because serious harm has been caused by past offending does not necessarily mean that there is a significant risk of such happening in future (and vice versa).[92]

You will notice that there is discretion built into the scheme, but the judicial hand is led by the legislation very specifically towards a life sentence in these most serious and risky of circumstances. Still, such sentences will be rare.

ii. Dangerous recidivists (second 'listed' offences): s 224A CJA 2003

This is another route to the imposition of a life sentence. It was added in 2012[93] and (somewhat annoyingly) makes use of its own separate list of offences.[94] Broadly speaking, the conditions (again for adult offenders) are that if:

- the offender is convicted of an offence of a *violent or sexual nature* (the 'new offence'), which is serious enough to justify a sentence of ten years or more,[95] *and*
- at the time the new offence was committed, the offender had previously been convicted of a similar such offence (the 'previous' offence),[96] for which he had been sentenced to a custodial sentence of ten years or more,

- then the court must impose a life sentence, unless there are particular circumstances

91 See generally s 229 CJA 2003 and BCrP E 4.5ff

92 See principles in *R v Lang* [2006] 1WLR 2509 discussed at BCrP E 4.19-4.22

93 By s 122 LASPO Act 2012

94 Set out in Sch 15B to CJA 2003

95 Listed in Pt 1 of Sch 15B

96 The previous offence can be one of those listed anywhere in Sch 15B (not merely Part 1).

relating to the previous or new offence, or to the offender, which would make it unjust to do so.

This provision is obviously geared to the notion of dangerous recidivism,[97] although offenders who might 'qualify' for a life sentence under these provisions would be apt, it would seem, to qualify equally well under the s 225 scheme (discussed above). Again, there is a fair bit of room here for judicial discretion, which is why life sentences given under both schemes are often referred to as 'discretionary life sentences'. Just bear in mind that (as George Orwell might say) some life sentences are more discretionary than others.

(c) ***Extended sentences for (slightly less) dangerous offenders: s 226A CJA 2003***

The extended sentence is essentially for dangerous offenders who present a risk to the public, but on whom the courts are not required, by operation of either of the provisions discussed above, to pass a life sentence. The extended sentence is the next best (or safest) option.

An extended sentence is a term of imprisonment (not exceeding the maximum for the offence) which is equal to the sum of two parts, namely (i) the appropriate custodial term (the term of imprisonment which would otherwise have been imposed) plus (ii) a further term ('the extension period') to be served on licence, of such length as the court considers necessary to protect members of the public from the prisoner's potential future offending. The extension period may be up to five years for a specified violent offence, and up to eight years for a specified sexual offence. Where the offender is an adult, the court *may* (not must) impose an extended sentence where:

- the offender has been convicted of a specified offence

97 See guidance in *A-G's Ref (No 27 of 2013) (Burinskas)* [2014] 1 WLR 4209 cited at BCrP E 4.18

of a *violent or sexual* nature[98] *and*

- the court considers there is a significant risk of serious harm being caused to the public by that offender's reoffending in future, *and*
- the court is not required to pass a life sentence by operation of either s 125 or 124A (discussed above), *and*
- either
    - the appropriate custodial term for the offence in question is at least four years; *or*
    - the offender had (at the time this offence was committed) previously been convicted of one of the *most* serious offences of a *violent or sexual* nature (listed in Sch 15A).

The objective is clearly to keep a better 'eye' on dangerous offenders, even in the absence of a life sentence. The way in which this is achieved is by adapting the release provisions. Normally, a prisoner is released (on licence) half-way through his custodial sentence. Where an extended sentence[99] has been passed, the release will be *two-thirds* through the custodial term. However, for the *most serious of cases* (the custodial term exceeds ten years, or the sentence has been imposed for one of the most serious of violent or sexual offences) there is *no automatic release* at the two-thirds point, but the case will be referred to the Parole Board so that consideration can be given to the prisoner's release. The prisoner would, of course, be entitled to automatic release at the end of the custodial term if he has not been released already.

(d) 'Three strikes and you are out' and other mandated minimum sentences

These are a (not uncontroversial) import from our American cousins. In effect,

98 In other words, an offence specified in Sch 15 CJA 2003

99 Passed on or after April 2015. See BCrP E 4.10/11

statutory provisions dictate a minimum sentence outcome in two sorts of situations. One is where the offender has been convicted for the *third* time of certain offences, namely:

- *trafficking in class A drugs* (for example heroin): the mandatory minimum sentence is at least seven years' custody where the offender is convicted for the third time;[100] *or*
- *domestic burglary*: the mandatory minimum sentence is at least three years' custody where the offender is convicted for the third time;[101]

- unless, in either case, 'particular circumstances' (relevant to the offence or the offender) make this unjust.[102] There is thus a residual element of discretion built into the schemes. In addition, an early guilty plea can operate to reduce such sentences, although not below 80% of the prescribed minimum (of seven or three years).

There is also a statutory minimum for certain serious firearms offences,[103] resulting in a minimum custodial sentence of five years for an adult offender (the minimum period is three years for offenders aged 16 and 17 at the time of offending). This minimum - which, crucially, applies *even for a first offence* - must be imposed unless the court considers that there are exceptional circumstances (relevant to the offence or the offender) which makes this unjust. These firearms offences are so serious in their nature, that such exceptional cases will be rare.

4. MISCELLANEOUS AND ANCILLARY SENTENCES

Finally, bear in mind that there are additional sentencing powers which work in tandem with other mainstream sentences and/or do some specific job which the mainstream sentences cannot. In outline, they include the following.

100 PCC(S)A 2000, s 110
101 *Ibid*, s 111
102 For an example, see *R v Stone* [2011] EWCA Crim 2823
103 Firearms Act 1968, s 51A

A. BIND-OVERS

These can be a convenient way of dealing with offenders. It is most commonly deployed in the magistrates' courts, but the Crown Court can also bind a person over 'to be of good behaviour and to keep the peace'. This effectively requires him to pay a specific sum of money if he misbehaves within a specified period of time.[104] This sort of 'bind-over' tends to be used in cases of petty violence (for example, in a dispute between neighbours which gets out of hand) or activities of protesters (for example, hunt saboteurs). It may be used in addition to, or in lieu of, another sentence, and can even be imposed where there has been no finding of guilt. It is, after all, not a punishment, but essentially a promise not to offend.

In the Crown Court only, the judge has the power to bind an offender over to 'come up for judgment'. This is an alternative to remand on bail when there will be a gap between conviction and sentence.

B. COMPENSATION ORDERS

These are something akin to an order for damages in a civil court, and it comes under the umbrella of so-called 'restorative justice'. A compensation order in the criminal courts, which can be used in addition to or in lieu of some other sentence, allows a court dealing with an offender to make an order requiring him to pay compensation for any 'personal injury, loss or damage' *resulting from that offence* (or any other offence 'taken into consideration').[105] If the crime caused a death, such an order could include payment of funeral expenses and/or a sum for bereavement.

Courts are now under a statutory duty to consider making a compensation order in relevant cases.[106] Of course, such orders will not always be appropriate - the court must hear representations about whether, and if so in what amount, to make a compensation order. Clearly an offender must have the means to pay any such

104 It must be clear what, in the circumstances, would be bad behaviour: see *Hasman v UK* [2000] Crim LR 185 and generally BCrP E 13.1-13.3

105 See generally PCC(S)A 2000, s 130

106 *Ibid*, s 130(2A) as inserted by LASPO Act 2012

amount (if only by installments). The order should not be made if there is any real doubt about the offender's responsibility for the harm caused.

Note that if an offender has limited means, and the court is debating whether to impose a fine or make a compensation order, the *latter should be given priority*, so that any fine should be reduced, or if necessary dispensed with entirely, to enable a compensation order to be paid.[107] This is only sensible. A fine only punishes (and goes into the general fund); but the compensation order has the added (intended) benefit of actually doing the victim some good. It sometimes means victims do not need to resort to claiming damages in the civil courts.

There is no limit to the amount of compensation which can be ordered in either the Crown Court or the magistrates' court, unless the offender is aged under 18 years old, when the maximum is £5,000.[108]

C. DEPRIVATION AND OTHER FORFEITURE ORDERS

There is a general power to deprive criminals of the tools of their trade or other property, found on or lawfully taken from them when apprehended for the offence for which they are being sentenced.[109] If the court is satisfied that the property was used to commit or facilitate the commission of the crime (or was intended to do so), then it may make a deprivation order in respect of such property. Typical examples would be the car the handler used to transport stolen goods, and the specially adapted pump a petrol thief used to siphon off petrol from various car tanks. When making such an order, the court should have regard to the value of the property and the effect such order would have on other aspects of sentencing, bearing in mind (as always) the totality principle.[110]

Certain specific legislation contain their own forfeiture provisions, for example the Firearms Act 1968 and Misuse of Drugs Act 1971.

107 *Ibid*, s 130(12). Otherwise, compensation orders are not to be used to 'buy' one's way out of a penalty for the commission of a crime: see BCrP E 16.11

108 For a helpful summary of the main principles behind compensation orders, see *R v Stapleton* [2012] EWCA Crim 78 and SG-369

109 PCC(S)A 2000, s 143. The power does *not* extend to *real* property.

110 See, e.g., *R v Scully* (1985) 7 Cr App R(S) 119 and BCrP E 18.2. The property must belong to the perpetrator.

D. CONFISCATION ORDER

Such orders are available in the Crown Court[111] and are intended not to deprive criminals of the tools of their trade, but the proceeds of their criminal lifestyle. They are usually reserved for big-time fraudsters, lucrative scams and fat-cat criminals. The court needs to decide, in any given case, whether the offender has benefited from their criminal lifestyle generally (if they have one) or from their specific criminal conduct (for example, a one-off heist). The relevant legislation sets out a rather complex mechanism for determining these issues. If the court so decides, then it will determine what is a 'recoverable amount' and can make an order requiring the offender to pay that amount. Confiscation orders, if applicable, are normally made before otherwise sentencing the offender for the offence, and should be taken into account before making orders like fines, compensation orders and the like, but not taken into account when imposing any other kind of sentence (for example, imprisonment).[112]

E. REGISTRATION OF SEX OFFENDERS

Certain sexual offences trigger off an automatic notification of details (name, address and so on) to police so that the offender can be 'put on the sex offenders register'. The relevant offences are listed in Sch 3 of the Sexual Offences Act 2003, and include the usual - rape, indecent assault, offences relating to child pornography and so forth. The duty to register sex offenders is imposed not just on sentencing courts, but also on those cautioning an offender. Once registered, an offender will stay on the register for an amount of time which will vary depending on the gravity of offence/sentence imposed. An unreasonable failure to comply with registration requirements is itself a criminal offence. Where the offence leading to registration involves children, an order disqualifying the offender from working with children will usually follow.[113]

111 Magistrates may commit an offender to the Crown Court to be made subject of a confiscation order.

112 But the court can postpone confiscation hearings for up to two years from the date of conviction. The rather complex procedure is set out in CrimPR Pt 33

113 See generally, BCrP E 23.1

F. ENDORSEMENT OF DRIVING LICENCES AND DISQUALIFICATION[114]

You may have some experience of the joys of penalty points being endorsed on your driving licence. If not, no doubt there is a traffic camera out there waiting just for you. Most road traffic offences are endorsable, so that in the absence of 'special reasons' the court must order that particulars of such convictions be 'endorsed' on the driver's driving licence. Unless the offender is already disqualified from driving when the endorsement is ordered, the number of points ordered will be commensurate with the gravity of the offence (and is prescribed by law).[115] 'Special reasons' are notoriously difficult to show, and must relate to the offence, not to the offender. Racing an expectant mother to the maternity ward might work, but *"I am a great driver, was momentarily distracted and did not notice the speed restriction sign"*, will not.[116]

By virtue of the so-called 'totting up' procedure, if the court is required to endorse penalty points onto an offender's licence, and that endorsement (plus any others already on the licence, provided those offences were committed within the last three years) reaches the magic figure of 12 points or more, then that offender must be disqualified from driving for at least six months (12 months if he has already been disqualified once), *unless* the court, in light of all the circumstances, thinks it appropriate to disqualify him for a lesser period, or not at all.

Certain serious offences bring automatic disqualification (unless there are 'special reasons'). The minimum is usually one year, but can be greater (for example, causing death by dangerous driving carries a minimum two year ban).[117]

G. COSTS ON CONVICTION

Finally, a convicted defendant will (as the 'loser' in the litigation) be liable to pay such prosecution costs as the court considers 'just and reasonable'.[118] This applies to both summary trial and trial on indictment. Not surprisingly, whether and the

114 For detail (which can get complex) see BCrP Pt C if necessary.

115 See Sch 2 Road Traffic Offenders Act 1998

116 See *Chatters v Burke* [1986] 1 WLR 1321

117 See BCrP C 7.8 and 7.10

118 Prosecution of Offences Act 1985, s 18(1)

extent to which a defendant is ordered to pay prosecution costs will depend on his means, ability to pay, conduct during trial, and whether he has been acquitted of some offences and convicted of others. The amount of any costs payable must be specified in the order.[119]

revision tips

- Know the basic limits on sentences in the magistrates' courts. Especially watch out for a question where that court is sentencing in respect of a combination of summary and either-way offences. Only if the magistrates are sentencing in respect of two+ either-way offences is the overall custodial limit raised to 12 months.
- Do not confuse the consequences of breaching a conditional discharge with that of breaching a suspended sentence.
- Sentencing is a vast area. Check your exam syllabus so you know where to focus your revision.
- Know the basic sentencing implications of a few key offences (e.g. maximum sentence). Robbery seems to come up a lot in exams.

It is worth reading...

The Crown Court Compendium (Pt II Guide to Sentencing) is worth consulting to reinforce your understanding. Ditto the Sentencing Council's Guidlines for Imposition of Community and Custodial Sentences (Feb 2017), available at sentencingcouncil.org.uk

R v Hawkins (1985) 7 Cr App R (S) 351. This is a short and amusing judgment about the need (or not!) of a *Newton* hearing. The offender said he was not involved with the worst of the offending because he had just gone off to the loo (yeah, right!).

119 See generally Ch. 12 and BCrP D 33.21ff

CHAPTER 11

Children and young people: trials and sentencing

Young offenders pose a special dilemma for criminal justice. It seems unfair to treat them just like an adult, since they are often as much of a victim (of immaturity, poor parenting, poverty, prejudice) as a perpetrator. But the public may still need protecting from these individuals and the system which deals with them must be answerable to it. The compromise we in England and Wales make is to adapt our court procedures to accommodate juveniles when and where we need to.

We try to do this in a number of ways. First, we have a specially adapted magistrates' court, known as the Youth Court, dedicated to hearing cases against juveniles. Secondly, it is a stated 'aim of the youth justice system to prevent offending by children and young persons'.[1] Thirdly, the courts are under an *obligation* to have regard to the *welfare* of juveniles whenever they are called upon to deal with them.[2] Fourthly, when sentencing, we try even harder with children to keep them out of custody, and where possible attempt to address underlying problems which may be causing or contributing to the offending. In short we try (with limited success, some would say) to keep youngsters from becoming gangsters.

1 Crime and Disorder Act 1998, s 37

2 Children and Young Persons Act (CYPA)1933. The notion of the 'welfare of the child' permeates the whole of the law relating to children. See Part 18 Sentencing Guidelines, (SG-522), and especially para 2.9 for list of factors which can impact on the young.

1. TERMINOLOGY

One has to be careful not to be confused by the terminology, which is sometimes used a little inconsistently. The age of majority (that is, legal adulthood) is 18 in England and Wales, but for some purposes distinctions are made between older teens and younger children. Thus, a *juvenile* is essentially anyone under the age of 18.[3] Once a person becomes 18, he or she is treated (for most purposes[4]) like any other adult defendant/offender. But as we all know there is a big difference, say, between a 12 year old and a 17 year old, and so the law sometimes sub-divides this juvenile population (for criminal justice purposes). Those under ten effectively fall off of the criminal courts' radar. This is because, however badly they have behaved, they are legally incapable of committing a criminal offence.[5] Otherwise, a juvenile *under* the age of 14 is often referred to as a *child*; and if aged 14-17, as a *young person*.[6] The main function of this latter division will become clearer when discussing sentencing options.

2. ALTERNATIVES TO PROSECUTION

In 2013, a system of 'youth cautions' and 'youth conditional cautions' (which mirror the adult cautions) was created as a formal way of dealing with juvenile crime without actually prosecuting the juvenile in question.[7] This method of 'pre-court disposal' means that the matter effectively goes no further than the police station (and the youth offending team). There has to be sufficient evidence to prosecute, but where it seems better not to do so, then if the child admits to the offending and understands the implications of resolving the matter in this way, then a caution (with or without conditions) may be administered.

3 CJA 1991, s 68

4 See Ch.10 re sentencing option specific to those aged 18-20

5 Adults and older children who (because of this rule) use the under-ten's to do their dirty work for them can be tried as 'manipulators'.

6 CYPA 1969, s 70. As the name of the legislation indicates, this is an historic sub-division. It does not stop different rules applying to different ages of juveniles for different purposes. See below about ordering parents of juveniles to attend Youth Court.

7 See generally BCrP D 2.28ff. *'Community Resolution'* is an *informal* way of responding to minor crime and anti-social behaviour.

3. YOUTH COURT TRIALS

The vast majority of charges brought against juveniles are tried summarily in the Youth Court, which is a specially constituted magistrates' court whose procedures are particularly adapted for the purpose. Procedurally, summary trials[8] in the adult magistrates' court and proceedings in the youth court have a lot in common, but there are important differences.

A. SPECIAL BENCH

Youth Courts normally consist of three magistrates, often (but not necessarily) including one man and one woman,[9] who have been selected from a 'youth panel' of magistrates. These will have had experience of and special training in dealing with juvenile defendants.

B. PRIVACY

The general public are excluded from youth courts.[10] Only the juvenile concerned, his or her parents and legal representatives, officers of the court, bona fide members of the press, witnesses (after giving evidence), others directly concerned with the case (for example, probation officer, social worker[11]), and anyone else whom the court may specially admit shall be allowed into a youth court in session.[12] The latter category makes it possible for the court to allow in persons who are not otherwise participants, but who have a genuine interest in seeing justice being done in the particular case: for example (non-testifying) victims, community representatives - and even law students!

C. STRICT REPORTING RESTRICTIONS

Strict reporting restrictions *automatically apply*. The media may not report or broadcast

8 For summary trial procedure see Ch. 8

9 The requirement for a mixed gender bench was removed by the Justices of the Peace Rules 2016, No. 709.

10 Contrast this with adult courts where the public has a general right to attend, unless exceptionally proceedings are adjourned to sit in private.

11 It is common to see relevant staff from social services in youth court. The defendant may be 'known' to social services, even in the care of social services, and social workers and the like who know the child and his ciricumstances can be a very useful resource for the court or defence team.

12 CYPA 1933, s 47(2), replicated effectively in CrPR, r 24.2(1)(c)

anything which reveals the name, address or other identifying details of the juvenile defendant and any other juvenile concerned in the proceedings.[13] This is why the cases involving children are reported using letters and not names.[14] The ban may be lifted in three circumstances:

(i) If the defence apply to lift the ban and the court agrees it is necessary to do so in order to avoid causing the juvenile injustice (for example, to encourage defence witnesses to come forward), *or*

(ii) If the prosecution (in the form of the DPP) apply to lift the ban, the offence is serious enough,[15] the juvenile is 'unlawfully at large' and the court agrees it is necessary to do so in order to apprehend the juvenile, *or*

(iii) After a conviction, the youth court (after allowing representations from the parties) may remove the restriction if it considers it is in the public interest to do so (not perhaps to 'name and shame', as such, but to show the public that justice in a particular case 'has been done'). The court will thus need to consider whether publicity would, in fact, enhance the youth's celebrity status among his peers and so be counter-productive.

In any case, the restrictions cease to apply once the person concerned reaches the age of 18.

D. ATTENDANCE OF PARENTS

When children get into trouble, their parents will usually want to 'be there' for them. Quite naturally, therefore, many parents voluntarily accompany their child appearing in youth court. Those not so minded (which may partly explain why their child is appearing in youth court) can be compelled to attend. If the juvenile is aged

13 CYPA 1933, s 49. See BCrP, D 24.14/15

14 In the adult courts, such a ban in respect of young offenders is not automatic, but the court may well (and typically would where children are concerned) impose similar restrictions. See below as to trying young people in adult courts.

15 Either a specified offence of a violent or sexual nature, or other offence carrying a maximum term in prison of at least 14 years. See generally Ch. 10

under 16, the court *must* order a parent to attend, unless it would be unreasonable to do so. With older defendants (aged 16 or 17), the court *may* order a parent to attend. One reason for requiring parents to attend is to get them to engage with their son or daughter's offending where possible. The parents may not be directly responsible for what their child did, but they may be part of the problem. If so, it is sometimes a good idea to make them part of the solution. This can even extend to a sentence which actively impinges on the parents (or their wallets), which is discussed below.

E. INTERMEDIARIES AND SPECIAL MEASURES

Juvenile defendants (especially those with additional special vulnerabilities) may need to have an intermediary appointed to ensure that they can understand what is going on, communicate effectively with their lawyers and, if they choose to give evidence, do so coherently. A vulnerable accused may also be allowed to give evidence by live link. This is catered for in the Criminal Procedure Rules.[16] Otherwise, it is as well to remember that defendants (whatever their age or vulnerability) were expressly excluded from the range of special measure directions available to qualifying witnesses laid down by statute. This is discussed in more detail in Chapter 17.

F. RELATIVE INFORMALITY

Proceedings in the youth court are a little less formal even than in the adult magistrates' courts. For a start, the defendant does not go into a dock, but sits on a chair facing the magistrates, his parents (or other responsible adults[17]) beside him. The magistrates themselves do not sit on a raised platform, but on ordinary chairs behind an ordinary table (albeit slightly raised in some courts). They address juveniles (accused or witness) by their first name, and usually attempt to express themselves in clear and simple terms, if still serious in tone.

16 See CrimPD V 18B

17 Where a juvenile does not have legal representation, the court may permit a parent or other 'suitable supporting adult' to assist him in conducting his defence, although this may not be the best solution to the problem.

The vocabulary is also less formal. Thus, witnesses 'promise' rather than 'swear' to tell the truth. Magistrates do not 'convict' juveniles, but 'find the case proven'. The magistrates do not 'sentence' such offenders, they 'make a disposal'.[18] The different terminology is really purely semantic, but it may make the entire episode less traumatic and stigmatising for the young person. That is its purpose.

4. SENTENCES IN THE YOUTH COURT

Much about sentencing in the youth court is similar to that which takes place when sentencing adults. How the court deals with a juvenile will depend on his offence, his culpability, his record, his mitigation and so on, although the court *must* have regard to his welfare and must obtain (and have regard to) a pre-sentencing report, unless there is one in front of it which is still applicable.[19] The usual thresholds apply, but age is a much bigger part of the equation in the youth court (not surprisingly), and some of the sentencing options (and a lot of the vocabulary) are specific to this court. The goal is to avoid 'criminalising' young people while 'ensuring that they are held responsible for their actions and, where possible, take part in repairing the damage they have caused'.[20] What follows is a brief outline of the youth court's options when dealing with juvenile offenders.

A. DETENTION AND TRAINING ORDER (DTO)

The DTO is the youth court's version of custody. The name itself says a lot about what such an order is meant to achieve, although some might say it represents the triumph of hope over experience. This is the most serious sentence which the *youth court* can pass, and the criteria get more onerous the younger the offender gets.

18 The same terminology would be used if dealing with a juvenile in an adult court, as to which see below.

19 There is thus less scope for dispensing with such reports (usually compiled by the Youth Offending Team) when dealing with juveniles: CJA 2003, s 156. The report should recommend intervention on one of three levels: standard, enhanced and intensive. See Sentencing Guidelines, Pt 18, para 10.11ff (SG-530)

20 Sentencing Guidelines, Pt 18, para 1.3 (SG-521)

The first thing to remember is that (subject to the intervention of the Secretary of State[21]) a juvenile must be *at least* 12 years old for such a sentence to be passed. A ten or 11 year old who is sentenced in the youth court may *not normally* be given a DTO.[22] Secondly, the DTO is a custodial sentence and so the court must be satisfied that the *custody threshold*[23] has been crossed before imposing such an order. Where juveniles are concerned, this may involve looking even more closely than one would with an adult at all the implications of such a sentence and especially whether it really is the best way of preventing re-offending, given the 'circumstances, age, and maturity' of the juvenile concerned.[24] There really should be no meaningful alternative.

In addition, if the offender was *under 15 years of age* at the time the offence was committed, then a DTO can only be ordered if (in addition to the custody threshold having been crossed), the juvenile is also a '*persistent offender*'. The latter tends to translate into his having been dealt with for the commission of 'imprisonable offences on at least three occasions in the past 12 months'.[25] This could, in principle, include a single 'spree' of offence(s) in respect of which the DTO sentence is being considered.[26]

The possible total length of DTO's come in conveniently even numbers starting from a minimum of four months to a maximum of 24 months. This is so the term can be cut in two, since one half of the period is spent in detention (and training), at which point the offender is released to spend the other half of the time under supervision. The court must, as always, take account of any time spent on remand when imposing the order (while still keeping to the period options).

Note that a DTO cannot therefore be imposed where the maximum sentence for an adult is less than the four month minimum, (or where factors like mitigation would bring a time in custody below four months).[27] For summary offences, a DTO must not exceed six months.

21 And only if necessary to protect the public: s 100(2)(b) Powers of Criminal Courts (Sentencing) Act 2000 (PCC(S)A 2000). In such cases, more heavy duty sentencing will be in order anyway (see below).

22 Offences calling for more serious sentencing need to go to the Crown Court (see below).

23 See generally Ch. 10

24 Sentencing Guidelines, Pt 18, para 11.12 (SG-531)

25 *Ibid*, para 6.5 (ii) (SG-526)

26 See *R v Charlton* (2000) 164 JP 685

27 This would include, for example, criminal damage cases which must be tried summarily, since the maximum sentence in such cases is 3 months. See BCrP E 7.18. As to consecutive DTOs, see E 7.20

B. YOUTH REHABILITATION ORDER (YRO)

This is the youth court's version of the adult community sentence.[28] The name of course is more descriptive of its good intentions, but it works in the same way. Thus the order is always the generic YRO, which is then 'personalised' by including one or more 'requirements' as appropriate to the situation.[29] Again, the appropriate threshold *must* be crossed.[30] Moreover, although the order is not a custodial sentence, it does curtail the offender's freedom to an extent, and so it must be no more restrictive than is proportionate to the seriousness of the offending. Some of the requirement possibilities for juveniles tend (not surprisingly) to be a little less onerous than their adult equivalent; others are particularly geared to likely needs of young offenders. Some typical examples (with their limitations) are:

(i) An 'unpaid work requirement' is *only possible* where the offender is aged 16 or 17 at the date of conviction. The number of hours must be between 40 and 240 hours, to be completed (normally) within 12 months.

(ii) A programme requirement for young offenders, which would tend to focus on life skills, job skills or other positive intervention to prevent re-offending.

(iii) A supervision requirement (not to exceed three years), where the youth is supervised by a social worker or probation officer.

(iv) A residence requirement (this requires the offender to reside with a specified individual or, if 16 or over, at a specific place). It is also possible, in certain circumstances, for a juvenile to be made subject to a local authority residence requirement of up to six months. This might be appropriate where the offender's current residence seems to

28 See Ch. 10

29 Criminal Justice and Immigration Act 2008, s 1

30 Sentencing Guidelines, Pt 18, para 10.3ff (SG-530)

be contributing to his offending (and this option might really do some good.)

(v) An attendance centre requirement. This requires the young person to attend such a centre for a specified period, and while there to engage in some guided instruction or activity. The period to be imposed by this requirement must be *at least 12 hours* in any event. The maximum which can be imposed depends on age: 36 hours for a 16 year old, 24 hours for those 13-15 years old; 12 hours for those aged ten or 11.

(vi) A curfew requirement (to remain at a specified location for specified periods between 2 and 16 hours in any day).

And so on.[31] As with adults (and for the same reasons), certain requirements (for example, mental health treatment, drug testing, substance abuse treatment) require the consent of the offender. Similarly, failure to comply with an YRO requirement is dealt with in much the same way as with adults breaching community sentences.[32]

C. FINES

It is possible to order that a fine be paid, but this is not often a very viable option for obvious reasons. The maximum amount which may be imposed on a young person by the youth court is £1,000; the limit in the case of a child is £250. Where the offender is under 16, the court *must* order that the fine is paid by the offender's parents (and so should take into account the latter's means when deciding whether a fine is an appropriate sentence). Where the offender is 16 years or older, the court may order the parents to pay.[33] Only very exceptionally would a fine seem a very germane order - especially if the offender does not even have to pay it!

31 For complete list see BCrP E 9.2ff

32 As to which see Ch. 10

33 PCC(S)A 2000, s 137 and see BCrP E 14.7

D. MISCELLANEOUS ORDERS

Absolute and conditional discharges are available in the youth court, as are bind-overs - we have looked at these briefly already in Chapter 10. Two other orders which the youth court can impose are as below.

(i) Referral order

This is an order 'referring' an offender to a youth offender panel, primarily in the hopes of nipping nascent juvenile offending in the bud. It is intended as a pro-active sentence for offences which are neither trivial nor so serious as to warrant detention, and is intended to stand virtually alone as a sentence. It is discretionary in some circumstances, but mandatory in others. Where a juvenile *pleads guilty to a first offence*, the youth court *must* make a referral order, unless it is considering either a custodial sentence or an absolute discharge.[34] The youth offender panel, which comprises persons with experience of dealing with young people, makes a 'contract' with the offender and his family, including certain obligations (set by the panel, not the sentencing court) which might typically include apologising or making reparation to the victim. The offender will have meetings with the panel over a period of between three to 12 months.

(ii) Reparation order

The youth court has power to require a juvenile offender to make reparation to a victim of his crime or to any person affected by it, or the community at large. 'Reparation' does not mean compensation. The idea is that the offender does some *non-monetary* act to make up for his crime. Such orders may not be made if the court is intending to pass either a custodial or community sentence,[35] although there seems to be no reason why the act of reparation could not resemble one of the less onerous

34 See BCrP E10 for details
35 PCC(S)A 2000, s 73(4)

YRO requirements. Before making such an order the court would have to consider the written views of a probation officer, social worker or member of a youth offending team as to what act of reparation would be suitable. In any case, whatever the offender is asked to do should be commensurate with the seriousness of the crime, and not (so far as possible) interfere with the offender's schooling, work or religious beliefs.[36]

5. DEALING WITH JUVENILES IN OTHER COURTS

Sometimes juveniles, even very young children, commit dreadful crimes or present a danger to society. Fortunately, this is pretty rare, but it happens - perhaps most infamously (and shockingly) with the murder by two ten year olds of the toddler James Bulger in 1994. In such cases, more severe sentences than the youth court can hand down are necessary. These are:

(i) 'Detention at Her Majesty's pleasure'.

This is the official name for the mandatory life sentence given to the under 18's who commit murder. Only the Crown Court can deal with such offences. A juvenile so sentenced will be detained in such a place and under such conditions as the Secretary of State may direct. In its nature it cannot attract a 'whole life' direction (the sovereign's pleasure may change). The usual starting point for a minimum term[37] is 12 years. In the case of Jon Venables and Robert Thompson, the boys who killed James Bulger, this was originally set at eight years, quite possibly (at least in part) so their case could be re-visited when they were 18 and would be transferred to a Young Offenders Institution.[38] Remember that all the minimum term does is set

36 *Ibid*, s 74(2) and (3). For detail see BCrP E11

37 See generally discussion in Ch. 10

38 Setting the minimum term in that case caused all manner of angst and anxiety. See, e.g., *R v Home Secretary, ex parte Venables and Thompson* [1997] 3 WLR 23. The boys were eventually released on licence at 18 because it was feared transfer to a more adult prison would undo any rehabilitation and re-education which had gone on previously. They had to assume new identities because of the notoriety of the case and public disgust at their behaviour. One has been back in prison since. And see the case of *R v Cornick* [2014] EWHC 3623

the time to be served before release on parole can be *considered*. It does not mandate a release date.

(ii) Long term detention

This is shorthand used for sentences handed down to juveniles under s 91 PCC(S)A 2000, which is also commonly referred to by the section number of the statute. In effect s 91 allows the under 18's to be sentenced like adults when the circumstances warrant it and something more draconian than the DTO is called for. It can include a (discretionary) life sentence. In practice, such sentences are reserved for a small minority of the most grave offences. The court must be of the view that no other method of dealing with the juvenile is appropriate.[39]

It is important to note that such sentences can only be passed by the Crown Court. In order for it to be able to do so, the case must either have been tried there or the defendant committed there for sentencing.

How cases involving juveniles get to the Crown Court for either of these purposes is really very similar to how it works for adults. Thus juveniles, like adults, make their first appearance in the magistrates' court. If they are alone or with other juveniles, they will first appear in the youth court. If a juvenile is charged jointly with an adult, the two will both first appear in the (adult) magistrates' court. It will then be for the magistrates to decide on trial venue. It is important to note that a juvenile (unlike an adult) *never* has a right to elect trial by jury in the Crown Court.[40] But very exceptionally, this is where he may end up.

A. SENDING YOUTHS TO CROWN COURT *FOR TRIAL*

The youth court is designed and intended for the summary trials of youths, and so juveniles must always be tried there, except in *very specific and limited* circumstances.

39 See cases discussed at BCrP E 7.12ff and D 24.27ff

40 His legal representative can of course make representations to the court on venue. Life can get a bit complicated when juveniles become adults during a prosecution. For a useful summary see Sprack, *Practical Approach*, 11.32-33

Thus a juvenile *must* be sent[41] to the Crown Court for trial if:

(i) he is charged with homicide (that is, murder, manslaughter); *or*

(ii) he is charged with an offence which (in the case of an adult offender) is punishable with 14 or more years in prison (robbery for example) and the magistrates consider that he could properly be sentenced to long term detention under s 91; *or*

(iii) he is charged with a serious firearms offence which carries a mandatory minimum sentence[42] *or*

(iv) where notice has been given for a transfer[43] of the case to the Crown Court (cases involving child witnesses or complex fraud) *or*

(v) where the offence is one of those offences of a violent or sexual nature which fall within the ambit of the dangerous offender provisions;[44] *or*

(vi) he is charged alongside an adult who is sent to be tried on indictment and it is in the interest of justice that both are tried there together (discussed below).

In other words, the case has to be a serious one (or it must otherwise be in the interest of justice) to send a child or young person for trial on indictment. The presumption is very much against trying juveniles in the Crown Court unless clearly required.[45]

On those rare occasions when a juvenile is tried in the Crown Court, the latter should 'take all possible steps' to assist the young defendant 'to understand and participate in the proceedings'. In effect, it should replicate youth court procedure and presentation where possible.

Note that reporting restrictions are *not* automatic as they are in the youth court, but the court has a *discretion* to impose restrictions as necessary to prevent

41 Under s 51 and 51A of Crime and Disorder Act 1998 (CDA 1998). See Ch. 5

42 See Ch. 10

43 Under s 51B or 51C CDA 1998. See Ch. 5.

44 See Ch. 10

45 See BCrP D 24.38-40

identifying details of the accused being published (while under the age of 18). In deciding whether to impose restrictions, the court will have to balance the right to privacy, family life and the interest of the child against the important public interest in open justice. Generally speaking, it is for the party seeking to derogate from the principles of open justice to convince the court of the need for anonymity.[46] Ground rules, intermediaries or other SMD[47] (including hearing evidence in private or restricting attendance by members of the public) may be necessary. The courts have come a long way since the trial of Jon Venables and Robert Thompson, who really had few effective concessions made to their vulnerabilities.[48]

If a juvenile is sent to the Crown Court for trial under any of these provisions, then if he is charged with other related offences, whether indictable or summary (if serious enough), these may go along with him to be dealt with there at the same time. This is merely one of those efficiency measures which we discussed earlier when considering mode of trial for adults. They work in the same way for children.[49]

Crown Court's power of sentencing youths

The Crown Court has all the sentencing options open to it (including those of the youth court) when dealing with a juvenile who has been convicted there. But strictly speaking, the Crown Court is supposed to remit the juvenile to the youth court to be sentenced (except in homicide cases) unless it would be 'undesirable' to do so.[50] More often than not, however, it is considered undesirable (for example, either because it would cause unnecessary delay, or the trial judge is better informed about the case than the youth court would be[51]). There will be exceptions (where proper sentencing needs to await a proper pre-sentence report, for example), but juveniles are *not normally* sent to the youth court to be sentenced following conviction in the Crown Court.

---

46 Juvenile victims and witnesses (not the accused) may be protected for life: s 45A YJCEA 1999. See also s 45, replacing s 39 YJCEA 1999 (since April 2015). See also *Reporting Restrictions in the Criminal Courts* (revised in May 2016) at judiciary.gov.uk

47 See CrimPR 3.9. Not all SMD are available to vulnerable defendants, but some are. See above and Ch. 17

48 The ECHR was not impressed: see discussion and possible modifications to be made nowadays BCrP D 24.88ff

49 s 51A(4) and (5) CDA 1998 and see Ch. 5

50 PCC(S)A 2000, s 8

51 See, e.g., *R v Lewis* (1984) 6 Cr App R (S) 44

B. COMMITTING JUVENILES TO THE CROWN COURT *FOR SENTENCING*

The Crown Court may be able to sentence like a youth court when the need arises, but it does not work the other way around! Thus, the magistrates' court may commit a juvenile appearing before it to the Crown Court for sentencing where:

(i) he is charged with an offence to which either s 91 (long term detention) or relevant provisions of the dangerous offenders scheme applies *and*
(ii) the juvenile indicates a guilty plea.[52]

Juvenile plea before venue

Thus, there may be times when the magistrates' court has a case in front of it which may require sending a juvenile to the Crown Court for trial or committing him there for sentencing. Getting an indication of plea at this stage is part of the decision-making process. If a guilty plea is indicated in the circumstances described above, then if the court considers that only the Crown Court can pass an appropriate sentence, it will commit the juvenile there for sentence. If a not guilty plea or no clear plea is indicated, then the court will have to decide whether the appropriate venue for trial is the Crown Court. Clearly the juvenile must be present at this hearing to indicate his plea, although if he is represented (and his representative can indicate a plea on his behalf), then the court could proceed in his absence if, for example, his behaviour was so disruptive that it interfered with due process.[53] As with other indication of plea scenarios, there may be scope for a change of mind, either by the court or the individual, as the case progresses.

52 This plea before venue procedure for juveniles was introduced by s 24A-D MCA 1980. But it does not apply to all offences, so that if the charge were manslaughter, the guilty plea would have to be taken in the Crown Court.

53 S 24A(3) and s 24B MCA 1980 and generally BCrP D 24.24ff

6. ADULTS AND CHILDREN

A practical dilemma arises when a juvenile and an adult appear together, charged with the same or related offences. Defendants charged together ought usually[54] to be tried together - especially if jointly charged with the same offence. But youth court is for youths only; adults can never be tried there. So how is this tension between togetherness and separation resolved? Where an adult and juvenile are charged together, is it ever possible for the adult to go one way and the youth another? This depends on the circumstances, and in particular on whether the two should (or will) be *tried* together. *If they stay together*, the *adult* will dictate the trial venue and the youth will go where the adult goes. If, however, the youth can 'separate' himself from the adult somehow (for example, one pleads guilty and the other pleads not guilty), then the gravitational pull will work towards his being dealt with in the youth court (unless, of course, the case is too serious for the youth court, as discussed above).

So let us assume, for the sake of the discussion below, that an adult and a juvenile have been jointly charged or otherwise appeared together in respect of an offence(s) for which, had the juvenile appeared alone, the youth court would be the appropriate venue for trial.

A. JOINTLY CHARGED WITH INDICTABLE OFFENCES

Ideally persons jointly charged with the same offence should be tried together. To require the adult to forego his right to trial by jury (because it would be too upsetting for the juvenile) would be unacceptable. On the other hand, to insist that the youth must always join the adult in the Crown Court when the latter either must be (indictable only) or elects to be (either-way offence) tried on indictment,

54 See discussion in Ch. 6

would also be rather draconian. So the compromise is this: the juvenile will be sent to be tried with the adult in the Crown Court if it is in the '*interests of justice*'. Deciding this will involve balancing the desirability of a joint trial against the undesirability of exposing young people to the possible trauma of a Crown Court trial. This in turn will depend on common sense factors like the age of the child, the inconvenience of two separate trials, the roles played by the juvenile and the adult in the alleged offence and so on. If the magistrates decide that a joint trial is not in the interests of justice, the adult will go to the Crown Court alone. The juvenile will stay behind and be asked for his plea to the charge(s):

(i) If he pleads not guilty, the adult magistrates could try him, but will almost always exercise their discretion to send him to the youth court for trial.[55]
(ii) If he pleads guilty, the powers of the adult magistrates to sentence a juvenile are very limited and so if the full range of options available to the youth court are needed, that is where he should be sent to be sentenced.[56]

If the juvenile and adult are *both convicted* in the Crown Court, the latter has the full range of sentencing powers open to it (including those of the youth court), and so can sentence the two together when (as is often the case) this is desirable, for example to reduce unnecessary delay and expense and/or (particularly in such cases) to ensure that there is no unacceptable disparity in sentencing. Otherwise the Crown Court should remit the juvenile to the youth court for sentencing.[57]

55 MCA 1980, s 29

56 For example, the adult magistrates' court has no power to order a DTO or YRO. See CYPA 1969, s 7(8)

57 But curiously, you might think, the Crown Court does *not* have the power to remit a juvenile (who has been sent there for trial with a jointly charged adult) back down to the Youth Court for trial, even if, for example, the adult subsequently pleads guilty, thus leaving the juvenile to be tried in the Crown Court alone: *R(W)(a minor) v Leeds Crown Court* [2012] 1 Cr App R 162, cited at BCrP D 24.50.

B. CHARGED TOGETHER IN RESPECT OF OFFENCES TO BE TRIED SUMMARILY

Where the offences are to be tried summarily, the same dilemma arises, but on a lesser scale, because we are not worried about depriving an adult of trial by jury, and adult magistrates' courts are less scary than the Crown Court. But an adult still cannot go to the youth court, so again a decision has to be taken about whether the youth goes by himself to the youth court, or stays in the adult magistrates' court with the adult. What happens depends, unsurprisingly, on the *need for or desirability of* a joint trial.

If the juvenile is *jointly charged* with the adult, then the magistrates' court *must* try the two *together.* This assumes they both plead not guilty. If one pleads guilty and the other not guilty, then again they may go their separate ways, and the gravitational pull would tend to draw the juvenile down to the youth court to be tried (if he pleaded not guilty) or sentenced (if he pleaded guilty), as the case may be.[58]

Finally, there may be circumstances where the juvenile is not jointly charged with the adult, but the offences with which they are both charged are linked in some way, for example, one or other is accused of aiding and abetting the other, or the charges arise out of the same or connected circumstances. If they plead differently, they can go their separate ways. But in such cases, if both plead not guilty, then the adult magistrates' court has a *discretion* to hear the cases together if it chooses. And if that court began to hear the case against the co-defendants before realising that one was in fact a juvenile, then again it has a discretion to complete what was started.

In any event, if a juvenile is tried in the adult magistrates' court, then the court has a discretion to put reporting restrictions and other appropriate measures in place.

58 Again the adult magistrates has power to try the juvenile and limited powers to sentence him, but would most often remit to the youth court.

revision tips

- Be aware of the basics of youth court sentencing options. Know the important distinctions (especially as between children and young people) and check your exam syllabus so you know where to focus your attention. Note carefully the ages of offenders in exam questions: this is the detail the examiner wants to test (e.g., as regards DTOs).
- Remember that juveniles are sometimes tried in the adult courts, but adults are *never* tried in the youth court. Juveniles have *no right* to elect trial by jury.
- You are almost bound to get a question involving an adult and juvenile accused. It might help to think of them as holding hands if they appear or are kept together for their trial: in such cases the adult always dictates where the two start out (adult magistrates' court) and end up. But if the two become dis-engaged (often by one pleading guilty and the other not guilty), then the two can go their separate ways and the juvenile will usually be 'pulled down' to the youth court (if that is where, without the adult's involvement, he would have naturally ended up).

It is worth reading ...

The judgment of Coulson J in the tragic and well-publicised case of *R v Cornick* [2014] EWHC 3623. It is (as always) very readable. It clearly demonstrates the mechanics of sentencing and contains useful insight into reporting restrictions.

Dip into Part 18 of the Sentencing Guidelines. Note what is covered, especially the bits in bold.

CHAPTER 12

Costs and legal aid

Before going on to consider appeals and so on, it remains to say a few words about public funding and costs - a very few words, as it happens, since this aspect of procedural law tends to be changeable. Because these two aspects of litigation impinge on one another to such a degree, it makes sense to cover them together. Certainly the changes wrought by LASPO 2012 make inroads into both. What follows is a brief outline, so you can grasp the fundamentals and watch for further developments.

1. PUBLIC FUNDING

A person with the means to pay privately for legal advice and representation can, of course, choose to do so if arrested or charged with a criminal offence. For many people, however, this is not an option; any help they receive must be financed by public funds (often called 'legal aid'). The body who (since 2013) administers funding for such services is the Legal Aid Agency (LAA),[1] which (in a previous incarnation) was created 'for the purposes of securing that individuals involved in criminal investigations or criminal proceedings have access to such advice, assistance and representation as the interests of justice require'.[2]

Just how such services should be dispensed (especially, the Ministry of Justice

1 Headed by a Director of Legal Aid Casework. Many of these organisational changes were brought about by LASPO 2012, Pt 1, which came into effect in April 2013.

2 Access to Justice Act 1999, s 12(1)

would no doubt add, in an age of 'austerity'), and what the interests of justice in fact require, is hotly debated by the legal profession and the government. For some years now, these services have been 'contracted out' to firms of solicitors on the basis of 'standard crime contracts' (including set rates of pay and so forth). Concerns were heightened in 2013 by government proposals to reduce rates of pay and introduce 'price competitive tendering' into the equation. To many this would have translated into 'cut price' justice. In 2016 these plans were dropped following two consultations and legal action by the professionals delivering the service.[3] But legal aid for Crown Court cases is now subject to a means-test, which has resulted in a worrying increase in the number of defendants acting without the benefit of legal representation.

In a few areas, a 'Public Defender Service', apparently modelled on its American namesake, has operated (initially as a pilot scheme). It has its own salaried staff to 'provide independent advice, assistance and representation on criminal matters.' This has been controversial, and so far is not co-existing very happily with law firms and other self-employed practitioners doing legal aid work.[4]

At the police station, legal aid is offered under an 'initial' advice and assistance scheme. Where it has been ascertained that an individual 'qualifies' for such help, then the 'sort of advice and assistance that an individual might need whilst in custody' must be made available to him. Qualifying requirements should focus, and be based, on the interest of justice. The trend has been to move towards a system where help is dispensed (initially at any rate) by telephoning the Defence Solicitor Call Centre, where it will be decided whether a solicitor should attend, or if legal advice will be given over the phone: a sort of 'DSCC 111 service', if you will.

Entitlement to legal aid for those needing legal help in other contexts, and especially representation at court,[5] is determined both by reference to the merits of the application (the 'interest of justice' test) and the means of the applicant.

3 For more information see researchbriefings.parliament.uk/ResearchBriefing/Summary/SN06628 and lawsociety.org.uk/news/stories/new-legal-aid-crime-contracts-for-2017-what-you-need-to-know. The 2017 contracts are not dissimilar to the 2010 contracts.

4 See, e.g. lawgazette.co.uk/practice/call-to-review-public-defender-service/5039489.article

5 Defined broadly by LASPO 2012, s 14

Recipients of certain welfare benefits will automatically meet the means test. Where the interests of justice lie depends on common sense factors: for example, how likely is the person to lose his liberty? Are there substantial questions of law to be considered? How important to the outcome of the case is the skill of witness handling? Can the individual understand what is going on?[6] Crudely put, they amount to asking: does this person (and/or the court) really need a lawyer in attendance? Some cases are sufficiently serious that, *if* the means test is satisfied, legally aided representation would likely follow - defendants in the Crown Court are automatically deemed to have passed the interest of justice test.[7]

2. COSTS

Costs are inextricably linked to public funding, because commonly the state is often the only viable source of funds with which to make payments in respect of legal costs. The idea of the loser paying the winner's costs applies in principle to criminal cases, but losing defendants tend to be impecunious, so it can be something of a one-way street (and one which the government would like to be less trodden). Public prosecutors have financial backing in the form of 'central funds' if defendants are entitled to a costs order, but the prosecution are more likely to win than defendants, many of whom do not have the means to pay costs. That is one reason why they need legal aid! This is the government's dilemma as they see it: lots of money going out, but little coming in. And so another way of reducing the costs of legal aid (besides capping amounts paid to lawyers dispensing legally aided services) is to limit how much can be paid by way of costs to successful defendants who paid privately for their legal services.

6 *Ibid*, s 17(2) which effectively replicates its legislative predecessor.

7 See Criminal Legal Aid (Contribution Orders) Regulations (SI 483 No 2013) as amended. And see the gov.uk website for basic information of criminal legal aid means testing. Some recipients of public funding may be asked to make a 'contribution' to their legal costs (depending on means).

There are thus two aspects of payment of costs: *who pays* and *how much.* The principles in criminal cases apply in much the same way whether the case was tried in the magistrates' court or the Crown Court (and indeed in much the same way as in civil cases, adapted to the exigencies of criminal cases).[8]

DEFENDANT'S COST ORDER

As to who should pay: in principle, a 'defendant's costs order' should normally be made whenever (an individual) defendant has been acquitted or is successful on appeal, unless there are 'positive reasons for not doing so'. An example of a 'positive reason' for not making such an order might be where the defendant's conduct brought suspicion on himself so that the prosecution was knowingly misled into thinking the case against him was stronger than it was.[9] A court must state its reason whenever denying a defendant a costs order on this basis.

In the case of public prosecutions, such costs are paid by the State out of central funds for 'such amount as the court considers reasonably sufficient' to compensate the defendant for any expenses 'properly incurred by him in the proceedings.' For these purposes, legal costs are defined as 'fees, charges, disbursements and other amounts payable in respect of advocacy services or litigation services including, in particular, expert witness costs.'[10] So *only* legal costs are covered, not costs like loss of earnings because of the time spent in court *defending* the case.

As to how much should be paid: in practice, capped legal aid rates will (usually) apply but where appropriate, a defendant's costs order may be for such 'lesser amount as the court considers just and reasonable' - such may be appropriate, for example, when an accused is acquitted on some but not all charges.[11]

So, in the magistrates' court, *privately paying* defendants may, if acquitted, be entitled to recover their legal costs, but will in any event recover no more than

8 The CrimPr rules on costs (which sound, at times like their civil counterpart) are found at Pt 45.

9 Practice Direction (Costs in Criminal Proceedings) [2015] EWCA Crim 1568, as amended (2015 Costs PD) and see BCrP D 33.9

10 Prosecution of Offences Act 1985 (POA 1985), s 16 and 16A(10)

11 *Ibid* s 16(7) and see BCrP D 33.13

amounts payable under prevailing legal aid rates.[12] This is now also the position in the Crown Court, but for a time (cases brought between 2012 and 2014, roughly) privately paying defendants were not able to recover any of their legal costs following an acquittal. This was justified by the fact that all defendants in the Crown Court were then entitled to legal aid, whatever their means (subject in some cases to a contribution), thus rendering it (theoretically) unnecessary for defendants to pay for what was usually far more expensive private legal representation (which the state would have to repay if a costs order was made against it). There were lots of complaints about this blanket ban. In 2014 legal aid in the Crown Court was also made subject to means testing and so, where legal aid has been applied for and refused (*this is an important pre-condition*), a defendant's costs order can be made there, but again with relevant amounts capped at legal aid rates.[13]

A defendant's costs order will often be redundant for a legally aided defendant, but where such a person was late getting public funding or was required to make contributions to his costs, it will still be important to him to be able to recover the amount he is out of pocket.[14]

PROSECUTION COSTS

Where the defendant is convicted, he may be ordered to pay the prosecution such costs as the court considers 'just and reasonable'. This will vary depending not only on his means and ability to pay, but also the nature of the case, how reasonable the not guilty plea was, and so on. The amount of costs payable should be specified in the order.[15] Usually the costs payable by a losing defendant are considerably less than the actual costs of the proceedings because the court has to take into account the means of the offender and the effect of any financial order it makes. Public prosecutors are rarely paid out of public funds, of course, since this would effectively

12 See BCrP D 33.6
13 2015 Costs PD, para 2.2.4
14 See BCrP D 33.19
15 POA 1985, s 18(1),(5)

amount to the state paying itself! Costs orders against convicted defendants should not be used to punish those who had the choice and elected trial on indictment, although of course the fact that the Crown Court was the more expensive option will necessarily figure into the calculation.

Where the offence is indictable, a *private* prosecutor may be awarded costs, out of central funds, in an amount the court thinks reasonably sufficient to compensate him or her for expenses properly incurred. As with the defendant's costs order, in appropriate circumstances, such lesser amount as the court considers just and reasonable may be ordered.[16]

Whoever wins or loses, a costs order should always reflect the fact that costs have been incurred by an 'act or omission' on the part of a party. So if, for example, a day was wasted because prosecution witnesses were not at court, the costs wasted would be ordered against the prosecution even if ultimately the defendant was convicted.

revision tips

- Check your exam syllabus to know where to focus your detailed attention.
- This area of law is changeable and prone to being buffeted by the political winds, so keep your eye on the on-going debate.

It is worth reading ...

R v Penner [2010] EWCA Crim 1155 is a good read on all sorts of levels. It reinforces the importance of the (previous edition of the) Criminal Procedure Rules and includes some evidential revision as well. But notice the conversation at the end (between the bench, who were not best pleased with Mr Penner, and counsel) about legal aid and costs. It includes the understatement of the year by Thomas LJ to the effect that 'these regulations sometimes change'.

16 *Ibid*, s 17(2A), inserted by LASPO 2012

CHAPTER 13

Appeals

The outcome of a trial is important not just for the individual accused, whose liberty may be at stake, but also for public confidence in the criminal justice system. We all need to know that judicial decisions derive from due and proper consideration under the law. An effective appellate system helps not only to correct errors but to maintain faith in the process. A vital aspect of your job as legal advisor and advocate will be to know when and whether, in your particular case, an appeal is advisable. You can be pretty sure a client who has just been sent to prison will want to know.

You might think that only convicted defendants launch appeals, but you would be very wrong. Sometimes the prosecution can ask for an aspect of a case to be reviewed, and the courts even have self-correcting mechanisms.

Subject to a court's ability to 'tweak' its own decisions, the natural direction of travel for appeals is, of course, up the chain of command, so that generally appeals from the decisions of magistrates go to the Crown Court; appeals from Crown Court decisions go to the Court of Appeal; and (when warranted, which is rare) appeals from the Court of Appeal go to the Supreme Court. But sometimes appeals can take something of a side trip to the High Court, which is off crime's everyday beaten path, lying (in hierarchical terms) somewhere between the Crown Court and the Court of Appeal. It is as well to have a clear idea of these relationships.[1]

1 There is a neat little diagram in *Practical Approach*, Fig 26.1

Appeal procedure can be quite complex, and when you are first learning the topic you can easily be overwhelmed by the technicalities. Start by getting a basic, but confident grip on the 'who, what, when, where, how and why' of criminal appeals: for example, who can appeal, where does appeal lie, when can the appeal be made, what form does the appeal take, is permission required, what is to be lost or gained from appealing.

To help you on your way, what follows is a brief guide and introduction.[2]

1. APPEALS FROM THE MAGISTRATES' COURT

A. POWERS OF MAGISTRATES TO 'RECTIFY' MISTAKES: S 142 MCA 1980

S 142 MCA 1980 effectively gives magistrates the power *to correct their own errors*. This is a convenient and inexpensive way of dealing with a mistake which everyone, the magistrates included, agree has been made. So, where a person has been convicted by a magistrates' court (whether by pleading or being found guilty) and it subsequently appears that it would be *in the interests of justice* to do so, the magistrates' court itself may direct that the case be re-tried before a differently constituted bench.[3] The order for a re-trial can be made by the very same magistrates who convicted the defendant (and made the mistake), or by a different bench.

The mistake might be procedural or legal, and the decision to retry a case is entirely a matter for the magistrates,[4] but the power is not a wide or generalised one. It has been described as one which should be used in relatively limited situations - something akin to a 'slip rule'.[5] A good example would be where an accused has been convicted in his absence, which was later explained by his having been in prison at the time.[6] The point is to avoid an expensive appeal where a simple and

2 You will find more detail, as always, in BCrP.

3 MCA 1980, s 142(2)

4 Although the decision could itself be the subject of appeal.

5 See, e.g., *R (Williamson) v City of Westminster Magistrates' Court* [2012] EWHC 1444 (Admin) and see BCrP D 22.73

6 See, e.g., *R (Morsby) v Tower Bridge Magistrates' Court* (2008) 172 JP 155

non-controversial error can easily be put right.

There is no time limit for asking the magistrates to exercise this power (they may also act on their own initiative), but their ability to do so is lost once an appeal has been made to either the Crown Court or the High Court,[7] as discussed below.

In similar fashion, the magistrates can also vary or rescind their sentencing decisions following a plea or finding of guilty.[8] This is essentially a power to 'tweak' a sentence where 'the mistake is quickly identified and it is accepted on all sides that a mistake has been made'.[9] It would only be 'very exceptionally' that this power could be used to increase a sentence.[10]

B. APPEAL TO CROWN COURT BY DEFENDANTS

Only convicted persons may appeal to the Crown Court. The extent to which such an appeal may be brought depends, essentially, on whether the accused pleaded guilty, or was found guilty after summary trial.

(i) Appeal followed a guilty plea and sentence imposed by magistrates

Generally speaking if an accused pleaded guilty, he may only appeal against his sentence - no matter how lenient.[11] Clearly a convicted person would be more apt to be grateful for, rather than critical of, a sentence like an absolute or conditional discharge, but the option is left to him.

The logic of usually only allowing appeals against sentence following a guilty plea is obvious. If an accused pleads guilty it is hardly surprising or objectionable that he was convicted. Of course, as we have seen, it is important that a plea of guilty is given freely and unequivocally, so if the Crown Crown agrees that the guilty plea was 'equivocal' (that is, ambiguous or given under duress),[12] it can 'remit' the case back to the magistrates' court for it to be tried on a not guilty plea.

7 MCA 1981, s 142(2A)

8 *Ibid*, s 142 (1). The power can be exercised on its own initiative or on written application by a party: see CrimPR, r 28.4(2)

9 *Holme v Liverpool City Justices* (2005) 169 JP 306, per Collins J at [30]

10 *Ibid*, see [42]-[43] and BCrP D 23.23/24

11 MCA 1980, s 108(3)

12 See Ch. 8 and BCrP D 29.4

(ii) Appeal following a guilty plea and committal for sentence

The situation is slightly different if the accused pleaded guilty and then was committed to the Crown Court for sentence. Because, in effect, the Crown Court has got its hands on the case, it retains a general discretion to direct the magistrates to rehear the case on a not guilty plea. The latter may feel aggrieved by such a command, but (as the lower court) they must comply.[13]

(iii) Appeal following a not guilty plea

A person found guilty following a not guilty plea and summary trial, may appeal to the Crown Court against conviction and/or sentence. Notice of appeal must be given in writing to the prosecutor and the clerk of the relevant magistrates' court within *21 days of sentence* being passed (even if the appeal is only against conviction and there was a gap in time between conviction and sentence).[14] If proper notice is given in time,[15] *no leave to appeal is required.*

The magistrates will be asked to grant bail pending appeal, if they have just passed an immediate custodial sentence.[16] If they refuse, the Crown Court can be asked to grant bail. Given how relatively short sentences in the magistrates' court tend to be, it can matter a lot to an appellant to be out on bail during this time; otherwise he might find that he has served much of his sentence before the appeal is even heard. For this reason (amongst others), appeals of those in custody are usually prioritised in the Crown Court list.

Constitution of court

Such appeals are heard by a circuit judge (or recorder), who will normally sit with two lay magistrates.[17] An appeal against conviction takes the form of a *rehearing*, so in effect the entire case is re-run. The defence may ask for a copy of the clerk's

---

13 *Camberwell Green Justices ex parte Sloper* (1978) 69 Cr App R 1

14 CrimPR, r 34.2(2)

15 And the Crown Court can extend time for giving notice and so on: *ibid*, r 34.2(3) and see generally BCrP D 29.6

16 MCA 1980, s 113(1)

17 Senior Courts Act 1981 (SCA 1981), s 74 and see BCrP D 29.7

notes of the evidence given in the summary trial, and this request should be met if practicable. But neither side is limited to the evidence called at the original trial. If the appeal is against sentence alone, it is essentially only the bit of the process between conviction and sentencing which is repeated.

Powers of Crown Court on appeal

As you might expect, the Crown Court's powers on appeal are very extensive. They can do just about anything; they can confirm, reverse or vary any part of the decision appealed against. They can remit the case back to the magistrates' court (for example, if the plea was equivocal) or substitute their own finding.

So far as sentence is concerned, the Crown Court has the power to pass any sentence which the magistrates themselves *could have passed, even if more severe* than the sentence the lower court had in fact passed - even if only the conviction was appealed against.[18] It is fair to say that it is unusual for the Crown Court to increase an appellent's sentence, but this power (along with the risk of an order to pay the prosecutions costs) acts as something of a disincentive against the pursuit of silly, unmeritorious appeals just for the sake of doing so. Given that no leave is required to appeal from the magistrates to the Crown Court, it is important that *some* deterrent is operative.

C. APPEALS TO HIGH COURT ON LEGAL OR JURISDICTIONAL QUESTIONS

There are two methods, open to *both defence and prosecution*, of appealing aspects of magistrates' decisions to the High Court: (i) by asking the justices to 'state a case' for the opinion of the High Court on a question of law or jurisdiction, or (ii) by an application for judicial review.

18 SCA 1981, s 48(1). This power should be carefully deployed to avoid injustice. If the appeal is formally abandoned however, there is no power to increase the sentence. See BCrP D 29.10-29.13

(i) Appeal by way of case stated

This is a venerable, if somewhat arcane means of seeking guidance from the Administrative Court[19] of the High Court on a legal or jurisdictional question which has arisen from a case in the magistrates' court. This method of appeal is available to both prosecution and defence, but must await the final outcome of the case. Typically it is used to attack either a conviction[20] or an acquittal following summary trial, on the grounds that the magistrates either made a decision which was *wrong in law* or *in excess of their jurisdiction*.[21] The magistrates' court effectively gives leave to appeal when it agrees to 'state the case' to the High Court, which it does in the form of a question after having set out in some detail the findings of fact (but not the evidence) which have given rise to it.

The sorts of issues which might properly be raised for the High Court's consideration are: whether the magistrates were entitled to hear the case; whether inadmissible evidence was admitted or admissible evidence wrongly excluded; whether there was, on the evidence, a case to answer.

Sometimes it can be difficult to know where the line is to be drawn between bad decisions (on the facts) and wrong decisions (on the law); but strictly speaking only the latter may form the basis of an appeal by way of case stated. If, for example, the defence contend that the justices' decision was against the weight of the evidence (as opposed to one no reasonable tribunal could have arrived at), then their only remedy is to go to the Crown Court for a rehearing of the evidence.[22]

An application for the magistrates to state a case must be made within 21 days of the decision being appealed against and is served on the relevant magistrates' court and all parties. Magistrates can refuse to state a case (for example, because they consider it frivolous), but if they agree to do so it is usually the court's legal adviser who drafts it, after which the magistrates sign it and send it to the appellant.[23]

---

19 Also still known as the Divisional Court of the Queen's Bench Division.

20 It could also be used to attack a sentence handed down by magistrates, if it were in excess of their jurisdiction. But this rarely happens.

21 MCA 1980, s 111(1)

22 See, e.g., *Oladimeji v DPP* [2006] EWHC 1199 (Admin)

23 A district judge may well draft his own. There is a useful example set out in *Practical Approach*, Ch. 27, para 27.21 and see useful summary features at BCrP D 29.18

Again, bail may be granted pending the hearing in the Administrative Court, which must consist of at least two judges, but will usually have three. The court decides entirely on the basis of the facts set out in the written 'case stated' and legal argument by counsel - no new evidence is adduced. If there are two judges sitting who do not agree, the one who agrees with the court below prevails, so the appeal will fail.

(ii) Judicial review

This too is a venerable route to the Administrative Court, but is not so much a method of appeal, but a means of invoking the High Court's inherent *supervisory jurisdiction* over the acts and omissions of public bodies, including inferior judicial tribunals, to ensure they are lawful.

Broadly speaking, the purpose of judicial review is to prevent magistrates' courts (and other inferior tribunals) from breaching natural justice or exceeding their jurisdiction, and/or to insist that they exercise their proper functions appropriately. The High Court exercises this jurisdiction by issuing one or other of the three following orders (known as 'prerogative orders'):

(a) A quashing order (which quashes the decision of an inferior tribunal)
(b) A prohibiting order (which prevents an inferior court acting unlawfully or in excess of its jurisdiction)
(c) A mandatory order (which compels the inferior tribunal to act)

Permission to apply for judicial review is always required; this in itself is an involved procedure. The time periods are also very tight. Application must be made within three months of the decision complained of, and in any event, 'promptly'.

Judicial review is not an easy option, but occasionally it is the right one.[24]

2. APPEALS FROM THE CROWN COURT

Most[25] appeals arising from trial on indictment go, in the first instance - and only with permission - to the Criminal Division of the Court of Appeal.[26] The vast majority of these are brought by defendants seeking to quash convictions and/or reduce sentences. But there are other avenues to the Court of Appeal open to prosecutors or the state. A Crown Court judge also has a limited ability to fine tune his or her own sentences (without troubling the Court of Appeal).

Work preliminary to an appeal (for example, applications for leave to appeal or for bail pending appeal) is usually carried out by a single judge, on the papers. Vital administrative support comes from the Registrar of Criminal Appeals, who is essentially the first port of call in respect of applications to the Court of Appeal and is in charge of navigating the case through the appeal system.

A. CROWN COURT JUDGE'S ABILITY TO VARY OWN SENTENCE

The Crown Court cannot itself decide to re-run one of its own trials, as the magistrates' court can, but the sentencing judge[27] in the Crown Court has a limited ability to 'tweak' the sentence he or she personally has passed. There is a strict time limit too, so that a sentence imposed or order made by the Crown Court judge when dealing with an offender 'may be varied or rescinded within 56 days of being passed or made'.[28] If this time has passed, the self-correcting ability is lost.

The obvious use to which this power is put is to correct minor errors made by the court when passing sentence. It can also be used to reduce a sentence if, on

24 Judicial review is a vast topic and beyond the scope of this book. See generally BCrP D 29.25ff. There is a neat little comparison of appeal by way of case stated and judicial review in BCrP D 29.42

25 Appeals by case stated or judicial review, discussed above, are generally used to correct errors in the magistrates' court, but can also be used to challenge decisions by the Crown Court which do not concern trial on indictment (for example, decisions on appeals from magistrates).

26 The jurisdiction, powers and procedure there are primarily governed by the Criminal Appeal Act 1968 (CAA 1968) and CrimPR, parts 36ff

27 Only the sentencing judge has this power. Any lay justices who may have been involved (if the case was heard on appeal from

reflection, the judge feels he or she was too harsh. It is possible to use the power to increase or substitute one sentence for another, although only exceptionally would it be appropriate to replace a non-custodial sentence with a custodial sentence.[29]

B. APPEALS AGAINST CONVICTION OR SENTENCE BY DEFENDANTS

This is the mainstay of the work of the Court of Appeal. Appeals can be against conviction only, sentence only - or against both. *Permission and grounds of appeal are always required.* The hearing consists of submissions on errors of law or process - evidence may be, but is rarely, heard. In all these aspects, appeals heard in the Court of Appeal could not be more different to appeals heard in the Crown Court. This is not surprising really, given that the Court of Appeal (unlike the Crown Court) is not a trial venue!

(i) Appeal against conviction

(a) Permission to appeal is necessary

Unless the trial judge certifies the case as fit for appeal, the Court of Appeal must be asked to grant leave.[30] As you can imagine, it is rare for the judge to certify his or her own case for appeal, but a novel point may have emerged or there may be some other cogent reason[31] for the judge to consider it appropriate for an aspect of the case to be reviewed by the appellate court. Most often, however, leave must be sought from the Court of Appeal itself.

(b) Notice Procedure

Appeals (or application for leave to appeal) against conviction should be made within *28 days* of conviction.[32] Notice, plus grounds in support, are lodged at the Crown Court where the proceedings took place, which will forward them on to the Registrar

the magistrates' court) do not need to be present. Powers of Criminal Courts (Sentencing) Act 2000 (PCC(S)A 2000), s 155(4) and see *R v Morrison* [2005] EWCA Crim 2705

28 PCC(S)A 2000, s 155. The power cannot be exercised (rather obviously) if an appeal or request for permission to appeal have already been determined: BCrP D 20.95

29 See examples at *ibid*, D 20.96

30 CAA 1968, s 1(2)(a)

31 See BCrP D 26.8 and CrimPD III 14H.1-4

32 The 28 day period may be extended: see BCrP D 27.12

of Criminal Appeals. If counsel has advised this course of action, he or she will draft the notice and grounds. This nearly always involves three separate steps: drafting 'initial grounds' based on counsel's trial notes, then requesting a trial transcript, upon receipt of which (assuming the appeal still seems viable) the initial grounds can finally be 'perfected'.[33] The papers, which by this time will be very detailed, are put before the single judge, who acts as a kind of filter. The prosecution's view may be sought. If that judge refuses leave to appeal, the application can be renewed before the Court of Appeal itself. Applicants[34] who are refused leave by the single judge, often take it no further. One reason is that if they are in custody, they become vulnerable to a 'loss of time' direction, discussed below. For obvious reasons, leave to appeal against conviction will rarely be granted if the conviction was the result of a guilty plea.[35]

(c) The 'loss of time' direction

The Court of Appeal has at its disposal an important (if not necessarily very effective) means of discouraging hopeless appeals from offenders who have been given prison sentences. It is known as a 'loss of time' direction. Unless and until such an order is given, the time that an appellant spends in custody while his appeal is being considered is obviously part of any custodial sentence he is serving. But *if* the court makes a loss of time direction, the amount of time specified in the order (which will be time which the court considers it wasted dealing with an appeal which was devoid of merit) *will not be counted* as time spent serving his custodial sentence. In effect, the amount of time 'lost' gets added back onto the appellant's time in custody.

Such directions can be given by the single judge when refusing leave to appeal (which is usually effective in stopping any renewed application for leave being made) or by the full court when dismissing an appeal (which could also increase the amount of time to be 'lost', if such a direction had already been given by the single judge).

33 See CrimPR, r 39.3 and BCrP D 27.1-27.13 for procedural detail. Note that counsel should never draft grounds which are not properly arguable.

34 Strictly, an applicant only becomes an 'appellant' once leave to appeal has been given.

35 But it is possible if the plea was ambiguous, based on an incorrect ruling of the court or followed inappropriate legal advice. See generally BCrP D 26.9

It will not help if counsel has encouraged a hopeless appeal lacking 'substantial and particularised' grounds, and defendants should always be warned about the risks of a loss of time direction being made. Equally, the court should use the power fairly and wisely. In the case of *R v Hart*,[36] the court expressed the view that this particular disincentive needed to be employed more often, and in four unrelated applications gave the same direction, namely that 28 days of the period in custody should not count as having been served. Still, one might wonder if most appellants might think an extra month 'added on' to a sentence calculated in years might well be a price worth paying for a chance of a successful appeal.

(d) Grounds of appeal against conviction

There is only one single ground of appeal: that the conviction is 'unsafe'.[37] This can cover a multitude of sins, however, in particular that the trial judge made an error of law or there was a material irregularity in the course of the trial or an error occurred which so prejudiced the fairness of the trial that the conviction should be quashed. A defendant's right to a fair trial is obviously an important part of this equation; even guilty people are entitled to due process. As Mantell LJ put it in *R v Davis*:[38]

> The court is concerned with the safety of the conviction. A conviction can never be safe if there is a doubt about guilt. A conviction may be unsafe where there is no doubt about guilt, but the trial process has been vitiated by serious unfairness or significant legal misdirection. That being so, there is no tension between s 2(1)(a) of the Criminal Appeal Act 1968 and s 3(1) of the Human Rights Act 1998.[39]

36 [2006] EWCA Crim 3239. And see CrimPD IX 39E 1.1/2

37 CCA 1985, s 2, which replaced an earlier, more detailed description of three grounds of appeal. There seems little doubt that the generic description 'unsafe' includes the specific grounds set out previously. The closest analogy is family law, where the one ground for divorce is that the marriage has 'broken down' irretrievably, but this can be manifested in a number of different ways. See BCrP D 26.15/16

38 [2001] 1 Cr App R 8

39 Article 6 of the ECHR (right to fair trial) is incorporated into British law by the Human Rights Act 1998, s 3(1)

Grounds of appeal tend to sub-divide into two sorts of mistakes:

- those manifested by what the judge did or did not *do* when conducting the trial (for example, excluded admissible evidence, admitted inadmissible evidence, or wrongly rejected a submission of no case to answer and so on), *and/or*
- those manifested by what the judge did or did not *say* in summing up to the jury (for example, failed to direct the jury properly on the burden and standard of proof, failed to put the defence case fairly to the jury, misdirected the jury on the law and so on).[40]

(e) The appeal hearing

A full Court of Appeal hearing appeals against conviction will usually consist of (at least) three Lord Justices of Appeal, although in especially important cases five, or even seven, will sit. Unsurprisingly, the number must be uneven.

The Crown will almost always be represented by counsel where there is an appeal against conviction. If the accused is in custody, bail is unlikely to be granted pending consideration of the appeal, unless the circumstances are exceptional, since the risk of having to return to prison might disincline the appellant to do so. The accused need not be present at the appeal hearing, but is usually entitled to be there if he wishes (via live link if appropriate).

The hearing is based on legal submissions focused on the grounds of appeal, which should be drafted ('settled') with 'sufficient particularity'.[41] These will be repeated and possibly amplified and/or clarified in skeleton arguments.[42] These appeals do not take the form of a rehearing. Having said that, the Court of Appeal may hear additional evidence if it is 'necessary or expedient in the interests of

40 As to the Court of Appeal's approach to the most common errors, see BCrP D 26.21ff

41 See Guide to Proceedings in the Court of Appeal (Criminal Division) available at justice.gov.uk/downloads/courts/court-of-appeal/criminal-division/proc_guide.pdf

42 See CrimPD IX, 39 F 1-3

43 CAA 1968, s 23

44 *Ibid*, s 23(2)

45 See *R v Smith* [2014] 2 Cr App R 1 (1) and discussion at BCrP D 27.24ff

justice'.[43] This discretion is wide, but will be exercised with care. In considering whether to receive any additional evidence the court should ask itself common sense questions, including: is the evidence credible?; would hearing it assist the court in making its decision?; would it have been admissible at trial?; is there a reasonable explanation for the failure to adduce the evidence at trial?[44] The Court of Appeal is not, generally speaking, the place to fill in evidential gaps left at trial; the appeal courts would grind to a halt if evidence which could or should have been produced at trial is routinely admitted when convictions are being reviewed. It is the jury, not the Court of Appeal, who is supposed to hear the evidence and determine the facts of the case.[45]

(f) Possible outcome of appeals against conviction

Following appeal against conviction, the Court of Appeal has, as you might expect, a range of options, including the following:

- Dismiss the appeal. This might, but will not necessarily be coupled with a loss of time direction (discussed above).
- Allow the appeal and quash the conviction.
- Allow the appeal, and order a re-trial.[46] A re-trial will be ordered if the Court of Appeal considers this to be in the *interests of justice.* Much will depend on the length of time which has elapsed since the original trial, how long the defendant has been in custody, the state of the evidence and public opinion.[47] When a new trial is ordered, a fresh indictment is preferred, usually for the same offence alleged in the original indictment, but the Court of Appeal could order that the accused be tried for a lesser or alternative offence. It will also remand the accused in custody or on bail, as it thinks fit. Note that if the appellant is convicted on the fresh indictment, the sentence passed *must not be more severe* than first time around. It could, of course, be more lenient.[48]

46 This produces the same effective outcome as declaring the trial a nullity and issuing a writ of venire de novo, a common law power which still exists.

47 See, e.g., *R v Taylor* (1994) 98 Cr App R 361

48 See CAA 1968, Sch 2

- Allow part of the appeal, and dismiss the other part. If they do this, the Court of Appeal may pass a new sentence on the remaining conviction (but this cannot exceed the totality of the sentence imposed by the trial court[49]).
- Find the appellant guilty of a lesser/alternative offence. If the jury could have convicted of a 'lesser offence' than that contained in the indictment, the Court of Appeal could effectively do the same thing; for example, quash a murder conviction and replace it with manslaughter. Similarly, if there are two counts on the indictment and the jury acquitted on count 1 and convicted on count 2, the Court of Appeal could reverse the verdicts.[50]
- Make any relevant ancillary orders. For example, as to costs or permission to appeal to the Supreme Court.

(ii) Appeal against sentence

The procedure for appealing against sentence[51] is very similar to that for appealing against conviction. Often the two are pursued in tandem. So far as an appeal against sentence is concerned, note the following differences:

(a) Notice of application

Leave to appeal is required for an appeal against sentence just as it is for an appeal against conviction (discussed above), although it is even less likely that the sentencing judge would grant a certificate that the issue is fit for appeal. This would be a little like saying to the Court of Appeal, *"I've just passed a silly sentence - see if you can spot the mistake"*. If only appealing against sentence, the 28 day notice period runs from the *date of sentence*, which may be later than the date of conviction. If appealing against

49 *Ibid*, s 4(3)
50 See discussion at BCrP D 26.40
51 Which has the same broad meaning as in appeals from the magistrates: CAA 1968, s 50. Procedure is set out (in detail) at BCrP D 26.42ff

both, however, time runs runs from the date of conviction. Again, the 28 day period can be extended.

(b) Ground for appeal against sentence

A large degree of discretion resides in the sentencing judge, and the appellate courts will be loath to interfere with a sentence which falls within an acceptable range given the circumstances of the case. Some judges sentence at the harsher end of the scale than others, and it is not the Court of Appeal's job to pass judgment on the rights and wrongs of individual judges exercising their legitimate discretion. There has to be some fundamental mistake for an appeal against sentence to succeed.[52] Thus, the grounds most likely to succeed in this context are that:

- The sentence passed was wrong *in law* (typically the judge had no jurisdiction to pass the sentence under appeal).
- The sentence passed was wrong *in principle* (for example, if it can be argued that the appellant was sent to prison when the custody threshold had not been crossed[53]) and/or the sentence was *manifestly excessive* (such a sentence would also be wrong in principle. The sentencing guidelines should keep sentences within reasonable bounds, but this is a common ground of appeal).
- The *approach* to sentencing was wrong (for example, the judge took into consideration factors irrelevant to sentence).
- The *procedure prior to sentence* was wrong (for example, the judge did not wait for a pre-sentence report).
- There is an *unacceptable disparity of sentence* between co-accused (this ground usually needs to join forces with one of the others to be successful).
- *Legitimate sense of grievance* (this might happen, for example, where an accused was led to believe that a particular type of sentence would follow the

52 See, e.g., *R v Gumbs* (1926) 19 Cr App R 74 and see generally BCrP D 26.50 for a review of typical grounds of appeal. Note that it is hoped that fewer mistakes will occur if and when the sentencing regime is rationalised and codified.

53 See Ch. 10 (Ch. 11 for juveniles)

recommendation of a pre-sentence report - even if the sentence actually passed was not, of itself, too severe).

(c) Conduct of hearing

Appeals against sentence may be determined by a *two* judge court, although if they are not in agreement, the matter will need to be reheard in front of a three judge court. The prosecution is rarely represented by counsel when the defendant appeals against his sentence, because it is not the prosecution's job to lobby in favour of a particular sanction. However, as we shall see there are occasions when the state, in the form of the Attorney-General, can make its own application to the Court of Appeal regarding the sentence handed down by the Crown Court judge.

(d) Possible outcomes on appeal against sentence by the defendant

On appeal against sentence, the powers of the Court of Appeal are very broad, with one important caveat. It can quash any sentence or order which is the subject of the appeal and replace it with any sentence or order it considers appropriate so long as:

- the sentence it passes/order it makes is one which the Crown Court *could have* passed/made *and*
- taking the case as a whole, the appellant is *not more severely* dealt with on appeal than he was by the Crown Court.

So, unlike appeals from magistrate's courts, the Court of Appeal does *not* have the power to increase the appellant's sentence (looking at the case holistically). This is logical, given that the court has given the appellent leave to appeal, and so must have thought there was something to argue about. Note, however, that court could make a loss of time direction, which can definitely make a sentence seem a little longer, so there are still some risks.

C. PROSECUTORIAL ROUTES TO THE COURT OF APPEAL

Most of the time the Court of Appeal is being asked to quash convictions and reduce sentences. There was a time when that was virtually all it did - prosecutors barely had a look-in! In the 1970s, however, this tide began to turn. Nowadays there are several important ways in which the prosecuting authorities may challenge decisions in the Crown Court.

(i) Prosecution seeking retrial on fresh evidence

Since 2004, the prosecution have been able to seek to retry a defendant acquitted of certain serious offences, if new and compelling evidence has come to light and it is in the public interest to proceed again against him.[54] This is not a complaint about the original trial; rather, it is a limited exception to the principle of 'autrefois acquit'.[55] In effect, the prosecution applies for an order quashing the acquittal and directing a retrial for the offence. The DPP must agree that the application is warranted and leave to appeal must be sought from the Court of Appeal.

(ii) Attorney-General's reference on a point of law (following acquittal)

Except for the very limited circumstance described above, prosecutors have never been able to appeal against an acquittal on indictment in the same way that a defendant could appeal against conviction. This could mean that the trial judge might make an erroneous ruling in the course of the trial which goes unchallenged (because the defendant won't want to). To avoid this, it is possible for the Attorney-General to refer a point of law to the Court of Appeal for their opinion.[56] The idea is to ensure that errors of law are not replicated and so assist in *future* prosecutions, but whatever the appellate court decides on the legal point, the acquittal giving rise to it

54 CJA 2003, s 75-97. For an example of this provision in operation, see *R v A* [2009] 1 WLR 1947.

55 See discussion in Ch. 9

56 CJA 1988, ss 35-36

is unaffected. It cannot be overturned.

The defendant is given 28 days notice of the application, although he personally will likely be totally unconcerned with the outcome. His counsel may, however, wish to argue the point in front of the Court of Appeal on behalf of future defendants.[57]

(iii) Attorney-General's reference of 'unduly lenient' sentence

Normally, prosecutors are not concerned with the sentencing outcome of a case. They provide the trial judge with information to assist in sentencing, but they do not advocate for a particular outcome. In certain circumstances, however, there may be a feeling (possibly shared with the general public) that a convicted person has received a sentence which is far too lenient in the circumstances. If the offence is sufficiently grave (in other words, indictable only or a serious either-way offence specified in the legislation[58]), the Attorney-General can ask the Court of Appeal to review a sentence which he or she considers to be 'unduly lenient', that is, if it 'falls outside the range of sentence which the judge, applying his mind to all the relevant factors, could reasonably consider appropriate'.[59]

The *Court of Appeal* must grant *leave* before the matter can be argued in front of it. The procedure is the same as a defendant's appeal against sentence, discussed above.

On review, the Court of Appeal may (but need not necessarily) impose a more severe sentence than imposed at first instance, so long as it is a sentence which the Crown Court could lawfully have passed. In determining *whether* a sentence was unduly lenient, the Court of Appeal will not look at new material which was not available to the sentencing judge (since one cannot criticise a judge for not taking into account information he or she did not have). If, however, they decide the sentence *was* unduly lenient, they may then take into account any new information in deciding

57 See generally CrimPR, Pt 41. A good example of this procedure in action is *Attorney-General's Reference (No 1 of 1975)* [1975] QB 733, cited in BCrP D 28.6ff

58 The specified offences are set out in BCrP 28.11. A memorable example is the broadcaster Stuart Hall, whose sentence for historic sex abuse offences was doubled on the Attorney-General's reference: guardian.co.uk/uk-news/2013/jul/26/stuart-hall-sentence-sex-attacks.

59 See comments in *Attorney-General's Reference (No 4 of 1989)* [1990] 1 WLR 41, at 45-46

the extent, if any, to which it should be increased.[60] Any increase which the Court of Appeal is minded to pass may in part be mitigated by the stress of facing the prospect of being re-sentenced more harshly. So, for example, if the Court of Appeal was minded to increase a sentence from five years to eight years imprisonment, it might make allowance for the anxiety the proceedings may have caused the offender by settling on an increase to seven years.[61]

This procedure can also be used to increase a minimum term set by the court in a murder case. The life sentence itself, of course, is immutable.[62]

(iv) Prosecution appeals against adverse rulings (before acquittal)

The CJA 2003 introduced provisions[63] to give prosecutors the general ability to appeal against certain adverse rulings made by a judge trying a case on indictment - not after an acquittal (see above), but before, that is any time *before* the start of the judge's summing up. Leave is required, either from the trial judge (who would naturally be approached first) or the Court of Appeal. Two different types of rulings will be capable of challenge once these new provisions are fully in force: 'terminating rules' (in force) and 'evidentiary rulings' (not in force at the time of writing).

(a) 'Terminating' rulings

These are so called because if the appeal does not succeed, the ruling is so fatal to the prosecution case that it will be stopped dead in its tracks. A good example would be a half time ruling that there is no case to answer. When seeking leave to appeal a 'terminating' ruling, the prosecution must agree, in open court, that if leave to appeal is refused or the appeal abandoned, then an acquittal must inevitably follow. Given that the ruling to be appealed would terminate the prosecution case in any event, there is not really much to be lost in giving this assurance. The procedure is

60 *Attorney-General's reference (No 74 of 2010)* [2011] EWCA Crim 873

61 As in *Attorney-General's reference (No 1 of 1991)* [1991] Crim LR 725

62 CJA 2003, s 271 and see Ch. 10

63 CJA 2003 ss 57-74. For more details see BCrP D 16.74ff

complex, and beyond the scope of this book, but suffice to say that such appeals can be expedited (in which case the trial may be adjourned pending the decision) and the Court of Appeal in rendering its decision may confirm, reverse or vary the ruling appealed against (and make such ancillary orders as may be necessary). Obviously, if it reverses the terminal effect of the judge's ruling, the prosecution case may well be capable of resurrection.

(b) Evidentiary rulings

Such rulings relate to the inclusion or exclusion of evidence which 'significantly weakens' the prosecution case. The ruling must relate to a qualifying offence (that is, only the most serious) and the application must be made before the close of the prosecution case. Again leave to appeal is required. There is no obligation on the prosecution to agree that if the appeal fails, the accused should be acquitted, but this could well follow naturally. Again the Court of Appeal can confirm, reverse or vary the ruling appealed against and make any necessary ancillary orders. This appeal route was not yet operative by the summer of 2017, but watch this space.

It seems likely that an appeal against these two types of rulings may often be combined. For example, the judge may have excluded prosecution evidence (evidentiary ruling) and as a result ruled that there was no case to answer (terminating ruling).

In making its decision, the Court of Appeal should not reverse a ruling of the trial judge unless satisfied that it is wrong in law, involved an error of law or principle or was not a reasonable one to have been made.[64] The position of the trial judge should be respected. It has been said that the hurdle which the prosecution must overcome is a 'high' one, because the Court of Appeal is 'so much worst placed to make the sort of assessments and judgments' which a trial judge must make.[65]

64 CJA 2003, s 67
65 *R v M* and T [2009] EWCA Crim 2848, per Moses LJ at [25]

D. REFERENCES FROM THE CRIMINAL CASES REVIEW COMMISSION

The Criminal Case Review Commission (CCRC), which was set up to investigate and process allegations of miscarriage of justice, may refer a conviction on indictment to the Court of Appeal, when it considers that there is a 'real possibility' that the conviction, verdict, finding or sentence, as the case may be, will not be upheld.[66] Generally speaking the impetus for the referral will come from an argument or evidence not raised in the original trial or during any appeal process. Once the Commission refers a case, it will be treated as any other appeal from the court where the original trial was conducted.[67]

3. APPEALS FROM THE COURT OF APPEAL

For most practical purposes the Court of Appeal is the final appellate court. However, there may be occasions when a further appeal to the Supreme Court (either by the prosecution or defence) is warranted. This is only possible if leave to appeal is given either by the Court of Appeal or the Supreme Court) *and* the Court of Appeal certifies[68] that the case raises a point of law of general public importance which ought to be considered by the Supreme Court.[69]

If a case goes all the way up to the Supreme Court, a defendant might find, for example, that his conviction is quashed in the Court of Appeal, only to be restored in the Supreme Court.

66 CAA 1995, s 13

67 Note that the CCRC can also refer a summary conviction to the Crown Court, but if it does so that court has no power to increase the sentence: *ibid* s 11(5) and see generally BCrP D 28.1

68 There is no appeal against the refusal to grant such a certificate: *R v Tang* [1995] Crim LR 813

69 CAA 1968, s 33

4. REFERENCES TO THE COURT OF JUSTICE OF THE EUROPEAN UNION

Sometimes cases tried before our national courts raise issues about the application or interpretation of the laws of the European Union, by which (as members) we are bound. The idea is that these should be applied consistently throughout the EU. If the domestic court (of whatever level) cannot answer the question without doing so, a reference to the Court of Justice of the European Union (CJEU[70]) may be necessary. The court in question makes the request, and will usually do this before any trial starts (treating the matter as a preliminary issue); in any event, the domestic proceedings will need to be put on hold until a 'preliminary ruling' is given. A good example of this in operation is the pub landlady in Portsmouth, Karen Murphy, who was taken to court by the English Premier League for screening football matches via a Greek satellite instead of paying Sky, which holds the broadcasting rights in the UK. Sky's fees were considerably higher than those charged Ms Murphy by the right's holder in Greece. The case began in the magistrates' court but raised the issue of 'freedom of movement of services' within Europe, which required a reference to the CJEU.[71]

Since the referendum in June 2016, our days as members of the EU are (presumably) numbered. Once 'Brexit' has been achieved, such references could become otiose.

70 Just to be confusing, this used to be known as the ECJ.

71 To find out what happened see, e.g., bbc.co.uk/news/business-17150054 (but note that she did not 'go' to the CJEU, the question was referred to it by a High Court judge).

revision tips

- Create your own table incorporating the basic 'who, what, when, where and why' of appeal procedure. Do not just mindlessly copy the information (or worse, someone else's table). The idea is to get the knowledge into *your head* - not simply transfer it from one piece of paper to another.
- In the process, note important distinctions between appeals to Crown Court and appeals to Court of Appeal, especially regarding:

  (a) whether leave is required or not,
  (b) the nature of the hearing (retrial or legal submissions),
  (c) time limits,
  and
  (d) the appeal court's powers regarding sentencing (especially whether the sentence can be increased or not on appeal).
- Note which routes of appeal are open to defence only/prosecution only/to both. This information can sometimes help you find the correct answer.

It is worth reading …

BCrP still recommends reading the 2008 guidance on appeal procedure at justice.gov.uk/downloads/courts/court-of-appeal/criminal-division/proc_guide.pdf. It is an easy read.

DPP v Chajed [2013] EWHC 188 (Admin) is a neat little case on s 142 and inventive ways of failing to provide a breath specimen.

R v Ahmed [2010] EWCA Crim 2899, as to when and whether fresh evidence might have rendered a verdict unsafe. The case reads like an episode of *Law and Order* … motive, opportunity, means. And there are a few evidential points and a review from the Criminal Cases Review Commission thrown in for good measure.

PART TWO

criminal evidence

CHAPTER 14

Prove it!

Introduction to criminal evidence

We have looked at the procedural rules: now we must, as they say, consider the evidence! As with any litigation, the view to be taken of the facts in a criminal case will largely depend on the extent and quality of the evidence[1] placed before the tribunal charged with returning a verdict. It is therefore vital to have a firm grasp of the rules and principles about the relevance, reception, and possible exclusion, of items of evidence in criminal cases, not only for the examinations you will be required to pass (that goes without saying) but also as a foundation for embarking on practice with confidence.

The key to understanding these rules and principles is having a secure knowledge of the nature, purpose and rationale behind them (even as they change). This will make them a lot easier to apply in a factual setting and to recall in a closed book test. I hope that the way in which this section of the book is set out, and the explanations and examples offered, will help you to do this.

More and more, the trend in evidence is to codify relevant rules and principles. But the case law is still very important, especially in illustrating how the rules actually work in practice. But a word of warning: do not expect all of the appellate cases you read to line up in a neat intellectual row. Appeals in criminal

1 Keane's definition of evidence as 'information by which facts tend to be proved' has the virtue of clarity: Keane & McKeown, *Modern Law of Evidence* ('*Modern Law*') p. 2. The brief introduction which follows is interesting.

cases sometimes produce a certain tension between a desired outcome in a specific case and the application of general principle, the two of which may not always seem to pull in the same direction. By and large, where there is a will there is a way, and the law is usually flexible enough, and judges creative enough, to allow a court to get to the outcome it thinks is fair in the circumstances. This may or may not be a good thing for cases which follow. The infamous case of *R v Kearley*[2], for example, might well have been decided differently on appeal had it involved other facts and had the judges been less sceptical about the nature of the police evidence. You need to take this creative tension in your stride - if you try to get all the case law to form a coherent, complementary and consistent whole (especially in this area of law), you will drive yourself crazy!

What follows, of necessity, is an introductory overview, which will provide both a springboard for learning the subject, as well as a useful revision tool when the time comes. The devil is often in the detail, of course, so always check your exam syllabus and, where necessary, consult the practitioner (or other) text of your choice.[3]

Let's start with the basic principles, a review of some fundamental evidential terminology, and a brief word about facts which do not require proof by evidence.

2 [1992] 2 AC 228, discussed below in Ch. 20

3 See discussion of practitioner and other texts in Ch. 1

4 A fact in issue is essentially one which (if disputed) must be proved in order for the party who bears the burden of proving it to succeed. See below and BCrP F 1.1

1. BASIC PRINCIPLES

It is important to understand the basic principles underlying the law of evidence and, in particular, to carefully distinguish between the three 'hurdles' to the reception of evidence in any given case, namely relevance, admissibility, and the discretion to exclude.

A. RELEVANCE

Only information which is *relevant* to a fact in issue[4] in a case is capable of being admitted into evidence. Put crudely, to be relevant, the information has to have some bearing one way or the other on the matter at hand. As Lord Steyn described it, all that is required for an item of evidence to be relevant is that it should have 'some tendency in logic and common sense' to advance (or defeat) the proposition in issue.[5]

Relevance is thus essentially an *objective* concept and involves making rational connections between a general observation[6] and the specific issue to be proved. For example, the gregarious nature of a person would be relevant to whether that person's sudden and persistent failure to contact friends was sinister or not.[7] This is because we generally accept the idea that something *might* be wrong if a communicative person stops communicating. Thus, an argument about relevance will essentially boil down to the correctness or not of the assumption which underpins it, so it is important to be able to identify this and scrutinise its validity - a denial of relevance can be a useful tool for an advocate.

Relevance vs weight

It is essential to remember, however, that *an item of evidence can be relevant without actually proving very much. Do not confuse relevance with weight.* The latter has to do with how

5 *R v A* (No 2) [2001] 2 Cr App R, 21, at [31]. So evidence of motive, for example, is irrelevant to the prosecution of a strict liability offence. See BCrP F 1.11

6 As Christopher Allen put it (in the 4th edition of his *Practical Guide*, p. 11), 'the key to relevance is an understanding of the importance of generalisations about the way things are in the world' p. 11ff. The examples and discussion about relevance and weight (also in the 5th edition, p.10ff) are interesting and very illuminating.

7 As in the famous case of Dr Crippen, which is vividly described in the opening paragraphs of *Practical Guide*.

persuasive an item of evidence is, and will determine its 'probative value'. Weight is thus the more subjective concept, which brings common knowledge and experience into the equation. Having said that, although relevance and weight are distinct features of evidence, they do interact with one another in the sense that the more bland the generalisation underlying the argument for relevance, the less compelling the evidence in question is likely to be. For example, in a rape case, the fact that the defendant is a male will be relevant in the sense that 'men are more apt to commit rape than women'; this is a generalisation with which most people would agree. But the evidence carries little weight because this statement is very generic and says nothing at all about whether a particular male committed a particular rape in particular circumstances. There are a lot of men in the world. A more targeted assertion would increase its evidential value, but only if it remains accurate. The bolder the generalisation, the weightier the evidence is likely to be, but 'the trouble with bold generalisations is that they are less likely than cautious ones to be true'.[8]

Be prepared, too, for judges to fudge the boundary between relevance and weight. Sometimes they will pronounce evidence to be 'insufficiently' relevant to be admitted.[9] This is rather like describing a woman as being a 'little bit' pregnant. Strictly speaking, evidence either is or is not relevant. What does vary (again, like a pregnant woman) is the weight - it could say very little about guilt, or it could say a lot. This will be an important factor in the court's discretion to exclude evidence, discussed below.

B. ADMISSIBILITY

This is the second hurdle. Evidence must be relevant, but relevance does not guarantee *admissibility*. Indeed, the heart and soul of the law of evidence has historically been the exclusionary rules which render otherwise relevant evidence

8 *Ibid*, 4th Edn, p. 22

9 Sometimes the distinction is made between 'legal' relevance and 'logical' relevance. The former is really more of a comment on weight than relevance, but excluding evidence of 'insufficient' relevance does save juries from being distracted by information they would never give any credence to. See, e.g., *R v Robinson* [2006] 1 Cr App R 221, CA, cited at BCrP F 1.11

inadmissible. These rules grew up by virtue of three historical imperatives: (i) the harshness of the criminal law in the 18th and 19th centuries, which the rules were intended to mitigate; (ii) the prevalence of the jury system, which was thought to bring with it risks of prejudice and misunderstanding; and (iii) the fear of fabrication and the assumption that people will say anything to get out of trouble. The trend in the last ten years has been to ease up on these rules, but the fact remains that relevant evidence still has to meet strict admissibility criteria, as we shall see in the chapters which follow.

C. DISCRETION TO EXCLUDE

Even if an item of evidence is relevant (hurdle 1) and does not fall foul of the admissibility rules (hurdle 2), there is still a judicial *discretion to exclude* evidence. This is hurdle number 3. At *common law*, the court has a general discretion to exclude otherwise admissible *prosecution* evidence, where its prejudicial effect *outweighs its probative value.*[10] This discretion involves an important *balancing act*, and the weight of the evidence in question is an important factor. Of course, if the evidence is probative of the offence charged then it will also be prejudicial. In that situation the scales are more or less evenly balanced - this is not a problem for criminal justice. What this common law discretion is geared to is excluding evidence which may inflame a jury's prejudice while not actually proving very much. It is of general application and a useful string to defence counsel's bow.

In addition, there is the *statutory discretion* to exclude under s 78 of the Police and Criminal Evidence Act 1984 (PACE 1984). This provides that a court may refuse to allow *prosecution* evidence to be given if it 'appears to the court that, having regard to all of the circumstances, *including* the circumstances in which the evidence was *obtained*, the admission of the evidence would have such an *adverse effect on the*

10 *R v Sang* [1980] AC 402

fairness of the proceedings that the court ought not to admit it'. This is a different sort of discretion. It is of general application, but especially comes into its own, as we shall see, when considering the admissibility of confessions.[11] Because of the explicit reference to how evidence is obtained, s 78 is particularly germane whenever there is an argument that evidence to be tendered by the prosecution has been acquired oppressively or improperly or unfairly, for example after an illegal search or as a result of the activities of an agent provocateur. But it is *not limited* to such cases; the court may exercise the s 78 discretion *whenever* admission of an item of prosecution evidence would be unfair, whatever the circumstances.[12]

The importance of these two general discretions cannot be over-emphasised.[13] Furthermore, although they can overlap, *it is important not to confuse or conflate them.* Each helps to ensure a fair trial in its own way. The common law discretion does its part by looking at the probative value of a specific item of evidence to ensure that it justifies the prejudice its reception will cause. The s 78 discretion is rather more holistic in its approach, ensuring fairness by being protective of both the defendant (especially against the power of the state) and the integrity of the proceedings.

It is also crucial to note that these general discretions can *only operate to exclude prosecution evidence.* They are designed to protect defendants from prosecutors, but not from co-defendants. We will see time and time again, that when it comes to one defendant wanting to admit evidence against another defendant, then laissez faire is fair.

11 See Ch. 21

12 For example, because the evidence is critical but cannot be effectively tested in cross-examination. This might arise with certain kinds of admissible hearsay evidence. See Ch. 20

13 More detailed discussion can be found at BCrP F 2.1ff

2. TERMINOLOGY

Before going on to look in more detail at the various admissibility and related rules of evidence, it may be helpful to begin with a brief guide to some of the technical terms we might encounter along the way.[14]

A. FACTS IN ISSUE VS COLLATERAL FACTS

The nature of the offence charged, and any special defences raised, will determine the *facts in issue* in any given criminal case. These are the facts which (if disputed), must be proved by the party who bears the burden of proof, in order to succeed in the case.[15] *Collateral facts* are those which relate to a subsidiary matter which, while not among the facts in issue, nevertheless affect the question of whether a fact in issue has been proved or not. The most common example of a collateral fact is that which affect a witness's *credibility*.[16] Although, as we shall see, there are times when evidence relevant to credibility merges with evidence directly relevant to a fact in issue (and indeed evidence may be relevant to both), it is important to understand the conceptual difference between the two.

B. TYPES OF EVIDENCE

Evidence comes in various forms - things, words, documents - and it is useful to look at some of the descriptions practitioners use. But beware the curse of classification; nothing is that simple, and often the same word is used to describe different things. So be prepared.

(i) Direct vs circumstantial evidence

In this context, evidence is direct if it speaks *directly to a fact in issue*. For example

14 You can find further detail in BCrP F 1 and F 8

15 See generally Ch. 15

16 A fact affecting a witness's competence to give evidence is another example of a collateral fact. So too are facts relevant to the admissibility of evidence. Where the issue needs resolving *before* the evidence in question can be adduced (or not, as the case may be), such collateral facts are also known as *preliminary facts*.

if the witness saw the accused strike the victim, he could give direct evidence of the physical attack. A confession is direct evidence of the incriminating conduct which it admits. In contrast, circumstantial evidence requires an *inference* to be drawn before it can achieve its purpose; it is evidence of a relevant fact from which conclusions *about* a fact in issue *can be drawn*. Typical examples are evidence of motive or alibi or fingerprint evidence. In the absence of a confession, states of mind like dishonesty can only be established by circumstantial evidence. The list goes on and on. Most cases turn on some if not quite a lot of circumstantial evidence. Remember, too, that (no matter what they say on TV) there is nothing inferior about circumstantial evidence; its probative value depends on its quality, not its classification. A coherent cluster of circumstantial evidence can be more compelling than an item of direct evidence. Pollock CB famously compared circumstantial evidence to a rope comprised of several strands, and put it like this: '... there may be a combination of circumstances, no one of which would raise a reasonable conviction, or more than mere suspicion; but the whole, taken together, may create a strong conclusion of guilt, that is, with as much certainty as human affairs can require or admit of'.[17]

(ii) Direct vs hearsay evidence

In this context, *direct evidence* refers to evidence given by a witness about relevant events which he or she personally or directly perceived. *Hearsay evidence*, by contrast, comes in a form which is at least one removed from that source: in other words, it is an assertion not made by a person while giving oral evidence in a case, the truth of which the tribunal is being asked to believe. There are risks attached to hearsay evidence, and so strict rules apply to its reception.[18]

17 Cited and discussed at BCrP F 1.18

18 See Ch. 20

(iii) Original evidence

Original evidence is another description which changes depending on context. Sometimes it is also used, in contrast to hearsay evidence, to refer to words uttered by someone other than a testifying witness which are put forward not to prove the truth of what was said, but merely to prove that the assertion was made. This might be pertinent if the state of mind of the speaker or the reaction of the person who heard the assertion is relevant.[19] The term is also used, when describing documents, to distinguish between the 'original' and some derivative, for example, a photocopy.

(iv) Documentary evidence

This refers to evidence contained in documents. Typical examples are written contracts, letters, diary entries. But it can extend to anything on which evidence is recorded, for example, films, CDs and video recordings.[20] The original document is usually considered the best version of the evidence,[21] but copies or other secondary evidence may be admissible. Remember that what is relevant about such evidence is the truth of the *information contained* in the document; if what is important about the document is its physical state, then evidentially it becomes an item of real evidence.[22]

(v) Real evidence

This term is used to describe something which is evidentially useful because of the way it looks, feels, smells and so forth. The tribunal thus needs to evaluate the evidence using its own senses, often with the help of expert evidence to explain its significance. Typical examples include the murder weapon or the burglar's balaclava. It can be very powerful evidence. A notable illustration is OJ Simpson's glove, which was accompanied by his lawyer's famous admonition: *"If it doesn't fit, you must acquit"*. And so they did.

19 See *ibid*

20 s 134(1) Criminal Justice Act 2003

21 Sometimes called 'primary evidence'. See also the so-called best-evidence rule, which, if it still exists, only really pertains to documents. See BCrP 1.30/31

22 And so a copy would not serve any useful purpose!

If the real evidence cannot easily be brought to court, then the court will go to it. This is known as a 'view'.[23]

C. TRIBUNAL OF LAW AND FACT

In trials on indictment in the Crown Court, the judge and jury neatly divide into the tribunal of law and fact respectively. The judge thus decides matters of *law* (for example, admissibility of evidence), controls the conduct of the trial and gives the jury careful directions on their role.[24] The jury, as the tribunal of *fact*, has the job of deciding the facts in issue, including the ultimate issue of whether the accused is guilty or not. In the magistrates' courts, both of these functions reside in the bench. Legal decisions are still legal decisions and a determination of guilt still depends on findings of fact, but both tasks are completed by the same person(s) in the magistrates' court.[25]

D. VOIR DIRE

This is the so-called 'trial within a trial' where the court hears evidence of disputed *facts* in order to determine a preliminary matter such as the competence of a witness or the admissibility of a confession. In the Crown Court, a voir dire takes place in the absence of the jury, since the decision is a legal one, for the judge. No such division of labour exists, of course, in the magistrates' courts (although a different bench from that hearing the main case may have determined the preliminary issue).

3. ESTABLISHING FACTS WITHOUT EVIDENCE

Generally speaking, facts are proved by adducing evidence at trial. There are two important exceptions to this rule: formal admissions and judicial notice.

23 See BCrP F 8.45-8.51
24 See *ibid* F 1.32
25 Lay justices will be assisted on legal questions by a legal advisor. See Ch. 8 and BCrP F 1.38

A. FORMAL ADMISSIONS

This is a means by which uncontroversial aspects of a case are formally admitted and so cease to be an issue at trial. Do not confuse *formal admissions* with *informal admissions* (for example, something incriminating said at the police station) - the latter are capable of being explained away (if not necessarily easily), and can be excluded by the court itself.[26]

Under s 10 Criminal Justice Act 1967,[27] a formal admission may be made of any *fact* of which admissible evidence would have been admitted at trial.[28] Such can be made by or on behalf of prosecutors *or* defendants, and are *conclusive* evidence of the facts admitted in the proceedings (including any appeal or re-trial relating to the same matters).

As you might expect, there are plenty of safeguards built into the process, including the fact that *unless made orally in court*, the admission must be *in writing*,[29] signed by the person purporting to make it.[30] If made on behalf of an individual *defendant*, the admission must be made by his *counsel or solicitor*.[31] Finally, such admissions may only be withdrawn with leave of the court. The need for formality and the role of legal advisors in the case of defendants is important to ensure that the admission is made knowing the full implications of doing so. The point of formal admissions is to avoid wasting time unnecessarily, not to bamboozle an accused into admitting culpability.

B. JUDICIAL NOTICE

Judicial notice may be taken of facts either with or without inquiry. Judicial notice *without* inquiry is taken of facts which are regarded as common knowledge, for example, that a fortnight is too short a period for human gestation; that cats are ordinarily kept as domestic pets; that the streets of London are full of cars; that Elvis

26 See generally Ch. 21

27 Criminal Justice Act 1967 (CJA 1967), s 10(1)-(4)

28 Thus it seems one cannot admit evidence by way of a formal admission, if it would otherwise be excluded by some other rule of evidence (e.g. because it is inadmissible hearsay). See BCrP F 1.1-1.3

29 In which case it would be read to the jury if there is one.

30 If made on behalf of a company, for example, it should be signed by some appropriate person on its behalf: s 10(2)(c) CJA 1967

31 If the admission was made by a defendant before trial, it must later be approved by his solicitor or counsel (for example, where it was made before the defendant had legal representation): *Ibid*, s 10(2)(d)/(e)

Presley lived and (mainly) performed in the USA.[32] Why waste time and money proving the obvious?

Where certain sorts of facts (for example, meaning of words, diplomatic custom, historical events) are not a matter of common knowledge, and there is disagreement, the doctrine of judicial notice *after* inquiry allows the judge to make a determination as to the disputed meaning, custom or event, using such works of reference as might assist. This process is very different from proof by evidence in the normal course of events, although the relationship between the two is not without its ambiguities and complexities. What is clear is that judicial notice after inquiry is not intended to usurp the function of the jury as the tribunal of fact, and so Crown Court judges tend to be very careful to stay on the right side of the division of labour.[33]

revision tips

- Be clear about the 'hurdles' to the reception of evidence in a criminal case, and the importance of the discretion to exclude.
- Do not confuse relevance and weight.
- Be comfortable with the conceptual distinctions (and basic vocabulary) set out above.

It is worth reading ...

Taylor CJ's judgment in *R v Sultan Khan* [1995] 1 Cr App R 242. This is an older case where evidence of heroin importation had been obtained by bugging private premises (in accordance with existing guidelines). When discussing relevance and admissibility, it is focused only on the type of evidence in question, but the observations about the discretion to exclude are of general application. It reinforces the important message that so far as that (and indeed any) discretion, each case must be judged on its own merits. The evidence was clearly probative, but was its use fair? The appellate court thought so.

32 See, generally, list of examples in BCrP F 1.5

33 See, generally, discussion in Keane & McKeown, *Modern Law*, p. 733ff

CHAPTER 15

Burden and standard of proof in criminal cases

The outcome of a case will usually 'turn on its facts', as the saying goes. More particularly, where contested versions of events have been put forward, a verdict will depend on the view taken by the tribunal of fact of what happened, and why. The rules about the burden and standard of proof tell us who has the job of proving the facts in issue - and to what extent. This needs to be clearly understood by a jury.

The *burden of proof* is the obligation imposed on a party to prove a particular fact in issue, failing which that party will lose on that issue. This is often referred to as the 'legal burden'[1] and must be clearly distinguished from the so-called 'evidential burden', which is an obligation of sorts, but *not* an obligation to *prove* anything.

In criminal cases following a not guilty plea, the constituents of the offence(s) charged will be the initial guide to what facts need to be proved. In any given prosecution, the facts in issue are effectively those aspects of the actus reus, mens rea, and identity (of the perpetrator), including any special defences raised, which are disputed.

It is important to appreciate that only *one* party will bear a burden of proof on any given fact in issue.

Because of the interplay between the legal and evidential burdens in criminal cases, it may be as well to begin with the latter.

1 There are several other expressions describing the legal burden of proof, e.g., 'the persuasive burden', the 'ultimate burden'. This can be confusing for the beginner, since they all effectively mean the same thing.

1. EVIDENTIAL BURDEN

It is vital to remember that an evidential burden is *not* a burden of *proof*.[2] Rather, it is a requirement to put forward (or be able to point to[3]) enough evidence on a particular issue to give the tribunal of fact something to decide; the obligation is discharged when there is sufficient evidence to justify, as a *possibility*, a favourable finding. The evidential burden is thus a *low* threshold; certainly discharging it does not by any means prove anything. A party bearing a legal burden of proof on an issue, who could not even manage to discharge the evidential burden, will lose on that issue (and so probably outright) without the other side having to say or do much of anything.[4]

By and large, the party with the legal burden of proof on an issue also bears the evidential burden, so they tend to go together as a twin-set. There are, however, several instances where the defendant in a criminal case, although he or she does not bear a legal burden on an issue, nevertheless has an obligation to point to sufficient evidence on that issue to make it worthy of consideration. These will be matters which the prosecution is not required to raise as part of its case, but on which a defendant may wish to rely to excuse or mitigate his behaviour - typically, for example, common law defences such as duress or self-defence, and statutory defences such as 'loss of self-control'.[5] Alibi works in much the same way. If defendants did not bear an evidential burden on such issues (which do not form part of the offence charged), it would make life very difficult for prosecutors. Defendants are not forced to raise these particular defences; but nor are prosecutors asked to second-guess all possible answers to a charge.[6] The imposition of an evidential burden in such cases is thus merely a matter of common sense. It is important to remember, however, that the burden of *proof* on issues of this kind *remains squarely on the prosecution*; once the evidential burden has been discharged, it is for the prosecution to *disprove* the defence raised.[7]

2 As explained, e.g. in *L v DPP* [2003] 3 WLR 863, para 22

3 The party with the evidential burden need not necessarily be the one adducing the evidence. The evidence may emerge during the presentation of an opponent's case. See, e.g., *ibid*, para 23

4 The usual context is a defence submission, at the end of the prosecution case, that there is 'no case to answer'. If allowed, the case would collapse at that stage and there would be no need to hear the defence case. See Ch. 8 (Summary trial) and Ch. 9 (Crown Court trial).

5 A much less common example is the defence of 'marital coercion' as recently raised (unsuccessfully) in the Vicky Pryce trial (see fn 27). See also complete list of such defences and discussion at BCrP F 3.36ff

Whether an evidential burden has been discharged is a matter for the judge alone. It is sometimes said that the evidential burden governs what the judge *does* (for example, in leaving the question to a jury or withdrawing it from their consideration), whereas the legal burden governs what he or she *says* when directing the jury about how to consider their verdict.[8] This is another useful way of clearly differentiating between the two.

2. THE LEGAL BURDEN OF PROOF

In criminal cases, the starting point, so far as the incidence of the legal burden of proof is concerned, is the overarching principle that a defendant is presumed innocent until proven guilty. The general rule, therefore, is that the *prosecution* bears the *burden of proving each and every element of the offence in question.*[9] As Viscount Sankey LC put it in the famous case of *Woolmington v DPP:*[10]

> … it is sufficient for (the defendant) to raise doubt as to his guilt; he is not bound to satisfy the jury of his innocence … the principle that the prosecution must prove the guilt of the prisoner is part of the common law of England and no attempt to whittle it down can be entertained …

It has in fact been 'whittled down' quite a lot. The *Woolmington* case itself referred to exceptions to this general rule, namely the common law defence of insanity and 'any statutory exception'. The use of the word 'any' makes the latter sound like a wide category, but it is important to appreciate that further constraint has since been imposed by the effect of the European Convention on Human Rights (ECHR), incorporated into English Law under the Human Rights Act 1998 (HRA 1998),

6 In these days, the nature of the defence case should not remain a mystery for long, because of the early disclosure rules and the effects of s 35 of the Criminal Justice and Public Order Act 1994 (see Ch. 7), but the evidential burden still obliges a defendant to point to some evidence on which such defence is based.

7 To the criminal standard, as to which see below. So in such cases the burdens are split, with the defence having an evidential burden, but the prosecution ultimately bearing the legal burden of proof on the issue.

8 See Glanville Williams', *Evidential Burdens on the Defence* (1977b) 127 NLJ 182

9 Even if this involves proving a negative. So it is for the prosecution to prove lack of consent on a rape charge. A defendant bears no burden at all (evidential or legal) on

specifically, by Art 6(2): 'everyone charged with a criminal offence shall be presumed innocent until proved guilty according to law'. This is clearly consistent with the general principle, and so Parliament's ability to transfer, by way of statute, a legal burden of proof on a particular issue from prosecution to defence[11] is limited - *only burdens on a defendant which are compatible with Art 6(2) will be lawful.*

A. EXCEPTIONS

Statutory exceptions sub-divide into two categories, and so it is convenient to think in terms of the three types of situation where the onus of proof may (or may not) be 'reversed'.

(i) Insanity defence

This is the common law's only exception to the general rule, as mentioned in the *Woolmington* case. If the accused raises insanity as a defence, he bears the burden of proving it.[12] This is a rarely invoked and, unlike statutory exceptions, is not very controversial.

(ii) Statutory exceptions

(a) Express statutory exceptions

These tend to be easy to recognise in the sense that it is clear from reading the relevant statute that the intention is to impose on the defendant a burden of proof on a particular fact in issue. An example is s 2 of the Homicide Act 1957, which explicitly states that on a charge of murder, it shall be 'for the defence to prove' that the accused was (at the material time) suffering from diminished responsibility (if that is being raised to reduce murder to manslaughter). The rationale for this particular imposition of a burden of proof on an accused is the assumption that he

the issue of consent, as this forms part of the description of the offence (*Horn* (1912) 7 Cr App R 200)

10 [1935] AC 462 at 481-2

11 Any statutory provision seeking to do this is sometimes referred to as a 'reverse burden provision'.

12 *M'Naughton's Case* (1843) 10 Cl & F 200. The standard of proof is the civil standard (see below). If unfitness to plead and stand trial is raised, and this is disputed, the burden of proof rests on whoever raised it: BCrP F 3.8

knows his own mind better than the prosecution.[13]

Similar provisions appear in statutes dealing with drug offences (Misuse of Drugs Act 1971, s 28), offensive weapons and knife crime (Prevention of Crime Act 1953, s 1; Criminal Justice Act 1988, s 139) and trademark offences (Trade Marks Act 1994, s 92(5)).

Before the HRA 1998, one could be confident that a statutory provision explicitly requiring the defendant 'to prove' something had the effect of reversing the legal burden on that issue. However, any such provision is now open to challenge as being incompatible with Art 6(2), and if it is found to be so (and some have) the pragmatic result has been to decide that such wording is capable of imposing an evidential burden only, and so does not, in fact, place an onus of proof on the defendant. You might think it odd to find that the words 'to prove' can mean '*not to prove, really, but just to present some evidence*', but the solution is a practical one - and avoids having to re-draft a raft of legislation![14] Not surprisingly perhaps, this demotion is known as 'reading down' the legislation. As Lord Styne put it in *R v Lambert*:[15]

> It is clear that the 1998 Act must be given its full import and that long or well entrenched ideas may have to be put aside, sacred cows culled.

Having said that, it is important to realise that *not every statutory imposition of a burden of proof on a defendant will infringe Art 6(2), and so not every such provision will (if challenged), need to be 'read down'.* Some have stood up to scrutiny; others have not.[16] Through a series of cases on the subject, it seems well settled now that, despite the strict wording of Art 6(2), it does not act to ban reverse burden provisions absolutely and in deciding whether such a provision is or is not compatible with Art 6(2), the court must view each case *on its own merits.*[17] Fairly obviously, any derogation from the general rule must be kept within reasonable limits; in essence, the court will need to balance the interests

13 Rather like the common law insanity plea.

14 Equally the words 'to show' might be thought to be more elastic, but in *R v Johnstone* [2003] 1 WLR 1796 The House of Lords said the provision employing these words imposed a legal burden of proof and this was not (in this instance) incompatible with Art 6(2)

15 [2002] 2 AC 54, at [6]

16 Compare, e.g., *Lambert, ibid* with *L v DPP* [2002] 2 All ER 854

17 'The justifiability of any infringement of the presumption of innocence cannot be resolved by any rule of thumb, but on examination of all the facts and circumstances of the particular provision as applied in a particular case,' per Lord Bingham in *Sheldrake v DPP* [2005] 1 AC 264 at [21]

of the individual defendant against the public good to which the offence is directed. The court will ask itself whether the reverse burden is justified in the circumstances and, to answer that question, will look at a range of factors,[18] including:

- Is there a 'compelling reason' for departing from the general rule? How important is the social evil which the offence addresses? Is the imposition of a burden of proof on the defendant fair and reasonable? It is a *proportionate* method of achieving the legitimate aims of the legislation?
- How serious is the punishment should the accused be convicted? The more serious the punishment, the more compelling the reason for the reverse burden should be.
- How does any burden of proof imposed on the defendant compare to the matters requiring proof by the prosecution? Even if it is difficult to decide what are constituents of the offence and what are not, the defendant should not be asked to do the prosecution's job for it.
- *How easy* (or difficult) would it be for the defendant to discharge the burden of proof? Does he have easy access to the facts? Are they within his own knowledge? Matters going to an accused's state of mind at the time of the offence can pose difficulties, since to know your state of mind is one thing; being able to prove it may be another. Showing a licence or permit, on the other hand, is usually thought to be pretty straightforward (although in this day and age of computer based public records, it might be as easy for the prosecution to access such information as the defence).
- The *overriding* concern is that a trial should be *fair*. The 'presumption of innocence' underpins this aspiration and so the further away one gets from it, the more objectionable the reverse onus provision will be.

18 See *AG Reference (No 1 of 2004)* [2004] 1 WLR 2111, para 52. See also *R v Sheldrake* [2005] op.cit. [22] cited at BCrP F 3.18

In one sense these are all logical common sense considerations, but applying them is not always straightforward. Sometimes they conflict with each other. For example, if the offence in question is very serious it will be in the public interest to convict perpetrators, which might be some justification for a reverse burden on a particular aspect of the case. However, such an offence would also carry a serious punishment, which would militate against such an imposition. New cases which arise (real or in an examination question) must be viewed holistically and argued on their own merits. If the court finds that a provision does conflict with Art 6(2), then it will be 'read down' to impose an evidential burden only, which, as you know by now, is not a burden of proof!

(b) Implied statutory exceptions

As discussed above, express statutory exceptions are usually easy to identify; the question is whether they need to be 'read down' if an Art 6(2) challenge is made. Other statutory provisions are not so clear. Sometimes the issue is whether, even if not expressly stated, a reverse burden has nevertheless been imposed by *implication.* And if, as a matter of construction, a burden has been cast on the defendant, then the *supplementary* question now is: what sort of burden is imposed? If the imposition of a reverse burden of proof would be incompatible with Art 6(2), then it is likely to be interpreted as an evidential burden only.

S 101 of the Magistrates' Court Act 1980 provides that where a defendant relies for his defence 'on any exception, exemption, proviso, excuse or qualification', whether or not it is part of the description of the offence, 'the burden of proving' such a defence shall be on him. Strictly, this legislation governs summary trials, but it has been held to apply equally to trials on indictment.[19]

In the case of *R v Hunt*,[20] the appellant was convicted of unlawful possession

---

19 *R v Hunt* [1987] AC 352
20 *Ibid*

of morphine, contrary to the Misuse of Drugs Act 1971, s 5(2). Under applicable regulations,[21] any preparation containing 'not more than 0.2% morphine' was exempted from the possession prohibition. The question arose as to who had the burden of proof on this issue: was it for the prosecution to prove the amount seized contained more than 0.2% morphine, or was it for the defendant to prove that he came within the exemption? Earlier cases had spoken of answering this question by reference to a careful analysis of the statute to determine which words described the offence (which was for the prosecution to prove) and which, the exemption (which was for the defendant to prove); [22] but the House of Lords in *Hunt* thought a broader approach should be taken. Lord Griffiths set out guidelines which foreshadow the later cases on compatibility with the HRA 1998. He said that:

- The courts should be 'very slow' to classify a defence as falling within s 101 because Parliament would never lightly intend to impose an obligation on a defendant to prove his innocence.
- The *ease* with which a defendant could discharge a burden of proof is a highly relevant factor. In the *Hunt* case, it was thought very difficult for the defendant because he was no longer is possession of the substance. Had he been, the outcome might have been different.
- The gravity of the offence is a relevant consideration. The more serious the implications of a conviction, the more likely it is that any ambiguity should be resolved in favour of the defendant.

As with the 'reading down' cases, these guidelines are at times easier to articulate than apply consistently, and again every case must be decided on its merits. If a court determines that a provision does fall within s 102, the question then arises

21 See Misuse of Drugs Regulations 1973, Sch 1, para 3

22 See *R v Edwards* [1975] QB 27

23 This additional requirement for compatibility with HRA 1998 has largely neutralised the controversy which previously surrounded reverse burdens arising by implication.

as to whether this construction of the legislation is compatible with Art 6(2), which brings into play the principles and guidelines discussed earlier. If a legal burden of proof would infringe Art 6(2), then it would follow that only an evidential burden will be imposed.[23]

3. STANDARD OF PROOF

Once it is determined on whom a burden of proof lies, the next question is to *what standard* must that burden be discharged. In civil cases, the standard of proof is the 'balance of probabilities'.[24] In criminal cases, the prosecution must discharge their burden of proof 'beyond reasonable doubt'. The criminal standard is the more onerous standard, because the consequences and implications of a criminal conviction for an accused are, generally speaking, that much more serious.[25]

The criminal standard of proof should be explained to juries by telling them that they must be satisfied so that they feel '*sure*' of the accused's guilt. This is thought to be the best way of describing 'beyond reasonable doubt', an expression which judges are now discouraged from using, much less elaborating.[26] If both expressions have been referred to during the trial (counsel, for example, may well refer to the standard of proof in their speeches), it should be made clear to jurors that they mean the same thing.

'Being sure' is thought to be the safest direction, but there is no precise formulation which a judge must use, and it is important to appreciate that it is the *overall* effect of the summing up which matters. If a jury is unsure what 'unsure' means, then it is appropriate to explain simply that they should exclude fanciful possibilities and act only on realistic ones.[27] A judge may refer to the standard of proof on more than one occasion, and it is possible to correct an earlier inadequate

24 See *Be Civil!*, by the author, Ch. 17

25 See, e.g., useful explanation by Woolf, LJ in *R v B* [2003] 2 Cr App R 197, p. 204

26 As the judge in the first Vicky Pryce trial rather grumpily told the jury when they asked him to explain again what 'reasonable doubt' means. Whatever the press might think, this is not an unusual question for jurors to ask. Sweeney J's initial instruction that 'the prosecution must make you feel sure of guilt' was fine, but perhaps undermined slightly by his adding, parenthetically, that 'this is the same as, but no more than, proof of guilt beyond reasonable doubt'. See www.crimeline.info/news/pryce-jury-summing-up.

27 *R v Majid* [2009] EWCA 2563, CA at [12]

direction. But it is also possible to say too much. As Lawton LJ put it in *R v Ching*: [28]

> … judges would be well advised not to attempt any gloss upon what is meant by 'sure' or what is meant by 'reasonable doubt'. In the last two decades there have been numerous cases before this court … which have come here because judges have thought it helpful to a jury to comment on what the standard of proof is. Experience in this court has shown that such comments usually create difficulties. They are more likely to confuse than help.[29]

We have seen that there are occasions when, as an exception to the general rule, a defendant bears a legal burden of proof[30] on an issue. In such cases, that burden is discharged on the *civil* standard, *not* the criminal standard of proof. It is important to appreciate that defendants *never* have to prove anything beyond reasonable doubt. *That standard is for prosecutors only!*

4. PRESUMPTIONS

So-called 'presumptions' can have an effect on the burden and standard of proof. They operate, to a greater or lesser degree, by allowing (sometimes obligating) fact finders to draw certain conclusions ('the presumed fact') from other facts ('the primary facts'). One tends to refer to three 'types' of presumption, although the term is used rather loosely. They are as follows.

A. 'PRESUMPTIONS OF FACT'

These are not presumptions so much as inferences to be drawn, as a matter of common

28 (1976) 63 Cr App R 7

29 He went on to say that 'exceptional cases' do arise where further explanation is justified, as in *Ching* itself. See discussion at BCrP F 3.50. See also *R v Majid* [2009] EWCA Crim 2563, which BCrP cites as a cautionary tale at F 3.48

30 This, of course, is to be distinguished from an evidential burden (see above).

31 When no, or no plausible, explanation is given. The fact that as a general rule, adverse inferences may now be drawn where circumstances call for an explanation, makes this presumption a little old-fashioned. See generally Ch. 23

sense, from certain facts. In reality, such are just examples of commonly recurring items of circumstantial evidence. The way they operate is that if the primary fact is proved, the presumed fact *may* logically be presumed. But there is *no compulsion.*

Examples well known to criminal lawyers are the 'doctrine of recent possession', which is an inference of guilt (as thief or handler) which may be drawn from the fact that a person is found in possession of recently stolen goods;[31] and the notion that people intend the natural consequences of their actions.[32]

This presumption can also operate in individual cases. Remember the case of John Darwin, the missing canoeist who 'came back from the dead'?[33] He was presumed dead on the basis that the apparent circumstances of his disappearance (parts of a broken canoe, clothes found washed up on the beach and so forth) and the fact that he had seemingly not reappeared, made this a logical conclusion to draw.[34] However, the coroner had been under no compulsion to make the declaration because less than seven years had passed.[35]

B. IRREBUTTABLE (OR CONCLUSIVE) PRESUMPTION OF LAW

This is not a presumption so much as a rule of substantive law. If the primary fact is proved, the presumed fact *must* be presumed. This kind of presumption is compulsory and so is incapable of being rebutted. An example in criminal cases is the fact that children under ten years of age are incapable of being found guilty of an offence.[36]

C. REBUTTABLE PRESUMPTIONS OF LAW

These are true presumptions, of which there are many examples.[37] Their purpose is two-fold: (i) to *save time and effort* when in 99 cases out of 100 the presumed fact follows from the primary fact (for example, the presumption of legitimacy) and/or (ii) to *resolve a dilemma* (for example, the presumption of death).[38] Bear in mind that the

32 Another matter of common sense, put on a statutory basis by s 8 Criminal Justice Act 1967 (reversing *DPP v Smith* [1961] AC 290).

33 See, e.g., Telegraph Online for 4 December 2007, which includes a video of him looking very much alive!

34 As it happened he hid in the house next door while his wife waited to claim the life insurance money, then they both fled to Panama. The defence of marital coercion did not work well for her either: news.bbc.co.uk/1/hi/england/tees/7520803stm

35 At which point the rebuttable 'presumption of death' could have been relied upon. See below.

36 Children and Young Persons Act 1933, s 50

37 See generally discussion at BCrP F 3.69ff

38 Discussed in *Be Civil!*, by the author, Ch. 17

latter are only applicable when there really is a dilemma. If the court will make the inference you want from the facts at hand, there is no dilemma which needs resolving!

Rebuttable presumptions operate as follows. If the primary fact is proved, the presumed fact *must* be presumed, *unless* there is evidence to the contrary. Thus a rebuttable presumption casts a burden on the party against whom it operates. How onerous this burden is depends, in criminal cases, on who benefits from the operation of the presumption. If it operates in favour of the accused, the prosecution will always bear a legal burden of proof, which must be discharged beyond reasonable doubt. If, however, the presumption operates in favour of the prosecution, the defendant will either bear an evidential burden to 'neutralise' the presumption (if common law) or a burden of proof on the civil standard (if statutory).[39]

revision tips

- Do not confuse an evidential 'burden' with the legal burden of proof.
- Remember that defendants rarely have to prove anything; when they do, they only need do so to the civil standard (balance of probabilities). Only prosecutors are held to the criminal standard.
- Consult the Crown Court Compendium I Ch 5.

It is worth reading …

The judgment in *R v Majid* [2009] EWCA Crim 2563, CA. This is good little case (although perhaps not so pleasant for the victim who needed his head 'stapled' after being run over by the appellant) about the perils of over-analysing the criminal standard of proof for juries. It also contains useful comments about improper cross-examination, which are worth noting.

The judgment in *R (on application of Cuns) v Hammersmith Magistrates' Court* [2016] EWHC 748 (Admin). This is a short little case on defendants discharging evidential burdens imposed on them. Something went a bit awry with the transcript (all the paragraphs have the same number). But the message is clear.

39 See BCrP F 3.69

CHAPTER 16

Privilege
and related concepts

Many of the rules of evidence spring from a desire to ensure a fair trial. For the same reason, openness underpins many of the rules of criminal procedure, and is most obviously manifest in the form of strict disclosure requirements.[1] The principles relating to *privilege* and *public interest immunity* have less to do with these motivations, important though they are, and more with a competing idea: namely that there are times when the benefits in withholding evidence from the court or an opponent should prevail over the public interest in openness. Occasionally, secrecy will trump transparency.

It is important to distinguish between the various forms of privilege and between privilege and public interest immunity claims. There are two important, but different types of privilege: privilege against self-incrimination and legal professional privilege. These privileges are *personal* - they must be claimed or waived by the party or person whom they protect.

Public interest immunity is not a privilege as such. It imposes a *duty*, not a right to withhold disclosure, and gives the court power to exclude evidence on the grounds that its disclosure would damage the public interest. It can, and should, be distinguished from legal professional privilege.[2]

1 See generally BCrP D 9, and above, Ch. 7

2 See general principles at BCrP F 10.1

1. PRIVILEGE

A. PRIVILEGE AGAINST SELF-INCRIMINATION

The privilege against self-incrimination is as old as the rule of law. It is designed to protect a person from being compelled by the state to 'convict himself out of his own mouth' and is available whenever the risk to exposure to future prosecution or penalty from a question or request for information is a 'real and appreciable' one. In criminal cases, the privilege only protects the person claiming it.[3]

An obvious manifestation of this privilege is that an accused cannot be compelled to testify in his own trial.[4] It is important to note, however, that if an accused *does* elect to give such evidence, then he waives the privilege to this extent: he may be asked questions in cross-examination, even though his answers may tend to incriminate him as to the offence(s) charged. This is only sensible - it would be odd if a defendant could tell his own side of the story, but could not then be challenged on it.[5] What he would be protected against, however, is answering questions which tended to expose him to risk of prosecution for some *other* offence.[6]

Over time, statute has chipped away at the privilege in some specialist areas where the public interest in obtaining the information is thought to outweigh the 'right to silence'. Thus there are various legislative provisions which require specified persons in specific circumstances to answer questions or produce documents or information, notwithstanding that compliance may incriminate them. Examples include proceedings involving the care or protection of children, breach of intellectual property rights, and actions for the recovery of property and so on arising out theft and fraud cases. Although the privilege against self-incrimination may not be relied upon in such cases to avoid complying with relevant orders or answering questions, there is a protective quid pro quo offered: namely that the answers and information

3 *R v Khan (Mohammed Ajimal)* [2007] EWCA Crim 2331, [29] and BCrP F 10.3

4 Although there may be risks to him in taking this option. See Ch. 23

5 See 1(2) Criminal Evidence Act 1898, which was designed to cope with the many risks which arose when defendants, as a general class, were first allowed to give evidence on their own behalf.

6 The privilege also extends to exposing a person to risk of penalty or forfeiture, but the more common risk in criminal cases is exposure to a criminal charge.

supplied as a result of these provisions may not be used in evidence in any resulting prosecution. The latter would have to be pursued using other evidence.

B. LEGAL PROFESSIONAL PRIVILEGE

There are two 'heads' of legal professional privilege. It is important to distinguish between them:

(i) Head 1: 'Legal advice privilege'

Confidential communications between professional legal advisor and client (or any person representing that client) made in connection with the giving or receiving of legal advice to that client are protected by legal professional privilege. *This is so whether or not litigation is contemplated or underway at the time.*[7] Here the communication is a two-way street and can be thought of in the form of a straight line, with the client at one end and the legal advisor at the other.

Legal advice is not confined simply to telling a client about the law; conversely, not all advice (and certainly not every communication) is privileged.[8] In particular, communications in furtherance of crime or fraud are a well-recognised (and sensible) exception to the principle - it is no business of lawyers to be hatching criminal plots![9] In complex cases, issues can arise about who is a client (if not an individual) and what is legal (as opposed, say, to financial[10]) advice. But the essential idea is straightforward enough; it is in the public interest that people should be able to get legal advice in complete confidence. Others are therefore not entitled to know of the content of such communications, unless the privilege is waived *(by the client)*. One important context when this might happen is when an accused opts[11] to give details of the legal advice he was given in order to explain why he did not answer questions put to him when interviewed by the police. Judges should warn counsel, or the accused, when the

7 Compare this with Head 2. See BCrP F 10.16

8 See the interesting list in Blackstone's *Civil Practice*, para 48.47

9 See discussion at BCrP F 10.32

10 See, e.g., *Three Rivers District Council v Bank of England* (No 6) [2004] UKHL 48, [2005] 1 AC 610)

11 There is a difference between *volunteering* information about legal advice and being *forced* to do so, e.g. to rebut an allegation of recent fabrication. The latter will not amount to a waiver: see BCrP F 10.38

latter is at risk of waiving his privilege.[12]

(ii) Head 2: 'Litigation privilege'

This brings a third person into the equation. *Confidential communications* between a professional legal advisor and/or his client *and a third party* are privileged where the *dominant* purpose was to enable the legal advisor to advise or act in connection with *litigation* which at the time was at least reasonably in prospect.[13] The typical example is an expert's report. So long as the right person (that is, the person commissioning the document) has the right motivation (litigation), then the privilege attaches, even if no trial ever takes place. Here the lines of communication usually form a triangle, involving three people instead of two.

The rationale here is that parties should be free to *conduct* litigation confidentially. A party who obtains an unhelpful expert's report, for example, need not disclose it (or its contents) to his opponent. Only if the evidence is to be *relied upon* in the litigation, must it be disclosed pre-trial.[14] In effect, the party seeking to adduce the evidence must waive his privilege in the information *before* (not merely as) the evidence is adduced. This is so no-one is taken by surprise, and everyone can respond sensibly to the evidence at trial. But a party who does not want to rely on such a privileged document, can bin it.[15]

Waiver of legal professional privilege

A client may elect to waive legal professional privilege. Often the purpose and degree of the waiver is clear; two typical circumstances when this might happen have been referred to above. Sometimes, however, a document may be disclosed for a limited purpose, and the question may then arise as to the extent to which the privilege has been waived. The answer is usually determined by fairness and the importance of

12 As to the risk to the defendant of not telling their story as soon as possible see e.g. *R v Loizou* [2006] EWCA Crim 1719 and Ch. 23 below

13 *Waugh v British Railway Board* [1080] AC 521 and BCrP F 10.22ff

14 See CrimPR r 19.3

15 Although it might well provoke a re-evaluation of the case! And it does not prevent that expert/ evidence being called by the other side, unless the views expressed are based on privileged information. See BCrP F 10.27

legal professional privilege to the proper administration of justice.[16]

C. WITHOUT PREJUDICE PROTECTION

In a sense this can be viewed as something of a 'mirror image' of litigation privilege, because it also involves the solicitor or client and another person: specifically the other party to (usually civil) litigation. Without prejudice *communications (oral or written) made in a genuine attempt to seek a settlement of a dispute*, are protected[17] from disclosure *to the court* at trial (the other side, of course, knows all about it). The purpose of this rule is to encourage open and effective negotiation by removing the fear that, if attempts to settle fail, any admissions apparently made during the negotiations will be used at trial against the party who made them.[18]

But what about admissions made in the course of attempting to settle a civil case, which reveal criminal behaviour? In *R v K(A)*[19] the question arose whether a third party, who had come by evidence of damning admissions made in the course of 'without prejudice' negotiations, was entitled to rely on them in subsequent criminal proceedings against the party who made them. It was held that the 'without prejudice' rule is intended to enable parties to negotiate freely without being prejudiced in respect of the *dispute to which the negotiations relate*. Although it may be justifiable to extend the protection to subsequent proceedings between those same two parties, the public interest becomes weaker the further away from the original dispute one gets. Criminal proceedings will involve different parties and are necessarily at least one removed from the original civil dispute. In general, therefore, the public interest in prosecuting crime is sufficient to outweigh the good which comes from promoting the settlement of civil disputes. In appropriate situations, however, it may be possible to exclude the evidence in the interest of fairness under s 78 PACE 1984.

16 See *R v Ahmed* [2007] EWCA Crim 2870, summarised at BCrP F 10.36

17 The 'without prejudice' rule is more of a protection than a privilege, but you will find practitioners describing it both ways.

18 See generally *Be Civil!*, by the author, Ch. 17

19 [2010] 2 WLR 905

2. PUBLIC INTEREST IMMUNITY (PII)

This is a very different concept to those discussed above and involves a court making a decision about, if not the lesser of two evils, then the greater of two goods. There is, on the one hand, a public interest in withholding from disclosure material which, if revealed, would harm the nation in some way. Typically such information relates to national security, terrorism intelligence, the identity of police informers and so on. On the other hand, there is a public interest in fair trials and justice not only being done, but being seen to be done. When these two public interests collide, if the court decides to keep secret or exclude otherwise admissible evidence, it will do so on the basis of public interest immunity.

Public interest immunity has thus been described as a *duty, not a privilege*, and should only be asserted if it is believed that the public good is better served by concealment than disclosure. In criminal cases the public interest most typically cited is the effective investigation and prosecution of serious crime, which is furthered by not revealing the names of informers or investigative processes when doing so would expose individuals to harm or put future operations in jeopardy. This may justify some derogation from the 'golden rule' of disclosure, but a fair trial should not ultimately be put at risk. If the accused cannot get a fair trial, better not to try him at all.[20]

Prosecutors seek a PII ruling from the court in accordance with CrimPR, r 15.3. A copy of the written application, setting out reasons why disclosure is not in the public interest, will be served on the defendant unless even that degree of disclosure is considered problematic. It is for the *court* in each instance to *balance* the competing risks and determine where the public interest lies.[21] This is a completely different exercise than the assertion or waiver of privilege. In criminal

20 *R v H and Others* [2004] UKHL 3, discussed in *Practical Guide* p. 437; Keane & McKeown, *Modern Law*, p. 649ff

21 *Conway v Rimmer* [1968] AC 910

cases it is also at times a painfully difficult exercise, since in many cases the liberty, and sometimes the lives, of individuals may be at stake.[22]

revision tips

- Distinguish clearly between privilege (in its various forms) and (*if* it is on your exam syllabus) public interest immunity. The distinctions are important.
- Remember that the privilege against self-incrimination is about a person not being forced to expose himself to *criminal* proceedings.
- Remember that if a defendant gives evidence in his case (and he cannot be forced to do so), he must answer questions put to him in cross-examination - even if they tend to incriminate him (which is the general idea of cross-examination!). This is a kind of waiver.
- Be aware generally of typical situations in which privilege might be waived.

It is worth reading ...

R(DPP) v Leicester Magistrates' Court [2015] EWHC 1295 (Admin). A short and useful review of the privilege against self-incrimination on facts which are easy to grasp. But note comment at BCrP F 10.3

Paras 65-69 of *The Attorney-General's Guidelines: Disclosure of Information in Criminal Proceedings* (Appendix 4 of Blackstone's *Criminal Practice*). In five short paragraphs, you can get a real sense of the exceptional nature of a PII claim in criminal cases.

22 This is a complex area of law. See generally BCrP F 9.1ff

Witnesses I

Pre-trial considerations

Generally speaking, witnesses give their evidence *sworn*, whether by taking an oath or making an affirmation. Both methods are accorded equal status[1] - the point is the solemn promise to tell the truth, not the belief (or lack of it) in a god.[2] The modern law of oaths and affirmations is governed by the Oaths Act 1978 which covers a multitude of matters, from the way in which the oath (which varies according to religious belief) is to be administered, to the fact that its validity is unaffected if the person who took it actually has no religious belief. The provisions make clear that the important thing is that the witness *feels* bound by any oath or promise that has been given, not its form as such.

In certain circumstances, evidence will be received *unsworn*. This is commonly the case with young children, which is discussed below in the context of the competence and compellability of witnesses.[3] There follows a review of the measures which a court can put into place to help certain witnesses when they give their evidence. Finally, once it is clear who is to give evidence, how, and with what assistance, it is necessary to look at the various rules which govern the course of testimony. These are discussed in Chapter 18.

1 The Oaths Act 1978, s 5(4). Thus, a perjury charge can flow from a witness who, having taken an oath or affirmed, wilfully gives false evidence: Perjury Act 1911, s 1

2 It follows that it would be improper for a judge, when summing up, to make any distinction between a witness who has affirmed and a witness who has taken the oath.

3 See also the position of a witness called merely for the purpose of producing a document at BCrP F 4.32

CHAPTER 17

1. COMPETENCE AND COMPELLABILITY IN CRIMINAL TRIALS

When preparing for trial, it is important to know whether the witnesses you want to call are *legally capable* of giving evidence; and, if so, whether they can *be required* to give evidence[4] if they are unwilling to do so voluntarily. 'Competence' refers to the first of these concepts; 'compellability', to the second.

The *general rule* is that *all* persons are *both competent and compellable* to give evidence.[5] Exceptions peculiar to criminal cases involve the accused and spouses/civil partners of the accused. Another important exception relates to children (and persons of unsound mind), which applies in *both* criminal and civil cases. The tests differ, although they borrow from and interact with each other.[6]

It is important not to confuse these three exceptions. They are commonly the subject matter of examination questions, often in combination with each other to test your ability to distinguish between and apply them simultaneously. Let's look at each one in turn.

A. THE ACCUSED

It is convenient to look at the exceptional status of the accused as witness by reference to the persons or party who may wish to call him.

(i) As witness *for the prosecution*

A defendant cannot be forced to incriminate himself,[7] and so accused persons are *not competent* as witnesses *for the prosecution*. In other words a defendant cannot give evidence on behalf of the prosecution even if for some bizarre reason he wanted to. This is so whether the defendant is charged alone, or with others.[8]

4 This includes answering questions asked, not just turning up!

5 If it were otherwise, the availability of crucial evidence would be unpredictable, at best. See BCrP F 4.1/2. Basic competence is defined in terms of ability to understand and give understandable answers to questions asked. See fn 33 below.

6 See also *Be Civil!*, by the author, Ch. 17

7 See generally Ch. 16

8 Youth Justice and Criminal Evidence Act 1999 (YJCEA 1999), s 53(4)

A co-accused can, however, give evidence for the prosecution if he *ceases* to be a co-accused. Thus where several people are charged in a case, and the prosecution want to use the evidence of one of them against the others, it is necessary to separate that potential witness from the pack so that he is not (or is no longer) liable to be convicted of any offence *in those proceedings*.[9] This can happen in a variety of ways, but in effect the case against that potential witness must be dropped, stopped, or completed, whether by an acquittal being entered or a guilty plea taken. If an accomplice decides to plead guilty, he is no longer 'liable to be convicted' in the proceedings in which it is proposed he gives evidence, since he has already formally admitted his guilt.[10] This would also be the case, of course, if the accomplice were simply to be *tried* separately, but the evidence in such circumstances is likely to be so tainted by self-interest that in practice this latter course is never taken.[11]

(ii) As witness *on his own behalf*

At every stage of criminal proceedings, a defendant is *competent* to give evidence on his own behalf, but *not compellable*.[12] A defendant who goes into the witness box[13] to tell his side of the story is open to cross-examination, whether by the prosecution or, if there is one, a co-accused, and in the process may well incriminate himself (or a co-accused). In other words, the evidence a defendant gives (assuming it is otherwise admissible evidence) can be used for *all purposes* - for, as well as against his case. A defendant cannot therefore be compelled to give evidence on his own behalf, because this too could conflict with his right not to incriminate himself.

A defendant who does not opt to tell his side of the story, however, will run the risk of a jury deducing from this that he has no story to tell. The 'adverse inferences' which may be drawn from a defendant's exercising his so-called 'right to silence', are discussed in detail in Chapter 23.

9 *Ibid*, s 53(5), BCrP F 4.8

10 Whether the accomplice is sentenced before or after the evidence given at the trial of the remaining accused might affect the view a jury takes of the evidence he gives, but it does not affect his competence as a witness.

11 The risks of such evidence being excluded by the judge (or rejected by the jury) would be very high. See e.g., *R v Turner* (1975) 61Cr App R 67. The sensible explanation of the position, given in that case by Lawton LJ, is usefully set out at BCrP F 4.9

12 'Every stage' includes post conviction (e.g. on sentencing) and, in practice, on a voir dire. See BCrP F 4.10

13 See Criminal Justice Act 1982, s 72 which sets out the general rule that a defendant electing to give evidence does so from the

(iii) As witness *for a co-accused*

An accused is *competent, but not compellable* as a witness for a co-accused who is being tried together *in the same* criminal proceedings.[14] Co-defendants running their cases in tandem might want to give evidence *for* each other; however, a defendant seeking to put the blame on his co-accused obviously would not. Remember too that an accused who agrees to give evidence on behalf of a co-accused is just as open to incriminating cross-examination (on behalf of the prosecution or another defendant) as he would be when giving evidence on his own behalf, so it is not a risk-free option.

Note, however, that a co-accused who *ceases*[15] being a person charged in the *same* proceedings becomes both competent *and compellable* as a witness for any former co-defendants who remain standing in the dock where he once stood. This is similar to the way in which an accomplice who is separated from the other co-accused can become available as a witness for the prosecution, although in this context a defendant will need to weigh up the pros and cons of calling such a witness, who may not perform well, especially under cross-examination. Much might depend on how and why that potential witness ceased to be a co-accused in the proceedings in question.

B. SPOUSE/CIVIL PARTNER OF THE ACCUSED

Again, it is convenient to look at the exceptional status of an accused's spouse as witness in criminal cases by reference to the person or party who may wish to call the evidence. This matter is governed by the Police and Criminal Evidence Act 1984 (PACE 1984), s 80, and applies equally to a spouse or civil partner of an accused.[16]

witness box and sworn, unless the law requires that the evidence be given unsworn.

14 A person charged in criminal proceedings shall not be called as a witness 'except on his own application': Criminal Evidence Act 1898, s 1(1)

15 Because, e.g., he pleads guilty or is tried separately or there is found to be no case against him.

16 s 84(1) Civil Partnership Act 2004

(i) Spouse/civil partner of accused as witness *for the prosecution*

Historically, it was not thought to be very conducive to marital harmony to force people to give evidence *against* their spouses, and so there has long been a *general* rule (applicable also to civil partners) that the spouse of the accused is *competent* to give evidence for the prosecution (and so may if he or she chooses), but *cannot be compelled* to do so.[17] Over time, however, it became clear that there were certain types of crimes where the public interest in successfully prosecuting offenders outweighed that of protecting the spousal relationship. These are the *'specified'* offences, described in PACE 1984, s 80(3), as being those where:

(a) the offence charged involves an assault on, or injury or a threat of injury to, *the spouse of* the accused *or* a person who was at the material time *under the age of 16*,

(b) the offence charged is a sexual offence alleged to have been committed in respect of a person who was at the material time *under the age of 16*,

(c) the offence charged consists of attempting or conspiring to commit either of the above, or being a secondary party to or inciting either of the above.

In a nutshell, these translate into crimes of domestic violence (that is, abuse by the accused on his or her *own* spouse/civil partner) and/or child abuse (on *any* child). In such cases, the spouse is often the only witness to the event, either because she[18] is the victim herself, or the mother of the child in question.[19] For that reason, *in these exceptional cases only*, the spouse of the accused (assuming she is not jointly charged) is not only competent, but also *compellable* as a witness for the prosecution.[20] They are thus also known, in this context, as the 'compellable offences'.[21]

---

17 There is no obligation to tell a wife who is competent but not compellable that this is the case before interviewing her about the crime of which her husband is suspected. But if the question were to arise as to whether it is in the interests of justice to admit her statement as hearsay, it would assist the argument for doing so if it could be shown that she had made the statement knowing she was under no obligation to do so. See *R v L* [2009] 1 WLR 626 and Ch. 20 on hearsay generally.

18 The legislation is gender neutral, of course, but men are most often the perpetrators and women the victims of domestic abuse.

19 But note that the injury or threat to children extends to *any* child; it need not be the child of the accused or his spouse.

20 PACE 1984, s 80(2A)

For some time it was not clear how the requirement of s 80(3)(a) that the compellable offence '*involves* an assault on, or injury or a threat of injury', was to be interpreted. Must the 'involvement' be legal (and so part of the legal definition of the offence charged) or simply factual (where violence is not necessarily alleged, but has in fact occurred in the commission of the offence)? In the case of *R v A(B)*[22] the Court of Appeal decided that a narrow, but sensible construction was needed. A balance had to be struck between the competing interests of protecting the spousal relationship and protecting spouses generally (in this context, by convicting perpetrators of domestic violence) and this was best achieved by keeping s 80(3)(a) within purposeful bounds. Thus the offence charged does not have to have as one of its ingredients 'an assault on, or injury or a threat of injury' to the spouse or person under 16. It is sufficient if the offence 'encompasses the real possibility' of such an assault. But the focus must be on the '*legal nature of the offence and not the specific factual circumstances' of its commission*. As the court pointed out, if it were otherwise, not only could a very wide range of offences be caught by the s 80(3) exception, which was not Parliament's intention, but it might be very difficult to determine at the outset of any case whether the spouse was truly compellable or not, as the evidence might not emerge in the way envisaged.[23]

(ii) Spouse/civil partner of accused as witness *for a co-accused*

An accused's spouse or civil partner (so long as not a co-defendant) is *competent* to give evidence for a co-accused, but is *not compellable unless the offence in question is a specified offence.*[24] In other words, the spouse of an accused is only compellable for a co-accused in those cases where he or she would be compellable for the prosecution. This is to stop the latter achieving indirectly (by means of cross-examination) what they are otherwise precluded from doing in presenting its own

It would seem that if compelled to give evidence about a specified offence, a spouse cannot be made to answer questions about any other offences charged, however factually related, unless they too are 'compellable offences'. This can make things a little awkward procedurally. The point was raised but not resolved in *R v L*, op. cit., see [22]. See BCrP F 4.14/15.

21 This should also help you remember both the general rule and this exception.

22 [2012] 1 WLR 3378

23 *Ibid*, paras 18 and 19, per Sir John Thomas P and BCrP F 4.16

24 s 80(2A)(a)

case. But watch out for multiple defendants, each with spouses/civil partners, in an exam question - if D1 is charged with violence only against D2's wife, D1's wife cannot be compelled to give evidence against her husband[25] because the relevant specified offence only extends to violence allegedly perpetrated on the accused's *own wife*, and not the wives of others or women generally. In this respect it differs significantly from the 'compellable' offence affecting children under the age of 16.

(iii) Spouse/civil partner of accused as witness *for the accused*

It is not thought to be particularly harmful to marital relations to be required to give evidence *for* your spouse, so the overarching general rule prevails: an accused's spouse (or civil partner) is *both competent and compellable as a witness for that accused*, unless he or she is a co-accused in the trial. Whether it is tactically wise for a defendant to compel his spouse to give evidence is another matter altogether. Much would depend on the nature of the case, the importance of the evidence and what the spouse might (or might not) be inclined to say!

(iv) Spouses/civil partners *jointly charged*

It is important to note that if spouses or civil partners are *jointly* charged in the *same* proceedings, then the interplay with the privilege against self-incrimination means that:

(a) *neither* are competent to give evidence for the prosecution (because they are both accused persons), *and*

(b) although otherwise competent to give evidence (for example, on their own behalf or on behalf of each other), neither *in any circumstances* can be compelled to give evidence in the case, whatever the offence.[26]

---

25 Either as witness for the prosecution or called by her spouse's co-accused.

26 s 80(4) PACE 1984.

As with co-accused generally, however, if one such spouse is not (or is no longer) to be tried in the same proceedings with the other, then this blanket prohibition no longer operates and the normal *spousal* rules will apply.[27]

Finally, note that unmarried partners, other than civil partners, are *not* given any special protection from the general rule that witnesses are both competent and compellable.[28] Nor are persons who were, but are no longer married or in a civil partnership.[29]

C. CHILDREN

(i) Competence

Children[30] who are competent to give evidence will give that evidence either sworn or unsworn, depending (mainly) on their age. In determining these matters, there is some interplay between civil and criminal procedure. You may remember that to be competent to give sworn evidence in a civil case, a child must pass the test set out in the case of *R v Hayes*;[31] namely, does the child understand the 'solemnity of the occasion' and the 'special duty to tell the truth, over and above the ordinary social duty to do so'? This is sometimes referred to as being '*Hayes appreciative*', and at one time (as the case name suggests) applied equally to criminal trials. The idea behind the *Hayes* test was to move away from the need for belief in the divine sanction against lying, and so secularise the test for the giving of sworn evidence.[32]

So far as criminal cases are concerned, these matters are now governed by the Youth Justice and Criminal Evidence Act 1999 (YJCEA 1999), ss 53-55. To summarise:

(a) Like all witnesses, children are competent to give evidence if they can understand questions and respond so as to be understood, that is, give

27 *Ibid*, s 80(4A)

28 The Grand Chamber of the European Court of Human Rights recently held that although this may interfere with the cohabitee's right to family life (Art 8), it was excusable as being 'necessary' for the 'prevention of crime': See PACE 1984, BCrP F 4.15

29 s 80(5) PACE 1984. Some commentators think the spousal non-compellability rules are rather outdated: see e.g. Keane & McKeown p.131

30 A person is a child in the legal sense if under the age of 18.

31 [1977] 1 WLR 234

32 Children's evidence in civil cases is discussed further in *Be Civil!*, by the author, Ch. 17

intelligible (not necessarily intelligent) answers to questions. A child (or indeed anyone) who cannot meet this modest standard is not competent to give evidence.[33]

(b) Children who are competent, *at least* 14 years old and '*Hayes appreciative*' will give their evidence *sworn*. Because it is often the case, witnesses who are competent to give evidence will be presumed to be '*Hayes appreciative*', if no evidence to the contrary is adduced by any party.[34]

(c) Children who are *under 14* years of age are not able to give sworn evidence under any circumstances (whatever their intelligence or morality), so assuming such a child is competent, the evidence must be given *unsworn*.[35] Note that an older child/person (14 years or older) who is competent, but nevertheless unable to satisfy the *Hayes* test, would also give evidence unsworn.[36]

It will be for the judge to form an opinion on these matters, if they arise - ideally before the child is to give evidence. The beauty of the criminal regime is that children aged 14 and older are effectively treated like adults for these purposes, so there is nothing the judge need do unless a doubt is raised (supported by evidence) about their competence or capacity to give sworn evidence. And if they are under 14, children can only give their evidence unsworn, so the only issue which can arise is their ability to give evidence at all.

Issues of competence (of any witness) can be raised by either party, or by the court itself, but at the end of the day it is for the person who wishes to call the evidence to establish, on the balance of probabilities, that the witness is competent.[37] Obviously, the younger the child, the more likely it is that questions of competence will arise, but *every witness (and every trial) is different*.[38] The procedure in such cases is

33 s 53(1) YJCEA 1999

34 Our friend the time-saving rebuttable presumption (see Ch. 15). See YJCEA 1999, s 55(3) and BCrP F 4.23

35 YJCEA 1999, s 55(2)

36 *Ibid*, s 56

37 Whether it is the prosecution or defence who seeks to call the evidence. *Ibid*, s 54(2), and see generally BCrP F 4.3

38 The question of competence is witness and trial specific: it is about the ability or capacity of the particular witness in a particular trial to comprehend, and provide comprehensible answers to questions asked in court, including those put in cross-examination. The quality of those answers is a matter or credibility and cogency, not the competence of the witness. See the guidelines set out in *R v Barker* [2010] EWCA Crim 4/BCrP F 4.21

governed by s 54 YJCEA 1999. The judge will typically ask the child appropriate questions (or watch relevant video recordings) - in the presence of the parties, but in the absence of the jury if there is one.[39] Special provisions can be put in place to help children to give evidence, and when deciding competence it should be assumed that any such assistance as may be necessary, will be available.[40] Expert evidence is admissible on the question of competence,[41] but will rarely be necessary with child witnesses who otherwise have no mental impairment. A decision that a child is competent may need to be revisited after his or her evidence is commenced or completed, especially if the initial decision was based on an ABE[42] interview. The child's behaviour under cross-examination some time after that initial interview could tell a different story, in which case the competence ruling could be reversed and the evidence excluded.[43]

The position and procedure is much the same when the issue in question is not the child's competence, but the manner in which the evidence should be given.[44] Again, if any question arises as to a child's eligibility to give sworn evidence, it will be for the person seeking to have that witness sworn to satisfy the court on the balance of probabilities that the relevant conditions have been met.[45]

(ii) Compellability

A child who is judged competent to give evidence (whether sworn or unsworn) will also be *compellable* to give that evidence. There are *no special rules for children and their parents* as there are for husbands and wives! If this seems a little harsh, remember that special arrangements are available to assist children in giving their evidence. These are discussed later.

39 YJCEA 1999, s 54(4) and 54(6)

40 *Ibid*, s 54(3). Special Measures Directions, available for children and other vulnerable witnesses, are discussed below.

41 *Ibid*, s 54(5)

42 Pre-trial interviews are conducted under specific guidelines with the objective of Achieving Best Evidence from young and vulnerable witnesses, and so are known as 'ABE interviews'. And see *R v F* [2013] EWCA Crim 424, especially para 39: not a child witness but an adult with special needs. The procedure and principles are the same.

43 As in *R v Malicki* [2009] EWCA Crim 365

44 YJCEA 1999, s 54(6)

45 *Ibid*, s 55(2) and (4)

D. PERSONS WITH MENTAL INCAPACITY

In criminal cases, the position here is also governed by the YJCEA 1999. The tests and procedure are the *same as for children*, although clearly chronological age is not so likely to come into the equation. On the other hand, expert evidence (to assist with questions of competence) is more likely to be relevant and necessary when the witness is mentally impaired in some way. It is important to remember, however, that mental illness does not necessarily render a witness incompetent to testify. Each case must be decided on its own merits. Again, if the witness with mental incapacity is found to be competent, that witness is also compellable to give evidence (unless any of the restrictions discussed above apply). Special measures should be put into place as appropriate.

E. SECURING ATTENDANCE OF WITNESSES AT TRIAL

It is essentially the parties' responsibility to ensure that their witnesses turn up at trial.[46] If either prosecution or defence requires the presence of a witness, but it looks as if that person might not attend as asked, then an application may be made for a *witness summons*.[47] This is effectively an order of the court that the witness attend to provide the required evidence. The court may issue a summons if satisfied (i) that the witness is likely to be able to give, or produce, *material* evidence and (ii) it is in the *interests of justice* to summons him or her to attend on the specified date.[48]

A *warrant* may be issued if the court is satisfied that a witness who was properly the subject of, and served with, a witness summons, nevertheless failed to attend without 'just excuse'. A warrant may even be issued if the court is satisfied (by evidence on oath) that a summons itself would probably not result in the witness attending. Note that magistrates' clerks may issues summonses, but not warrants.[49]

Failure to obey a witness summons without just excuse is a contempt of the

46 All witnesses whose evidence is being relied upon should attend to give oral evidence unless the parties agree to its being read out or the court rules otherwise.

47 s 2 Criminal Procedure (Attendance of Witnesses) Act 1965 (CP(AW)A 1965). Procedure is set out in CrimPR Pt 17

48 The test is the same in the Crown Courts and magistrates' courts: CrimPR 17.1/3

49 The test for 'just excuse' is very strict. See *R v Abdulaziz* [1989] Crim LR 717. For service of witness summons see CrimPR Pt 4, cited at BCrP D 21.28

court which issued the summons.[50]

Witness summons obviously have their place (and they can be useful when a person wants to be seen to have been compelled), but one should always think carefully about calling reluctant witnesses. Without a game plan in mind,[51] they can be difficult to handle and may do more harm than good.

2. SPECIAL MEASURES FOR VULNERABLE AND INTIMIDATED WITNESSES

At common law, the courts have always had some inherent ability to make special provision for certain types of witness who, either because of an innate vulnerability or the nature of their evidence, required assistance to give their evidence.[52] But as the need for a more coherent and comprehensive system increased, so too did the intervention of statute. The YJCEA 1999, Pt II, Chapter I sets out a detailed framework for court ordered 'special measure' directions (known colloquially as SMDs) for 'vulnerable and intimidated witnesses', but the system continues to evolve - the legislation has been significantly amended at least twice, and is further augmented by requirements of active case management and the obligation to ensure full participation of all those appearing in court.[53] This makes a rather unwieldy set of provisions even more difficult to navigate, so be patient in your approach to them. What follows is a brief introduction to assist you in understanding the nuts and bolts.

The idea behind the YJCEA system is to facilitate the giving of testimony by certain identifiable classes of vulnerable witnesses who might otherwise be too incapacitated, fearful or victimised to give their evidence effectively. The aim is not to enhance the content of the evidence as such, but to maximise the accuracy and coherence of its transmission to the tribunal. Some measures are geared specifically

50 Punishable with imprisonment or fine. See generally BCrP D 21.27ff and D 15.91ff

51 A prosecutor, for example, might knowingly call a witness likely to be 'hostile' (see Ch. 18) in order to get that person's earlier statement admitted as hearsay (see Ch. 20)

52 See, e.g., *X, Y and Z* (1990) 91 Cr App R 36

53 See BCrP D 14.1/2

to assisting witnesses who are very young or in some way disabled and need help communicating their evidence; others are intended for witnesses who are so scared or distressed by the idea of testifying in court that assistance is needed to minimise the trauma involved. A witness could, of course, require both kinds of help.[54]

As a general proposition, once the court (on application[55] or on its own accord) determines that a witness is 'eligible' for an SMD, it will then go on to consider whether, and if so what, special measures are needed to maximise the quality of the evidence to be given.[56] There are some circumstances, however, where the legislation requires that a *particular* direction be given.

A. THE RANGE OF SPECIAL MEASURES

It may be as well to begin with the sorts of measures which may (and in some cases must as a first resort) be available to a witness eligible for special measures,[57] starting with the most basic:

(i) Removal of wigs and gowns[58]

This is often done for the benefit of young children while they give their evidence, so they do not feel intimidated by the court process, or worse, be distracted by its resemblance to a fancy dress party

(ii) Screening the witness from the accused[59]

This is an appropriate measure when the witness can cope with the hub-bub of the courtroom, but may feel intimidated or upset if the accused watched the evidence being given. Note that it is *only the accused* who will be prevented from seeing the witness (and vice versa): not the bench, the lawyers, the jury (if there is one) or other relevant court personnel, who will go about their business as usual.

54 Advocates must now adapt to witnesses, not the other way round. See, e.g. *Achieving Best Evidence in Criminal Proceedings: Guidance on interviewing victims and witnesses, and guidance on using special measures* (2016) (*ABE Guidance*) cited in BCrP D 14.4

55 Application is made in writing, using a specially designed form for the purpose. The procedure is governed by Part 18 of the Criminal Procedure Rules, which focuses on how the form is to be completed and when it should be submitted. This is summarised at BCrP D 14.6ff. A look at the form itself will tell you a lot.

56 YJCEA 1999, s 19(2)

57 Depending on the basis of eligibility, which is discussed below

58 YJCEA 1999, s 26

59 *Ibid*, s 23

Because the use of screens could give jurors a negative impression, the judge should given them an appropriate direction when summing up so the defendant's case is not prejudiced.[60]

(iii) Exclusion directions in sexual offence and other special cases

Named people (or members of the press) may be *excluded* from the courtroom while a vulnerable witness gives evidence, thus achieving a *degree of privacy*.[61] This measure can *only* apply in *sexual offence cases* or where the court has reason to believe that the witness may be *intimidated* by the presence of the named individual(s). As you might expect, persons who may *not* be excluded under this provision include the accused, legal representatives acting in the proceedings, or any persons appointed to assist the witness.

(iv) Aids to communication[62]

This provision is *only* available to witnesses who have trouble *communicating* with the court because they *are young or otherwise mentally or physically impaired*.[63] The idea is that the device in question is one which, if used, will help compensate for any incapacity suffered by the witness and thus enhance the transmission of the evidence. Use of normal hearing aids might not need to be the subject of such measures any more than spectacles would, but more technical or complex aids would (for example that used by Stephen Hawking to speak). This special measure is essentially about *things* which assist communication. The next one is about *people* who do this.

(v) Examination of witness through an interpreter or approved intermediary[64]

Use of a signer for the hearing impaired would be an example of this type of special

60 See Crown Court Conpendium Pt 1 Ch. 3-6

61 See YJCEA 1999, s 25, which sets this measure out under the heading 'evidence given in private'. This description is a little broad since only those persons described in the direction are excluded (one member of the press is often allowed to stay) and the direction does not stop the proceedings being public for other purposes. Whatever element of privacy is achieved, it only lasts during the giving of the evidence in question.

62 *Ibid*, s 30

63 This measure is thus not applicable to the fearful or distressed witness: *Ibid*, s 18(1)

64 *Ibid*, s 29

measure, which again is *only* available to those needing help *communicating* their evidence because they are *children or otherwise physically or mentally incapacitated.*[65] Both interpreters and intermediaries facilitate communication, although the latter's job extends beyond mere translation. The function of the intermediary is to ensure that the meaning of questions asked of - and answers given by - the vulnerable witness is effectively conveyed, whether in a police station or a courtroom.[66] Theirs is a holistic and proactive role, which is to assess the abilities and needs of a vulnerable witness (which can be wide-ranging), advise on how best to communicate with that person, and help to ensure that quality of communication is maintained.[67]

The importance of the intermediary in helping witnesses, especially young children, to communicate their stories in court, has gained prominence over the last decade. Most registered intermediaries are speech and language therapists, but a wide variety of professions are represented, including social work, mental health and psychology. The idea is to match the relevant expertise to the given witness's communication deficit, which could be the product of any number of factors, including immaturity and learning difficulties.[68]

(vi) Evidence by 'live link'[69]

This is a means by which a witness, who is somewhere other than the courtroom (often somewhere else in the building), gives evidence in real time, but via a two-way television (or similar) link set up to communicate with those involved in the proceedings. The witness can see on one screen the person asking the questions, and be seen by the relevant people (judge, jury, lawyers) on another screen in the courtroom.[70] The witnesses may be accompanied by a specified person to support them while giving their evidence - often someone from the court's witness support scheme, but a young person, for example, may do better having a parent (or other

65 Thus this measure too is not applicable to a witness eligible merely due to fear or distress: *ibid* s 18(1)

66 See *ibid*, s 29(2)

67 For example, by alerting the judge that a line of questioning may be confusing the witness. Such interventions are made to the judge, in front of a jury if there is one, since they need to assess the quality of the evidence given.

68 As to how intermediaries work see the tool kit *Intermediaries Step-by-Step* (2015) on The Advocate's Gateway at theadvocatesgateway.org and generally BCrP D 14.43-44

69 YJCEA 1999, s 24

70 *Ibid*, s 24(8)

71 So long as such person does not interfere with the process. See *ibid*, s 24(1A) and (1B)

72 See below on previous consistent statements

known adult) present.[71] If evidence is directed to be given in this way, the witness cannot give evidence any other way without the court's permission. This is to avoid witnesses, in effect, getting to tell (or re-tell) their one story in two different ways.[72]

(vii) Video recorded evidence[73]

In an increasing number of situations, the court may order that the *evidence-in-chief* of a young or vulnerable witness should take the form of a video-recorded interview (and when this happens, the cross-examination which follows is often, although not inevitably, by live link). Clearly not just any taped conversation with the witness will do; the conduct of such examinations is governed by the Achieving Best Evidence guidelines, which is why they are known as 'ABE interviews'.[74]

It may be useful to think of such recordings as the audio-visual equivalent of witness statements which stand as evidence-in-chief in civil trials. In the same way, inadmissible evidence should be edited from the recording and the witness must normally be available for cross-examination.[75] The big difference, of course, is that the cross-examination will usually also be subject to an SMD (at present, often a live link: video recorded cross-examination was still being piloted in 2017 e.g. for complainants in rape cases).[76] And of course the judicial discretion to exclude evidence[77] applies equally to recorded, as to live evidence-in-chief.

B. WITNESSES ELIGIBLE FOR SPECIAL MEASURES

Eligible witnesses under the YJCEA 1999 fall into five categories (none of which include the accused). They are not necessarily mutually exclusive.

(i) Children[78]

All witnesses under 18 at the time of hearing or recording (except the accused) are

---

73 YJCEA 1999, s 27 (evidence-in-chief). A provision allowing for video recording of cross-examination and re-examination (s 28) has not yet been brought into force for all courts: see BCrP D 14.46

74 The ABE Guidance (2016) is available on the CPS and MoJ websites. In the legislation, reference is made to 'relevant recordings' which is defined as 'a video recording of an interview of the witness made with a view to its admission as evidence-in-chief of the witness': see, BCrP D 14.32. As to cross-examination, see Ch. 18

75 *Ibid*, s 27(5)

76 In civil cases, witness statements standing as evidence-in-chief is not special - it is the norm. See *Be Civil!*, by the author, Ch. 17

77 See Ch. 14

78 YJCEA 1999, s 16(1)(a) (as amended)

eligible for an SMD by virtue of s 16 YJCEA 1999. Unless the child or the court feels that some other direction, or no direction is preferable,[79] or the interests of justice dictate otherwise,[80] there is a presumption or *'primary rule'* that in all such cases the court must direct that: (a) the witness's evidence-in-chief shall be given by means of a relevant video recording, and (b) any other evidence (cross-examination and re-examination), if not also video recorded,[81] shall be given by means of a live link.[82] Where this primary rule is displaced, and the evidence is to be given in court, then the use of screening must be ordered, unless this is not in the circumstances felt necessary.[83] In either case, the court should also consider whether any other special measures (for example, the use of an intermediary) are warranted.[84]

(ii) Complainants in sex, modern slavery and trafficking cases[85]

Complainants in sexual offence and related cases are, generally speaking, known to be particularly vulnerable witnesses, and so they too are given a special status under the YJCEA 1999. Like children (and sometimes they are children), such witnesses are by definition eligible for an SMD unless they inform the court that they do not wish to be eligible on this basis. If the case is heard in the Crown Court, then s 22A also applies, which effectively says that if a party applies for a direction that the complainant's evidence-in-chief be given by means of a relevant video recording, then this is the direction the court should make, unless such a direction is unjust or some other direction is thought more able to maximise the quality of the evidence.[86] As to cross- and re-examination of the complainant, the court should consider whether, and if so what special measures might be made. Although not mandated, it would be common to direct that this aspect of the complainant's evidence be given by live link, although in time pre-recorded cross-examination and re-examination may well be on the menu of possibilities.[87]

79 What sway the child's own views on the matter holds will depend on factors like his age, his relationship to the accused, and so forth. *Ibid*, s 21 (4C)

80 *Ibid*, s 21 (4)

81 The legislation is worded to cater for the bringing into force of s 28 (which extends video recording to cross-examination and re-examination of witnesses), which may now happen sooner rather than later, at least in certain sex offence cases, following the pilot scheme referred to in fn 73 above.

82 YJCEA 1999, s 16(3)

83 Again taking into account any views expressed by the witness and bearing in mind the aim of maximising the effective communication of the evidence. *Ibid*, s 21(4A)-(4C)

84 *Ibid*, s 21 (2)(b) and BCrP D 14.13ff

85 *Ibid*, s 17.4 and ss 1 and

(iii) Witnesses in proceedings involving weapons[88]

This is a category which confers eligibility on *any* witnesses (other than the accused) in proceedings relating to a 'relevant offence' (which at present includes an *array of firearm or knife crimes*[89]), unless the witness in question informs the court that he or she does not wish to be eligible on this basis. There is no 'primary rule' or presumption in favour of ordering video recorded evidence-in-chief, but this remains one of the options. If a witness is eligible under this head, it will be for the court to decide whether and, if so, what special measures to order in the circumstances.

In a sense, these first three categories each describe an objective status conferring *automatic entitlement* to an SMD. The next two categories are not age or case specific, and involve an assessment of some sort by the court as to the eligibility of the witness.

(iv) s 16: Witnesses eligible on grounds of *incapacity*[90]

As we have seen, children are automatically entitled under this head, but under s 16 an adult witness will also be eligible for an SMD if the court considers that he or she has a physical or mental impairment which would 'diminish' the quality of the evidence to be given. The court should have particular regard to the witness's ability to answer questions coherently, completely and accurately when assessing the likely quality of his or her evidence.[91] If the court finds the witness eligible on this basis (and assuming the witness is in fact competent to give evidence), it will go on to determine whether and, if so, what special measures should be directed to maximise the transmission of the evidence.

(v) s 17: Witnesses in *fear or distress* about testifying[92]

A witness will be eligible for special measures under s 17 if the court considers that

---

2 of the Modern Slavery Act 2015. See BCrP D 14.17/18

86 *Ibid*, s 22A(5)-(9). Ironically, it might suit some accused tactically to reduce the complainant to a disembodied face on a small screen. Also some victims may wish to testify in open court.

87 See fn 81

88 YJCEA 1999, the recently added s 17(5)-(7)

89 'Relevant offences' are described in Schedule 1A. The list can be added to or otherwise amended in future by virtue of s 17(6)

90 YJCEA 1999, s 16(b)

91 *Ibid*, s 16(5)

92 *Ibid*, s 17(1) and see BCrP D 14.19

the quality of the evidence in question will be diminished because the witness is fearful or distressed about testifying in court. In deciding whether the witness is eligible on this basis, the court will take into account common sense matters such as the age, background, and other circumstances of the individual concerned, as well as the nature of the offence charged and any relevant behaviour towards the witness on the part of the accused or his family (any of which may explain why the witness is scared or distressed).[93] Again, if the witness is found eligible on this basis, the court will go on to determine whether and, if so, what special measures should be directed to assist the witness.

It is important to note that in making decisions about whether an SMD should be made, and if so on what terms, it is important for the court not only to consider any relevant views expressed by the witness, but also whether the measures under consideration would tend to inhibit such evidence being *properly tested* by the accused or other party to the proceedings. Special measures are intended to maximise the evidence by assisting witnesses, where assistance is needed and wanted, but they are *not* intended or designed to interfere with effective cross-examination or a fair trial.[94]

C. THE ACCUSED AS WITNESS

There may be times when a vulnerable defendant needs assistance from the court to ensure that he has a fair opportunity to put forward his defence as best he can, and to understand and participate meaningfully in the proceedings. But the accused as witness was explicitly excluded from the ambit of s 16 and 17 of the YCJEA 1999,[95] and so it has been left to the inherent power of the court, human rights obligations, piecemeal legislative tinkering and the case management rules to try and fill the void. For example, s 33A of the YCJEA 1999 (as amended)[96] permits

93 *Ibid*, s 17(2)

94 The special measures scheme was held to be compliant with Art 6 of the European Convention on Human Rights in *R (D) v Camberwell Green Youth Court* [2005] 1 AllER 999, HL, although its half-hearted extension to vulnerable defendants still gives cause for concern: BCrP D 14.25

95 This is thought by some to be an unsustainable omission, especially in youth courts, although it is fair to say that the defendant as witness always throws up special considerations. One could also begin to imagine cases where, if the accused were also generally eligible, there might be no-one in the courtroom but the police, advocates, judge and jury! See also Hoyano, L. '*Special Directions Take Two: Entrenching Unequal*

the court to make a 'defendant's evidence direction', allowing an accused to give his evidence through live link (where this would assist) if his ability to participate in the proceedings as a witness is impaired by limited intellectual or social functioning or (in the case of adults) through mental illness. But the use of intermediaries for vulnerable defendants has been undermined by funding considerations and recent Practice Directions.[97] Trial judges are expected to do all they can to assist a vulnerable defendant, adapting the normal procedure as necessary,[98] but attempts to extend the SMD regime more comprehensively and so give 'equality of arms' to accused witnesses remains somewhat stymied.[99]

D. ANONYMOUS WITNESS ORDERS

The sorts of special measures we have been discussing so far are not especially controversial. Even where allowed to give evidence-in-chief by video recording, the witness, whose identity is known, will be available for a comprehensive cross-examination.[100] The same cannot be said for the anonymous witness order (AWO), which is an entirely different species of special measure. Clearly there will be times when the safety or evidence of a witness would be seriously compromised if that person's identity were known, but if a defendant does not even know who his accuser is, this has very serious implications, not only for him but for natural justice.

Having said that, in appropriate circumstances, to protect witnesses and induce them to give evidence, various measures can be ordered,[101] ranging from use of pseudonyms, screening witnesses and modulating voices to withholding specific information and banning certain questions in cross-examination which might enable the witness to be identified. In a nutshell, such orders may only be properly made if *three conditions* are met: (i) the order is *truly needed* to protect the safety of the witness, prevent serious damage to property or prevent real harm being done to

Access to Justice?' [2010] Crim LR 345

96 Inserted by the Police and Justice Act 2007, s 47: BCrP D 14.22/23

97 Crim PD1, 3 F.12 and see generally BCrP D 14.25

98 See e.g., *R v Cox* [2012] 2 Cr App R 6 and generally BCrP D 14.21

99 In part, no doubt, because of the funding implications. See generally, Cooper, P & Wurtzel, D, '*A Day Late and a Dollar Short: in Search of an Intermediary Scheme for Vulnerable Defendants in England and Wales*' [2013] Crim LR 4 and *R(OP) v Sec State for Justice* [2014] Cr App R 70 at [46]

100 Even if/when pre-recorded, such cross-examination can be thorough.

101 Coroners and Justice Act 2009 (CAJA 2009), s 86 (2)

the public; (ii) the proposed order would in the circumstances be consistent with a *fair* trial; and (iii) the order is needed to ensure that *important* witness testimony is given.[102] Further, if an order is made, it will clearly be necessary for the judge to give such warning to the jury as appropriate to ensure that the defendant is not prejudiced by it.[103]

The current law is found in the Coroners and Justice Act 2009. Section 89(2) sets out the matters which the court should look at when deciding whether to make an AWO, which include all sorts of common-sense considerations, including whether the evidence could be admitted in some other way than by testimony in court, the importance of the credibility of the witness to the case, whether other lesser measures would protect the witness and whether the evidence is the sole and/ or decisive evidence against the accused. *R v Mayers*[104] gives detailed guidance on how the courts should approach these statutory provisions,[105] and highlights two facts, namely that there must really be no alternative to the order and that the outcome of most applications will boil down to whether there can be a fair trial if the order is made. It also gives guidance on the warning to be given to juries, and in particular the need to direct them about the 'obvious difficulties facing a defendant who is challenging either the credibility or accuracy of an anonymous witness'.[106] Although hundreds of witness anonymity orders (mostly in respect of undercover police officers) have been made since they were first given legislative endorsement in 2008,[107] it is still important to observe that they should not be regarded as routine, but rather as a special measure 'of last resort'.[108]

---

102 *Ibid*, s 88

103 *Ibid*, s 90

104 [2009] 1 WLR 1915

105 These are usefully summarised in Keane & McKeown *Modern Law*, p. 170

106 *R v Mayers*, op. cit., cited in Crown Court Compendium Pt 1 Chs. 3-8

107 The predecessor to the CAJA 2009 was the nearly identical Criminal Evidence (Witness Anonymity) Act 2008

108 *R v Donnovan* [2012] EWCA Crim 2749 and BCrP D 14.50

revision tips

- Distinguish clearly between the rules about competence and compellability as they affect

  (a) the accused
  (b) the spouse/civil partner of the accused *and*
  (c) children/those with mental impairment

- You may well get a combination of such witnesses in an exam question, and will need to differentiate between them. Read exam questions carefully and note relevant detail - especially who is being asked to give evidence, and for (or against) whom - and in what sort of case!
- Remember the rationale for the competence/compellability rules (and the exceptions). This should help you to remember them.
- Make sure you can identify arguments for and against an SMD in any given case, as well as the eligibility requirements.

It is worth reading ...

R v A(B) [2012], a recent case on the spousal compellability rules. It is easy to understand factually, and the judgment is short. It shows clearly how priorities can clash and also alludes in a post-script to the difficulties of keeping the law in this area consistent and up-to-date. There is some reference to special measures legislation which has since been amended but, given that the current law is set out in this chapter, you will no doubt figure that out!

R v Lubemba [2015] 1 WLR 1579. Two cases really - both easy to grasp. In one the judge's approach was fine, in the other it was not. A good review of best practice with vulnerable witnesses. See especially para [45]

Witnesses II

Testifying at trial

In the last chapter, we looked at evidential matters affecting witnesses which arise before a trial. This chapter will concentrate on the law governing the giving of oral evidence by witnesses. Beginners can find this aspect of evidence law confusing, in part because the rules really only come alive in a courtroom.[1] Once in practice, you will learn to identify and deal with any contravention as it is occurring. Experience will eventually be your best guide, but until then it may help you to make sense of what might seem a disparate set of topics, to bear in mind the following:

(a) The three stages of oral testimony are *examination-in-chief, cross-examination* and (if necessary) *re-examination.* I have used these as the main sub-divisions for this section, although the focus is on the first two. Context is important, and so you should learn to differentiate the rules which pertain *only* to examining your own witness, those which pertain *only* to cross-examination and those which apply *across the board.* This will help you to understand and remember them.

(b) It is important to remember that a witness's credibility, or 'credit' as it is sometimes called, is a relevant fact in any given trial because it is something which makes that witness's version of events more or less likely to be true. Some of the witness handling rules require an appreciation of

1 So take all opportunities to see (real) trials in action. Watch and listen carefully.

the difference between questions going *solely* to the credit of the witness and questions which are relevant to a fact in issue in the case[2] - even (or especially) when the line between the two virtually disappears.

(c) There is always a rationale which, even when rather outdated, lies behind each of the rules of witness handling. Understanding the former will help you remember the latter. Three principles, which particularly impact on witness handling, are: the notion that *justice delayed is justice denied* (so trials should be over as quickly as possible and not get bogged down in side-issues); *evidence is best heard live and on oath* (hence pre-trial accounts of what happened are only received in certain circumstances); and *a person's moral character can tell us something about his credibility.*

Finally, do not confuse fictional and factual representations of witness handling. It could make matters worse if you have been watching American television.

1. EXAMINATION-IN-CHIEF

There are some important rules relating to the course of presenting one's own evidence and examining witnesses in chief. It is as well to remember that, although a judge may, from time to time, ask questions of a person testifying (especially an unrepresented accused to help him), it is essentially the advocate's job to question witnesses. Moreover, the credibility of the evidence of a witness is an important aspect of getting one's case across. There are, however, *limits* on what a party may do to bolster the quality of the evidence being presented in support of his own case.

2 The latter might at the same time also affect the witness's credibility, of course.

3 See *Be Civil!*, by the author, Ch. 17

4 Even if pre-recorded by virtue of a Special Measures Direction (SMD). See Ch.17

5 Or assumes the existence of facts not yet in evidence. An example of this might be (assuming it is not established a knife was used): Q: *"When he pulled out the knife, what did you do?"*

6 A question need not necessarily be in this form to be leading. Even *"And was it stormy that night?"* is very suggestive of the preferred answer (unless

In civil cases, examination-in-chief is something of a dying art, since a witness's pre-trial statements will usually (but not inevitably) stand as his or her evidence before cross-examination.[3] This is not the case in criminal trials, where generally speaking, witnesses still give their evidence-in-chief orally,[4] and so it is especially important in this context to know and understand the rules governing the conduct of this phase of questioning any witness. They include the following.

A. THE GENERAL RULE AGAINST ASKING LEADING QUESTIONS IN EXAMINATION-IN-CHIEF

Leading questions suggest to the witness a particular answer.[5] An obvious example might be: *"It was stormy on that night, wasn't it?"*, which (assuming the weather was as suggested and the issue is controversial) invites the curt response: *"Yes"*.[6] The purpose of the general prohibition against asking leading questions in chief is obvious, and really just a matter of common sense. The evidence is meant to come from the witness, who directly perceived the event in question; not the advocate, who did not. The idea behind questioning your *own* witnesses, who may well be inclined to want to give helpful evidence, is to *elicit* the evidence from them, not put words in their mouths.[7] This is not always easy to do, and there is great skill involved in effective examination-in-chief.[8] The rule, however, is not applied strictly where introductory or formal matters are concerned, or when the subject matter of the question *is not* in dispute. So if it is not a vital piece of the evidential puzzle that it was stormy on the night in question, the suggestion from counsel that it was will not be of any consequence.

B. THE SO-CALLED 'HOSTILE WITNESS'

An advocate conducting examination-in-chief should know what the evidence of that witness will be.[9] Nevertheless, sometimes witnesses get muddled or say the

---

the answer one seeks is a negative!).

7 The matter is quite the reverse, of course, when it comes to much cross-examination: see below.

8 The judge can give the advocate some leeway in the interest of justice. See BCrP F 6.13 (see also examples in *Practical Guide* p.99-103)

9 From the witness's statement, which the questioner will always use as a guide. There is also an old legal adage: 'Never ask a question to which you do not know the answer'. Without a strategy in mind (depending on what is said), it can certainly be risky to do so!

10 See below.

11 Although other witnesses can be called to try and repair or counteract the damaging testimony: see BCrP F 6.47

12 This could happen as late as re-examination,

wrong things or suddenly remember something differently. This is known as 'not coming up to proof'. Beyond inviting him to refresh his memory, [10] there is little an advocate can do about a witness who is 'unfavourable' in this sense, except soldier on as well as possible. This is because there is a general rule against impeaching or contradicting your own witness. You cannot put a person forward as a truthful witness for your own cause, and then turn around and suggest that the testimony is not to be believed when that witness does not say what you wanted or expected him to say.[11]

However, it can become apparent[12] that the witness you have called actively does not wish to tell the court, truthfully, what he knows. In such cases, that witness may, with the court's permission,[13] be declared 'hostile'. This allows the advocate in effect to cross-examine his own witness to the extent of asking leading questions and putting to him and, if necessary, proving, 'that he made at other times a statement inconsistent with' what he is (or is not) now telling the court.[14]

If the hostile witness adopts the evidence in the previous statement under questioning, then it simply becomes his evidence on the day. If he does not, then the previous statement will be proved against him and is admissible as evidence of the truth of the matters stated in it.[15] In the latter case, where there is conflicting evidence from the same witness, the question then arises as to what the judge should tell a jury. In short, they will usually be told to consider the reliability of the witness evidence, in view of the contradictions and surrounding facts, and then decide whether they prefer the evidence in court or the previous statement - or neither![16]

Unless you are prepared, it is not generally an ideal situation to have a 'hostile' witness on your hands (after all, the witness is supposed to be on your side), and mercifully it does not happen too often.[17] However, knowing what to do, and making the best of it,[18] is a lot better than just sitting down with a puzzled look on your face.

see BCrP F 6.49. If one can anticipate (and do something about) a witness's reluctance to give evidence, so much the better. But prosecutors faced with witnesses who have 'second thoughts' about giving evidence are often only too happy to have them declared 'hostile' on the day. See, e.g., *R v Mazekelua* [2011] EWCA Crim 1458.

13 The judge's discretion is virtually unappealable. The application should usually be made in front of the jury. *R v Khan* [2003] Crim LR 428. It may be sensible to first invite the witness to 'refresh' his memory. See below and BCrP F 6.50.

14 Criminal Procedure Act 1865, s 3. However, one is not allowed to discredit such a witness more generally, for example, by adducing his previous convictions. See BCrP F 6.51 and discussion

C. THE RULE AGAINST PREVIOUS CONSISTENT STATEMENTS

A 'previous consistent statement' is a statement made by a witness on an occasion before the trial which is consistent with that witness's later testimony in court. The general rule, in both civil and criminal cases, is that evidence of such statements (also called self-serving statements) is not admissible to bolster the *credibility* of the witness. The rationale for the rule is that the evidence does not improve with repetition and is most reliable when heard on the day in court; the fact that the witness previously told others the same story does not confirm the evidence he is telling in the witness box. More importantly the rule prevents witnesses from manufacturing evidence or attempting to make their version of events seem more plausible by merely rehearsing it several times.[19]

Exceptions

As ever, there are exceptions to this rule. They are: (i) a defendant's innocent reaction on accusation, (ii) evidence of previous identification, (iii) a victim's complaint, (iv) rebutting allegations of recent fabrication, and (v) memory refreshing documents. The first three of these are only applicable in criminal cases; the last two apply to both criminal and civil proceedings.

(i) Self-serving statements made on accusation

This survives as a concession to a defendant to show consistency with his not guilty plea. We will see that incriminating statements by defendants are admissible as evidence of guilt;[20] it would be rather harsh if an earlier protestation of innocence were to be excluded for all purposes. Strictly speaking all that such (wholly exculpatory) statements show is that the defendant's 'attitude' or 'reaction' when first accused of the crime is consistent with innocence. This exception is not strictly

of cross-examination and previous inconsistent statements below.

15 CJA 2003, s 119(1) and see below Ch.20

16 See, e.g., *R v Joyce* [2005] EWCA Crim 1785 and Crown Court Compendium Pt 1 Ch.14-7

17 The risks are higher when that witness had to be compelled to give evidence.

18 If the evidence is important, the earlier statement will be of some evidential value as a hearsay statement. If it is unimportant, it might be more sensible to stop the questioning, rather than reveal the witness to a jury as an unwilling one.

19 Hence the rule is also known as the 'rule against narrative'. See, BCrP F 6.38 and *R v Roberts* [1942] All ER 187 for an example of its application and rationale.

20 See Ch.21 on confessions.

limited to an initial reaction, although the more time which has elapsed between the first encounter with his accusers and the assertion of innocence, the less weight it will carry.

Sometimes, defendants make statements which partly incriminate and partly exonerate. These are known as 'mixed statements'. Because it is difficult, if not impossible to explain to a jury that the parts of the statement which assist the defendant's case have some lesser status than those which incriminate him, the position now is that *a mixed* statement is admissible in its *entirety* for the tribunal of fact to decide where the *truth* lies.[21] In directing a jury, however, the judge would be entitled to point out that human nature more readily makes excuses than accepts blame.

(ii) Statement of previous identification

The reason for the emergence of this exception is the obvious importance attached to identification evidence and ensuring that the right person is convicted of the crime. By the date of the trial a lot of time may have passed since the commission of the offence and anything which excludes 'the idea that the identification of the prisoner in the dock was an afterthought or mistake' is to be encouraged.[22] As a matter of common sense, an earlier identification is likely to be more cogent than a later one, and a so-called 'dock identification' should be avoided in any event.[23] Thus, the common law allows a witness to give evidence of having identified the accused on a previous occasion.[24] As you might expect, the usual practice is to do this before asking the witness whether that person is in court.

The Criminal Justice Act 2003 (CJA 2003) extended this principle so that it is no longer limited to the identification of the accused, or indeed to the identification of a person. The exception now covers a previous oral or written statement of

21 See BCrP F 6.39 and *R v Aziz* [1996] AC 41 and see Ch. 20

22 See famous explanation of Viscount Haldane LC in *R v Christie* [1914] AC 545, at 551

23 If you had to speculate as to who in the courtroom had done something wrong, the person standing in the dock might seem a pretty good guess.

24 Anyone who witnesses the identification could also give this evidence.

a witness which 'identifies or describes a person, object or place', provided the witness, while giving evidence, 'indicates that to the best of his belief he made the statement, and to the best of his belief it states the truth'.[25]

(iii) Earlier statement of victim's complaint

This exception, which used to be known as 'recent complaint', dates back to the time when corroboration of a victim's evidence was needed in sexual abuse cases. The latter requirement has long gone, but the permissive exception to the rule against self-serving statements remains. Note, however, that by operation of the CJA 2003, it is not limited to sex cases. Moreover, it is now no longer a statutory requirement that the complaint be particularly recent![26] To reflect this it should perhaps be re-branded 'victim's complaint'.[27]

Thus, this exception now covers any previous statement, whether oral or written, made by the victim of the offence being prosecuted, which 'consists of a complaint (whether to a person in authority or not) about conduct which would, if proved, constitute the offence or part of the offence' to which the proceedings relate.[28] There is no limitation in the 2003 Act on the number of complaints which could be admitted in evidence this way, although clearly a court would have to guard against the possible unfairness of 'complaint upon complaint'.[29]

Remember too that the point of allowing in evidence of recent complaint at common law was to show consistency with the victim's evidence. It thus follows that there must be evidence from the victim with which to be consistent and so the requirement remains that this exception to the rule against previous consistent statements can only be invoked if the witness *first* gives the evidence *orally* in court.[30]

Finally, at common law, a complaint made as a result of a leading question was inadmissible, but this no longer applies unless a threat or promise is involved.[31]

25 Criminal Justice Act 2003 (CJA 2003), s 120(1), (4) and (5)

26 s 120(7)(d) CJA 2003, which required that the complaint was made 'as soon as could reasonably be expected after the alleged conduct', was repealed by the Coroners' and Justice Act 2009, s 112

27 The Crown Court Compendium refers to it simply as 'statement of complaint'. See Pt 1, Ch.14-12

28 CJA 2003, s 120(1), (4) and (7), cited at BCrP F 6.32

29 Which brings us back to the policy behind the general rule itself! See *R v O* [2006] 2 Cr App R 405

30 CJA 1003, s 120(7)(f)

31 *Ibid* s 129(8)

Having said that, the manner in which a complaint is elicited is likely to affect the *weight* to be attached to it, as might the time which had elapsed since the incident and/or the source of the evidence of the previous complaint - the more independent that source and the more spontaneous the complaint, the better.[32]

(iv) Statement rebutting an accusation of recent fabrication

This is a common sense exception. If, under cross-examination, a witness's version of events is challenged as being a 'recent' invention, it would be very unjust if the general rule prevented that witness rebutting this allegation by pointing to (and adducing in re-examination) earlier statements which are consistent with the evidence he is now giving. If, however, the allegation is that the story has been untrue from the outset, then the general rule would prevail.[33]

(v) Refreshing memory

A person's memory of an event may understandably fade between the time of making a statement about it and the date of trial. The rules of evidence recognise this and have designed ways and means to allow a witness's memory to be 'refreshed'. This can happen before giving evidence ('out of the box') or while giving evidence ('in the box'). It is useful to distinguish conceptually between the two, as I have done below, although the CJA 2003 has all but eliminated the practical difference between them.

(a) In the box

- This is all about *facilitating* the giving of oral evidence by reference to a memory refreshing document; typically, in criminal cases, a police officer's notebook. A witness who experiences difficulty in recollecting the events to which his evidence relates may, with the court's *permission*, refer, while

32 See, e.g., *R v AA* [2007] EWCA Crim 1779, at [16]

33 For a readily understandable example see *R v Oyesiku* (1971) 56 CrAppR 240. And see BCrP F 7.61-7.64

giving that evidence, to a document or other written statement in order to refresh his memory provided certain conditions are met. Before the CJA 2003, to be used for these purposes, such documents had to pass the test of 'contemporaneity', which was taken to mean having been made as soon as possible after the events in question, when the events were 'fresh in the mind'.[34] These conditions were relaxed for criminal cases by s 139 of the CJA 2003, which requires only that the statement was 'made or verified' by the witness, who states in his oral evidence that the document was made at an earlier time, records his recollection at that time, and his recollection at that time is likely to be *significantly better* than at the time of giving testimony.[35] Clearly this last requirement is not usually very hard to comply with and many documents would qualify. In practice this means most witnesses would be permitted to refresh their memories from their witness statements while giving evidence, although the court retains a residual discretion to disallow this even if the statutory conditions are met.[36]

- Applications to make use of memory refreshers will normally be made by counsel during examination-in-chief (when the deficit first becomes obvious), but a witness may refresh his memory 'at any stage of proceedings' and the judge can be the one to make the suggestion that such a document might assist. Ultimately it is for the court to decide whether the recollection of the witness is likely to have been significantly better when that document was made, whatever the witness himself thinks.[37]
- A witness who wishes to make use of a memory refreshing document in the box must produce it for the judge and the other side to inspect. As we shall see below, in some circumstances the document can itself become an item of evidence. Unless and until this happens, it is important to remember that it is

34 *R v Richardson* [1971] 2 QB 484

35 See CJA 2003, s 139 (1) (my emphasis). There is an equivalent (and very practical) provision allowing the memory to be refreshed from the transcripts of sound recordings: s 139(2). See BCrP F 6.14ff

36 *R v McAfee* [2006] EWCA Crim 2914

37 *R v Mangena* [2009] EWCA 2535, CA

the testimony of the witness which constitutes the evidence in the case, not the document (which should be referred to, not mechanically recited).

(b) Out of the box

It is a matter of common sense (and practice) for witnesses to refresh their memories from notes made by them, and in particular their own witness statements, before going into court to give their evidence. Care should be taken that several witnesses do not compare notes while reviewing their own statements. And it is desirable, but not essential, that opposing counsel know that the memories of the witnesses they will cross-examine have been refreshed in this way - most will assume this has happened. But otherwise, it is done routinely and is uncontroversial; the giving of evidence is a test of veracity, not a feat of memory.[38]

It is open to the judge, as a matter of discretion and in the interests of justice, to permit a witness who has started giving oral evidence-in-chief, to take a break and refresh his or her memory (out of the box) from a statement made by that witness closer to the time of the events in question - again, usually the witness statement. The common law allows this if:

- the witness says he cannot now recall all of the details of the event because of lapse of time
- the witness made a statement much nearer the time of the event, which records his/her recollection at that time
- the witness did not read this statement before giving evidence *and*
- the witness wishes to read the evidence before continuing.

If the judge gives permission, the witness can either withdraw or read the statement in

38 *R v Richardson*, op. cit.
And see BCrP F 6.26/27

the box (during a sort of 'time out'), but in either case the common law position is that the document must again be removed before the witness continues to give evidence.[39]

Having said all of that, given how much more relaxed the rules about refreshing memory in the box are under s 139 of the CJA 2003, in practice it would now be rare to resort to these common law rules.

When does a memory refreshing document become evidence?

A document used to refresh the memory *does not, as such, become evidence* in the case. It merely *facilitates* the witness in giving his or her oral evidence. When a document is used to refresh the memory of a witness, cross-examining counsel may inspect it. This in itself will not make it evidence in the case. Equally, opposing counsel is entitled to cross-examine on the contents of the document without making it evidence, *provided* the questioning does *not go beyond* the parts used for refreshing the memory of the witness. However, where the advocate's cross-examination strays *beyond* the parts of the document referred to by the witness in examination-in-chief, this entitles the party calling the witness to put the entire *document* into evidence so that the tribunal of fact see it.[40] Because of this, an advocate will always have to weigh up the possible advantage of cross-examining beyond the memory refreshing parts of such a document against the possible disadvantages of the entire document being put in evidence. This is especially so in jury trials.

Evidential status of admissible previous consistent statements

It is important to remember that the rule against previous consistent statements (and exceptions (ii) - (iv) above), are all about earlier statements being admitted (or not) to show *consistency* with, and so bolster the *credibility* of, the *oral evidence which the witness gives in court.* This rule make no sense without a witness present and testifying

39 *R v Da Silva* [1990] 1 WLR 31. The witness can only do this once!

40 *Senat v Senat* [1965] P 172 and see BCrP F 6.30

in court. It collides with, but should *not be confused* with the hearsay rule, which is concerned with when out-of-court statements are admissible as evidence of the facts stated in them (or 'truth of contents', as it is sometimes described).[41]

The hearsay rule covers a wider range of out-of-court statements than the rule about previous consistent statements, including many where the maker of the statement is *not* present in court. Where a hearsay statement is admitted for truth of contents, it can of course also be evidence of consistency, if the maker has given evidence. But at common law, the reverse was not necessarily the case, so until the intervention of statute, if a previous consistent statement was admitted by way of exception to the general rule, it was (strictly speaking) only relevant to the collateral issue of the credibility of the testifying witness. This somewhat artificial distinction between consistency and truth of contents disappeared in the civil courts many years ago with the abolition there of the rule against hearsay, and eventually in criminal cases it became difficult to sustain, much less explain to juries. Thus the CJA 2003 now says that where statements of the kind described in (ii) - (v) above are admitted into evidence to show *consistency* (by way of exception to the general rule against this), they are *also admissible as evidence of the truth* of the matters stated therein.[42]

So, let us suppose that V is a victim of an assault by D. Immediately after the attack, V went to her mother and told her what had happened and that D was responsible. D is subsequently arrested and charged with the offence. After V gives evidence against D at his trial, V's mother can also give evidence about what her daughter had told her about the alleged attack soon after it occurred, which supports the evidence which V herself gave when in the witness box. The earlier statement by V is a victim's complaint and so is admissible as an exception to the general rule against previously consistent statements (see (iii) above). As such it is able to

41 See Ch.20

42 See CJA 2003, ss 120 (2)-(7). In the case of previous identification and victim's complaint, the witness will also have to attest to the making and the truthfulness of the statement (s 120(4)(b)). The 2003 Act thus not only extends some of the exceptions to the rule against previous consistent statements, it also 'upgrades' their evidential status when they are admitted into evidence. A defendant's wholly innocent response to accusation is considered evidence of demeanour, and not a statement capable of being true. That exception to the rule against previous consistent statements does not, therefore, intersect with the hearsay rules (or require the defendant to give evidence). See discussion in Keane & McKeown, *Modern Law*, pp.187-8

support the credibility of V's testimony in court. But (so long as V confirms in court the making and truthfulness of the statement to her mother) the statement can also (by virtue of s 120(4) CJA 2003) be admitted as evidence that what she said to her mother did in fact happen.[43] The judge will, of course, need to remind a jury that the complaint cannot give independent confirmation of the victim's version of events (because the source of the complaint is the victim herself) but the fact that it was made and the circumstances in which it was made can assist them in deciding whether the victim's account is true.[44]

The same is true of previous statements made about a relevant event, where the testifying witness has *no independent recollection* of the facts in question, but can attest to the accuracy of the pre-trial statement. The common law struggled to cope with this situation within the remit of memory refreshing documents, but in fact if someone has no memory of something, there is no memory to refresh - and if the witness cannot testify to some aspect of the case (because he has completely forgotten about it), then strictly speaking there is nothing with which to show consistency. Various fictions had been created over the years to accommodate this situation, but the CJA 2003 swept these aside and simply made such statements admissible hearsay[45] if certain conditions are met. Thus such statements will be admissible as evidence of the truth of the matters stated in them so long as (i) the witness testifies that he made the statement and believes it to be true,[46] and so long as the court accepts that the statement was (ii) 'made by the witness when the matters stated were fresh in his memory but he does not remember them, and he cannot be expected to remember them well enough to give oral evidence of them in the proceedings'.[47]

This sounds a wide provision, but remember that the witness has to be *in the box to attest to these details*, and can be cross-examined on convenient lapses in memory and so forth. The courts are entitled to be sceptical![48]

43 And of course the evidence of both witnesses (V and her mother) can be tested in cross-examination, as to which see below.

44 See Crown Court Compendium Pt I Ch.14-12, para 3

45 See generally Ch.20

46 CJA 2003, s 120 (4)

47 CJA 2003, s 120(6)

48 See *R v Chinn* [2012] 2 Cr App R 39 on the court's approach to such statements, cited at BCrP F 6.21

49 Rare exceptions would include a witness who dies after examination-in-chief (not, one hopes, as a result of it!) but before cross-examination.

50 This useful description is used in the 4th Edn of Chris Allen's *Practical Guide* (2008), p.107

51 See BCrP formulation at F 7.5 and generally F 7.1/2. For the role of the judge in restraining and controlling cross-examination, see F 7.6 and 7.14/15

2. CROSS-EXAMINATION

Virtually all witnesses[49] must be made available for cross-examination, the purpose of which is to 'complete and correct'[50] the version of events recounted in examination-in-chief. Thus the questioner's job is essentially two-fold: (i) to elicit and highlight the facts which support the case of the party on whose behalf the cross-examination is being conducted, but also (ii) to cast doubt on the accuracy and/or truthfulness of the evidence given in chief which does not. In doing the latter, it is sometimes necessary to attack the credibility of the witness personally, as well as his or her testimony.[51]

Unlike examination-in-chief, cross-examination works on the assumption that the witness does *not* favour the case of the party on whose behalf it is conducted. So some of the limitations imposed on the former do not apply to the latter. For example, there is no general ban on leading questions since it is not thought that the witness will be very motivated to follow the cross-examiner's lead.[52] Similarly, because the witness has not been called in support of the case of the party conducting the cross-examination, the latter is free, by all proper means,[53] (and subject to some very important restrictions discussed below) to discredit the witness.

It is also the case that cross-examination is not limited to the ground covered in the examination-in-chief, but can extend to any relevant matter.[54] The first point to make in this regard is that it is always relevant, and usually necessary, to 'put'[55] one's case to the witnesses in cross-examination, where the opposing parties' version of events are at odds with one another. In other words, as a general proposition, a witness *must* always be given the opportunity to respond to any challenge made to his evidence before a jury can be invited to disbelieve it, or contradictory evidence can be adduced.[56] This is especially important if appearing for a defendant in a criminal trial, since such challenges will often be the jury's first introduction to the

52 Indeed, a line of cross-examination often concludes with a statement in support of the case of the cross-examining party, with a rhetorical 'tag' at the end (*"You never saw the knife, did you?"*) or without (*"So you never saw the knife … !"*).

53 As a matter of professional conduct, as well as good tactics, cross-examination should be conducted with restraint and courtesy. Cross-examination need not be offensive to be effective - quite the reverse, in fact. Vulnerable witnesses usually require special consideration, as discussed below.

54 Subject to rules of admissibility and so on.

55 One does not need to use this word, of course, and the less often you do so, the better. In one sense, all cross-examination is a putting of the case of the party on whose behalf

nature of the defence.[57] If done effectively, it will lay a useful groundwork for the subsequent presentation of the defendant's case. But again, *how* (and the extent to which) a party's case may be canvassed with a witness in cross-examination may be dictated by a witnesses' special status or particular vulnerability, as discussed below.

Secondly, always remember that a witness's *credibility* is also a relevant matter in any given case because this will affect the extent to which that witness's evidence is to be believed. Thus, questions in cross-examination might relate solely to a fact in issue *("He wasn't carrying a gun when you saw him, was he, Mr. Smith?")* or solely to credit *("You suffer from night-blindness, don't you, Mrs. Jones?")* and the distinction between the two is an important one to grasp. Having said that, bear in mind that the line between them at times becomes very hazy, when it does not seem to disappear altogether, and it is perfectly possible for a line of cross-examination to be relevant *both* to credibility and a fact in issue, especially when cross-examining defendants in criminal cases.

Credibility can be tested in a variety of ways, but questions will be apt to focus either on (a) the ability (or not) of the witness to have perceived or remembered accurately the evidence given in chief, or (b) some aspect of the witness's character or circumstances which would make their testimony unworthy of belief - an obvious example being where he or she has been convicted of perjury. As to the second of these, for some centuries all manner of character failings, which today might be considered mundane and/or unrelated to truthfulness, were considered relevant when cross-examining a witness as to their entitlement to be believed.[58] Over time, this very permissive approach to a party's ability to refer to the bad character of witnesses in order to impugn their credibility has been curtailed and constrained, both by the common law,[59] but primarily by statute. Chapter 19 looks specifically at the limitations placed on attacking the character of witnesses in criminal cases

such questioning is being conducted, for example by bringing out details, omitted from examination-in-chief, which assist the cross-examining party. The important thing is that a witness has a chance to respond to the extent that his or her evidence is being challenged. This need not be offensive or aggressive.

56 A failure to put your party's version of events to the witness you are cross-examining amounts to tacit acceptence of the latter's accounts. See *Wood Green Crown Court, ex parte Taylor* [1995] Crim LR 897 r C7.2 of the Code of Conduct of the Bar of England & Wales, and discussion in BCrP F 7.8

57 This is also required, of course, by Art 6.1 (fair trial) and 6.3(d) (right of challenge) of ECHR.

(whether the accused or not) under the CJA 2003. Another very important restriction relates to cross-examination of complainants in sex cases, which is discussed below. There follows a brief look at how the special needs of children and other vulnerable witnesses can be recognised and accommodated, especially in cross-examination. This section then concludes with two other more general matters which commonly arise on cross-examination, applicable both to civil and criminal cases: previous *in*consistent statements and rebuttal on collateral issues.

Finally, remember that when considering the rules relating to cross-examination, it is important to bear in mind that there are often two aspects of the process to think about. The first is: *"Can I put the question at all to the witness?"* This is because some of the rules will prevent certain matters even being raised in cross-examination. But, even if the answer to the first question is *"Yes"* (and only if it is *"Yes"*), you may still need to consider a second question: *"If I do not get the response I want, is there anything I can do to prove the witness wrong?"* You may be surprised to learn that the answer to this question is sometimes *"No"!*

A. SPECIAL RESTRICTIONS IN SEX OFFENCE CASES

Historically, morality was regarded as relevant to credibility, and until relatively recently any witnesses in any type of criminal case (other than the accused) could be cross-examined about their sexual proclivities or promiscuity merely in order to show that they were not the sort of person whose evidence was worthy of belief. In some contexts, such suggestions might today simply come across as silly or of little consequence or even rather desperate, but when cross-examining complainants in sex cases, this line of questioning poses particular problems. There are several points to bear in mind.

---

58 See, e.g., *R v Castro* (1874) cited in *Practical Guide*, p.109

59 In *Hobbs v Tinling* [1929] 1 WLR 207 it was made clear that questions put to witnesses to undermine credibility should not be so remote in time or minor in nature that the imputation cast could not seriously affect the court's opinion of the witness.

(i) The issue of consent

Such cases, and especially rape cases, are very apt to turn on the issue of consent, that is, the physical act is not disputed as such, but whether or not the complainant consented is. Because sexual activity tends to occur in private, the issue of consent can therefore come down to a question of the complainant's word against that of the accused, which in turn gives credibility a heightened relevance.

(ii) The need to protect the complainant at trial

Defendants in criminal cases have long had some protection from the admission of evidence of bad character intended merely to impugn their credibility, for fear of unfairly prejudicing them in a jury's eyes.[60] It was only much later that it was thought necessary to give complainants in rape and related cases an analogous kind of protection.

(iii) Interests of justice

Complainants who expect to be personally attacked in cross-examination will be disinclined to seek justice; often they feel it is they who are on trial as much, if not more than the accused.[61] It is not conducive to the public good if victims of rape and other such offences do not come forward and give evidence for fear of being harassed and bullied when they do so. For obvious reasons, complainants in sexual offence cases are protected from being cross-examined by their alleged attacker (the accused) personally.[62] But it is not enough to limit the questioners. It is also necessary to control the *questions*, and in particular those in cross-examination which are intended only to vilify the complainant.

---

60 They now have less protection than they once had. See generally Ch.19

61 The problem is magnified if there are several defendants, each with cross-examining counsel.

62 S 34-39 YJCEA 1999 protects three classes of witnesses from cross-examination by an accused in person. See BCrP F 7.3

(iv) Merging of credibility and issues of fact

In rape and related cases, however, the line between cross-examination as to an issue in the case and cross-examination as to credit can easily become obscured. As Lord Hutton put it in *R v A (No 2)*, 'issues of consent and credibility may well run so close to each other as almost to coincide'.[63] Promiscuity in itself, for example, does not really prove very much so far as consent to sex on a given occasion is concerned.[64] One is always entitled to say 'no'. But there may be aspects of an allegation of sexual behaviour - the circumstances, say, or timing of such behaviour - which gives the evidence probative value, so that it extends beyond merely showing a proclivity or otherwise discrediting the complainant and goes some way towards assisting the jury in deciding what actually happened in the particular case. It would be unfair to a defendant to disallow relevant evidence of probative value merely because it might also cast the complainant in a bad light.

All of which makes framing rules about limiting cross-examination of complainants in sex cases important, but very difficult. The first attempt, in the 1970's,[65] essentially banned questions in rape cases about the complainant's sexual experiences with anyone other than the defendant, unless the court gave permission, on the assumption that the sexual history between victim and accused was always likely to have some relevance. This may be so in the technical sense, but it still allowed questioning which did not prove very much so far as the guilt or innocence of the accused was concerned. In particular it was apt to confuse or conflate a tendency to give consent to sex with the accused, with evidence of having actually done so on the occasion in question. It could not, in effect, cater to a complainant's right to say 'no' and so eventually these rules were repealed and replaced by ss 41-43 of the YJCEA 1999.[66]

These later provisions significantly increased the restrictions on how

63 [2002] 1 AC 45, at [138] p.108ff

64 See discussion in *Practical Guide*, p.109

65 Sexual Offences (Amendment) Act 1976

66 We have already discussed this (multi-purpose) legislation when considering competence and special measures in Ch.17

defendants[67] conduct their cases. They apply to 'sexual offence' cases generally, and not just rape,[68] and generally preclude questioning about a broader range of what is now called the victim's 'sexual behaviour'.[69] Moreover, the scope of the general ban on rooting around in the complainant's sexual past is extensive. Put very broadly, the scheme created by ss 41-43, which attempts to balance the competing interests of complainant (male or female) and accused, works like this:

(i) The wide general exclusion

Section 41(1) begins with a wide general exclusion: where a person is charged with a sexual offence, then, *unless the court gives permission, no* evidence may be adduced and *no* question may be put in cross-examination *by or on behalf* of the accused at trial *about any sexual behaviour* of the complainant *(whether with the defendant or not).*

(ii) Court must give permission

Thus, the *court must give permission* before such evidence can be given or question put. Permission must be sought by or on behalf of the accused. For obvious reasons, the application is made in private, and in the absence of the complainant, who might otherwise be alerted to what will be coming in cross-examination if permission were to be granted.[70]

(iii) Permission only possible in limited circumstances

More pertinently, the court *may only give permission* in certain *very prescribed* situations as set out in ss 41(2)-(5).[71] It is important in this context to distinguish between cases where consent is at issue, and those where it is not. The legislation is very much focused on the former, since it is in such cases that the line between credibility and disputed facts in issue is hardest to maintain.

---

67 The scheme only restricts defence questions and evidence: YJCEA 1999 s 41

68 The 1976 Act was limited to cases of rape, including attempts and aiding and abetting rape.

69 'Sexual behaviour' seems to be wider than 'sexual experience': s 42(1)(c). See discussion at BCrP F 7.22ff. The definition is, of course, gender neutral: *R v B* [2007] EWCA Crim 23

70 The court's decision will be given in open court, but in the absence of any jury and presumably in the absence of the complainant as well. Reasons must be given: s 43(2). Application is in writing in accordance to CrimPR Pt 22

71 And if allowed, only evidence of *specific* acts of sexual behaviour are allowed: s 41(6). Thus evidence to the effect that 'the complainant is a slag' would not be allowed on any basis.

Where consent is a relevant fact in dispute (s 41(3)(b) and (c))

In such cases, what the legislation seeks to do in the first instance is to anticipate and delineate the sorts of circumstances where the evidence of previous sexual behaviour would, of necessity, be sufficiently probative of a relevant fact in issue to justify its reception in such cases. Essentially, it provides *only two possible* situations where a judge may give permission for the general ban to be lifted, namely:

(a) where the complainant's sexual behaviour is so *proximate in time*[72] that it helps explain the context of the act in question. The actual wording is 'at or about the same time', and this will rarely include behaviour which has occurred beyond 24 hours either side of the alleged offence.[73] The idea is to exclude behaviour which amounts to nothing more than previous voluntary sexual acts with (but not limited to) the accused, which say nothing about whether consent was or was not given on the occasion which is the subject of the charge. But if, say, consensual love-making began before dinner, it may help explain what happened after,[74] although of course it does not by any means rule out a change of mind over dessert: *or*

(b) where the complainant's sexual behaviour is *so similar* to some other sexual behaviour which occurred *as part of or about the same time* as the assault in question[75] that it cannot be put down to coincidence (and so again helps explain the particular context of the sexual act). Staying with the dinner analogy, suppose the victim and accused had established a pattern of sexual foreplay where consent (or lack of it) was signalled by what the complainant wears at the table. If appearing in a French maid's uniform was their habitual code for 'oui', and this is what was worn by the complainant on the occasion in question, this information might help explain what happened

72 s 41(3)(b)

73 See *R v A* (No 2), op. cit., cited at BCrP F 7.33/34

74 And see Lord Steyn's example in *ibid*, at [40]

75 s 41(3)(c)

next, although again it does not rule out the withdrawal of consent by some other (possibly more orthodox) means. The behaviour in question need not be bizarre, but it should not be banal. So, for example, it would not include a taste for one-night stands or previous consensual sex in a car or a preference for Continental lovers.[76] These are all far too ordinary to tell us much about a specific incident. To be heard, the sexual behaviour must be telling.

Where relevant issue is not consent (s 4.1(3)(a))

(c) The legislation makes an important distinction between cases where the proposed evidence or cross-examination relates to a relevant issue, and that issue is consent (as discussed above) and those cases where the relevant issue is *not* one of consent. For example, the defence might be that the physical act did not take place and there is an alternative explanation for the complainant's injuries, or it might be alleged that the complainant is motivated by revenge and so is making the entire thing up. It might also be that the accused claims to have *believed* at the time that the complainant was consenting. S 42(b) makes clear that when s 41 refers to 'issue of consent' this means any issue as to whether the complainant *in fact* consented to the conduct constituting the offence charged and 'does not include any issue as to the belief of the accused that the complainant so consented'. The distinction is an important one because if the relevant issue to which the questioning relates is not one of consent, this in itself is an *entirely separate*, possible means of escape from the general prohibition.[77] The reason for this is, I suppose, rather obvious, since if the issue is the accused's belief in consent, it is *his* credibility which is essentially on the line, and not his victim's.[78]

---

76 Lord Williams during the debate on the bill in the House of Lords, Hansard, 23 March 1999, col 1218

77 YJCEA 1999, s 41((3)(a)

78 Even so, the court will be strict about what cross-examination is allowed and will be careful to differentiate between evidence that a person would have consented if asked and a belief that a person is consenting on a particular occasion: see, e.g., *R v Barton* [1987] 85 Cr App R 5, discussed in Allen's *Practical Guide*, p.119

Having said that, the line between the defence of consent and the defence of belief in consent can be rather hazy, since an accused who alleges consent presumably also believes that the complainant consented. The two defences are thus often run in tandem or as alternatives. When this happens the question then arises as to how the court will deal with permission to refer to the complainant's sexual history, since the restrictions are more severe when the issue is one of consent than when the issue is one of belief in consent. The short answer is that the court will take a pragmatic approach and decide which really is the central issue; if honest belief is a secondary issue, or merely follows logically from the allegation of actual consent, then the stricter regime will apply.[79]

To rebut prosecution evidence (s 41(5))

(d) Permission may also be given if the behaviour relates to evidence of the complainant's sexual behaviour which has been adduced by the prosecution[80] and goes no further than necessary to *rebut or explain* that evidence.[81] Let us say that in a rape case the complainant testifies that she has only had and would only have consensual sexual intercourse with her husband. It would be very unfair to a defendant if this assertion could not be challenged as a result of the general ban, and so evidence of or questions about previous consensual intercourse, whether with the accused or another person (neither of whom were the complainant's husband), either before or after the alleged rape, could be permitted, *so long as it goes no further than necessary to respond to the prosecution evidence.* Such rebuttal evidence would obviously damage the complainant's credibility at the same time as it speaks to the issue of consent, so the statute is alive to the need to keep the questioning within bounds.[82]

79 See, e.g., *R v W* [2004] EWCA Crim 3103, para 15

80 Or referred to in cross-examination, see *R v Hamadi* [2007] EWCA 3048

81 YJCEA 1999, s 41(5)

82 See, e.g., *R v F* [2008] EWCA 2859

(iv) Permission must be necessary to render verdict safe

Assuming that one of the four exceptional scenarios described above (in (a)-(d)) applies, the judge must, *in addition*, also be satisfied that a refusal to give permission to admit the evidence or allow the cross-examination might render *unsafe* the decision of the fact finder on any relevant issue in the case.[83] If the relevant issue is consent, this is likely to follow naturally if the rigorous constraints of ss (3) or (5) are (as they must be) already met. If the issue is not one of consent, then this additional requirement comes much more into its own as an important prerequisite to obtaining permission to put the questions to the complainant.

It is also worth remembering that there is no overarching judicial discretion (beyond that which may be said to be built into the requirements s 41) to exclude or limit evidence or questioning in respect of the complainant's sexual behaviour if the strict conditions of admissibility are met.[84] To this extent, ss 41-43 create a self-contained code. There may, however, be something of a discretion to *include* such questioning on behalf of the defence, even if on the face of it such is disallowed under s 41, where this would be consistent with the right to a fair trial under Art 6 of the European Convention on Human Rights (ECHR). Or at least, according to *R v A*,[85] which considered the relationship between s 41 and the Human Rights Act 1998 (HRA 1998), the former can be interpreted as not excluding any line of cross-examination required to ensure a fair trial. S 3 of the HRA 1998 requires the court, so far as possible to do so, to read and give effect to primary legislation in a way which is compatible with human rights. The House of Lords decided that s 41 could be interpreted as containing an implied proviso that evidence or questioning required in order to ensure a fair trial should not be excluded. Clearly this decision was a pragmatic one,[86] and probably only capable of being successfully evoked in very specific circumstances,[87]

83 See s 41(2)(b)

84 *R v F* [2005] 1 WLR 2848, para 29

85 [2002] 1 AC 45

86 The alternative would have been a declaration of incompatibility which no-one in the House of Lords (as it then was) had the stomach for.

87 It is unlikely to apply to sexual behaviour with other men or an isolated incident with the accused. See Laws LJ in *R v White* [2004] EWCA Crim 946, at [35]

but it can give a defendant an extra line of argument for admissibility in some cases.

Finally, the point behind the rules limiting cross-examination of complainants in sex offence cases is encapsulated in s 41(4) which says that 'for the purposes of (3), no evidence or question shall be regarded as relating to a relevant issue in the case if it appears to the court reasonable to assume that the purpose (or main purpose) for which it would be adduced or asked is to establish or elicit material for impugning the credibility of the complainant as witness'. However, the court must take care not to let s 41(4) defeat the purpose of s 41(3), because there will be times when the complainant's credibility is so relevant to a permissible issue in the case that the purpose of the cross-examination must logically be to try to impugn it.[88] To this extent s 41(4) may be best regarded as a policy statement rather than a strict additional hurdle.

B. CROSS-EXAMINATION OF VULNERABLE WITNESSES

We have looked at some of the ways in which the needs of vulnerable witnesses are catered for in the criminal justice system, whether by use of special measures (such as pre-trial recordings and use of intermediaries) or by statutory restrictions placed on the sorts of questions which may be asked of certain witnesses (for example, complainants in sex offence cases). Until recently, however, there had been little focus, in legal circles anyway, on helping vulnerable witnesses to give accurate evidence by adapting conventional cross-examination techniques to suit their individual needs.

Cross-examination is, quite rightly, a jealously guarded tool for testing evidence and discovering where the truth lies; but increasingly, social scientists have produced empirical research showing that traditional methods of cross-examination, deployed in a generic, 'one-size-fits-all' fashion, may hinder rather than assist vulnerable witnesses (including children, people with learning difficulties, and victims of traumatising events) to give cogent and accurate evidence. The use of leading questions, one hallmark of

88 See, e.g., Lord Hutton's comment in *R v A* (No2), op. cit., at fn 63. For an example of the operation of s 41(4) see *R v Islam*, cited at BCrP F 7.27

89 See good example in Adrian Keane, *Towards a Principled Approach to the Cross-Examination of Vulnerable Witnesses* [2012] Criminal Law review, 407-420 ('Principled Approach') at p.417

90 *Raising the Bar: The handling of vulnerable*

cross-examination, is a prime example. In suggestible witnesses or those wishing to please, these can merely encourage acquiescence, and so risk producing unreliable answers; in such cases it will be more appropriate to ask more open questions to ensure that the witness is able to recount accurately what they experienced.[89]

Recently there has been important progress in ensuring that questioning is properly tailored to young and vulnerable witnesses. Adaptation should be witness and case specific. New practice directions impose clear obligations on judges, and the Advocacy Training Council has produced guidance to enable practitioners 'to handle vulnerable witnesses and defendants in a manner which is sensitive to their needs', while recognising that the 'primary purpose' of calling witnesses remains to put evidence before the tribunal of fact and then to rigorously test those parts of the evidence which are controversial'.[90] This tool kit contains a checklist of issues to be considered for inclusion in a Trial Practice Note/Protocol, including what has become known as the 'ground rules' for advocates when questioning a specific witness.

Judges now have *The Judicial College Bench Checklist*, specifically for cases involving young children as witnesses.[91] Aside from identifying early the particular vulnerability of the witness and risks posed by traditional deployment of cross-examination techniques, it says the court should schedule a ground rules 'discussion' about questioning - such is required in cases involving intermediaries, but is also recommended in all cases involving any young witness.[92] Ground rules can range from length and sequencing of questioning and the number of breaks given to the witness, to specific directions on how best to put questions (short simple questions using common names for things) and more particularly, the sorts of questionning format to avoid (for example, 'tag' questions, restricted choice questions[93]). There might also be restrictions on how, and in what form, a party's case is put to a vulnerable witness. It is then up to the judge to ensure that the ground rules are followed.[94]

---

witnesses, victims and defendants in court, London: Advocacy Training Council, 2011, para 2.3

91 JCB Checklist: Young Witness Cases, available at judiciary.gov.uk/publications/jc-bench-checklist-young-wit-cases

92 See Keane & McKeown, p. 216ff and Crim PD 1 3D-F. Intermediaries are discussed in Ch.17

93 Examples might be: *"He was never in your room, that is right, isn't it?"* (see fn 52) or *"Tuesday or Wednesday, which one was it?"* (this sort of question gives, but also restricts choice). The danger with these sorts of classic cross-examination questions is that a young or vulnerable witness might just give the answer he or she thinks will best please the questioner.

94 *R v Wills* [2012] 1 CrApp R 2 at [22]

In setting ground rules, the court will, of course, have in mind not only the needs of the vulnerable witness, but also the interests of the accused and the need to ensure that the proceedings, as a whole, are fair.[95] Each witness and each case will have different demands, and the court will have to be alive to keeping the needs of the witness and the needs of a defendant *in balance*; for example by giving suitable directions (at a suitable juncture[96]) to the jury, excluding evidence in the exercise of judicial discretion, and so on. Some ground rules will need more 'counterbalancing' than others. This is a belated, but rapidly evolving area of criminal justice. For a useful and readable exploration of its implications, have a look at Adrian Keane's *Towards a Principled Approach to the Cross-examination of Vulnerable Witnesses*.[97]

C. THE RULE AGAINST REBUTTAL ON COLLATERAL MATTERS

If a party was allowed to call evidence to rebut a witness every time an unfavourable reply was given in cross-examination, trials might take a very long time indeed to complete. And if the time is not well spent, lengthy proceedings are not in the public interest. So, to keep trials efficient and focused, an important limitation is put on a party's ability to contradict a witness in this way. The rule, which is applicable at common law to both criminal and civil cases, is that answers given in cross-examination on *purely collateral* matters - typically, matters which go solely to the witness's credibility but which are *otherwise irrelevant* to any of the issues in the case - may not be contradicted by rebuttal evidence. This is sometimes called the rule of 'finality of answer', which is a confusing description, because the rule does not mean that the tribunal of fact must accept the truth of the answer given, nor does it mean that the questioner should not be given every reasonable opportunity to extract the admission in cross-examination which he or she seeks. What it does mean is that evidence may not be *adduced* by the party asking the questions to rebut the answer

95 See, e.g., *R v Lubemba* [2015] 1 WLR 1579

96 Some directions will be suitable for the judge's summing-up at the end of the trial, but others may need to be given before or after the relevant witness is questioned. *R v Wills* op. cit., at [36]

97 Op. cit., at fn 89. And see also BCrP F 7.10. SMDs were discussed in Ch.17

98 See Ch.19

99 It is entirely possible to be relevant to both. See discussion and cases referred to at BCrP F 7.42. As we have seen in discussing sexual offence cases, the more the matters in dispute boil down to one person's word against

given by the witness. Hence, it might be better described as the *rule against rebuttal.*

The purpose of the rule is to prevent advocates getting off topic and proceedings getting bogged down on peripheral and essentially irrelevant issues.

There are two points to bear in mind when considering the rule *against* rebuttal. First, *it can only apply to matters which have been properly put to a witness* in cross-examination. The interplay, for example, with the rules regarding bad character evidence is especially important.[98] If the question cannot be asked, then there will be no answer to rebut!

Secondly, the difficulty with applying the rule is that it is not always easy to determine what matters are relevant to an issue in the case, and what are relevant only to credibility or some other purely collateral issue.[99] It is important to appreciate (both in practice and for examination purposes) that the rule *only* precludes rebuttal evidence in respect of questions going *solely* to collateral matters. Even if a line of questioning speaks to a witness's credibility, if it *also* speaks to a fact in issue in the case, then the limitation *does not* apply.[100] In addition, there are, as always, the inevitable *exceptions* to the rule. They are:

(i) Previous convictions

If a witness is properly cross-examined about a previous conviction (which is usually only relevant to credit), and denies it or refuses to answer, then the conviction may be proved against him.[101] To be 'proper', any question to a witness about previous convictions would have to be permitted under s 100 CJA 2003 (for non-defendant witness) or s 101 CJA 2003 (for an accused). Again, if the question cannot be put, then the rule against rebuttal cannot arise! Remember too that just because you can do something, does not mean that it is necessarily sensible to do it. In particular, an accused with criminal convictions himself will need to think very carefully before casting aspersions on others, since to do so could render his own bad character admissible in evidence.[102]

---

another, the more facts in issue and credibility converge.

100 See, e.g., *R v Funderburk* [1990] 1 WLR 587 and BCrP F 7.43

101 Criminal Procedure Act 1865, s 6. The way to prove convictions is governed by s 73(1) and (2) PACE 1984, that is, by providing a duly signed certificate and proof that the named person is the person whose conviction is to be proved.

102 s 101(1)(g) CJA 2003. See generally Ch.19

103 *R v Richardson* (1968) 52 Cr App R 317

104 s 99(2) and s 118 (1)(2) CJA 2003

105 See, e.g., *Mendy* (1976) 64 Cr App R, 4. Although s 99 CJA 2003 abolished the common law rules

(ii) General reputation for untruthfulness

Whether or not a witness has been convicted of a dishonesty offence, that witness's credibility may be impugned by others speaking to his or her general reputation for untruthfulness.[103] This is a long-standing, common law exception, which has been expressly preserved by the CJA 2003,[104] but is not often invoked because of the limitations on attacking the character of non-defendant witnesses imposed by s 100, and the risk to defendants of attacking the character of others.

(iii) Allegations of bias

Evidence is admissible to contradict a witness's denial of partiality for or against one of the parties to proceedings, to show that he is prejudiced as to the outcome of the case.[105] For example, in *R v Shaw*[106] it was held that the accused was permitted to call evidence to contradict a prosecution witness who, in cross-examination, denied having threatened to 'get even' with the accused after the two had argued. This is a common sense exception to the rule against rebuttal. If a witness has a vested interest in the outcome of a case, the fact finder ought to know about it. But there has to be some basis to the allegation of bias (which brings the exception into play) beyond a mere attack on the credibility of the evidence, and this can sometimes seem a fine distinction. For example, it has been said that a denial that a bribe was *offered* to a witness could not be contradicted, whereas a denial that a bribe had been *accepted* could, because it was only the latter fact which actually said something about the partiality of the witness.[107]

(iv) Physical/mental disability affecting reliability

If a witness has a mental or physical impairment affecting the reliability of his evidence, then this is something which those whose job it is to assess that evidence should know. Thus if, for example, an identifying witness denies in cross-examination

governing admissibility of bad character evidence (as defined in the legislation) in criminal proceedings, s 98 defines 'bad character' in such a way as to exclude evidence of misconduct and so on (if that is what giving biased testimony is) which 'has to do with' the offence charged or the 'investigation or prosecution of that offence'. Most allegations of bias in the context of the rule against rebuttal will thus fall outside this definition (or be allowed independently under s 100, as discussed at Ch.19). At the end of the day, therefore, this exception remains pretty intact. See generally BCrP F 7.51ff

106 (1888) 16 Cox CC 503, Assizes

107 See *A-G v Hitchcock* [1847] 1 Exch 91, cited at BCrP F 7.52

that he suffers from night blindness or is prone to hallucinate, then evidence may be called to prove that he does suffer from such disabilities. As Lord Pearce observed in the leading case of *Toohey v Metropolitan Police Commissioner*:[108]

> Human evidence ... is subject to many cross-currents such as partiality, prejudice, self-interest and above all, imagination and inaccuracy. Those are matters with which the jury, helped by cross-examination and common sense, must do their best. But when a witness through physical (in which I include mental) disease or abnormality is not capable of giving a true or reliable account to the jury, it must surely be allowable for medical science to reveal this vital hidden fact to them.

The evidence of disability can itself be rebutted, although only insofar as is necessary to meet a specific challenge to the witness's reliability and should not extend beyond this in an attempt merely to bolster the credibility of that witness.[109]

D. PREVIOUS INCONSISTENT STATEMENTS

Clearly, one of the most effective ways of rebutting witnesses in cross-examination is to prove that they made a statement on an earlier occasion which contradicts the evidence they now give at trial. Unsurprisingly, these are known as *previous inconsistent statements*, and so long as the statement is *relevant to an issue* in the case, it may be admissible to contradict the witness's testimony in court. There are precise rules about how to go about doing this. These are found in ss 4 and 5 of the Criminal Procedure Act 1865, which set out the manner in which such statements are to be put to a witness, and (surprisingly, you might think) apply to civil as well as criminal cases. The point of the procedure is to protect witnesses from being unfairly surprised during cross-examination and to give them a chance to correct their testimony.

108 [1965] AC 595

109 This is known as 'oath-helping'. See, e.g., *R v Robinson* [1994] 3AllER 346, cited at BCrP F 1.11

In essence, what should happen is this. The circumstances of the making of the previous statement are put to the witness, who is first given a chance to accept that the earlier statement was made and that it is true (and so, in effect, to correct his testimony). According to s 5, which relates to documents only, a witness who is being contradicted should be shown the earlier statement, asked to read it and then asked if he stands by his oral evidence. This may be enough for the witness to see the need to change his testimony. If not, the advocate may put the document into evidence to establish, at the very least, inconsistency. But by virtue of the CJA 2003, such a document is also admissible for truth of contents, even in criminal cases.[110] Again, an advocate may have to weigh up the pros and cons of this happening (for example, other aspects of the document may support or confirm the other side's case).

Finally, a jury who is, as a result of this process, confronted with inconsistent evidence from the same witness, will be directed to make a judgment about which account, if any, they accept. The direction will vary depending on whether the previous statement assists the prosecution or the defence, to ensure that the accused is given any benefit of doubt.[111]

3. RE-EXAMINATION

A witness who has been cross-examined may be re-examined by the party who called him, within the *same constraints as apply in examination-in-chief.* This will not always be necessary. The point of re-examination is to repair any damage done in cross-examination, which may have left the witness's version of events ambiguous or incomplete. It is *not* an opportunity to repeat matters raised in examination-in-chief which were not covered in cross-examination or, worse, to embark on an entirely

110 CJA 2003, s 119. See generally BCrP F 7.46-7.50

111 *R v Billingham* [2009] EWCA Crim 19 at [68]. See also Crown Court Compendium Pt 1 Ch.14-6

new subject. It is very important to remember that an advocate is *not allowed*, in re-examination, to ask questions which do *not* arise from the cross-examination, unless the court gives permission.[112]

revision tips

- Know which rules about the giving of testimony pertain particularly to evidence-in-chief or re-examination (for example, the rule against previous consistent statements) and those which are specific to cross-examination (for example, the rule against rebuttal) - and why. The same goes for the exceptions to the rules.
- Understand the rationale behind the rules/exceptions. This will help you to remember and apply them to a factual scenario in an exam.
- In any test, highlight the detail in the questions carefully so you are clear about which aspect of which rules you are being asked about.

It is worth reading ...

R v AA [2007] EWCA Crim. This is an interesting appeal on several levels. I mention it here because it concerns proper directions to a jury when evidence of a victim's complaint is admitted in evidence. For a bit of added value, note the conversation between counsel and the bench regarding re-trial and bail. You will feel like you are in the room!

Have a look at some of the sample directions concerning the matters discussed in this chapter in the Crown Court Compendium Pt 1, Ch. 14-6 to 14-12. Because of the interplay between the rules about previous statements and their evidential value under CJA 2003, they are set out in the hearsay section.

The ghastly case of *MH v Regina* [2012] EWCA Crim 2725. A hideous and graphic child abuse case if you can stomach the details. It covers a lot of evidential ground including the rule against rebuttal, vulnerable witnesses and victim's complaint.

112 See BCrP F 7.60. The court has a discretion to permit re-examination to show consistency if there is a risk that the jury might be positively misled after cross-examination: see BCrP F 6.38

CHAPTER 19

Character evidence
in criminal cases

Evidence about a person's character, whether good or bad, may be *relevant* to a criminal case in any one of three ways. It might be:

(i) *a fact in issue*. For example, on a charge of driving while disqualified, an essential ingredient of the offence is the fact of disqualification;[1] *and/or*

(ii) *relevant to guilt or innocence*. Evidence that an accused has a relevant *propensity* to act (or not act) in a particular way would, logically, go some way (not necessarily a long way) towards establishing that the offence in question was (or was not) committed by him; *and/or*

(iii) *relevant to a witness's credibility*, or 'credit'.[2] A witness's character can have a bearing on whether, or the extent to which, the evidence given by that person is worthy of belief. In other words, evidence of bad behaviour on the part of any witnesses may serve to *discredit* their testimony.

It is important to be able to differentiate, conceptually at any rate, between (ii) and (iii) above. The distinction can, at times, be difficult to maintain, especially if a case turns on one person's word against another as to what transpired in private between

1 See, e.g., *DPP v Agyemayang* [2009] EWCA 1542, DC

2 Be prepared for these expressions to be used interchangeably: the more credible a witness is, the more 'credit' his evidence is given.

amount to a defence, the jury ought to weigh it into the balance when deciding whether the defendant is the sort of person to have committed the offence of which he is accused. It is especially important when character is a central aspect of the defence. In *R v Moustakim*, for example, where an alleged drugs mule claimed to be an 'innocent dupe', a failure to give a sufficiently robust propensity direction was considered fatal to the conviction.[12] A case involving serious allegations having occurred many years previously (for example, historic sexual abuse claims), will require especially clear instructions - in particular, to explain that because so much time has since passed without the accused committing any offence (assuming this to be the case), he may be less likely to have committed the offence charged.[13]

(iii) Impact of and principles in *R v Hunter*

One of the challenges over the years has been knowing what amounts to 'good character' for the purposes of a *Vye* direction. For example, an absence of convictions does not necessarily mean a person is of good character, if he or she has engaged in other misconduct. Equally, previous convictions will not necessarily prevent an accused being treated as a person of good character, especially where these are old, relatively minor or irrelevant to the case. When is a defendant entitled to a full *Vye* direction, and when is he not? And what if the accused is somewhere in-between good and bad - can the judge give a 'qualified' direction?[14]

The case law was comprehensively reviewed in *R v Hunter*,[15] which declared the law to be as follows:

1. An accused is *entitled* to a full and unqualified *Vye* direction if he is of 'absolute' good character, that is, if he has no convictions and no other reprehensible conduct is alleged, admitted or proved. The accused

12 [2008] EWCA Crim 3096

13 *R v GJB* [[2011] EWCA Crim 876. This is especially important where the defence is a straight denial and the accused has little more than his good name to rely on. This additional 'component' is sometimes referred to as a 'third limb' direction, but really it is just a *Vye* direction carefully adapted to the circumstances.

14 For example, to explain that although the accused cannot put himself forward as a man of good character, the fact that he has no convictions for offences of violence could count in his favour. See Crown Court Compendium Pt I Ch. 11, example 3.

15 [2015] 1 WLR 5367 and see commentary in BCrP F 14.5ff

does not need to prove his good character.

2. A judge may decide, in the circumstances of the case, to treat an accused with minor, spent or irrelevant convictions or cautions and such like, as *effectively* being of good character.[16] If an accused is judged to be of 'effective good character,' then the *Vye* direction *must* be given, although it can be modified if necessary to ensure that a jury is not misled (eg into thinking that he is of absolute good character).
3. An accused who is not judged to be of effective good character may, at the judge's *discretion*, be given a modified good character direction, where this is thought necessary to ensure fairness. The judge has a broad and 'open-textured' discretion whether to give any part of the direction, and if so on what terms.
4. Judges should take care not to give an absurd or meaningless direction.[17] If, for example, the judge is required to give a bad character direction, it may be possible to weave that together with any pertinent good character observations, so long as this does not render the entire direction ridiculous.

(iv) Inadequate direction not necessarily fatal

Provided the judge explains to the jury, in sufficiently positive and fair terms, the respect(s) in which the accused's good character (or aspects of it) may be helpful to him, the appeal court will be 'slow to criticise' any exercise of discretion and/or any qualifying remarks made given the facts of the individual case. Whether a failure to direct (or adequately direct) on good character is fatal to a successful prosecution, will depend on context and fairness and the effect on the safety of the conviction.[18]

16 See, e.g., (pre-*Hunter*) case of *R v Goss* [2003] EWCA Crim 3208, where a previous conviction for lack of insurance was considered irrelevant to a charge of possessing a firearm.

17 As was first made clear by the House of Lords in *R v Aziz* [1996] AC 41.

18 *R v Singh* [2006] 1 WLR 146, PC at [30], approved in *Hunter*, op.cit.

(v) Good defendant/bad defendant

Where there are two or more defendants, some with good character and some without, *those with good character are entitled to an appropriate Vye direction*, notwithstanding the implications for the others, about whom nothing very positive in this regard may be able to be said. It had been argued in the *Vye* case itself that the defendant(s) with bad character would be unduly prejudiced[19] in the eyes of the jury by the obvious contrast, but this was not thought to be a good reason to deprive the co-defendant with good character of the direction to which he would be entitled had he stood alone in the dock. This is consistent with a theme which runs through the rules of evidence, namely that they are essentially there to protect defendants from prosecutors, but not from each other. What the judge, having given a *Vye* direction in respect of one co-defendant, should tell a jury about the others, if anything, is a matter of judicial discretion. It may be necessary to warn the jury not to treat the absence of information as damning, or to speculate on the reasons why they have heard nothing about other co-defendants' characters. But sometimes it will be better to say nothing at all about it.

2. EVIDENCE OF BAD CHARACTER

This aspect of criminal evidence is now almost entirely governed by statute - The Criminal Justice Act 2003 (CJA 2003). Nevertheless, it may assist the understanding of this topic to begin with a brief overview of the development of this rather complex area of the law.

At common law, the prosecution was generally prevented from adducing (or eliciting from a witness in cross-examination) evidence of the *accused's* previous convictions or other tendency to misbehave (other than that directly relating to the

19 The risk of prejudice might be a ground for ordering separate trials, but there is no presumption in favour of doing so in cases of co-defendants with disparate characters. See BCrP F 14.24

20 It could be relevant in the sense that it must follow that a person in the habit of committing the offence charged (or offences like it) is more apt to be guilty than someone who does not have that habit. How much it actually proves, however, is another matter.

21 *DPP v Boardman* [1975] 421, at 454 per Lord Hailsham.

22 Clearly if the evidence is highly probative of the offence charged it will naturally point to the defendant's guilt and so prejudice his case. It is 'improper' or disproportionate prejudice that is the problem.

23 *DPP v P* [1991] 2 AC 447.

offence charged) in order to show guilt - not because such information is irrelevant,[20] but because it might distract the jury from the other evidence in the case and prejudice the defendant disproportionately in its eyes. The anxiety was that, having heard this sort of 'propensity evidence' - which was once memorably described as apt to shed 'more heat than light'[21] - a jury would convict for the wrong reasons (and possibly as a public service!). As the saying went: you should not give a dog a bad name and then hang it.

Only if its probative value justified the inevitable prejudicial effect,[22] was such evidence admissible against a defendant at common law.[23] Typically this was achieved when the similar fact evidence, as it was called, showed highly idiosyncratic (or 'signature') behaviour linking the accused to the offence charged[24] or provided necessary 'background' evidence[25] or otherwise performed a particularly effective probative task (for example, rebutting a specific defence[26]). In short, to be admissible at common law, the bad character evidence had to have some probative[27] job to do *beyond* merely showing a defendant's tendency to commit offences like that with which he was charged. The rule was strict - so strict that there was no scope for the common law exclusionary discretion[28] to operate independently of it.

In stark contrast, the common law was historically very liberal in allowing *others* appearing as witnesses in criminal cases to be cross-examined about *their* criminal convictions (and if necessary have them proved against them[29]) in order to impugn their credibility. This caused problems, however, once defendants were given a general right to give evidence in their own defence. If the accused could be treated just like any other witness in cross-examination, this would mean that the prosecution could achieve through the 'back door' (cross-examination) what it was prevented from achieving through the front (as part of the presentation of its case). In effect it was almost impossible to impugn the defendant's credibility as a witness

Before this case, attempts had been made to define more precisely when such evidence would be so probative as to justify the prejudice it would cause. Eventually it became easier to state the principle, which was phrased identically to the common law discretion to exclude evidence, thus rendering the latter otiose.

24 Often referred to as 'strikingly similar' fact evidence. See Lord Hailsham's unforgettable examples in *Boardman* [1975], op. cit.

25 See below.

26 For a startling example, see *R v Mortimer* (1936) 25 Cr App R 150

27 Note that when a court is considering the relevance or probative value of an item of evidence, the latter is viewed 'at its highest', that is, it is assumed (for this purpose) that the evidence is true (unless obviously

without also giving the dog a bad name.

A defendant witness thus required special protection and the Criminal Evidence Act 1898 gave it to him in the form of a 'shield' against cross-examination on his own bad character, unless either (a) the evidence was admissible anyway as an exception to the general rule excluding such evidence (in which case it could come in both front and back doors) or (b) the shield was 'lost', which could happen if, *in conducting his defence*, an accused gave evidence against a co-defendant *or* put his own credibility in issue[30] (either by blaming others or asserting his own virtue). In short, the accused was protected under the 1898 Act unless the evidence was admissible at common law in any event or he put his (or someone else's) character on the line.

The end result was that whereas most[31] non-defendant witnesses were generally considered fair game insofar as having their characters attacked in cross-examination, an accused was often effectively off-limits. Over time, it was felt that the law had got this balance wrong. In particular it was thought that juries were more sophisticated than had been supposed; judges were well able to exercise their discretion and give clear instructions to juries; and both could be trusted to ensure that relevant evidence was given the weight it deserved. Various proposals for reform were put forward and the end result was the CJA 2003, which in effect made it more difficult to impugn the character of a non-defendant witnesses (so they would be more willing to give evidence) but easier to introduce evidence of the accused's propensity to offend, in order (so it is said) to 'assist the evidence-based conviction of the guilty, without putting those who are not guilty at risk of conviction by prejudice'.[32]

A. BAD CHARACTER OF A *DEFENDANT*: s 101 CJA 2003

So far as the defendant's bad character is concerned, what the CJA 2003 did was to replace what had been an exclusionary rule, subject to narrow exceptions (*'not*

incredible). See, e.g., s 109 CJA 2003

28 See Ch. 14

29 This is one of the exceptions to the rule against rebuttal: see generally Ch. 18

30 There was a judicial discretion to exclude the cross-examination when the shield was lost in the latter case, but not the former.

31 One important exception was (and is) the special protection given to complainants in sex offence cases, as discussed above in Ch. 18

32 *R v Hanson* [2005] 1 WLR 3169, per Rose LJ, para 4

admissible, unless …') with a more inclusionary rule *('admissible if, but only if…')*, letting *judicial discretion play a much bigger role* in ensuring fairness in any given case. The net effect has been to greatly increase the admissibility into evidence of an accused's criminal disposition, usually in the form of previous convictions. There are specific 'gateways' to admissibility, and notice must be given of the intention to adduce the evidence, but so long as it is agreed or the judge determines that it meets a gateway requirement (some evidence might qualify for more than one gateway), it must be admitted through into evidence, subject (in some cases) to the judge's discretion to exclude it. Furthermore, once through a gateway (and not otherwise excluded or restricted), the evidence may be used for any relevant purposes - in other words, its use is *not necessarily confined* by the nature of the gateway through which it was admitted.[33] Judicial guidance is a critical part of the equation and when summing up, the trial judge must explain clearly to the jury for what purpose(s) the evidence may (and may not) be used.[34]

Much of the old law is echoed, at least conceptually, in the CJA 2003, which is why it is helpful to have a basic understanding of what went before. The biggest expansion is found in the widespread admissibility (unless excluded by judicial discretion) of facts which do no more evidentially than show a relevant propensity to offend. What follows is a brief outline of how the legislation works.

Meaning of bad character

For the purposes of the CJA 2003, bad character means 'misconduct' (that is, the commission of an offence or other 'reprehensible' conduct[35]) occurring before or after[36] the offence with which the accused is charged but which is *unrelated* to the *commission, investigation* or *prosecution* of that offence.[37] It is important to appreciate, if not always easy to make, the distinction between evidence of misconduct on *other*

33 See BCrP F 13.24/25. Note that gateway 101 (1)(f) is explicitly limited to using the evidence for a specific purpose: see below and BCrP F 13.79

34 See e.g., *R v Williams* [2011] EWCA Crim 2198, cited at BCrP F 13.25

35 … or disposition towards misconduct: s 98 CJA 2003. The word reprehensible connotes culpability or blame: *R v Renda* [2005] EWCA Crim 2826. See BCrP F 13.6/7

36 Most bad character evidence will involve conduct occurring before the offence charged ('prior bad acts' as American lawyers would say), but not all. Bad conduct occurring after the offence charged (but before trial) could qualify. See, e.g., *Re A* [2009] EWCA Crim 513

37 See CJA 2003, s 98(a) and (b)

(usually previous) occasions, which requires a gateway to admissibility, and conduct which *'has to do with'* the offence charged, which does not.

In *R v Graham,*[38] it was suggested that in a case of 'dealing', evidence of the possession of a substantial sum of cash might 'have to do with' the facts of the offence in question if, for example, it represents the proceeds of the sale of the drugs the defendant is charged with supplying. But where receipt of such money is not part of the prosecution's immediate case, its likely purpose is merely to demonstrate (by similar misconduct on 'other' occasions for which he was paid) that the accused is an active drug dealer, which is simply evidence of propensity. Some nexus in time can be an important guide, but even this may not be necessary for evidence relating to motive and similar aspects of a case.[39]

The end result may often be the same (in that the evidence would usually be admitted either way[40]), but the *route* to admissibility is different. If the evidence in question is not bad character evidence for the purposes of the CJA 2003, there is no requirement that it pass through a gateway - admissibility will be based on general principles of relevance, which should be easy to establish if the behaviour 'has to do with' the alleged offence.[41] But if a defendant can show the evidence in question is, *by definition*, evidence of bad character, then entry through an s 101 gateway is required.

The s 101 Gateways

There are seven gateways, s 101(1)(a)-(g). The first, 101(1)(a), (where all parties agree to the reception of the evidence) is self-explanatory. The second, 101(1)(b), (where the evidence comes from the defendant[42]) is geared to allowing an accused to gain whatever advantage he can from asserting control, where this is possible, over how his own bad character is presented. Both of these gateways require the active involvement of the accused in admitting the evidence, and so are not particularly controversial.

38 [2007] EWCA Crim 1499

39 *R v Sule* [2012] EWCA Crim 1130, approved in *R v Lunkulu* [2015] EWCA Crim 1350, cited in BCrP F 13.10-13.12

40 This prompted Toulson LJ to observe in *R v Graham*, op. cit., at para 25 that in many cases it was a 'distinction without a practical difference'. But examiners sometimes like to test these distinctions!

41 ... and so will not be very apt to be excluded by discretion of the judge

42 Either in-chief or in answer to a question put in cross-examination intended to elicit the information. See, e.g., *R v Tollady* [2010] EWCA Crim 2614

Gateway 101(1)(c) allows in evidence of the defendant's bad character where it is 'important explanatory evidence'. This is effectively a codification and re-branding of what the common law called 'background evidence', which is admissible where necessary to enable the jury *to make sense of* the events under consideration. Typically, such evidence will provide necessary context in which to place other parts of the evidential puzzle so as to render the whole picture comprehensible. It is commonly used to show a history of animosity, jealousy or controlling conduct, usually to rebut defences such as accident or self-defence. But if the jury can understand and decide the case without the additional evidence, then it is not admissible through this gateway.[43]

Evidence is said to be 'important explanatory evidence' if (i) 'without it, the court or jury would find it *impossible or difficult* properly to understand other evidence in the case' *and* (ii) 'its value for understanding the case as a whole is *substantial*'.[44] Adjectives like 'impossible' and 'substantial' set the bar fairly high and are intended to ensure that this gateway is not easily used to smuggle in propensity evidence. The latter should go through its own gateway,[45] which is linked to a specific statutory discretion for excluding the evidence in the interest of fairness.[46] Having said that, once evidence is through gateway 101(1)(c) as explanatory evidence it is capable of being used for any other relevant purpose, including propensity, and the jury will need to be instructed accordingly.

Again, there may at times be a fine line between explanatory evidence (which requires a gateway) and evidence which 'has to do with' the offence charged (which, because it is not 'bad character' as defined for the purposes of the CJA 2003, does not).

Typical cases of explanatory evidence relate to an historical relationship or pattern between the accused and (usually) his victim to reveal motive or some other reason for the commission of the offence. In *R v Phillips*,[47] for example, the accused denied murdering his wife and background evidence (as it was then called) was

43 *R v Lee* [2012] EWCA Crim 316, para 12-13

44 s 102 CJA 2003

45 See, e.g., *R v Davis* [2008] EWCA Crim 1156 where the Court of Appeal warned against admitting evidence with limited or no probative value as explanatory, when the real purpose was to suggest propensity without qualifying for the s 101(d) gateway. See BCrP F 13.29

46 Gateway (c) has no such linked discretion under the CJA, but there is scope for both the common law discretion and s 78 discretion to operate.

47 [2003] 2 Cr App R 528

admitted of their unhappy marriage over a number of years.[48] Such evidence may also explain other aspects of a case. In *R v Chohan*[49] an identifying witness knew the accused as a drug dealer. The Court of Appeal held that this fact was correctly admitted through gateway 101(1)(c) because the basis of her knowledge of the accused explained why the witness was able to give confident evidence of identification by recognition.[50] Evidence that the complainant in a rape case was sexually abused by the accused as a child may well help to explain whether a relationship between the two many years later was (or was not) truly consensual.[51]

Of the remaining gateways, it is important to note that three are for prosecution evidence only; one is for defendant evidence only. To reinforce this fact, I shall sub-divide the discussion below accordingly. The distinction is an important one, particularly since once through the defence only gateway, there is no discretion to exclude the evidence. Examiners like to test students on this aspect of bad character evidence.

Conceptually, s 101(1)(e)-(g) replicate, with modern refinements and language, the instances when an accused would have 'lost' his 'shield' under the 1898 Act. Of all of the gateways, it is s 101(1)(d) which represented the greatest departure from the past.

(i) Prosecution only gateways

(a) Important matter in issue between prosecution and defence: s 101(1)(d)

This gateway represents a 'sea change'[52] from the previous law because it is such a wide portal. 'Important matter' is defined as being 'a matter of substantial importance in the context of the case as a whole,'[53] which would seem to exclude very little. All but the most marginal evidence relevant to proving an element of the case against the defendant would seem capable of meeting this description. In the

48 But not so far in the past as to lose relevance: *ibid*, at 536

49 One of the conjoined appeals in *R v Edwards* [2006] 1 Cr App R 31; [2005] EWCA Crim 1815, para 62-78

50 It was probably also admissible under the propensity gateway (d), as to which see below.

51 See, e.g., *R v C* [2012] EWCA Crim 2034

52 See BCrP F 13.38

53 s 112(1) CJA 2003

54 Unlike s101(1)(e) and the requirement for non-defendant witnesses. See below.

55 Discussed below.

old days, the probative value of bad character evidence was a crucial part of the test of admissibility. *Gateway (d) does not even require any particular degree of probative value!*[54] Safeguards are to be found, not in the gateway itself, but in the discretion to exclude evidence[55] which would otherwise (quite easily) get through it.

s 103 goes on to highlight, in particular, two 'important' issues to which an accused's bad character may be relevant for the purposes of gateway 101(1)(d). The first is the defendant's *propensity to commit offences* of the kind with which he is charged.[56] This effectively reversed the previous law so far as evidence of a defendant's criminal disposition is concerned. As remarked in *R v Chopra*[57] whereas at common law evidence of the accused's propensity to offend in the manner charged was prima facie *inadmissible*, under the CJA 2003 it became prima facie *admissible*.

A second 'important' matter mentioned in s 103 is the accused's *propensity to be untruthful*,[58] which will be relevant if the prosecution seek to rely on this gateway to attack the credibility of the accused - something which happens with some regularity.

The point is that relevant evidence is admissible through gateway (d) (subject to a discretion to exclude) even if all it achieves is to show a propensity to offend as alleged or tell tales. Such evidence might, of course, also be capable of performing a more specific and potent probative job for the prosecution (for example, to rebut a specific defence, to establish identification, to provide evidence of system and so on[59]), and the judge must explain to a jury for what purpose the bad character evidence admitted through this gateway may be used. s 101(1)(d) is *thus not* limited to admitting propensity evidence, but those matters referred to in s 103(1) merited a special mention in the legislation because admitting bad character evidence merely for the sake of showing a relevant criminal disposition represented such a radical departure from the past. For that reason it is also worth making the following observations about them in particular, and gateway 101(1)(d) in general.

56 See s 103(1)(a), which is somewhat oddly worded in that it effectively deems propensity to be a matter in issue rather than merely a means of establishing a matter in issue (for example, identification or, more broadly, guilt). It also excludes such evidence when propensity is irrelevant to guilt (which is rare).

57 [2007] 1 Cr App R 225, CA. See principles in *R v Hanson* [2005] as summarised in Keane & McKeown, *Modern Law,* p. 528

58 s 103(1)(b) CJA 2003

59 These are situations where propensity evidence might well have been admissible under the old law, and so make it less likely that the court would exercise any discretion to exclude the evidence, as to which see below.

PROPENSITY TO COMMIT THE OFFENCE CHARGED

This is usually (but not exclusively) shown by establishing that the defendant has convictions for offences of the same 'description' or 'category' as that charged,[60] *unless* the court feels it would be *unjust* for some reason to use a conviction for this purpose (for example because the conviction is spent or happened too long ago).[61] Usually it will take more than a single conviction to establish a bad habit, but if one were very probative of the offence charged (for example because 'strikingly similar'), this could suffice.[62]

Remember too that propensity can be shown in other ways,[63] including using evidence of the commission of other offences on a multi-count indictment. This is known as cross-admissibility, and poses some of the most problematic use of this sort of bad character evidence. Where an accused faces two or more counts on an indictment, the evidence which goes to prove he committed one of the offences is, *so far as the others are concerned*, bad character evidence[64] and may be admissible to help prove that he committed the others (assuming it passes through a gateway on its own merits). This is in large part how cases against serial killers like Harold Shipman (the GP accused of murdering hundreds of his elderly patients in very similar circumstances) are established.[65] The underlying principle is that probative value of multiple accusations may derive in part from similarity but also from the unlikelihood that the same person would find himself falsely accused of the same sort of activity by different people on different occasions.

It is important, however, that juries reach verdicts on each count separately and the use to which such evidence may be put in achieving this requires clear instructions from the judge.[66] Juries must be careful not to 'overvalue the accumulation of inference'.[67]

60 See BCrP F 13.36. There are prescribed categories of offences listed in a Schedule to the CJA 2003.

61 See ss 103(2) and (3) CJA 2003. In a sense, where convictions are used here to establish propensity, there are two built-in discretions, ss 101(3) (general discretion to exclude evidence headed through gateway 101(d)) and 103(3) (added discretion to reject use of convictions as evidence of propensity where this seems unjust).

62 *R v Hanson* [2005] 1 WLR 3169. For an example where one offence was of such limited probative value it should have been excluded, see *R v Bennabbou* [2012] EWCA Crim 1256

63 Propensity evidence not supported by convictions requires care: see BCrP F 13.42

64 s 112(2) CJA 2003

PROPENSITY TO BE UNTRUTHFUL

Admitting evidence for this purpose under s 101(1)(d) poses risks to defendants and has caused some judicial difference of opinion. The Explanatory Notes[68] to the 2003 Act suggest that s 103(1)(b) 'is intended to enable the admission of a limited range of evidence such as convictions for perjury or other offences involving deception…as opposed to the wider range of evidence that will be admissible where the defendant puts his character in issue by, for example, attacking the character of another person.'[69] The case law is not entirely consistent, however, in interpreting the section, in part because decisions of this kind are inevitably 'fact sensitive.' Without some limitation, it could allow the prosecution to point to evidence of previous convictions (of any description) as showing a propensity to be untruthful merely because the accused pleaded not guilty, gave evidence, but was nevertheless convicted. The problem is that lying to avoid negative consequences of one's actions is a rather generic kind of propensity, especially amongst criminals.

Even so, it was thought that the Court of Appeal in *R v Campbell* [70] probably went too far in the other direction[71] when it said that in most cases a criminal's propensity for untruthfulness will not be an 'important' issue in a case, unless both the offence itself and the bad character evidence necessarily involved deceit. Because guilt was its own motivation for lying, Lord Phillips CJ did not think that it generally assisted much in assessing an accused's credibility that such a person might also be naturally inclined to be untruthful. A cautious test seemed necessary; otherwise defendant witnesses could be a lot more susceptible to attacks on their character than non-defendant witnesses, who usually have a lot less to lose.[72]

According to *R v Hanson*,[73] it is in any event important to appreciate that dishonesty is not necessarily synonymous with untruthfulness, and so past acts of dishonesty will not by themselves establish a propensity for untruthfulness. This is

65 Shipman saved the state time and money by killing himself while in custody pending trial.

66 See generally Crown Court Compendium, Pt 1 Ch. 13

67 See, e.g, *R v Nicholson* [2012] 2 Cr App R 405 and BCrP F 13.58ff

68 Explanatory Notes, para 374

69 See gateway s 101(1)(g) discussed below.

70 [2007] EWCA Crim 1472

71 See discussion in Keane & McKeown, p 542-43

72 See discussion of s 100 CJA 2003 below

73 Op. cit. fn 62

partly because the range of offences requiring an element of dishonesty is so great and varied, and the propensity should match as accurately as possible the issue to which it relates. A pattern of lying and deceitfulness might help with a dishonesty offence. But the reverse does not follow - a history of shoplifting, for example, will not necessarily reveal a propensity to tell lies.

What might be something of a middle ground is found in the recent case of *R v N(Norris)*, which declined to follow *Campbell.* N was accused of historic sex offences against the complainant when she was a child (and he, her babysitter). N's defence was that the complainant must have confused him with one of her other babysitters. N had a previous conviction for a sexual offence against an underage girl, where his version of events had clearly been shown to be untrue. It also transpired that, once convicted, he had lied about his war record to improve his chances of a lighter sentence. The Court of Appeal said the trial judge had rightly admitted both as evidence of N's propensity to be untruthful, since they revealed a pattern of sustained lying in a court context similar to the one in which he again found himself.[74]

The Supreme Court may well be asked one day to pronounce on the interpretation of s 103(1)(b). Until then, what one can take from the cases seems to be that for the bad character evidence to be admitted through gateway 101(1)(d) as evidence of a propensity to be untruthful, credibility must be a central issue in the case and the evidence in question should clearly speak to the accused's tendency to tell lies.

PROPENSITY AND CREDIBILITY

It is important to remember that propensity evidence admitted through gateway (d) is also capable of being used, as appropriate, to impugn the defendant's credibility. This is partly because (leaving s 101(1)(f) aside) evidence admitted through a gateway

74 [2014] EWCA Crim 419. The trial judge's directions to the jury were also said to be impeccable. It is well worth reading this short but evocative judgment.

can be used for *all* relevant purposes, and is not limited to the purpose described by the specific gateway through which it was admitted. One relevant issue will always be whether the defendant's evidence is worthy of belief, which can be affected (to greater or lesser degree) by evidence of criminal (or other bad) behaviour. The judge must carefully explain to a jury the various functions which such evidence may serve, so that both the distinctions between them, as well as their limitations, are clearly understood. The situation is not dissimilar to cases where the defendant is of good character. Where an accused's bad character is admitted through the propensity gateway (d), and he has put forward his own version of events, the jury will need directions about both propensity and credibility in order to understand fully how to approach the evidence.

SPECIFIC DISCRETION TO EXCLUDE: S 101(3)

S 101(3) provides a specific judicial discretion to exclude evidence which would otherwise be admitted through gateway (d), where the fairness of the proceedings dictate it. Specifically, the provision says that the court 'must not' admit evidence through this gateway if it appears that its admission would have 'such an adverse effect on the fairness of the proceedings that the court ought not to admit it'. This wording is reminiscent of the s 78 discretion,[75] recourse to which would therefore be rendered virtually redundant in this context, especially given s 101(3)'s use of the more mandatory words 'must not'.[76]

Curiously, however, the provision requires 'an application by the defendant', which would appear to preclude the court exercising the discretion on its own initiative. However, where gaps like this appear (and if advocates do not take hints or suggestions from the bench about making the appropriate application), it seems fairly clear that both the s 78, and the common law discretion to exclude where the

---

75 See generally Ch. 14

76 See *R v Chrysostomou* [2010] EWCA Crim 1403, CA. In any event s 78's 'may' is usually more of a 'must': see *R v Tirnaveanu* [2007], cited at BCrP F 13.19

prejudicial effect outweighs the probative value, can be exercised to fill the void.[77]

The discretion to exclude evidence of the accused's bad character is particularly important where gateway (d) is concerned, because propensity evidence can be very damning, thus making the jury's job of keeping an open mind difficult. No doubt this is one reason why the s 101(3) discretion is *specifically linked* to this gateway. In exercising this discretion, the court must pay particular attention to how much time has elapsed between the offence(s) charged and the bad behaviour which the prosecution proposes to admit through gateway (d).[78] Otherwise, there will as a matter of common sense be a link between the probative value of the evidence[79] and fairness - the less the bad character evidence has to say about the commission of the offence in question, the more apt a court will be to exclude it. In *R v Eyidah*, for example, the case concerned passport offences. The Crown had been allowed to adduce evidence of rent arrears, defaults on bank loans and even unpaid parking fines. The Court of Appeal held that this evidence ought to have been excluded. According to Hooper LJ, the jury had been 'wrongly deluged with a mass of prejudicial material', most of which 'had nothing to do with the case'.[80]

(b) Evidence to correct false impression given by defendant: s 101(1)(f)

Under the old law, a defendant who spoke well of himself could lose his 'shield' against cross-examination on his bad character. The logic is that where a man of bad character gives the impression that he is a man of good character, the jury is entitled to know the truth. This notion is replicated and refined in gateway (f), which in essence admits evidence of an accused's bad character in order to *correct* (and only for the purpose of correcting) a false impression given by (or on behalf of) the defendant. An accused can give a false impression in a variety of ways: by words or conduct, expressly or implicitly, in the witness box or in an earlier statement (for

77 See, e.g., *R v Weir* [2006] EWCA Crim 117

78 s 101(4) CJA 2003

79 See, e.g., *R v Benabbou*, op. cit.

80 [2010] EWCA Crim 987, CA, at para 13

example under questioning at a police station) which is relied upon in court. But one way or another, a *false* or misleading impression must have been *given* before the prosecution can make use of this gateway. This must, logically, involve more than a defendant putting himself forward as a person innocent of the charges brought against him - otherwise all defendants would be vulnerable to attack through this gateway.[81]

Note that a defendant's responsibility for the false impression may be avoided if he withdraws or disassociates himself from it. Thus where the false impression is given in a police interview, it can be neutralised by an agreed editing of the statement pre-trial (and not repeating it in court). If, however, a retraction is only made under cross-examination, this may be considered a concession to which the accused was driven, rather than a voluntary withdrawal or disassociation, as such.[82]

A typical example of evidence entering through this gateway is *R v Ullah*.[83] In that case, the accused stated in interview that he had never acted dishonestly and that he had been meticulous in his business dealings. He did not disassociate himself from these remarks and so at trial the prosecution were allowed to admit into evidence his previous convictions for deception-related offences. But remember, the bad character evidence admitted under this gateway should 'go *no further than is necessary to correct the false impression*', and be effective in doing so.[84]

The statutory discretion to exclude under s 101(3) does *not* extend to this gateway (f), but because it is a 'prosecution only' gateway, both the s 78 discretion and the common law discretion could be exercised where appropriate.

Note, too, that if bad character evidence admitted through gateway (f) would *not* otherwise be admissible through gateway (d), the jury will need careful directions about how to deal with it. If the evidence says little or nothing relevant about the accused's propensity to offend as alleged, then this should be made clear to them.[85]

81 See *R v D* [2011] EWCA Crim 1474 where it was said gateway (f) was too readily invoked by prosecutors. BCrP F 13.79/80 and see examples at 13.82-13.84

82 *R v Renda* [2005] EWCA Crim 2826

83 [2006] EWCA Crim 2003

84 s 105(6) and BCrP F 13.80

85 See Crown Court Compendium Pt 1 Ch. 12-8

(c) Defendant makes attack on another person's character: s 101(1)(g)

A defendant's speaking ill of others can have a similar effect to his speaking well of himself. Under the old law, a defendant could lose his 'shield' (and become liable to cross-examination on his own bad character) when he had impugned the character of a prosecution witness or the deceased victim of the crime. This idea lives on in gateway (g). The rationale is that juries should know about the sort of person making such allegations. The description of gateway (g) is a little more widely drawn than its predecessor, in that it can be opened by an 'attack' on the character of 'another person'. This could include a co-defendant, although the more usual object of attack is a prosecution witness.[86]

An accused can make an attack on another's character in any number of ways: by adducing evidence attacking another's character, or asking questions in cross-examination intended or likely to elicit such evidence, or where evidence is given of an imputation of another person made by the defendant on being questioned or charged with the offence in question.[87] The court will be alert, however, to prosecution attempts to use statements made in the heat of the cross-examination (when emotions may be running high) as an artificial device for getting an accused's bad character through this gateway.[88]

Bear in mind that the attack must be on another's *character* (for example, by saying that the other had committed an offence or had behaved, or was disposed to behave, in a reprehensible way[89]). A denial of guilt (or an aspect of the prosecution case) should not, however emphatically put, open the gateway, although it may be difficult at times to differentiate a vehement assertion of innocence from an attack on an accuser's character. The distinction usually turns on context and meaning. For example, to say a witness was mistaken should not open the gateway, whereas to say a witness was not to be believed because that person is a habitual liar, probably

86 See below re attacking the character of non-defendant witnesses.

87 s 106(1) CJA 2003

88 There is no provision for an accused to disassociate himself from an attack made under questioning, as there is for gateway (f). See, e.g., *R v Nelson* [2006] EWCA Crim 3412

89 s 106(2) CJA 2003 which links back to s 98

would. But each case much be judged on its merits.[90] Moreover, it does not matter how the attack is dressed up, but its effect. One could not avoid the gateway opening merely by alleging that the witness was known to be 'economical with the actualité'!

If an attack is made, it is irrelevant why it was made. So, if the defendant's case is that the victim's own behaviour was reprehensible, this will open the gateway. This happened, for example, in *R v Singh (James Paul)*[91] where it was a necessary part of the defendant's version of events that the complainant had invited him to her flat where the two of them spent some hours together smoking crack cocaine.

We saw how s 101(1)(f) limits the bad character evidence entering through that gateway to that which is necessary 'to correct' the wrong impression given by the defendant. Gateway (g) contains no such restrictions. Nor does it require the evidence to have any probative value. This gateway thus poses a special risk to defendants in terms of the prejudice the information revealed might cause in the eyes of a jury. No doubt it is for this reason that the s 101(3) discretion to exclude, which we have already seen applies to gateway (d), is also *linked specifically* to gateway (g), so that the court must not admit evidence through this gateway if it would be unfair to do so.[92] Judges should be particularly alert to the nature of the attack made and whether the revelation of bad character would be 'out of all proportion' to the damage done by it, and deploy the discretion to exclude such evidence where it is necessary to 'combat' the risk of improper prejudice.[93] To the extent that such evidence is admitted through this gateway, very careful directions should be given to the jury. If the evidence is only relevant to credibility, this must be made clear.[94]

(ii) Defendant-only gateway: s 101(1)(e)

s 101(1)(e) is the one gateway for *defendants only*. We saw earlier how gateway (d) gives the prosecution an opportunity to admit propensity evidence against a defendant.

90 See, e.g., guidance in *R v Britzman; R v Hall* [1983] 1 WLR 350

91 [2007] EWCA Crim 2140

92 See detail in discussion of gateway (d) above.

93 See, e.g., *R v Chrysostomou* [2010] op. cit., BCrP F 13.91 para 12.97

94 See, e.g., *R v Williams*, op. cit., fn 34 and Crown Court Compendium Pt 1 Ch. 12-9 para 4

Gateway (e) is a *defendant's* opportunity to do the same *against a co-defendant.* However, the bar to admissibility is set noticably higher than the prosecution's version, because, once evidence gets through this gateway, there is no discretion to exclude it.

To illustrate how gateway (e) works, let's assume a case against two defendants, whom we will call D1 and D2. D1 has no previous convictions, but D2 has. If the court allows it, gateway (e) permits D1 to admit evidence of D2's bad character if such evidence has '*substantial probative value* to an *important* matter in issue' between them. This often occurs when defendants deploy so-called 'cut-throat defences' *("I didn't do it - he did").* In such cases, credibility is usually an important issue because D1 will be asking the jury to prefer his evidence, which in turn requires them to decide that D2's version of events is less worthy of belief (and vice versa).

Note that where the co-defendant's credibility is *the* important issue between them, s 104(1) adds an *extra* requirement; D1 will *only* get evidence showing D2's propensity to be untruthful admitted through the gateway if D2 has conducted his defence in such a way as to *undermine* D1's case.

The point of gateway (e) is to give D1 as much scope, as is consistent with fairness to D2, to adduce evidence revealing his innocence. This is done either by allowing D1 to present evidence of D2's propensity to commit the offence in question or (assuming D1's defence has been undermined by D2's) to show why D2's version of events should not be believed. In both cases, the evidence must really have something convincing[95] to say about an important aspect of the case. There are several important points to make about this gateway.

(a) Establishing co-defendant's lack of credibility

The expression 'propensity to be untruthful' is used in s 104(1), but is interpreted more liberally for this gateway than it is the case for gateway (d), in part because

95 Substantial probative value has been described as meaning an 'enhanced ability' to prove or disprove the matter in issue: *R v Philips* [2011] 1 CrAppR 332 at [25]. See BCrP F 13.69

the law is less concerned to protect defendants from each other than it is to protect defendants from prosecutors. In this context it essentially equates to 'why the co-defendant shouldn't be believed'- in other words, it means credibility in the round. As Hughes LJ put it in *R v Lawson,* 'it is ... wholly rationale that the degree of caution which is applied to a *Crown* application against a defendant who is on trial ... [is not] applied when what is at stake is a *defendant's* right to deploy relevant material to defend himself against a criminal charge'. Thus, for the purposes of this gateway, a wide variety of unscrupulous conduct, not necessarily involving lying or cheating, might be capable of undermining a co-accused's version of events. Whether it is, and has substantial probative value, will be for the judge to decide on the facts of the case.[96]

(b) Nature of co-defendant's defence

Whether the nature or conduct of D2's defence (which includes the manner of cross-examination and so on) is such as to undermine Dl's defence really depends on the consequences to Dl if D2's version of events is believed. In *R v Davis,*[97] for example, D2 accused Dl of stealing a gold cross and chain which had disappeared from a house in circumstances where one or the other of them must have taken it. Any denial by D2 in those circumstances necessarily involved undermining Dl's chances of acquittal. This scenario is typical of cut-throat defences. But not all defences run in such stark opposition to each other - those that run in parallel will not necessarily involve co-accused undermining each other's defences. If, for example, D2's defence still provides Dl with an alternative version of events which, if believed, could result in his acquittal, than (for these purposes anyway) Dl's defence has not been undermined by D2's.[98]

96 [2007] 1 WLR 1191, [34], (my emphasis) and see BCrP F 13.74/75

97 [1975] 1 WLR 345: decided under the old law, but the idea is the same.

98 As in *R v Hendrick* [1992] Crim LR 427. In *Lawson* op. cit., the defences ran somewhat in parallel but nevertheless the co-accused had undermined each other's defence.

(c) Evidence of co-defendant's propensity to offend

The added requirement of s 104(1) does not bite where the bad character evidence is *not* primarily *directed at* credibility, but rather to the co-defendant's propensity to commit the offence charged. Generally speaking, however, the latter is the sort of evidence which the prosecution would already have got through its own (less constrained) gateway (d), and from which a co-defendant could, albeit indirectly, benefit. And of course such evidence might hit both targets - if the bad character evidence shows a propensity to commit offences of the type charged, it may well also have substantive probative value in relation to credibility since anything which points the finger of guilt at D2 must reflect badly on his assertion of innocence.

(d) No discretion to exclude

The test for admissibility through gateway (e) ('substantive probative value') is more stringent than the prosecution's gateway (d), which does not factor in any specified degree of probative value as an entrance requirement. The explanation (or quid pro quo) for applying a stricter test of admissibility for evidence against a co-defendant is that (*in contrast to* the prosecution-only, and indeed all of the other, gateways) there *is no judicial discretion of any description to exclude the evidence once the requirements of this 'defendants only' gateway (e) have been met.* This was the position before the CJA 2003 and remains the position today. It protects an accused's right to do all he can to defend himself. Having said that, it is still necessary to give proper notice of the intention to admit such evidence and there may very occasionally be scope on *procedural* grounds for a judge to disallow the evidence where the co-defendant would be unable to deal with it effectively.[99]

99 E.g., because the application made very late in the day as in *R v Jarvis* [2008] EWCA Crim 488

(e) Careful directions to jury

Juries will need clear directions on how to approach evidence coming through this defendant-only gateway. If the evidence is not relevant to propensity to commit the offence charged and there is a risk the jury may treat it as such, they will need to be warned against using it for this purpose. Otherwise, where the sole purpose of the evidence is to respond to D2's attempt to undermine D1's defence, then the direction 'can be given quite shortly'.[100] It is always important, however, to make the point that defendant-on-defendant evidence, as it were, cannot do the prosecution's job for it.[101]

Some general safeguards and limitations

There are, finally, some generally applicable safeguards and limitations on the admission of evidence of a defendant's bad character. In particular, the court has the power to stop a case where it feels such evidence has been 'contaminated' - this usually happens when evidence has been tainted by collusion between witnesses.[102] In addition, evidence of offences committed by an adult defendant as a child (when under 14 years old) is only admissible in very limited (and the most serious) circumstances.[103] This is because we are all apt to do silly things as a child or young person, when we are most impressionable and least in control of ourselves, and there should be some restraint on how much (and how long) this can be held against us.

Sec 27(3) Theft Act 1968

This was one of the exceptions to the rules prevailing before the major shift brought about by the CJA 2003, and still survives as a little world of its own where a specific sort of propensity evidence is admissible, in a specific sort of case, for a specific reason. If you are dealing with a case of handling stolen goods (or indeed if it comes

100 *R v Rosato* [2008] EWCA Crim 1243, para 26

101 See Crown Court Compendium Pt 1 Ch 12-7

102 See s 107 CJA 2003. Collusion is often a matter affecting weight, rather than admissibility of evidence, and so can be left to the jury, unless the evidence is so tainted that no reasonable jury could convict on it. See discussion at BCrP F 13.62ff

103 See s 108 CJA 2003

up in your examinations), then you will need to know about this provision.

In a nutshell, where:

(a) the accused is being tried for *handling* stolen goods *only,*[104] *and*

(b) there is evidence that the accused committed the *actus reus* of the handling offence charged,[105] *then*

(c) to help prove the necessary *mens rea* in respect of that offence (that he knew or believed the goods to be stolen), evidence is admissible *either* of his having committed the *actus reus* of handling in respect of goods stolen not more than 12 months before the date of offence charged *or* of his having been convicted of theft *or* handling stolen goods in the previous five years.[106]

It is important to notice that s 27(3) can *only be used for the purpose of proving guilty knowledge.* In effect, it allows in evidence of the propensity to *act* like a handler of stolen goods[107] in order to establish that the accused *thinks* like one too, thus making it easier for the prosecution to meet the *"I didn't know they were stolen"* defence. If the accused is in the habit of being on the receiving end of stolen goods, then it might follow that he knows what is really going on.

Problems can arise when the accused is charged with more than one count of handling, and judges have to take care when applying the provision and explain to juries how to use the propensity evidence they have heard; but in any event, prosecutors these days may find the relevant CJA 2003 gateway a simpler alternative.[108]

---

104 The provision does not apply if the handling charge is joined with another, such as theft.

105 There are a lot of variations (for example possession, retention, disposal, and so on, of stolen goods). See BCrP B 4.159

106 Written notice must be given of the intention to prove the conviction: s 27(3)(b) Theft Act 1968

107 Or thief, if there is a previous conviction.

108 See generally BCrP F 13.93

B. BAD CHARACTER OF *NON-DEFENDANT*: s 100 CJA 2003

At common law, witnesses other than an accused could be cross-examined about any manner of previous misconduct, for example, acts of dishonesty, immorality, drug addiction and so on, in order to impugn their credibility, unless the misconduct was so remote in time or nature as to have no bearing on the reliability of that witness in the eyes of the tribunal of fact.

Assuming, however, that such questioning was only relevant to the *(collateral)* matter of the witness's credibility, then if he or she denied the alleged behaviour then only in certain exceptional circumstances could evidence to rebut the denial be admitted into evidence, although this would not make accusatory cross-examination any more pleasant for the witness.[109] Evidence of previous convictions is one of those exceptional circumstances, of course, and this is the most typical way in which relevant bad character is manifested. This left non-defendant witnesses, in particular, very exposed to having their criminal past paraded in court in order to show that their testimony is not worthy of belief.

Over the years, certain types of witness have been accorded statutory or procedural protection from being asked questions in cross-examination on certain subjects (for example, complainants in sex offence cases) or in a certain manner (for example, vulnerable witnesses). These are discussed in Chapter 18. But it was still felt necessary, when reforming the law relating to bad character evidence generally, to impose more restrictions across the board to protect witnesses other than defendants, in order to encourage them to give evidence and to stop gratuitous cross-examination which has no other purpose than to intimidate, embarrass or 'muddy the waters'.[110] So, while s 101 CJA 2003 made it easier to admit evidence of an accused's criminal convictions, s 100 made it rather more difficult to do this in respect of other people. The point was to 'reduce kite-flying and innuendo ... in

109 The rule against rebuttal is discussed in Ch. 18

110 Law Com No 273 (2001), para 9.35. See also *R v Braithwaite* [2010] 2 Cr App R 1 and BCrP F 15.3/4

favour of a concentration upon the real issues of the case'.[111]

S 100 sets out its own mini-set of gateways for the admission of evidence of bad character of any person *other than* the accused, *whether called as a witness or not*, and irrespective of who (prosecution, accused or co-accused) seeks to elicit or adduce the evidence. The definition of bad character evidence is the same as discussed above.[112] The three gateways to admissibility will also sound very familiar.

One is where all the parties agree, which requires no explanation. A second gateway to admitting bad character evidence of a non-defendant is where the evidence is 'important explanatory evidence'. This bears the same meaning as it does for the equivalent s 101 gateway.[113] An example would be an abuse case where an explanation for the victim's failure to seek help from a particular family member or friend (not the accused) might be found in a history of violence perpetrated by that other person.[114]

The third sounds very like the defendant-only gateway discussed above in the context of an accused's bad character. This is because it tends to operate in situations analogous to gateway 101(1)(e), but in this context instead of an accused blaming a co-accused, an accused will usually be blaming a third party, typically the alleged victim of, or an apparently innocent bystander to, the crime. Thus, evidence of the bad character of a person *other than the defendant* is admissible through this gateway if it has '*substantial* probative value' in relation to a 'matter in issue in the proceedings which is of *substantial* importance in the context of the case as a whole'. This is a very high threshold and fact-sensitive. No specific examples are given of what issues might be of substantial importance in such cases, but quite clearly evidence admissible through this gateway can speak either to the credibility or the criminal propensity of the individual - or both.[115]

S 100(3) sets out common sense factors to assist the court in deciding whether

111 *R v Miller* [2010] EWCA Crim 1153, at para 20, cited at BCrP F 15.2

112 See BCrP F 15.6ff

113 s 100(1)(a). See also s 100(2) which is identically worded to s 102

114 See BCrP F 15.12

115 s 100(1)(b), (my emphasis) and see *R v Braithwaite*, op. cit.

the evidence in question (assuming it to be true) has substantive probative value, including the nature of the misconduct, when it occurred, how often it occurred and how similar (or not) it is to any behaviour which is relevant to the case at hand. Take, for example, the scenario where the victim of an alleged crime gives prosecution evidence against the defendant and the latter seeks to put some or all of the blame onto that victim. If the alleged victim has previous convictions which show he is capable or more likely to have been the aggressor, these could have substantial probative value in relation to the important issue of who in fact was the perpetrator.[116] At the same time, such convictions would serve the function of shaking the credibility of the victim's version of what happened.[117]

In other cases, only the credit of the person will be at issue; for example, has the witness accurately identified the perpetrator? For these purposes (just as with the defendant-only gateway to revealing the bad character of a co-accused) the broad notion that various kinds of bad character can undermine credibility prevails. In *R v Brewster*[118] it was said that whether convictions have persuasive value in undermining credibility will depend on their nature, their number and their ages, but it is not a prerequisite for admission that the conviction demonstrates a narrow propensity to untruthfulness. If a conviction follows a not guilty plea (or assertion of innocence), this may be relevant to the court in assessing the ability of the conviction to speak significantly to the credibility of the convicted person.[119]

Occasionally, of course, only criminal propensity will be at issue, although it would be unusual, if an accused seeks to blame another person, that the prosecution would either not charge that person as well or call them to give rebutting evidence (thus putting that person's credibility at issue too). An obvious example where it would be impossible to do either of these is where that other person is the deceased victim of the alleged offence. Whatever the precise purpose of adducing the bad

116 See *R v Platt* [2016] 4 WLR 51 for a good example of a case where the evidence did not have substantial probative value and should not have been admitted. The s 100(3) list of factors is not exhaustive, see BCrP F 15.16

117 See, e.g., *R v GH* (Criminal Propensity) [2009] EWCA Crim 2899

118 [2010] EWCA Crim 1194

119 See, e.g., *R v South* [2011] EWCA Crim 754, CA where an alibi witness had 53 convictions recorded between 1978 and 1996! The Court of Appeal said the trial judge should have distinguished between those which really assisted with the credibility of the witness and those which did not.

character evidence of someone other than the defendant, when it is allowed, juries should always have its significance carefully explained to them.[120]

Note too the interplay between this aspect of criminal evidence and others. In particular:

- A defendant who uses s 100 as a way of attacking the character of a non-defendant will risk evidence of his own bad character (if indeed there is any) being admitted through prosecution gateway s 101(1)(g), so he will want to think carefully before doing so.
- A request by a defendant for leave to cross-examine a complainant in a sex offence case may bring both s 100 and s 41 YJCEA 1999[121] into play. The latter prevents cross-examination of complainants on aspects of (not necessarily reprehensible) sexual behaviour except in very limited circumstances, and is thought to be the more formidable of the two obstacles.[122] But s 100 has broader application. So where, for example, the defence to a rape case is that the complainant is in the habit of making false allegations of sexual abuse, then so long as there is an evidential basis for the alleged falsity (which often there is not), s 100 will govern admissibility. This is because, even if the context involves sexual behaviour, the essence of the attack is that the complainant is a liar or a fantasist.[123]

Finally, except where the evidence is admitted by agreement, s 100 requires that *leave of the court* is given before the bad character evidence can be alluded to (in questioning) or adduced.[124] In this context, to be giving or refusing such permission might be as close as the judge will get to exercising any discretion, depending on who makes the

120 See Crown Court Compendium Pt 1 Ch. 12-10

121 See Ch. 18

122 *R v V* [2006] EWCA Crim 1901

123 See, e.g., *R v Stephenson* [2006] EWCA Crim 2325

124 If there were no admissible evidence to rebut a witness's denial, the cross-examination should normally not be allowed: *R v Miller*, op. cit.

application. Only if the *prosecution* seek to rely on evidence under s 100 (for example to attack a defendant's alibi witness) would it be open to a defendant to ask the court to exclude it under the s 78 discretion. There is no such discretion when defendants successfully make use of this gateway.

C. PROCEDURE

As mentioned above, a party seeking to cross-examine and/or otherwise adduce evidence of the bad character of a *non*-defendant must *apply* for *permission* to do so. Such applications, with copies to all parties, should be made as soon as 'reasonably practicable', and in any event not more than 14 days after the relevant prosecution disclosure. They are also opposed in writing.[125] Judges should give reasons for their rulings on applications under s 100 - they are *judgments*, not an exercise of discretion.

In the case of an *accused's* bad character, leave is not required as such, but *notice* must be given to the court and all other parties - not more than 14 days after the defendant in question pleads not guilty in the Crown Court (in the case of the prosecution) and not more than 14 days after prosecution disclosure (in the case of a co-accused). A defendant applying to exclude such evidence must do so not more than - yes, you guessed it - 14 days after receiving notice of intention to introduce or cross-examine on his bad character.[126]

All applications and notices should be made on the appropriate form. As you would expect, however, the court has the power to vary the requirements or excuse a failure to comply with these rules. This is only common sense, since issues of admissibility can arise unexpectedly, often at trial - for example, because of something a witness says. The court will be careful to ensure, however, that its ability to be flexible and forgiving is not exploited and that no defendant is unfairly 'ambushed' by an 11th hour attack.[127] It will also be astute to avoid distracting 'satellite litigation'.[128]

125 CrimPR r 21.3(3)/(4)

126 Prosecutors have 28 days from a guilty plea in the magistrates' court to serve notice: see *ibid*, r 21.4

127 See, e.g., *R v Ramirez* [2010] CrimLR 235

128 See, e.g., *R v O'Dowd* [2009] CrimLR 827

revision tips

- It is important to make distinctions when considering this aspect of criminal evidence, in particular between:
  - good character of accused (*Vye*) vs bad character of accused (s 101 CJA 2003)
  - bad character of accused (s 101) vs bad character of non-accused (s 100)
  - propensity vs credibility as relevant issues in a case
- You must clearly analyse and engage with the scenario the examiner is testing you on. You may be asked to identify the best route to admissibility or best reason for excluding otherwise admissible evidence
- As you revise, encapsulate the relevant gateway requirements. Note key words. Construct simple factual examples to help you differentiate between them.

It is worth reading ...

R v M [2009] 2 Cr App R.3, CA. Post *Hunter* this is a case of 'effective good character'. Moses LJ's judgment is short and to the point, and makes clear how important it is that an accused gets the fullest good character direction to which he is entitled. Juries need to be clear that good character actually operates in a defendant's *favour*.

R v Hoare [2016] EWCA Crim 1659. A short judgment, easy to follow. Several gateways get a brief mention and it makes clear how strict the courts are about protecting *non-defendants* from attacks on their character - even when they are no angels!

R v Benabbou [2012] EWCA Crim 1256. You get a lot for your money with this judgment. Take a moment to notice how prejudiced you begin to feel about the accused as you read about his bad character, but how little it actually proves about the event in question - it is a good reminder of the importance of the court's discretion to exclude evidence in appropriate circumstances. But compare it to *R v Montakhab* [2012] EWCA Crim 2012, where the previous behaviour of the accused said quite a lot about what he got up to on buses (that evidence would have been admissible even in the old days!).

Crown Court Compendium Pt 1 Chs 11-13 are a very valuable resource.

CHAPTER 20

Hearsay evidence
in criminal law

Just as with evidence of bad character, the rules about the admissibility of hearsay evidence are almost entirely governed by the CJA 2003.

Broadly speaking, hearsay evidence can be defined as a statement which is *not made by a person while giving testimony* in court proceedings, but which is nevertheless relied upon (in those same proceedings) to establish *the truth* of what was asserted.[1] So, for example, suppose A sees a person climbing through a window of a house at night. A later tells his friend B that the person he saw was D, who was wearing his hallmark gangland hoodie at the time. A also writes out a statement to this effect for the police. In order to prove that it was in fact D who climbed into the window that night, testimony from B of what A told him about this, is hearsay. So too (because it was not made in the course of giving oral evidence at the trial) is A's written statement.

The main objection to hearsay evidence springs from the fact that it is at least one remove from its immediate source.[2] Generally speaking, if the information comes straight from the horse's mouth, a court of law prefers to hear it directly from the horse. Far better for A in our example (who perceived the events) to tell the court directly what he saw - he can give sworn evidence and will be available for questioning so that its quality can be properly tested and evaluated. Maybe his view

1 See the precise wording of s 121(2) CJA 2003, which formulation does not vary much from earlier common law definitions.

2 And so includes an earlier statement made by that source whether in lieu of his testimony in court (see below) or in addition to it (see rule against previous consistent statements in Ch. 18)

was obstructed. Maybe someone else was wearing a hoodie like D's. Maybe A bears D a grudge. Historically, hearsay evidence played into the judiciary's worst anxieties - fear of distortion, as the story passes from one person to another, fear of fabrication and, especially, the fear that juries might give undue weight to evidence the truth of which could not be tested by cross-examination.[3]

Thus, at common law the rule operated strictly to exclude hearsay evidence, unless a specific exception applied. These attempted to cater to a variety of circumstances where hearsay evidence seemed to serve a useful purpose: for example, what if a witness has died? Aren't business records more cogent than the memory of the person who wrote the information down and promptly forgot it? Do we really need to be so strict where there are no juries? What if witnesses are intimidated? The exceptions to the rule eventually became so many and varied, and so complex in their operation, that by the time of the CJA 2003 it seemed a lot more sensible and straightforward to make them (or at least the best ones) part of the rule itself.

The criminal law did not go so far as the civil law, which effectively did away with the rule against hearsay altogether.[4] But (just as with evidence of bad character) it did move from a rigid exclusionary rule ('not admissible, unless') to a more *inclusionary* system ('admissible, if, but only if ...'), so that the so-called hearsay 'exceptions' are sometimes also referred to as 'gateways' to admissibility. The CJA 2003 codified and clarified much of the previous law, simplified its presentation, and introduced greater flexibility - in particular, it gave the courts the ability to admit hearsay in the 'interests of justice', even if no other route to admissibility is available. Such an *inclusionary* discretion was novel.

What follows is an overview of how the hearsay rules operate. The *first thing* you must be able to do is to identify whether the evidence in question is *hearsay or not*. This is not always easy. But it is important - practitioners often need to respond to this sort of

3 See, e.g., Lord Havers in *Sharp* [1988] 1 WLR 7, at p. 11, and discussion in BCrP F 16.1ff

4 See Civil Evidence Act 1995, s 1(1) and *Be Civil!*, by the author, Ch.17

issue as testimony is being given! Moreover, there is no point in looking at the gateways to the admissibility of hearsay evidence if the evidence is not, in fact, hearsay.[5]

1. IS IT HEARSAY OR NOT?

It is usually fairly straightforward to decide whether one is dealing with a 'statement not made by a person while giving oral evidence'. The shorthand often used for this aspect of the definition is 'out-of-court' statement, but all this means is that the statement relied upon was made on some earlier occasion (by the witness himself or by someone else) and not while directly testifying in the current case. Statements made in other court proceedings on a previous occasion can qualify as 'out-of-court' statements for these purposes, since, although made in a court, they were made earlier, and in a *different* court.

A 'statement' is broadly defined as a 'representation of fact or opinion by whatever means',[6] and so can be manifested in speech, documents, diagrams, drawings, sketches - even accusatory gestures.[7] The representation must be made 'by a person', so information generated by a machine, which is not based on information provided *by a person*, is not a 'statement' for these purposes.[8]

The trickiest part of the equation is deciding whether the out-of-court statement is being tendered 'as evidence of any matter stated in it'. There are two points here.

A. DOES THE STATEMENT HAVE 'TRUTH VALUE'?

First, is the statement *capable* of being believed as true? Does it, in effect, have 'truth value'?[9] Some utterances are in reality neither true nor false, they just are what they are - questions, for example, or greetings. *"Hi Tom, how are you?"* does not convey

5 And if not hearsay, the evidence will be admissible if relevant and not excluded by some other evidential principle or discretion.

6 S 115(2) CJA 2003

7 See, e.g., *Chandraskera v R* [1937] AC 220. The common law had considered photofit images and the like as non-hearsay (illogically, but understandably as a means of getting such evidence readily admitted at the time), but these have now been brought specifically under the general definition: s 115(2) CJA 2003

8 There are further requirements regarding accuracy where the statement is made by a machine on the basis of information supplied by a person. See s 129 CJA 2003

9 This useful expression is used by Chris Allen in the second edition of his *Practical Guide*, p. 136ff

believable factual information as such. At common law, however, the hearsay net had been (controversially) cast wide enough to include so-called 'implied assertions', that is, utterances which assert nothing factual, but from which, a believable fact could be inferred. So, for example, if Harry was seen approaching a person and heard to say to that person *"Hi Tom, how are you?"*, it could be inferred from what he had said that the person he approached was, as a matter of fact, Tom.

The leading case on this used to be *R v Kearley*,[10] which is interesting on many levels, including its having been a 3-2 decision in the House of Lords (as the Supreme Court was then known), which is as close as you can get there to a draw. Drugs had been found at the defendant Kearley's house. He was charged with possession with intent to supply and taken off to a police station. Meanwhile police officers stayed behind at his house, apparently answering phone calls from, and opening the door to, various people asking for drugs. At trial, the police officers were allowed to give evidence of these various requests, including what was said by the callers (for example, *"Is Kearley there?"* … *"I want my drugs"* - and so on), most of whom did not give evidence themselves. The question for the appellate court was whether this evidence should have been admitted. It was accepted that the purpose of the evidence was not to establish the truth of anything said by the callers per se, but rather to invite the jury to infer from the fact of the requests (not their content) that Kearley had been supplying drugs. There was, no doubt, some unease about the nature of this police evidence, which might well have put the House of Lords in, shall we say, an unreceptive frame of mind. In any event, a majority held that the evidence should not have been allowed because such 'implied' assertions were caught by the hearsay rule just as much as overtly believable statements.

The decision in *Kearley* was much criticised as an unnecessary and illogical extension of the rule against hearsay,[11] and the CJA 2013 seemed the ideal

10 [1992] 2 AC 228

11 And see Lord Griffith's powerful dissenting judgment, which in a different sort of case might well have carried the day: *Ibid*, at 238. He said in effect that the calls and requests were simply circumstantial evidence, directly perceived by the police, from which other relevant facts could be drawn, i.e. that Kearley's house was a place where buyers knew they could get drugs.

opportunity to lay the case (and the notion of 'implied assertions') to rest.[12] The method chosen for trying to achieve this was to say that for the hearsay rule to apply at all, the person who made the out-of-court statement must have done so with the *purpose* (at least in part) of '*causing another person to believe*' what had been stated or 'causing a person or machine to operate on the basis that' the matter stated is true.[13] The main case is now *R v Twist*, where Hughes LJ set out a useful three-step test to help navigate these statutory refinements: first, (i) ascertain what matter one seeks to prove. Assuming it is relevant, then (ii) ask whether there is a statement to this effect in the communication. If not, no question of hearsay arises. If there is such a statement, then (iii) ask whether one of the purposes of the maker was that some other person should believe the statement to be true, or act (or that a machine should act) on this basis. If yes, then the communication is hearsay; if no, then it is not.[14]

s\ 115(3), as interpreted by *Twist*, is not a perfect solution, but it has meant the removal of any number of (express as well as implied) assertions (for example, strictly private diary entries, text messages based on a presumed common knowledge, and indeed the *absence* of an assertion[15]) from the ambit of the hearsay rules, which of course does not make them inadmissible (or admissible). It just means they are not hearsay.[16]

B. WHY IS THE STATEMENT BEING PUT INTO EVIDENCE?

Even if an out-of-court staement is capable of being true, an important second point is this: is it being put in evidence *on the basis that* it is true? Or for some other reason? This is a crucial, if not always easy distinction, especially for beginners, who sometimes confuse the fact that a statement was made with its relevance to a case. One needs to focus on the job of proof the out-of-court statement is being asked to do. Always ask yourself: *does its evidential value depend on the statement being true?* Only if the answer to this question is 'yes', will a hearsay problem arise.

12 See BCrP F 16.16
13 CJA 2003, s 115(3)
14 [2011] EWCA Crim 1143, para 17 and see BCrP F 16.17-16.22
15 This deals with the problem of so-called 'negative hearsay'. See BCrP F 16.31/32
16 See, e.g., McCombe J in *R v KN* [2006] EWCA Crim 3309, at para 21. Applying s 115(3) can at times be tricky. See discussion at Keane & McKeown, p. 314-318

Quite often out-of-court statements are adduced not to establish the truth of what was stated, but for some *other* purpose - for example to show that the person who made the statement was capable of speech at the time, or was hysterical at the time of speaking[17] or even to show that the statement was false.[18] In such cases, the point is not the truth of the words spoken, but the fact that they were spoken at all[19] or the manner in which they were spoken. The person who heard them can give *direct* evidence of what he or she heard, felt and saw, which is perfectly capable of being tested in cross-examination. In such cases the statement is not hearsay, and is referred to variously as 'direct' or 'original' evidence or (in the case of things) 'real' evidence.[20]

Two cases which illustrate these points are *Subramaniam v Public Prosecutor*[21] and *R v Lydon*.[22] In the *Subramaniam* case, the defendant was charged with possession of ammunition contrary to emergency regulations. His defence was that he had been kidnapped by a terrorist gang and was acting under duress. He gave evidence about his capture, but the trial judge ruled inadmissible as hearsay any recounting he sought to give about his conversations with the terrorists. He was convicted and appealed. The Privy Council held that the trial judge had been wrong to exclude the evidence and indeed did not really seem to understand the hearsay rule! They explained:

> Evidence of a statement made to a witness by a person who is not himself called as a witness may or may not be hearsay. It is hearsay ... when the object of the evidence is to establish the truth of what is contained in the statement. *It is not hearsay...when it is proposed to establish by the evidence, not the truth of the statement, but the fact that it was made.* The fact that the statement was made, quite apart from its truth, is frequently relevant in considering the mental state and conduct thereafter of the witness or some other person in whose presence the statement was made.[23]

17 *Ratten v The Queen* [1972] AC 378 is a colourful and clear example.

18 See, e.g., *Mawaz Khan v The Queen* [1967] 1 AC 454

19 Sometimes the fact that certain words were spoken at all will be the fact in issue; because they have certain legal effect (such as words constituting offer and acceptance in the formation of a contract) or legal consequences (as in racial abuse cases, where the point is what was said. Whether the insult is true or not, is completely irrelevant).

20 See guide to terminology in Ch. 14

21 [1956] 1 WLR 965

22 (1987) 85 Cr App R 221

23 Op. cit., p. 970 (my emphasis). And see BCrP F 16.22/23

In other words, whatever the terrorists had said to the accused, whether true or not, might have caused him to fear for his life. This was relevant to the defence of duress and so should have been admitted.

R v Lydon concerned an armed robbery of a post office, committed in 1985. The question was whether Lydon had been one of the robbers. One item of evidence on which the prosecution sought to rely was a gun found about a mile away from the crime scene, in the grass by the side of the road down which the getaway car had been driven. Next to the gun, two pieces of rolled up paper were found, on which were written the words 'Sean rules' and 'Sean rules 85'. The defendant's first name was Sean. Experts said that ink found on the barrel of the gun was similar to, and so could have come from the same pen as that used to write on the pieces of paper.

The defence argued that the references to 'Sean' were hearsay, but the trial judge admitted the evidence and the Court of Appeal said he had been right to do so. The words written on the paper were not relevant for their truth. They were facts in themselves providing circumstantial evidence[24] from which a jury might conclude that the papers had been in the possession of someone who was named Sean or who was associated with a person of that name. The prosecution neither wanted nor needed to prove that Sean ruled anyone!

Lydon is a fairly simple example of what might be called the 'truth of contents' test. But it is an evocative one, and therefore useful while you still have on your hearsay 'L' plates. Other cases you come across may well be more complex, but you will be better equipped to understand both the basics and the importance of this aspect of hearsay evidence if you always keep in your mind that scrap of paper with 'Sean rules' on it, written with incriminating ink, lying in an incriminating place, amongst incriminating things.

---

24 Not necessarily strong evidence. Remember that admissibility of relevant evidence and its weight are different issues.

2. ADMISSIBLE HEARSAY

Assuming an out-of-court statement is hearsay, the next step is to decide whether the evidence is nevertheless admissible. The CJA 2003 creates four routes to admissibility in criminal cases:

(i) admissible by agreement
(ii) admissible by statute[25]
(iii) admissible by an expressly preserved common law principle
(iv) admissible in the interests of justice.[26]

All gateways are available to all parties as appropriate in the circumstances,[27] adapted as necessary to the relevant standard of proof. Reception by agreement of all the parties is not controversial, and so needs no more discussion, although do bear in mind that even when hearsay has been admitted in this way, a jury will still need a clear instruction about how to deal with it.

Remember, too, that hearsay can be oral or written as well as one or several times removed from the person making the original observation. Suppose, for example, that John sees a red Ford Mondeo speeding down the road. He writes down the model, colour and registration number, so he doesn't forget it. He tells Mary about the car he saw. Mary tells Franco what John told her about the car. If Mary gave evidence of what John said to her about the description of the car, this would be *first-hand, oral hearsay*. At trial, the information which John wrote down on the piece of paper would be *first-hand, documentary hearsay*. Franco's version of the same story would be *multiple* (specifically second-hand) *hearsay*. The differences between these various forms of hearsay are important, not only as a matter of common sense, but also in terms

25 Not only the 2003 Act itself, but others, such as s 30 CJA 1988, as to which see Ch. 22

26 s 114(1)

27 Compare this to certain of the bad character gateways which admit only prosecution or only defence evidence. See Ch. 19

of differentiating the various requirements for admissibility under the CJA 2003.

A brief outline of the most commonly evoked (and examined) gateways to admissibility are set out below, in a way which I hope will help you remember and distinguish between them.

A. THE UNAVAILABLE WITNESS: S 116 CJA 2003

In certain circumstances, a hearsay statement can be given in lieu of oral evidence from a witness. This is a sensible provision since witnesses do die or disappear or become unfit to testify. Therefore, hearsay evidence may be admitted where a person, who would otherwise have given the evidence in court, is *unavailable* to do so for any one of five reasons. The first four are *essentially objective* in their nature:

(i) the person is *dead*,
(ii) the person is *mentally or physically unfit* to give the evidence,
(iii) the person is *outside the UK* (and it is not *reasonably practicable* to secure his attendance),
(iv) the person *cannot be found* (and *reasonable steps have been* taken to find him).

Some of these reasons for unavailability will be easier to establish than others (death, for example, is usually obvious). The fact remains, however, that the need to resort to a hearsay statement on any of the grounds cited above must be clearly made out in the prevailing circumstances. For example, the fact that a witness is abroad is not enough. It must be shown (in this age of airplanes and Skype) that it is not reasonably practicable to bring the witness to court, in person or by video link.[28]

(v) The fifth reason for unavailability is *essentially subjective* in its nature and

28 The court will balance expense and inconvenience (and consider the effort taken to secure attendance) against the importance of the evidence in determining what is (or was) 'reasonably practicable'. See, e.g., *R v Riat* (and others) [2013] 1 Cr App R 2, at [15] and generally, BCrP F 17.13-17.15

> so contains *additional* requirements, namely that the person is *in fear* of giving (or continuing to give) oral evidence (either at all or on the subject matter covered by the statement) *and* the court gives *leave* for the hearsay statement to be given in lieu.

Note the *conjunctive* requirements. None of the other, more objective, reasons for unavailability requires permission of the court in order to meet the condition itself. 'Fear' is construed widely[29] but it will be important for the court to know what the witness fears and why. This can be proved[30] by means of the fearful witness's written statement, since requiring such witnesses to attend court to explain why they are too afraid to attend court might defeat the purpose of this particular route to admissibility. Having said that, judges 'must be astute not to skew a fair trial by a too ready acceptance of assertions of fear, since it is all too easy for witnesses to avoid the inconvenience and anxiety of a trial by saying they do not want to come'.[31]

Assuming the fear factor is made out, s 116(4) sets out common sense considerations for the judge when deciding whether or not to go on to give permission to adduce the hearsay statement instead. Especially important (and those counsel opposing the admission of such hearsay evidence would highlight) are the risk of *unfairness* to any party, how difficult it will be to *challenge* the statement, and whether the witness's fear could be overcome by any special measure directions.[32] This last question is very important, since a 'live' witness giving evidence, albeit with the benefit of an SMD, will be available for cross-examination, and this will always be preferable in this context to a hearsay statement. The decision whether or not to give leave should, like any discretion, be 'evaluative and fact sensitive'.[33] But all efforts should be made to get the fearful witness to court, even if only virtually - certainly such a person should never be assured in advance that their evidence will be read out.[34]

29 s 116(3) CJA 2003. And see discussion at cases referred to at BCrP F 17.17ff

30 The standard of proof will depend on whether the prosecution (beyond reasonable doubt) or defence (balance of probabilities) is seeking to rely on this particular reason for unavailability.

31 *R v Davies* [2006] EWCA Crim 2643, per Moses LJ, at [15]

32 See Ch. 17

33 *R v Doherty* [2006] EWCA Crim 2716, para 28

34 *R v Horncastle* [2010] 2 AC 373 cited at BCrP F 17.7ff. See also useful summary of the principles in *R v Shabir* [2012] EWCA Crim 2564, paras 64-65

There are several things to note generally about this s 116 gateway to admissibility. First, it is essentially about *first-hand hearsay*. The statement (which can be *oral or documentary*) effectively stands in for the unavailable witness, and so is only one removed from its source.[35] Second, the person who would have given the evidence had he or she been available must be *identified* to the court's satisfaction.[36] This allows the other parties to do what they can to counter evidence which cannot be impugned directly in cross-examination.[37] It is particularly important to note that the *fearful witness can be absent, but not anonymous.*[38] Thirdly, the oral evidence the unavailable witness would have given must itself have been admissible, and the witness competent[39] (at the time the statement was made) to give it. *In short, s 116 does not make admissible, evidence which would have been inadmissible coming from the mouth of the testifying witness.* Finally, if the person or party seeking to adduce the hearsay statement under s 116 is shown to have been the one to cause the witness to be unavailable, then the condition relied upon is deemed not to apply.[40] You are not allowed to send one of your own witnesses on an expedition to the North Pole just because you think his witness statement will stand up better than he will!

B. BUSINESS AND OTHER DOCUMENTS: s 117 CJA 2003

Often, when information has been recorded and kept safe in accordance with business practice or other professional protocol, it can be a more reliable source of evidence than the recollection of the person who supplied the original information. This is the rationale behind the s 117 gateway to admissibility.

35 If the unavailable witness's statement itself contains hearsay, then such evidence will only be admitted by agreement or with the court's permission: s 121 CJA 2003

36 s 116(1)(b) CJA 2003

37 See below for discussion of safeguards to ensure fairness.

38 Or a witness can be anonymous, but not absent. But he cannot be both. See discussion of Anonymity Orders in Ch. 17 and *R v Fox* [2010] EWCA Crim 1280

39 The word 'capable' is used in s 123 of the CJA 2003, but this is defined virtually identically to the test for competence.

40 s 116(5). If disputed, the standard of proof required to establish unavailability varies according to who (prosecution or defence) wishes to adduce the hearsay statement: see BCrP F 17.12

Thus, a statement contained in a document is admissible as evidence of any matter stated in it, provided that:

(i) the document was *created or received* by a person in the *course of a trade, business, profession or other occupation or as the holder of an office*, and
(ii) the person who *originally supplied* the information had (or may reasonably be supposed to have had) *personal knowledge* of the matters contained in it, and
(iii) any person through whom the information *may subsequently* have passed (en route to the document's ultimate creation) also *received it in the course of a trade, business* and so on.

These are the *basic* requirements for reception through s 117. It is important to note that this gateway admits *only documentary* (and so, not oral) hearsay. Having said that, 'document' is broadly interpreted as 'anything in which information of any description is recorded'[41] and so can include things like CDs, DVDs, and computer discs, from which it follows that documents can be 'created' in a number of ways (for example developing a photograph, typing a report, drawing a map, recording an interview). However achieved, what matters is that the creation of the document is in the *course of trade, business* and so on.

Remember too that s 117 can operate to admit *multiple* hearsay, although it is of course *possible* for the creator of the document and the supplier of the information to be one and the same person. *If* there is more than one link in the chain, then the *first link* will be the person who supplied the information and it is only this person who must have had (or reasonably be supposed to have had) *personal knowledge* of the matters contained in the document. All that is required of any subsequent links in

41 s 134(1) CJA 2003

the chain is that the information was *received by them, and the document created,* in the course of the *trade, business* and so on.

It is important also to note that there are *additional* requirements if the statement was prepared for use in pending or contemplated *criminal proceedings or for a criminal investigation.* In addition to the basic requirements, *either* one of the s 116 reasons for unavailability (dead, unfit and so on) must apply to the supplier of the original information *or* that person cannot in the circumstances 'reasonably be expected to remember the matters' dealt with in the statement.[42] This latter is especially useful to police officers, for example, who record aspects of their various criminal investigations, but may forget the detail as time passes and different cases intervene. Having said that, the point of this additional requirement is to ensure that if the person who supplied the original information has some memory of the event in question (which after all can be refreshed[43]) and is available to give first-hand evidence, he should do so.[44]

As with s 116, if oral evidence from the original informant would not have been admissible in any event, then s 117 will *not* make the evidence admissible.[45] But, unlike s 116, it is *not* necessary that the source of the statement be identified, as such. Under s 117, reliability comes not from challenging the information or the motivation of the informant, but from the 'regularity and repetition of business practice'.[46] As Thomas LJ put it in *R v Horncastle*, 'business records ... are compiled by persons who are disinterested and, in the ordinary course of events, such statements are likely to be accurate'.[47]

Even so, s 117 contains its own *in-built discretion* to exclude such evidence (whether tendered by prosecution or defence) if, in the circumstances, its reliability is considered doubtful. Common sense considerations apply, namely the source of the information, the contents of the statement and the way in which the information, or the document, was created or received.[48] For example, a letter travelling through the post could

42 s 117(4) and (5). Note that either defence or prosecution may seek to admit documents under s 117 for use in criminal proceedings.

43 See Ch. 18 for memory refreshing documents

44 *R v Horncastle*, op. cit.

45 s 117(1)(a)

46 As described in 2010 Crown Court Bench Book (predecessor to the Crown Court Compendium), p. 214 para 8

47 *R v Horncastle*, op. cit., at [15]

48 The court can 'direct' that the evidence is inadmissible 'if satisfied' that its reliability is 'doubtful': s 117(6), (7). Presumably the party seeking to rely on these sub-sections has the burden of proving unreliability, to the appropriate standard.

qualify as a business document, but if it arrived at its destination in a very degraded state, this could cast doubt on the reliability of its particular journey.[49] This residual discretion to exclude otherwise qualifying s 117 documents can cater for such situations.

C. HEARSAY ADMITTED IN THE INTERESTS OF JUSTICE: S 114(1)(D) CJA 2003

We have seen that there are many contexts in which the court may exercise a discretion to *exclude* evidence which might otherwise be admissible under the rules of evidence. One of the innovations of the CJA 2003 was to create, in effect, an *inclusionary* discretion so far as hearsay evidence is concerned, so that even if no other gateway to admissibility applies, the court may nevertheless admit the evidence if it is in the 'interests ofjustice' to do so. This does exist as a free-standing gateway, but nevertheless is viewed as something of a 'safety-valve' and is approached with some caution.

The 'interest of justice' gateway was created to deal with cases like that of *Sparks v R*.[50] This was an appeal to the Privy Council from Bermuda. The defendant was charged with indecently assaulting a young girl who was just under four years old. The victim, who was too young to give evidence herself, had told her mother that the man who assaulted her was 'a coloured boy'. The mother was not permitted to give this evidence because, coming from her, it was hearsay. The defendant, who was white, was convicted and appealed. He argued that it was 'manifestly unjust' for the jury to be left with the impression that the victim could give no clue as to the identity of her assailant. The Privy Council, however, held that the evidence had been properly excluded. It fell under no existing exception and justice was said to be best served by 'adherence to rules which had long been recognised and settled'.[51] The appeal was in fact allowed on other grounds. Had this not been possible, it may well have been decided half a century ago that the court had a discretion, in the

49 This was the example given in Law Commission No 245, para 8.74

50 [1964] AC 964

51 *Ibid*, at 978

interests of justice, to admit otherwise inadmissible hearsay evidence, since judicial sleep would not have been improved by the thought that a rigidly applied rule of evidence had helped to convict an innocent person. As it happened, however, this had to await the passing of the Criminal Justice Act 2003.

s 114(2) sets out a series of *common sense factors* to which the court *must* have regard (along with any other it considers relevant) when deciding whether to admit hearsay in the interests of justice. These include the importance of the evidence to the case, how probative the evidence is (assuming it is true), how reliable the maker (and the making) of the statement appears to be, the amount of difficulty involved in challenging the evidence and so forth. The focus is on the *reliability* of the evidence. It is clear that the courts should *carefully* scrutinise the evidence which a party seeks to admit through this gateway, and weigh up where the justice of the case lies, which can vary depending on the circumstances and especially whether the application is made by the prosecution or a defendant. As Hughes LJ put it in *R v Y*:[52]

> It does not necessarily follow that the interests of justice will point in the same direction upon an application by the Crown as they might upon application made by a defendant. Section 114(2)(i) moreover requires consideration of the injurious consequences of admission ('prejudice') to the party facing the evidence which will arise from the difficulty of challenging it. Since the burden of proving the case is upon the Crown and to the high criminal standard, very considerable care will need to be taken in any case in which the Crown seeks to rely on an out-of-court statement as supplying it with a case against the defendant when otherwise it would have none. In such a case if there is genuine difficulty in the defendant challenging, and the jury evaluating, the evidence, the potential damage to the defendant from that difficulty is very large.

52 [2008] 1 WLR 1683, at [59]

Thus, the s 114(1)(d) gateway should not be considered an easy option. 'Safety valve' remains an accurate enough description of its function - to be used when justice (and not a party to the proceedings) demands it. It is *not* to be treated as a means of circumventing the requirements of the other gateways or evidential principles.[53]

D. PRESERVED COMMON LAW ROUTES TO ADMISSIBILITY: S 118 CJA 2003

Several common law exceptions to the rule against hearsay have been expressly preserved by s 118 CJA 2003.[54] Some do not arise often; some impinge on other areas (for example, expert evidence).[55] Two of the most noteworthy, particularly for examination purposes, are 'res gestae' statements (discussed below) and confession statements (discussed in the next chapter).

(i) Res gestae statements

'Res gestae' roughly translates as 'things happening' and statements falling under this head are often referred to as 'forming part of the res gestae'. This category of admissibility actually divides into sub-species, which are now set out in s 118(4)(a)-(c). I propose to focus on (a)[56] which refers to utterances made by people who (at the time) were 'so emotionally overpowered by an event that the possibility of concoction or distortion can be disregarded'. This both describes the route to admissibility (sometimes known as 'excited utterances') and the justification for its existence. The idea is that the thoughts of the speaker (typically the victim of the crime or an observer) are so 'dominated' by what is going on, and the statement so spontaneous, that there was virtually no chance, opportunity or time to invent the evidence.

The leading case on this type of res gestae statement is *R v Andrews*.[57] It, and cases decided since make clear that both the nature of the incident and how soon

53 So anonymous hearsay should not get through this gateway either. *Fox*, op. cit, 1280 and see generally cases discussed at BCrP F 17.37ff

54 Those not preserved were abolished: s 118(2)

55 See list/discussion at BCrP F 17.42ff. Expert evidence is discussed in Ch. 22

56 The other two are statements which accompany an act and without which the act cannot be properly understood; and statements declarative of a person's physical or mental state (but not its cause). As to the latter see BCrP F 17.61ff

57 [1987] AC 281. See summary at BCrP F 17.52

afterwards the statement follows, are key aspects of this ground of admissibility. The less stirring the event and the greater the lapse of time between it and the statement, the less likely it will be that the latter will qualify as an 'excited utterance'. In *Tobi v Nicholas*,[58] for example, a statement made some 20 minutes after a relatively undramatic road traffic accident was held not to form part of the res gestae.

The case on the subject which all students seem to know is, of course, *R v Bedingfield*.[59] Bedingfield was charged with murder. His victim, her throat cut, had come out of the house where she had just been with the accused and immediately cried out: "*...see what Harry has done!*" Ironically, in the case itself the court ruled that the exclamation came after the event and so did not form part of the res gestae, but in the much later (and even more evocative) case of *Ratten v R*, Lord Wilberforce, commenting on the decision in *Bedingfield*, observed archly that 'though in a historical sense the emergence of the victim [from the room] could be described as a different 'res' from the cutting of the throat, there could hardly be a case where the words uttered carried more clearly the mark of spontaneity and intense involvement'.[60]

Every case will be different, of course, and the judge should always be alert to special features of a case which might add or detract from the risk of concoction. The maker of a res gestae statement need not necessarily (but usually will) be identified, but either way it is always important that the statement itself is reported reliably and accurately. Juries should be given careful directions.[61]

(ii) Confession statements

Conceptually, confessions belong here - they are a common law exception to the hearsay rule. They are such an important aspect of criminal evidence, however, and so often taught (and examined) discretely, that it seems sensible to deal with them separately. For that reason, they are discussed in the next chapter.

---

58 [1988] RTR 343, discussed at BCrP F 17.58

59 (1879) 14 Cox CC 341, Assizes

60 [1972] AC 378, PC at p. 390. *Andrews* overruled *Bedingfield*

61 See BCrP F 17.60 and Crown Court Compendium Pt 1 Ch. 14-13

E. STATUS OF PREVIOUS CONSISTENT AND INCONSISTENT STATEMENTS: SS 119/120 CJA 2003

It is important not to confuse the common law routes to admissibility preserved by s 118, discussed above, with the provisions of the CJA 2003 (ss 119 and 120) which deal with the interplay between the hearsay rules generally and previous statements (consistent and inconsistent) of testifying witnesses.[62] It is important to remember that the admissibility of the latter, which is also largely governed by the common law, only arises when the maker of the statement *is in court giving evidence.* This is in stark contrast to other types of hearsay (the unavailable witness, business documents and so on).[63] Indeed, ss 119 and 120 are not really gateways to admissibility as such, although they do update and modernise the rules about previous consistent and inconsistent statements. What the provisions do, in particular, is to provide that where such previous statements are admitted into evidence, they not only serve to bolster or undermine (as the case may be) the credibility of the testifying witness who made the statement, but they are also *admissible as evidence of the truth of the matters contained in them.*

3. THE SAFEGUARDS

We have already touched on some of these aspects of the CJA 2003, but it is important to have a good grasp of the range of safeguards built into the legislation, which are intended to address and 'counterbalance' any risk of unfairness resulting from the enlarged categories of admissible hearsay. They could come up in an examination question. In brief they are as follows.

62 Discussed in Ch. 18
63 Discussed above and see BCrP F 16.10

(i) Additional requirements for multiple hearsay: s 121(1)

Because hearsay can get less and less cogent the further away it gets from its original source, there are strict limits on the admissibility of multiple hearsay. Unless the parties agree, or the evidence is admitted through the business document gateway (s 117) or as a previous consistent or inconsistent statement (s 119/120), then in order for *multiple* hearsay to be admitted, the court must be satisfied that, given its *reliability*, the value of the evidence is *so high* that the *interest of justice* requires its admission. This is an especially important safeguard where an unavailable witness's statement itself contains hearsay.[64]

(ii) Capability of maker: s 123

As mentioned throughout this chapter, if the maker of the hearsay statement (or if one of the links in the s 117 'chain') would not have been competent[65] to give direct oral evidence at the relevant time, the legislation will not render the evidence admissible. In effect, evidence which would not have been admissible in non-hearsay form, cannot be made admissible by virtue of the CJA 2003. This is not a new safeguard, but has been replicated in the legislation.

(iii) Testing credibility of hearsay: s 124

One objection to a hearsay statement from an 'unavailable' witness is that it, and in particular its reliability, *cannot be directly tested in cross-examination.* To compensate somewhat for this, where such a hearsay statement is introduced, evidence which would have been admissible to impugn that witness or contradict the evidence had it been given 'live', is admissible for this purpose, including (with permission) rebuttal evidence which would normally offend the rule of finality.[66] This is a logical safeguard, giving opposing parties every opportunity to challenge the evidence as best they can in the absense of cross-examination. It plays an essential part in ensuring a fair trial.

---

64 As, for example, in *R v Friel* [2012] EWCA Crim 2871

65 The word used is 'capable', but it effectively translates as 'competence', as discussed in Ch.17. See BCrP F 17.8

66 Or the rule against rebuttal, as I have called it. See Ch. 18 *R v Horncastle*, op. cit., and BCrimP F 17.86

(iv) Stopping an unconvincing case: s 125

So, too, does s 125, which requires the Crown Court to stop a case which is largely dependant ('wholly or partly') on a hearsay statement and the evidence is so *unconvincing* that a conviction would be *unsafe*. In that situation, at the close of the prosecution case, the judge must direct the jury to acquit (or where appropriate discharge the jury and order a retrial).[67] Effectively, this provision ensures that *reliability* is at the heart of any assessment of the quality of the prosecution's case, where there is a legitimate argument that unconvincing hearsay evidence is central to it. It is important to look at the hearsay in the round and not in isolation, and in the context of *all* the evidence which has been adduced. The judge's role is to decide whether the hearsay evidence is reliable enough to be safely left to the jury.[68]

(v) Another discretion to exclude: s 126

There are several opportunities to ask the court, in its discretion, to exclude hearsay evidence. You will, of course, be well aware by now that the general discretions to exclude *prosecution* evidence on grounds of fairness under s 78 or where the prejudicial effect of admitting the evidence would outweigh its probative value, are of general application.[69] We will look again at the s 78 discretion in the next chapter when discussing confessions, and we have already referred in this chapter to the 'mini-discretion' to exclude evidence (whether tendered for prosecution or defence) linked to the s 117 gateway.

But there is more! The CJA 2003 contains what it calls a 'general discretion to exclude' hearsay evidence in the form of s 126(1). This provides that the court may exclude otherwise admissible hearsay evidence (again *irrespective* of whether it is tendered for the prosecution *or* the defence) if it thinks the *value* to be gained from the evidence's admission is *'substantially outweighed'* by the amount of time that would be

67 In such circumstances, the magistrates' court would simply dismiss the case.

68 *R v Riat*, op. cit., at [28]

69 These, which you will remember cannot be used to exclude defence evidence, are preserved by operation of s 126(2) CJA 2003

'wasted' in receiving it. This is a somewhat strangely worded provision, which has not had a lot of judicial consideration, but lack of probative value would seem to be key. In any case, the test is the same whether it is the prosecution or defence seeking to rely on the evidence.[70]

Right to fair trial under Art 6

An important aspect of a fair trial includes the ability to confront one's accuser and test evidence in cross-examination. This, of course is not usually possible with hearsay evidence - certainly not where the witness is 'unavailable'. Concern about this particular deficit is especially acute where the central evidence in a case is in this form. Whether it is possible to have a fair trial in such cases has been considered in a series of cases. It now seems clear, both on the basis of domestic and Strasbourg jurisprudence, that even where hearsay evidence is the 'sole or decisive evidence' against the defendant, the CJA 2003 statutory scheme is rigorous and robust enough on its own to protect the defendant's right to a fair trial.[71]

Starting with *Horncastle*, these cases confirm that while the CJA 2003 may have increased the opportunities to adduce hearsay evidence, it did not elevate the status of such evidence or mean it should be allowed in 'on the nod'. Such evidence is still hearsay, and is only admissible if it successfully navigates the various hurdles and safeguards which were introduced to allow judges to keep an eye on the risks posed by such evidence (especially as to its reliability), to assess the extent to which those risks are mitigated (for example by other evidence in the case) and to ensure that a fair trial is not compromised. Hearsay is thus neither admitted routinely (in other words, just because it passes through a gateway), nor excluded routinely (for example just because the evidence in question is central to the case), although as a matter of common sense the more 'critical' the evidence is, the greater is the vigilance

70 See interesting case of *R v Drinkwater* [2016] 4 WLR 42 and BCrP F 17.94/95 (which is headed 'Unconvincing and Superfluous Hearsay', so perhaps that says it all).

71 See *Horncastle, Riat, Friel* op. cit, discussed at BCrP F 17.89ff

required of the court. In *R v Riat*, the Court of Appeal sought to demonstrate how the statutory scheme works to safeguard a fair trial, by setting out something of a step-by-step guide to the judicial thought-process:[72]

(a) Is the relevant gateway requirement properly met (for example, ss 116-118)?
(b) What other material or evidence is there in the case to test or assess the reliability of the hearsay evidence (s 124)?
(c) Is there a specific 'interests of justice' test at the admissibility stage (for example, in respect of fearful witnesses under s 116)?
(d) If there is no other justification or gateway, should the evidence nevertheless be admitted in the interests of justice under s 114(1)(d)?
(e) Even if prima facie admissible, should the evidence be excluded (for example, under s 126 CJA 2003 or s 78 PACE 1984)?
(f) If the evidence is admitted, should the case be stopped later under s 125?

Each case, therefore, must be judged on its own merits. In *R v Horncastle* itself, the victim of a serious beating gave a statement about how his injuries occurred. Before trial he had died from an alcohol-related illness. His statement was critical evidence against the accused, but there was substantial independent evidence confirming its reliability, the accused had had ample opportunity to challenge its credibility, and the jury had been properly directed about its dangers, and so the Supreme Court held that a fair trial had not been compromised. The Court of Appeal came to the same conclusion in *R v Friel*, noting that the fact that the hearsay statement had been recorded on DVD served to 'temper' some of the drawbacks of the evidence, because the jury could take into account the demeanour of the witness as she told her story.

72 Op. cit., at [7]

By contrast, in the case of *R v Ibrahim*,[73] the evidence of the alleged victim of rape, who had made a statement but since died of a drug overdose, was said to have been rightly excluded because, although technically admissible, there were serious concerns about its reliability, in part because she had admitted making other statements of a similar nature to the police which were false.

It is clear from these cases, furthermore, how important it is that directions to juries about such evidence are both clear and comprehensive and speak to the particular deficiencies of the hearsay evidence, both in general terms and specifically in the case to be decided.[74]

Procedure

Advance notice in writing must be given of the intention to adduce *certain categories* of hearsay, that is evidence to be admitted through the unavailable witness gateway (s 116), the interests of justice gateway (s 114(1)(d), gateway s 117 (1)(c), and where multiple hearsay is concerned (s 121). This is only sensible, since other parties will want to examine the basis for admissibility and may well want to oppose it. The prosecution must give notice no more than 14 days after the defendant pleads not guilty (28 days if in the magistrates' court); defendants must do so 'as soon as reasonably practicable'. The appropriate form must be used and opposition is signified by service of a counter-notice.[75] The court, not surprisingly, has power to vary the form of notice or dispense with the requirement altogether; this is important, since the need to introduce (or oppose) hearsay may only become apparent at trial.[76]

73 [2012] 4 All ER 225

74 Crown Court Compendium Pt 1 Ch. 14 and BCrP F 17.96

75 Lack of a counter-notice may signal agreement to the admission of the hearsay evidence, but this does not inevitably follow.

76 See CrimPR Pt 20, and BCrP F 17.5

revision tips

- Make sure you understand what hearsay evidence is, and can recognise it when you see it (and know when you do not). Think in terms of the *purpose* the out-of-court statement is serving and the intention of the maker.
- Make sure you know (and can differentiate between) the various gateways to admissibility of hearsay. Know the relevant section and key words/ requirements. A memorable scenario for each gateway might help.
- Be aware of the rationale for, and the risks of, the admission of the various kinds of hearsay. Know the safeguards, including the all-important discretions to exclude. Be able to construct arguments for and against reception of an item of hearsay in the context of a specific set of facts.
- Do not confuse testimony from an anonymous witness (see Ch. 17) with the admission of a hearsay statement from an identified, but absent witness, under s 116 CJA 2003.
- Similarly, appreciate the difference between the admission of an out-of-court statement of a person who does testify and one who does not.

It is worth reading ...

Scott Baker LJ's judgment in *Maher v DPP* [2006] EWHC 1271 (Admin). Fun and games in the Sainsbury's car park. This fairly simple tale touches many bases, including multiple hearsay and the interests of justice gateway.

R v Friel [2012] EWCA Crim 2871. This story is easy to understand, the judgment is relatively short and it gives a clear and concise review of the relevant law.

R v Davis [2006] EWCA Crim 2643. This is a short, but evocative judgment in a s 116 (2)(e) fear case. It is easy to follow (and you can sympathise with the witnesses). It illustrates the fact that when the appeal court refers to your 'excellent' submissions, you know that you are about to lose... And compare it to *R v Shabir* [2012] EWCA Crim 2564, which went the other way. It is longer, but still easy to grasp and it contains some other evidential goodies.

The Crown Court Compendium Pt 1 Ch. 14 is also very illuminating.

CHAPTER 21

Confessions

One of the most important exceptions to the hearsay rule is confession evidence - another common law principle expressly preserved by s 118 CJA 2003. In this context, we are not talking about dramatic courtroom declarations exacted under cross-examination, which of course would not be hearsay at all; but evidence tendered of earlier statements made by an accused out-of-court (often during a police interview, but it need not be to a person of authority) which either wholly or partly incriminates him.[1] They are put forward (usually by prosecutors) as evidence of guilt, and so are classic hearsay statements. But, subject to the requirements of s 76 (and 76A) of the Police and Criminal Evidence Act 1984 (PACE), and any judicial discretion to exclude, they are nevertheless admissible.

The rationale behind the admissibility of hearsay in the form of out-of-court confessions rests on human nature, and in particular the fact that people are not apt to admit to doing something wrong, if in fact they did not do so. For this reason, such statements are thought to be reliable in their nature - at least hypothetically. It is, of course, very common for individuals to try to escape responsibility by blaming others, and so an important principle emerged at common law, namely that only the parts of the confession statement which *implicate the confessor* are admissible under this particular exception to the hearsay rule. Once the confessor begins to point the finger

1 A confession, according to s 82(1) of PACE 1984, is 'any statement wholly or partly adverse to the person who made it, whether made to a person in authority or not and whether made in words or otherwise'. This is a wider definition than had previously applied at common law. A retracted guilty plea can amount to a confession. See BCrP F 18.1-18.5

of blame at someone else, the justification for admissibility disappears. Thus, when admitted through this particular (s 118) gateway, any part of a defendant's confession statement which purports to implicate a co-accused *cannot* be used as evidence against that co-accused.[2] As discussed below, this will require careful explanation to a jury.

Of course, the reliability of a confession statement depends on the circumstances in which it is made. The idea is that the statement is made voluntarily, without fear or favour. Thus police Codes of Practice brought in under PACE 1984 (and the relevant provisions of PACE 1984 itself) are designed to ensure that guilty people are convicted on the basis of reliable evidence which has been fairly obtained. You should therefore be familiar with those aspects which particularly impact on confession statements (especially s 58 PACE 1984 and Codes C and D which cover access to legal advice and the protocols on detention, police questioning and identification, discussed in Chapter 2) because breaches *may* lead to exclusion of evidence under s 76 or 78 of PACE 1984. But bear in mind that breaches of PACE 1984 or the Code do *not automatically* lead to the exclusion of such evidence. Arguments for exclusion will have to look beyond any such breaches to the larger picture of unreliability and, ultimately, unfairness. We will look at ss 76 and 78 in turn.

1. S 76 PACE 1984

S 76(2) of PACE 1984 deals exclusively with confession statements. In essence, where the prosecution seek to rely on such evidence and the point is raised,[3] the court *must not* admit the confession statement into evidence *except insofar* as the prosecution establish *beyond reasonable doubt* that the confession was not obtained either (i) by *oppression or* (ii) in circumstances likely to render the confession *unreliable*.[4]

2 This is not the case should such a statement be admitted through another gateway, see below.

3 By the accused, or the court can raise the matter on its own initiative: s 76(3) PACE 1984

4 s 76(2)(a) and (b) PACE 1984

In other words, once challenged, the *burden of proof will be on the prosecution* to prove that the confession was not obtained in either of the ways referred to in s 76 (2) (a) or (b). In the Crown Court, applications to exclude evidence will be dealt with in the absence of a jury and at some appropriate point before the disputed evidence is to be called.[5] Magistrates have more discretion as to when to deal with such applications since if the trial is underway, they must necessarily hear the evidence when ruling on its admissibility. It is worth noting the following.

(i) Oppression

Oppression is defined in s 76(8) as including 'torture, inhuman or degrading treatment, and the use or threat of violence (whether or not amounting to torture)'. Thus the police behaviour has to be pretty extreme.[6] Most breaches of protocol or tricks of the police trade are unlikely to amount to oppression. But every case is different - the more vulnerable the suspect, for example, the more readily hostile questioning might become oppressive. And constant bullying and hectoring can qualify.[7]

(ii) Unreliability

S 76(2)(b) sets out a broader and more hypothetical test. The court is asked to consider whether the confession was obtained in circumstances ('anything said or done'[8]) likely to render *unreliable* 'any confession which might be made by him' as a result. Thus the test is not whether the actual confession was *itself* unreliable (or not[9]), but whether any such confession which the accused might have made in *those circumstances*[10] would likely be unreliable. Thus the focus is more on the circumstances and behaviour of the individuals concerned, rather than the precise confession statement itself. Threats, lies or inducements might but will not necessarily have

5 Usually on a voir dire: for relevant procedure see BCrP F 18.62ff

6 *R v Fulling* [1987] QB 426

7 See, e.g., the shocking case of *R v Paris and Others* (1993) 97 Cr App R 99 and generally BCrP F 18.10-18.14

8 By the police (or something 'external' to the accused). See, e.g., *R v Crampton* (1991) 92 Cr App R 372, cited at BCrP F 18.20

9 Indeed, the prosecution cannot avoid exclusion under s 76(2)(b) merely by pointing to evidence confirming the reliability of the confession: Re *Proulx* [2001] 1 All ER 57

10 Within reason. See Mance LJ's observations in *ibid*, at [46] and see BCrP F 18.21ff

the effect of rendering a confession unreliable, so it is very important in each case to think about, and be able to show, the *causal relationship* between the thing said or done to the accused and the potential unreliability of any resulting confession. This aspect of s 76(2)(b) is often overlooked by beginners.

For example, a typical police tactic is to tell presumed accomplices that each is trying to pin some or all of the blame for the crime on the other. That might be a lie, it might be inappropriate behaviour, but would it cause an innocent person to confess to something he or she had not done? Or would it merely provoke a more vehement denial? It is also important to remember that the circumstances of each case must be analysed carefully and on its own merits. A suspect's mental condition and/or vulnerability at the time of questioning is apt to be an important part of the equation and can even render otherwise appropriate questioning into something likely to result in an unreliable confession.[11] A seasoned veteran of police interviews, on the other hand, may be more able to 'handle' a breach of the Code.[12] Decisions under s 76(2)(b) are always fact, and in particular, defendant specific.[13]

(iii) Evidence admissable despite an excluded confession

It is important to realise that even if a confession is wholly or partly excluded under s 76(2), this will not necessarily affect the admissibility of any facts discovered as a result of the confession, or anything revealed about how the accused writes, speaks and so on.[14] Suppose Doris confesses to shoplifting designer clothes and tells the police she hid the clothes under a loose floorboard in her flat. The police search the flat and recover the clothes. Even if the confession statement is subsequently excluded, the fact that the clothes were found, and where they were found, is admissible (and useful) evidence against Doris.[15] What cannot be said (if the confession is excluded) is that the clothes were found as a result of what she had told the police.[16]

---

11 See, e.g., *R v Harvey* [1988] Crim LR 241, CC

12 E.g., *R v Alladice* [1988] 87 Cr App R 380, CA; *R v Saunders* [2012] EWCA Crim 1380 and comment in BCrP F 18.24. The codes are discussed at Keane & McKeown, p. 418ff

13 *R v Wahab* [2003] 1 Cr App R, 232, p. 241 per Judge LJ

14 S 76(4) PACE 1984. Unlike the USA, there is no blanket ban here on fruit from the forbidden tree. But, like any prosecution evidence, it could be excluded under s 78. See BCrP F 18.85-18.87

15 Unless this evidence is also excluded under the s 78 discretion. See below.

16 s 76(5) and (6) of PACE 1984

2. S 78 PACE 1984

The s 78 discretion, which we have looked at before, is of special significance in the context of confessions. This is because of the way it is worded, and in particular its reference to the court's 'having regard to *the circumstances in which the evidence was obtained*'. This usually makes an s 78 application for exclusion a logical alternative to one under s 76(2), although the latter will normally be the first port of call. Take care not to confuse the two - s 76(2) is a requirement focused on the *reliability* of the confession and puts a burden of proof on the prosecution. s 78 is a discretion going beyond reliability into the more general realm of *fairness*.

Both s 76 and s 78 concern evidence on which the *prosecution* propose to rely. And like s 76(2), arguments for exclusion under s 78 will be case specific. So again, breaches of the Codes (which, after all, are there to protect the individual from the state) may well assist in getting the evidence excluded, but will not guarantee it. Even a 'plain and obvious' breach, though deplorable, may not trigger exclusion if the accused has not been prejudiced by it. Lack of access to legal advice can be an important factor.[17]

What the judge must consider on an s 78 application is whether the reception of the confession evidence would so adversely affect the *fairness* of the proceedings that it ought to be excluded. This will inevitably involve weighing up aspects of a case: How reliable is the evidence? How serious is the offence?[18] How badly did the police behave? Were they acting in bad faith?[19] How vulnerable was the defendant? Have human rights been breached? Do the ends justify the means? Put crudely, can the defendant be convicted fairly and squarely if the confession is admitted?

It is also possible to try and have a confession excluded because its prejudicial effect outweighs its probative value. This common law discretion is effectively preserved by s 82(3) PACE 1984. This balancing exercise is not usually the point

17 *R v Canale* [1990] 2 All ER 187, cited in BCrP F 18.34

18 In *R v Veneroso* [2002] Crim LR 306, the defendant was charged with a drugs offence. Evidence of drugs was found after an illegal search, albeit that the police had entered the premises in good faith. The judge excluded the evidence saying that the defendant's right to privacy took priority over the public interest in securing a conviction. But the result might have been different, he said, if explosives had been found. Cf, e.g., *R v Ibrahim* [2014] ECHR Crim 1492 and see BCrP F 18.36ff

19 Bad faith can turn a relatively minor breach into a significant one, but the reverse does not follow: *R v Walsh* (1990) 91 Cr App R 161. And see BCrP F 18.40-18.42

when considering the court's discretion to exclude a confession statement (and clearly there is an overlap with the s 78 discretion), but it can be a useful line of attack where, for example, the accused was suffering from some sort of delusional or vulnerable state at the time of confessing.[20]

Finally, it is important to remember that even if the confession is not excluded under s 76 or s 78, the behaviour of the police and the reliability (or not) of the confession can (and should, if there is anything in the allegations) be the subject of *cross-examination of the police witnesses.* This is especially true in the Crown Court - one may not have convinced the judge, but there is still the possibility of convincing the jury that the confession statement is not to be believed in the circumstances.

3. CONFESSIONS, MIXED STATEMENTS AND CO-DEFENDANTS

Confession statements may be wholly damning. But often they contain assertions which both incriminate and excuse the confessor.[21] These are known as 'mixed' statements. Although strictly speaking, it is only the act of self-blame which forms the basis at common law for the admissibility of confessions as an exception to the hearsay rule,[22] it is a well established principle that the whole of a mixed statement, both the good and the bad, is admissible as evidence of the facts stated in it so that the jury can determine where the truth lies. This is partly a concession to fairness, but also a matter of common sense, and *applies whether the confessor gives evidence or not.* As Lord Lane observed in *R v Duncan*, 'It is, to say the least, not helpful to try to explain to the jury that the exculpatory parts of the statement are something less than evidence of the facts they state'.[23] Even so, it will usually be helpful, and appropriate, for the judge to point out to jurors that excuses may come more readily

20 As suggested in *R v Miller* [1986] 3 All ER 119, CA

21 A statement which is completely exonerating is, of course, no confession at all!

22 Strictly speaking, the exonerating aspects merely show consistency with the not guilty plea.

23 [1981] 73 Cr App R 359, at 365 approved by House of Lords in *R v Sharp* [1988] 1 WLR 7

than self-accusation to a defendant's lips, and so they may conclude that the more favourable part of the statement carries less weight - especially if he chose not to testify, which meant his explanation could not be tested in cross-examination.[24]

While making a confession statement, a defendant might say something about another person, who becomes a co-defendant in a joint trial. Whether what is said helps or hinders that co-defendant's case will dictate the enthusiasm felt by the latter if the confession is admitted into evidence. Let's look at each scenario in turn.

(i) Confession statements *implicating* a co-accused

In a confession statement, an accused often says something which incriminates a co-accused (often, but not necessarily, in the process of making excuses for himself). Because of the readiness with which people blame others for their problems, the normal principle is that an out-of-court statement by one defendant cannot be used by the prosecution as evidence against any other defendant. This remains the case for confessions admitted under s 118 CJA 2003, which will be the usual gateway for the prosecution. However, if the confession statement gets admitted by some other route - through the interests of justice gateway,[25] for example - then the statement can be used for all purposes, including as evidence against a co-accused.[26] This is because the statement is not being admitted under the gateway dealing explicitly with (and so applying the principles specifically related to) confession statements.

The implicated co-accused will probably not be best pleased, either way. We have seen that the whole of a confessor's mixed statement will always be admitted into evidence, so that a jury can decide where it thinks the truth lies. Even where jurors are told that the statement can only be used as evidence against the person confessing,[27] the co-accused would still prefer that the jury not hear what bad things

24 But care must be taken not to confuse the jury. See Crown Court Compendium Pt 1, Ch. 16-1, para 6

25 Under s 114(1)(d): see generally, Ch. 20. This would be rare. s 114(1)(d) should not be used to avoid other gateway requirements.

26 See *R v Y* [2008] 1 WLR 1683. The judge will, of course, have to think carefully about the implications for a co-accused of allowing evidence through 'interest of justice' or other 'non-confession' gateways. See BCrP F 18.81

27 If the same evidence were given at trial this would, of course, be entirely different. An accused can freely implicate a co-accused from the witness box!

the confessor had said about him in the out-of-court statement. It just doesn't look good. The confessor himself could agree that his statement be edited to remove the references to the co-accused, but the confessor is very unlikely to do so, since the aspects of the statement which blame the co-accused are apt to be the very same ones which (at least partly) excuse himself - and this is the part of the statement he will most want the jury to know about!

In either case, the jury will need to be given very careful directions. Just what those directions should be will depend on who wishes to adduce the evidence and why, and through which gateway it has been admitted. Thus:

(a) In the usual case, where the statement has been admitted by the prosecution, through the normal confession gateway (s 118), it should be made clear that what the confessor said out-of-court about the co-defendant is *not* evidence against that co-defendant.[28] The jury is free to use the mixed statement to excuse the confessor, but will have to find *other* evidence to convict the co-defendant.

(b) However, if the confession has been admitted through another gateway, the evidence is admissible for all relevant purposes. What the jury should be told will vary depending on who (prosecution or defence) will benefit from the evidence, but in any case the direction will focus on reliability and the possible motives of the maker of the statement, and be framed to reflect relevant burden and standards of proof.[29]

(ii) Confession statements *helpful* to a co-accused

Sometimes, what a confessor has said in his statement helps a co-accused's case. If the prosecution adduces the confession statement, then all well and good - the jury

28 This will partly involve a reminder of how easy it is to blame others to escape the consequences of one's own actions. See Crown Court Compendium Pt 1 Ch. 14-15

29 See examples at *ibid* and below, Ch. 24

will see the entire statement. But if, for example, the prosecution do not or are precluded[30] from admitting the confession statement of an accused, a co-accused may apply to do so. S 76A(1) PACE 1984 says that, where defendants are *jointly tried*, a confession made by one accused person may be given in evidence *for a co-accused* insofar as it is relevant and has not been obtained by oppression or in circumstances rendering such a confession unreliable. As you can see, these provisions mirror those in s 76(2), but where it is a defendant who must prove lack of oppression and so on, the standard of proof is the *balance of probabilities*,[31] which gives defendants a little more leeway for getting such statements admitted.

Sometimes a defendant might want to admit a confession statement of a person who might have been, but in the end was not, tried jointly with him - for example, where that person pleaded guilty after making a statement exonerating the remaining defendant. In such cases, s 76A(1) would not assist because the two are not jointly tried, but it might be possible to argue for the statement's inclusion in the 'interests of justice' under s 114(1)(d) CJA 2003. The defendant's reason for seeking to admit the evidence in hearsay form rather than calling the person who made it to give oral evidence under oath, will be an important factor in whether such an application is successful.[32]

(iii) No discretion to exclude defence evidence under s 78

A defendant, of course, may not be happy that a confession statement which speaks ill of or points blame at him will be admitted into evidence by a co-defendant. The worry, of course, is that (however careful the directions to the jury), the co-accused will inevitably be made to look bad, which could prejudice his case. Can a defendant apply to have the confession statement on which his co-accused seeks to rely excluded under the s 78 discretion? The answer, as you probably know by now, is a resounding *"No!"*. The general discretionary power(s) to exclude relevant evidence applies

30 E.g., following an s 78 application

31 Defendants rarely have to prove anything; they *never* have to do so beyond reasonable doubt. See generally Ch. 15

32 Since s 114(1)(d) should not be used to circumvent s 116. See, e.g., *R v Finch* [2007] EWCA Crim 36. Cf *R v Sliogeris* [2015] EWCA Crim 22, where the s 76A route to admissibility was barred (on grounds of relevance), but the co-defendant's partial confession was nevertheless admissible under s 114(1)(d)

only to evidence on which the *prosecution* seeks to rely. Beginners need to know (and examiners love to test) this proposition, so be clear both about the principle and its justification: the rules of evidence are generally predicated on the need to protect defendants from prosecutors, but not from each other. In order to give each co-defendant as free a hand as possible to conduct their respective cases, there is no overarching[33] discretion to exclude evidence brought by one defendant against another.

revision tips

- Be clear about why confessions are an exception to the hearsay rule. This will help you remember their value (and limitations) as evidence.
- Be able to distinguish between s 76 and s 78 as possible routes to excluding prosecution evidence
- Be able to construct arguments for and against the admission/exclusion of such evidence. In an exam, you may be asked to identify the 'best' basis for a judicial decision.

It is worth reading ...

One where the confession was excluded ...
Charles v DPP [2009] EWHC 3521 (Admin). Moses LJ's judgment (it takes a while to get to it) is short, covers both s 76 and 78 and is an example of impropriety leading to the exclusion of the confession evidence. It also shows how cases are 'stated' from the magistrates' court (see Ch.13), so you get two procedural gifts in one package!

And one where it was not ...
R v Alladice (1988) 87 Cr App R 380. This is a much older case, but still makes the point well (and based on simple facts) that mistakes made in bad faith may well produce a different result than those made in good faith insofar as excluding confessions obtained improperly go.
Again, the Crown Court Compendium is a useful (and readable) resource.

33 The 'mini' discretions, like s 117(6), built into the various sections of the CJA 2003 can operate on both prosecution and defence evidence. So can s 126, but a confession admissible against one defendant is unlikely to be excluded under this provision just because it puts a co-accused in a bad light.

CHAPTER 22

Opinion evidence and use of experts

As a *general rule*, opinion evidence is not admissible at trial. Witnesses must normally confine themselves to telling the court about the facts, and not express opinions or draw inferences from those facts. To do so would either be considered an irrelevance (unless the state of mind of the holder of the view is pertinent) or an intrusion on the role of those deciding the case, whose opinion is really the only one that matters. There are, however, *exceptions* to this general rule: namely,

1. the opinions of other tribunals:
2. the perceptions of witnesses of fact: *and, most importantly,*
3. the opinions of experts.

1. PREVIOUS JUDGMENTS

Judgments of a court are a form of opinion evidence, since a finding of guilt or innocence is really nothing more than the opinion of the tribunal trying the case. Before statutory intervention, there was a rule that verdicts in previous criminal or civil cases were not admissible in subsequent cases as evidence of the facts on which they were based. This is known as the rule in *Hollington v Hewthorn*,[1] which was at

1 [1943] KB 587

least partly explained by the fact that the opinion of a previous court, on matters not rehearsed in front of the present tribunal, is irrelevant; it is the view of the present tribunal that counts. Thus on a charge of handling stolen goods, the application of the principle meant that the conviction of the thief was inadmissible as evidence to prove that the goods allegedly received had been stolen.[2]

The rule had its obvious drawbacks, and in criminal cases it was reversed by s 74 PACE 1984, which operates much like its civil equivalent, s 11 Civil Evidence Act 1968.[3] Thus where the commission of an offence is relevant, the fact of the conviction creates a presumption that the offence was committed by the person convicted, 'unless the contrary is proved'.[4] The conviction is proved by producing a certificate of conviction duly signed by the clerk of the appropriate court and by proving that the person named on the certificate is the person whose conviction is to be proved.[5] If it is a defendant seeking to rebut the presumption (not an easy task at the best of times), proof will be on the balance of probabilities.[6] S 74 applies to previous convictions of the accused as well as persons other than the accused. It is also worth comparing both of these with the evidential status of previous acquittals.

A. CONVICTIONS OF PERSONS *OTHER THAN* THE ACCUSED[7]

A clear example of the application of s 74(1) is where proof of the commission of an offence by a person *other* than the accused is admissible to establish an essential *ingredient* of the case against the accused. So in the handling charge scenario mentioned above, if the thief pleaded or was found guilty, his conviction would be admissible in the case against the handler as evidence that the goods had been stolen. But the section can be used even if the relevance of the evidence falls short of actually establishing an element of the offence charged. For example, in *R v Castle*,[8] C and F were jointly charged with robbery. F pleaded guilty. At an identification

2 See, e.g., *R v Turner* (1832) 1 Mood CC 347 at 349, cited in BCrP F 12.6

3 Discussed in *Be Civil!*, by the author, Ch. 17

4 PACE 1984, s 74(2) and (3)

5 *Ibid*, s 73(1) and (2) and BCrP F 12.1ff

6 See generally Ch. 15. As to how such an exercise should be conducted so it does not simply become a retrial of the offence in question, see *R v C* [2011] 1 WLR 1942, discussed at BCrP F 12.20

7 PACE 1984, s 74(1) and (2)

8 [1989] Crim LR 567, CA

parade, the victim said 'yes' in picking out C, and 'possibly' in picking out F. At C's trial, evidence of F's guilty plea and conviction was admitted as being relevant to the reliability of the identification evidence; by confirming the correctness of the 'possible' identification of F, it also tended to bear out the accuracy of the more positive identification of C.

Having said that, the function of the conviction should always be made clear, especially to the jury; even if technically relevant, the evidence (if tendered by the prosection) will be excluded under the s 78 discretion if it would be unfair to admit it. This will, of course, be determined on a case-by-case basis.[9]

B. CONVICTIONS OF THE ACCUSED

As discussed in Chapter 19, an accused has some protection against the admissibility in evidence of any convictions he might have, lest the jury be unfairly prejudiced against him in the case they have to decide. S 74(3) does *not enlarge* the situations where such evidence is admissible against a defendant, but merely *simplifies* the process of proving the convictions whenever they are allowed into evidence. These could, for example, be admissible to help prove an element of the offence charged[10] or through one of the CJA 2003 s 101 gateways as bad character evidence.

C. PREVIOUS ACQUITTALS

Acquittals do not say nearly as much about a person's innocence as a conviction says about his guilt. For that reason, evidence of an acquittal is generally *not admissible* in a subsequent trial, unless there are exceptional features.[11] Sometimes the way in which the trial unfolded gives the acquittal a special significance[12] or leads to a clear inference that a central witness was not believed and that same person's credibility is in issue in the subsequent trial.[13] But even where, exceptionally, an acquittal is

9 See BCrP F 12.13 and discussion in *Practical Guide*, p. 405ff

10 For example, if a defendant was convicted of assault, and the victim later died, the fact of the assault could be proved by the conviction if the defendant was then charged with murder or manslaughter.

11 *Hui Chi-ming v R* [1992] 1 AC 34

12 See, e.g., *R v Doosti* (1985) 82 Cr App R 181

13 *R v Deboussi* [2007] EWCA Crim 684

admitted, it does not follow that it conclusively establishes innocence, nor that all issues in that trial were decided in favour of the accused.[14]

2. NON-EXPERT WITNESSES: PERCEPTION EVIDENCE

To an extent, we see the things we think we see, and so there is always some element of opinion in statements like *"It was dark"* and *"He is the man I saw"*. But it would be very time consuming (and rather tedious) to over-analyse such observations. Therefore, an ordinary witness will be allowed to express an opinion as a 'shorthand' way of describing things personally perceived, where attempting to differentiate fact and inference would be difficult, if not impossible. It is useful to think of this as *'perception' evidence*, and includes observations about a person's age, the state of the weather, even whether someone appeared to be drunk.[15] Where the 'opinion' best conveys the facts, it will be admissible. This is a common sense exception, which is about ordinary witnesses describing ordinary things. It is very different from the next exception.

3. EXPERT OPINION EVIDENCE

A. ADMISSIBILITY

Sometimes issues are raised in a case which require a level of knowledge which judges and juries do not possess, unless they have special training. Typical examples in criminal cases include understanding the significance of ballistics evidence, or DNA tests, fingerprint comparisons or blood alcohol levels. Without help, it can

14 *R v Terry* [2005] QB 996, CA and see generally BCrP F 2.21ff

15 See examples at BCrP F 11.2

16 See BCrP's list of expanding areas of expertise: F 11.9

17 *R v Browning* [1995] Crim LR 227

18 See, e.g., *R v Snell* [2006] EWCA Crim 1404 and discussion at BCrP F 11.8

be difficult for the court to know what conclusions to draw from the information provided. This is where the important role of the expert witness comes into play.

As an exception to the general rule, therefore, *relevant expert opinion* evidence is admissible where, without it, the fact finder could not be expected to come to an informed view on the issue to which the evidence relates. It is important to appreciate the prerequisites for admissibility and to note the following.

(i) Expert must be necessary

The first requirement for admissibility is that the fact finder needs the assistance of the expert in order to do its job properly, because the matter at issue is beyond ordinary human behaviour and experience. *If the tribunal of fact can form its own opinion without the assistance of an expert, then expert evidence is inadmissible because it is unnecessary.* Generally speaking, juries do not need help with commonplace emotions (like anger or grief) and their effect on human behaviour, nor with the sorts of everyday acts (or omissions) which might be careless or dangerous. But pathological conditions, accident reconstruction, technical analyses and so on will be apt to require specialist explanation.[16] So, for example, an expert is not permitted to express an opinion on the likely deterioration over time of the memory of a normal witness.[17] This is something we can all appreciate. But the effects of 'childhood amnesia' on memory recall is likely to be outside the experience of jurors, and so may well call for expert evidence.[18]

(ii) Expert must be qualified

The second requirement is that, if expert evidence is needed, it should come from a *suitably qualified expert* competent in a *relevant and recognised area of expertise*. How experts gain their expertise is not usually important,[19] so long as it has been acquired,[20]

19 Indeed, one can become an 'ad hoc' expert where special knowledge has been acquired just in the context of a particular case: see, e.g., AG's Ref (No 2 of 2002) [2002] EWCA Crim 2373. Occasionally statute prescribes qualifications needed to act as an expert. See BCrP F 11.4/5

20 Only rarely will it be necessary to hold a voir dire to determine whether a purported expert is suitably qualified to give such evidence. If the defence wish admissibility of expert evidence to be tested in a voir dire, it is for them to apply to the judge: *R v Francis* [2013] EWCA Crim 123 [36]

although these days most experts will be 'professionally' qualified. Usually, the more letters the better after the expert's name.

(iii) Experts must keep to their subject

It is important to remember that experts may only give expert opinion evidence on matters *within their expertise*. It is not uncommon for differently qualified experts to give evidence on the same or related issues. A pathologist, a neurosurgeon and an orthopaedic surgeon, for example, may all be able to give evidence on the cause of a death or serious injuries, but the trial judge needs to be 'watchful for experts *straying* outside their expertise'.[21]

(iv) The quirky expert

Some areas of expertise are more experimental or quirky than others, and the question can arise as to whether, and if so when, the court should refuse to entertain opinions of doubtful reliability. A witness's area of expertise must be one the court is prepared to recognise. But science is constantly evolving, and creating new areas of knowledge. The English courts have tended to be rather open-minded about these things, so that by and large unorthodox approaches are more likely to affect the weight than the admissibility of an expert's evidence. Even so, where the expert's opinion is pushing at scientific boundaries, or where medical knowledge is incomplete, courts should exercise caution, especially when the evidence is fundamental to the prosecution case.[22]

(v) Primary vs secondary facts

Remember that the job of the expert witness is to *express an opinion on certain facts in the case at hand.* It is important to appreciate that those underlying facts, known as the

21 Quoted in Bench Book 2010, Ch. 8, p. 153 (predecessor to Crown Court Compendium)

22 See *R v Holdsworth* [2008] EWCA Crim 971. In *R v I* [2012] EWCA Crim 1288 the Court of Appeal held that opinion evidence based on a test which was clearly reliable in one context could be admitted in respect of another, even in the absence of any evaluation of the test's reliability in that novel context. It was for the jury to determine the weight of such evidence. The issue of reliability and expert evidence is itself something of an evolving area and beyond the scope of this book. See, e.g., discussion in BCrP F 11.10ff

23 [1983] 1 WLR 126

24 Sometimes the primary facts are not established by the expert who gives the evidence, but by one of

'primary facts', must themselves be proved by admissible evidence. This is known as 'laying the proper groundwork'. Having said that, the research or reports or other materials ('secondary facts') which an expert uses or relies upon in *forming and explaining* his opinion need not themselves be admissible, but should be identified and made available for the court and the other parties to review.

The case of *R v Abadom*[23] provides a good illustration. The accused was convicted of robbery. The main evidence against him was that a pair of his shoes had glass fragments embedded in them, which the prosecution said came from the same window which was broken in the robbery. In support of this contention, the prosecution's expert relied on statistics collated by the Home Office in relation to the refraction index of broken glass. On appeal it was argued that these statistics, compiled by unidentified persons, were inadmissible hearsay. The appeal was dismissed on the grounds that once the primary facts on which an opinion is based are proved by admissible evidence[24] (here, the fact that the glass found in the defendant's shoe had the same refraction index as the glass from the broken window), the expert was entitled to (and indeed should) draw on the relevant work of others to help him arrive at his conclusion. Being an expert involves keeping up with, using and evaluating what others are doing in the field.[25] The Court of Appeal added that the material to which an expert refers should be identified so that it can be considered when evaluating the cogency of the expert's views, which requirement is now explicitly set out in the Criminal Procedure Rules.[26]

(vi) Jury decides the issues

Bear in mind too that the role of the expert is to *assist, not usurp*, the role of the fact finder. The ultimate decision in the case[27] and on the issues covered by the expert remains one for the jury (or magistrates), *not the expert.* Guidance on how a jury should

his team. S 127 CJA 2003 expressly allows hearsay statements from laboratory staff and others engaged in the analytical process to be used for the purposes of establishing relevant primary facts, unless the court orders it is not in the interests of justice for the evidence to be adduced in this way. It is not usually necessary to ask the testifying expert's helpers to attend trial to give this evidence!

25 This common law rule enabling an expert to 'draw on the body of expertise relevant in his field' is expressly preserved by s 118 CJA 2003

26 Rule 19.4 (1), CrimPD V, 19A.5 and see below.

27 Historically, the so-called' ultimate issue' rule meant that witnesses were prevented from expressing a view on matters which went directly to guilt or

handle expert evidence will be the subject of careful directions from the judge.[28]

B. PRE-TRIAL PROCEDURE

The criminal law has, quite sensibly, emulated some of the Civil Procedure Rules[29] insofar as certain procedural aspects of expert evidence is concerned. Thus r 19.2 of the Criminal Procedure Rules 2015 states that in criminal cases the *expert's duty* is to *further the overriding objective* by giving *objective*, *unbiased* opinion on matters *within his expertise*. This duty to the court takes *precedence* over any obligation to persons instructing or paying the expert, and includes informing the parties and the court if his opinion *changes* after having prepared a report which is served as, or given in evidence. These obligations, which are described in greater details in the case law,[30] are taken very seriously. In *R v Puaca*,[31] one reason a murder conviction was quashed was because the Crown's pathologist, in giving evidence on the cause of death following an initial first post-mortem, left it to others (in this case, an expert to be instructed by the defence) to present any contrary views and opinions, rather than setting out the possibilities himself and explaining his own opinion in that context.

The rules about the *contents* of expert's reports in criminal cases also mirror those in civil cases.[32] Thus, such reports must include the details of the expert's qualifications, the facts on which his opinion is based, the materials relied upon in making the report, a summary of any relevant range of opinion, reasons for his own conclusions and so forth.[33]

There are also rules aimed at narrowing the issues and a limited ability to order a single joint expert.[34] Thus, where more than one party wants to rely on expert evidence, the parties must *actively* consider seeking a meeting of those experts in an attempt to identify areas of agreement, to narrow the issues and thus avoid

innocence. The rule became so awkward to apply that it was abolished in civil cases and is largely ignored in criminal cases where expert evidence is concerned. But it is still for the factfinder to find the facts!

28 See guidance given in *R v Henderson* [2010] 2 Cr App R 185, summarised at BCrP F 11.43

29 See *Be Civil!*, Ch. 17

30 See *R v Harris* [2006] 1 Cr App R 55, as summarised in BCrP F 11.36

31 [2005] EWCA Crim 3001

32 One big difference is that they need not include any instructions given to the expert.

33 CrimPR, r 19.4

34 Although nothing like that in civil cases. There is no procedural 'fast track' to criminal justice!

unnecessary expense.[35] Where *more than one co-defendant* wants to introduce expert evidence, the court may direct that the evidence on that issue be given by one expert only.[36] This obviously pre-supposes that each defendant would be equally well served by the one expert. If the co-accused cannot agree on who that expert should be, then the court may select one for them (either from a list prepared by them or in some other manner). Where a direction for a single, joint expert is given, each co-accused may give the expert instructions and should send a copy of those instruction to the others. The court may also give ancillary directions (for example, regarding fees or any tests and so on which the expert wishes to carry out) as necessary.[37]

Pre-trial disclosure of expert evidence is very important and, as you would expect, the rules require that *both* prosecution and defence should alert *the court and each other* if they intend to adduce such evidence. This is achieved by disclosing the expert's report 'as soon as practicable' and in any event at the same time as any application to the court which is reliant on that evidence (for example, at the Plea and Trial Preparation Hearing).[38] Part of the purpose of the early disclosure is to give the other parties access to the information in the report in order to replicate experiments and/or otherwise test the accuracy of the evidence. The sanction for not complying with the rules can be severe. If pre-trial disclosure is *not made as required*, the evidence will *not be received* in evidence, *unless* either the parties agree or the court gives permission.[39]

C. PROCEDURE AT TRIAL

Section 30(1) of the Criminal Justice Act 1988 allows the court to admit into evidence an expert's report *whether or not* the expert who made the report attends to give oral evidence. If the expert does not give oral evidence, then the report (which would be hearsay,[40] of course) is only admissible with the leave of the court, and whether

35 The default position now is that the court will make such an order unless persuaded otherwise. See CrimPR r 19.6 and accompanying practice direction CrimPD V 19C

36 CrimPR r 19.7 (1)

37 CrimPR r 19.8 (3)

38 CrimPR r 19.3 (3). See also *R v Henderson*, op. cit., on case management in cases where expert evidence is the essential proof of guilt. Summarised at BCrP F 11.46

39 CrimPR r 19.3 (4) See, e.g., *R v Ensor* [2009] EWCA Crim 2519, where the prosecution was 'ambushed' by late disclosure of psychiatric evidence, and the defence was not permitted to rely on it.

40 See Ch. 20 and note that aspects of expert evidence can be agreed by the parties, including by means of a formal admission under s 10. See BCrP F 1.1

that permission is forthcoming will depend on the usual sorts of considerations, including why the person making the report does not attend; how easily (or not) it would be to contradict the evidence without the benefit of cross-examination; fairness to the accused and so on.[41] If the expert evidence is of any importance, and certainly if there is contrary evidence put up against it, then as a matter of common sense there would have to be a very good reason for not calling the expert as a live witness. If a matter calls for expertise, then generally speaking, expert evidence would tend to trump no expert evidence; and a live expert testifying (who stands up to cross-examination) would trump a piece of paper.

In any event, if the report is admitted, then by s 30(4) its contents 'shall be evidence of any fact or opinion expressed in it of which the person making it could have given oral evidence' - in other words, admissible hearsay.[42] If the expert also attends to give oral evidence, the report also, strictly speaking, amounts to a previous consistent statement,[43] but where the complexities and technicalities of expert evidence are concerned, courts make allowances in order that the evidence is fully understood. If it assists to read, see *and* hear it, then so be it!

Directions to a jury about the weight and purpose of expert evidence they have heard will be of considerable importance. Risks abound: in deciding the case (for that is their job) jurors (and indeed magistrates) should not be over-awed by the experts, yet should not be tempted to become experts themselves. Unchallenged and uncontradicted expert evidence from one side (which should only be rejected on some rationale basis) needs to be handled differently than dogmatic and entrenched disputes between opposing experts. How does one assess the reliability of an expert's views? How does one avoid being blinded by statistics? And so on. The judicial emphasis may well vary depending on whether the expert evidence supports the prosecution or defence, so as to be consistent with the required burden

41 CJA 1998, s 30(3)

42 You will remember that one of the four major categories of admissibility under s 114(1) includes hearsay admissible by 'any other' statutory provision. This includes 30 CJA 1988.

43 See Ch. 18

and standard of proof. Marshalling complex and disputed evidence so as to give juries an understandable summary of the issues for their determination can be difficult and requires careful preparation. Proposed directions on the expert evidence should usually be discussed with the advocates in the case.[44]

revision tips

- Remember that expert evidence is a form of opinion evidence, intended to *assist* the factfinder to come to a view on a matter requiring specialist knowledge - not do the factfinder's job for it.
- Be aware of the procedure around the reception of expert evidence in criminal cases. It is not unlike that in the civil courts, but has significant differences (not surprisingly).
- A jury needs to be reminded that they are not bound by any view expressed by an expert.

It is worth reading ...

Judgment in *R v Turner* [1975] QB 834. Aside from the murder itself, this is a neat and tidy little case about when juries do (and, more to the point, do not) require the help of an expert to do their job. Things have moved on a lot in the world of hearsay evidence, but what Lawton LJ says about matters within the experience and knowledge of ordinary people remains valid.

The general guidance on directions to juries about expert evidence in the Crown Court Compendium Pt 1 Ch. 10-3, is an excellent summary.

44 BCrP F 11.41 (the Bench Book referred to there has been replaced by the Crown Court Compendium). See also CrimPD V 19A.5/6 and R v Brennan [2015] 1 WLR 2060, especially [43]-[45]

CHAPTER 23

'Secrets and lies'

In previous chapters we have looked at the evidential implications of confessions and other statements made by an accused, both in and out-of-court. But what about things an accused does *not* say? And what if he invents stories which are later shown to be *untrue*? Both of these situations can have adverse evidential consequences for a defendant. Mike Leigh's famous film title is a good way to remember this important area of the law.

1. 'SECRETS'

There is a right to silence, of course, in the sense that a defendant cannot be compelled to give evidence and it is no job of his to prove his innocence, but the Criminal Justice and Public Order Act 1994 (CJPOA 1994) sets out certain occasions when the '*silence*' of a suspect or an accused might be held against him - when, as it is often described, '*adverse inferences*' may be drawn. As we shall see, certain stereotypical situations are catered for in the legislation,[1] and you must appreciate the differences between them, but they are essentially permutations on the same theme and predicated on the same idea: namely, that when accused of

1 Situations falling outside the legislation may still be covered by the old common law principles: see BCrP F 20.1ff

wrongdoing, innocent people who have an explanation will generally want to give it - and at the earliest opportunity.

Much of the focus of the law here is on *whether* the trial judge should give juries a direction on this aspect of a case, and if so, *what* should be said. Both aspects are matters which, in any individual Crown Court case, the trial judge will first discuss with the advocates in the absence (obviously) of the jury.

The relevant provisions of the CJPOA 1994 are ss 34, 35, 36 and 37. Silence is not really the point so much as a *failure to explain oneself*, and the circumstances in which explanations may be sought will vary. But for the sake of differentiation, and as another short-hand 'aide-memoire', let's thinks in terms of three scenarios: A. 'Silence at the station': B. 'Silence on the street' and C. 'Silence at trial'.

A. 'SILENCE AT THE STATION': S 34

Section 34 provides that if a defendant is *questioned under caution or charged*[2] with an offence, and *fails* to mention *a fact* later *relied on in his defence at trial* which, in the *circumstances existing at the time*, he could *reasonably have been expected to mention*, the court or the jury *may* draw such inferences from the failure *as appear proper.* For example, if an accused's defence at trial to a charge of affray outside a pub is that he was home at the time babysitting his little sister, then one would expect that he would have been keen to say so at the earliest opportunity; certainly he would have known then that he had been home with his sister. If he did not mention it, this might make his defence at trial look suspiciously like a late invention. On the other hand, the accused might have thought that babysitting for his sister made him look like a sissy, and he would lose 'street cred' if anyone found out. If this were the real reason he did not mention his alibi, then this would cast a different light on his failure to tell

2 Or officially warned he might be prosecuted: s 34(1)(b). The words of the caution explain the implications of 'silence'. See Ch. 2

the police about it. In the Crown Court, it is for the jury to decide what to make of a defendant's 'silence' in such circumstances, and so, if all of the s 34 prerequisites are met, the judge will have to give very careful directions about what inferences may or may not be drawn in the individual case.

If a s 34 situation has not arisen then, of course, there is no need for any direction to the jury about it. The object of s 34 is to deter 'the positive defence following a 'no comment' interview and/or the 'ambush defence'',[3] but it is to be applied with common sense. In *R v Adbdella,*[4] for example, the accused immediately disclosed his defence of self-defence, but failed to mention at that stage the fact that he had thought his victim had been armed with a hammer. The decision of the judge to proceed in a 'low key' way without giving a s 34 direction was said to be entirely justified and sensible in the circumstances. It is important to note the following.

(i) Failure to mention facts

The ability to draw adverse inferences under s 34 is aimed not at silence, as such, but the *failure to mention* facts later relied on at trial. Facts can be 'mentioned' in a prepared statement, rather than given as oral answers to questions. Adverse inferences may only be drawn if the defendant later seeks to rely on facts not contained in such a prepared statement.[5]

(ii) Facts later 'relied on at trial'

Facts can be *'relied on at trial'* even if a defendant does not give evidence. A positive case put in cross-examination on the defendant's behalf (or even by a defence witness in chief) can suffice.[6]

3 Per Hedley J in *R v Brizzalari* [2004] EWCA Crim 310

4 [2007] EWCA Crim 2495 and see generally BCrP F 20.3ff

5 *R v Brizzalari*, op. cit. If the defendant's account changes between the submission of the written statement and the evidence given at trial, there might be scope for a *Lucas* direction, as to which, see below.

6 *R v Webber* [2004] 1 WLR 404 (HL). But a defence admission (without more) of a fact relied upon by the prosecution, will not: *R v Betts* [2001] EWCA Crim 2643

(iii) Prevailing circumstances

The question of whether the defendant, in the *prevailing circumstances*, could reasonably have been expected to mention the relevant fact when questioned or charged, will *depend on a range of factors*, including 'the defendant's age, experience, mental capacity, state of health, sobriety, tiredness and personality' at the relevant time.[7] Defendants, and their circumstances, vary and must be looked at on an individual basis.

(iv) Legal advice

An added measure of protection for the defendant at the police station is found in s 34(2A), as a result of which *no* inference may be drawn *unless* the accused was given the opportunity to consult legal advice before being questioned and so on. But defendants who remain silent in interview often give as their reason the legal advice they were given.[8] If so, this is an explanation, like any other, which merits consideration. In essence a jury will have to decide whether the solicitor's advice was the *real* reason for the defendant's silence, or is merely being used as a convenient smoke screen.[9] This, again, will depend on the circumstances.

(v) Range of inferences

One of the possible inferences to be drawn from a failure to mention a fact which is later relied on at trial may be that the 'fact' is a late invention and so is untrue. If that 'fact' is central to the defence, then such an inference could undermine the whole of the defence case. It is important, therefore, that juries are aware of the *range* of inferences available to them in any given case, and are told to focus not on the truth of the fact as such, but the *reasonableness (or not) of the failure* to mention it earlier. In some cases, the reason for the defendant's silence may 'surrender no clue to the truth or falsity of his defence'.[10]

7 *R v Argent* [1997] 2 Cr App R 27, per Lord Bingham at p. 32

8 Legal professional privilege between solicitor and client is, of course, to be observed, but if either the defendant or solicitor gives evidence of the reason for advice to remain silent in the face of questioning, then the privilege will be waived to this extent: *R v Louizou* [2006] EWCA Crim 1719 at para 84

9 The question is whether the accused 'genuinely and reasonably' relied on such evidence: *R v Beckles* [2005] EWCA Crim 2766 and see BCrP F 20.18

10 Crown Court Compendium Pt 1 Ch 17-1, para 15ff

(vi) Use of adverse s 34 inferences

Adverse inferences drawn by reason of s 34 'silence' may be used, as seems proper in the circumstances, both in determining whether there is a case to answer and on the question of the defendant's guilt.[11]

(vii) Inference should not infringe Art 6

The ability of a factfinder to draw an adverse inference of guilt from the defendant's failure does not infringe the latter's Art 6 right to a fair trial, so long as the inference drawn *is just in the circumstances. No conviction should rest wholly or mainly on an adverse inference.*[12] The Crown Court judge is required to emphasise the defendant's right to silence, the prosecution's burden of proof, and to ensure that the jury understands that it can only draw an adverse inference if satisfied that the prosecution case clearly calls for an answer and the accused's silence when questioned could only 'sensibly be attributed to his having no answer - or none that would stand up to cross-examination'.[13]

(viii) 'May' not 'must'

It is for the trial *judge* to decide (having consulted counsel) *whether or not* to give a s 34 direction. *If* given, it should be detailed and crafted within the context of, and evidence in, the case as a whole, as summarised in *R v Petkar.*[14] It is then *for the jury to decide* whether, if at all, and to what extent, to draw any adverse inference. The wording of s 34 is *'may'* draw such inference - *not must.*

B. 'SILENCE IN THE STREET': ss 36 AND 37

These two sections are all about an accused's failure, once arrested, to account for himself in *suspicious circumstances.* Section 36 deals with suspicious *things* found

---

11 s 34(2)(c),(d) CJPOA 1994. In a jury trial, the question of whether there is a case to answer is one for the judge; the question of guilt is for the jury. Both functions reside in the bench in the magistrates' courts.

12 s 38(3) CJPOA 1994

13 See *Condron v UK* [2001] 31 EHRR 1 at [61] and see BCrP F 20.6 and 20.25

14 [2003] EWCA Crim 2668, at [51], usefully set out in Crown Court Compendium Pt 1 Ch. 17-1 para 23

on, near or in the possession of an accused; s 37 deals with an accused found in a suspicious *place*. The request for an explanation may well, but need not necessarily, occur at the scene of the crime.[15] A similar provision in s 62 of PACE 1984 regarding intimate body samples is also worth mentioning here.

(i) 'Objects, substances and marks': s 36

Where a suspect is *arrested* and the constable who arrests him (or another PC investigating the case) *reasonably believes* that the presence of any 'object, substance, or mark' on his person, clothing, footwear and so on[16] may be *attributable* to that suspect's *participation* in a specified offence, he may tell the suspect of his belief (by means of a '*special*' caution) and request that he account for its presence. If the suspect fails to do so, then the court or jury *may* draw such inferences as appear proper in determining whether there is a case to answer *or* on the question of guilt.

So, for example, let's suppose that police are called out to a house burglary. A back door window had been broken to gain access and an iPhone stolen. D is arrested near the scene. The arresting officer sees he has an iPhone and there is blood on his hand, which the officer suspects was caused when the broken window shattered. If D fails (when properly cautioned and asked) to account for his possession of the iPhone or the blood on his hand, then adverse inferences may be drawn if appropriate. You might think an innocent person would be only too eager to answer such questions; on the other hand, maybe D has a fear of the police or was drunk at the time. If entitled to do so, it is for the jury to draw such inferences, *if any*, that it thinks proper in all the circumstances.

(ii) 'Presence in a particular place': s 37

Similarly, adverse inferences *may* be drawn if a suspect refuses or fails to account

15 Which is why I have called this section '*Silence in the Street*'. But the refusal to account could happen (or be repeated) in interview at a police station.

16 CJPOA 1994 s 36(1)(a). See generally BCrP F 20.34ff

for his presence at a place at or about the time an offence was allegedly committed. Again, the suspect must have been *arrested* and the arresting officer must *reasonably believe* that the suspect's presence there may be *attributable* to his *participation* in the offence. If, having been informed of the arresting officer's suspicions, properly warned, and requested to give an explanation, the suspect fails or refuses to do so, the court or jury *may* draw such inferences as appear proper in determining either that there is a case to answer, or on the question of guilt.

So, in the example above, if D was found hiding in the bushes in the back garden of the house shortly after the burglary occurred, and refused to account for his presence there, then s 37 permits the drawing of adverse inferences. Note the following:

(a) Sections 36 and 37 concern a suspect's refusal or *failure to account* for himself. Do not confuse this with the fact that an accused, found with incriminating articles or in an incriminating place, *is itself an additional (and useful) item of evidence*. The latter is a separate item of circumstantial evidence, which would still be admissible (subject to any discretion to exclude) if for some reason statutory inferences were not permitted or appropriate in the circumstances.

(b) If the request to account for himself is made at an authorised place of detention (for example, a police station), no adverse inferences may be drawn if the defendant was not given the opportunity to consult *legal advice* before the request was made.[17]

(c) Many of the observations made above in relation to s 34 are applicable here. In particular, the judge should decide whether and in what terms a direction to the jury should be given;[18] but it is *for the jury to decide whether*, and the extent to which it is proper to draw an adverse

17 Ibid, s 36(4A); s 37(3A) CJPOA 1994. This mirrors s 34(2A) discussed above.

18 Crown Court Compendium Pt 1 Ch. 17-2 and examples there.

inference. Again, no court or jury may *convict wholly or mainly* on the basis of a failure by the accused to account for himself in circumstances set out in ss 36 and 37.

(iii) Failure to provide intimate body samples: s 62 PACE 1984

There is what you might think of as an analogous provision in s 62 PACE 1984, which is not so much about a defendant's accounting for himself, as about his *body* accounting for itself. In appropriate circumstances, *adverse inferences may be drawn* from a suspect's refusal, without good cause, to consent to the taking of *'intimate'* samples from his body. The taking of such samples, which include blood, semen, genital swabs,[19] pubic hair, dental impressions and so on, require consent because they are either intimate in their nature and/or require a significant physical interference with the body to obtain (for example, the use of needles to draw blood and so on). Non-intimate samples (for example, head hair, fingerprints) do not require consent, although appropriate prerequisites must be met.[20] Before a suspect is asked to provide an intimate sample, he must be warned that if he refuses without good cause, it could harm his defence if the case comes to trial. As you might imagine, what amounts to good cause will vary according to the circumstances, and juries will, where necessary, require clear directions.

C. 'SILENCE AT TRIAL': S 35

A defendant is not a compellable witness, but his failure to give defence evidence at trial (or failure, without good cause, to answer questions when giving evidence) can result in adverse inferences being drawn against him. The suggestion usually is that if an accused has a story to tell, he would stand up and tell it. There are several conditions to be met before this provision can apply.

19 For some reason swabs from the mouth are not considered 'intimate', probably because a suspect can spit saliva out into a cup, with his clothes on.

20 See ss 61 and 62 PACE 1984 and Crown Court Compendium Pt 1 Ch. 17-3

(i) There must be a case to answer

The defendant's guilt must be in issue.[21] If there is no case to answer or if the defendant has pleaded guilty, there is really nothing further that he need do on this issue. It is *important to note that s 35 inferences cannot be used to make a case to answer against the accused.*[22] This makes sense - if there is no case to answer, there is no need to say anything.

(ii) Defendant fit to give evidence

The defendant must be *physically and mentally fit to give evidence.* It would be harsh (to say the least) to construe a failure to testify as incriminating if in fact the trial judge decides that the accused's medical condition makes it undesirable that he do so.[23] A defendant who is fit to plead, will usually be fit to give evidence - but examples of conditions which might pose a specific risk in testifying are latent conditions like epilepsy or schizophrenia, where stress could trigger a full blown attack.[24] Medical evidence will almost always be required on this question and in assessing whether adverse inferences from a failure to testify are warranted, the judge is entitled to weigh up the defendant's condition (and the risk to him as revealed by the expert evidence) against the importance of the evidence in the case.[25]

(iii) Defendant aware of risks

The trial judge must *satisfy himself, in the presence of any jury*, that the *defendant is aware* of his options and the *risks attached to a failure* to give evidence or answer questions.[26] Precisely how one goes about making this clear to him will depend on whether the accused is represented or not.[27] Either way, it is a critical bit of the equation.

As usual, whether or not a s 35 direction should be given, and in what terms, should be discussed with the advocates before speeches. If the judge concludes that no

21 S 35(1)(a) CJPOA 1994

22 This is in distinct contrast to ss 34, 36 and 37

23 See actual wording of s 35(1)(b)

24 *R v Friend* [1997] 1 WLR 1433

25 *R v Tabbakh* [2009] EWCA Crim 464

26 s 35(2) CJPOA 1994

27 For the relevant procedure, see BCrP F 20.42/43. One way or another, the judge and jury must be satisfied (even if the judge has to do it himself) that an accused has been properly advised about the pros and cons of not giving evidence.

adverse inference is properly available, the jury may need to be explicitly told that this is the case. Otherwise, a s 35 direction must make clear that:

- the defendant is entitle to remain silent
- the burden of proof is on the prosecution
- an inference may only be drawn if the case for the prosecution is so strong that it clearly calls for an answer[28]
- The defendant's failure to testify cannot on its own prove guilt[29]
- the jury may draw an adverse inference against the defendant only if they think it fair and proper to do so

The essential message will be that if, in spite of any explanation for the defendant's silence (or in the absence of such evidence),[30] the jury conclude that the defendant's decision not to give evidence can only sensibly be attributed to his having no story to tell (or no story worth telling because it won't stand up to cross-examination), they *may* (not must) draw an adverse inference.[31]

Sometimes more than one section of the CJPOA 1994 may be applicable in any given case, and a judge will have to be careful to craft a direction which meets the various needs of the case but does not prejudice the defendant. Similarly, where a defendant fails to comply with procedural requirements regarding disclosure of the defence, adverse inferences may be possible. Like a failure to testify, a failure to provide a defence statement at all, or very late, cannot assist the prosecution to make a case to answer. And there may, of course, be a reason for late or lack of disclosure which stands up to scrutiny. But if not, a direction akin to a s 34 direction may be warranted, in the sense that the jury may be entitled to conclude that at the relevant time, the defendant either had not thought of his defence or had no defence which would stand up to scrutiny.[32]

---

28 If there had been no case to answer, the case would have stopped long before any summing up, but the point must be made to the jury that the weaker the prosecution case, the more a defendant may feel justified in failing to give evidence to contradict it. See, e.g., BCrP F 20.51

29 CJPOA 1994, s 38(3)

30 Defence counsel may not, in closing speeches, advance a reason for the defendant not testifying without an evidential basis to support it: *R v Cowan* [1996] 1 Cr App R 1

31 See generally Lord Taylor CJ in *R v Cowan*, *ibid* and Crown Court Compendium Pt 1 Ch. 17-5

32 See, generally, *ibid* Ch. 17-4. Defence Statements are covered by CPIA 1996. See Ch 7

2. LIES

Sometimes, of course, instead of saying nothing, suspects tell lies. This might be, and often is, intended to deflect suspicion and avoid blame. But from time to time, suspects lie for other reasons - for example, to maintain an image or keep up familial appearances. As Judge LJ put it in *R v Middleton*, '... while lying is often resorted to by the guilty to hide and conceal the truth, the innocent can sometimes misguidedly react to a problem, or postpone facing up to it, or attempt to deflect ill-founded suspicion, or fortify their defence by telling lies'.[33]

So, lying might or might not be motivated by the defendant's guilt; at the very least, being caught out in a lie would undermine his credibility as a witness, since a jury may well conclude that if he is prepared to lie once about something important, he may well do it again. Because of the complexities of human nature, the enthusiasm with which prosecutors will look to lying to support their cases, and the danger of rushing to judgment, juries require careful guidance on the evidential implications of a defendant's lies. This comes in the form of the so-called *Lucas*[34] direction, whose purpose essentially is to alert the jury to the fact that a lie told by an accused does not, of itself, necessarily point to his guilt, because he may have had some other reason for lying.

There are, importantly, certain prerequisites before a lie can have any evidential effect, namely:

(i) The fact of the lie must either be *admitted* by the defendant or it must be proved a lie *beyond reasonable doubt* by *independent* evidence before it can be taken into account;

(ii) The lie must be *deliberate* (not the result of confusion or mistake);

33 [2001] Crim LR 251, para 18

34 Named for the case *R v Lucas* [1981] QB 720, which discussed the matter in the context of the rules about corroboration, which for the most part have now gone. See generally BCrP F 1.21/22

(iii) The lie must relate to a *material issue* in the case. 'Material issue' does not mean a fact in issue or the ultimate issue of guilt or innocence, as such. Obviously, in weighing up a case against a defendant, juries must decide who and what they believe on the day. The risk that a jury may find the prosecution case ultimately proved (from which it might follow that jurors felt the defendant lied about what happened) is not what the *Lucas* direction is aimed at. *Lucas* is aimed at lies the defendant told about a matter which is *separate* from the commission (or not) of the offence charged, but which is capable of pointing to his guilt - an obvious example is giving a false alibi.

(iv) The jury must be warned that the *mere fact* of telling a lie is *not itself* evidence of guilt, because people sometimes lie for innocent reasons: for example, to 'bolster up a just cause or out of shame or out of a wish to conceal disgraceful behaviour from their family'.[35] Only if the jury is *sure* that the defendant did not lie for an innocent reason can the lie support the prosecution case.

(v) A defendant *cannot be convicted wholly or mainly* on the basis that he lied.

The trial judge will have to decide whether the *Lucas* direction is warranted in any given case. There are, nevertheless, certain identifiable circumstances (which may overlap)[36] when in the normal course of events it should be given, which are:

(a) Where the defence relies on an alibi

(b) Where the judge considers it desirable or necessary to suggest that the jury look for something to support an item of prosecution evidence which should be approached with caution (for example, identification

35 As explained in *Lucas*, *ibid*, per Lord Lane CJ

36 *Burge and Pegg* [1996] 2 CR App R 457

evidence)[37] and he points to the defendant's lie as one possibility.

(c) Where the jury are invited by the prosecution - *or may themselves be tempted* - to infer guilt of the offence charged from a lie the defendant has told about some other matter.

The *Lucas* direction is discretionary in the sense that if there is no risk a lie might be misconstrued, or if the lie is part and parcel of the offence, or if there has been no lie exposed on a material issue, then it need not be given. Indeed, if the direction is given unnecessarily it could do more harm than good. So it is important that judges consult with the advocates as to whether, and in what terms, the direction should be given. If the direction is given it should be case-specific; identifying the lie, the defendant's innocent explanations, if any, for the lie, and the fact that people may lie for some reason other than guilt and so forth.[38] While it may be difficult at times to distinguish between lies going to the ultimate issue between prosecution and defence (when the *Lucas* direction will not usually be appropriate) and those relating to a distinct but material matter relevant to the defendant's guilt or innocence (when it *may* be), the guiding principle will usually be that the judge should give a direction whenever there is a danger that the jury will assume that because he lied, the defendant must be guilty.[39]

37 See generally Ch. 24

38 See Crown Court Compendium Pt 1 Ch. 16-2

39 See *ibid*, para 2 and cases referred to there.

revision tips

- Remember that *inferences* which may be drawn from silence or lies are examples of *circumstantial* evidence. They can never be direct evidence of guilt.
- Know the key requirements for each situation where adverse inferences can be drawn. Note special caution for s 36/37 scenarios.
- *Differentiate* between the various statutory provisions in 'silence' (e.g. ss 36 and 37 only bite after arrest; failure to testify can never assist in making a case to answer etc) - use easily remembered scenario to trigger your memory.
- *Lucas* directions cater for a different situation, although it is not uncommon for an accused both to lie and fail to mention their defence at the earliest opportunity.
- Use the Crown Court Compendium Pt 1 to consolidate your understanding.
- The principles discussed apply in both the magistrates' and Crown Court, but it is obviously only in the latter that the importance of directions to juries arises.

It is worth reading ...

The Vicky Pryce case in 2013 is a good example of both issues discussed in this chapter. She took her husband Chris Huhne's speeding points, but hell did not break out until he left her many years later for another woman. The case was much publicised. He eventually pleaded guilty to the charge of perverting the course of justice, but Vicky Pryce pleaded not guilty, saying she had been the subject of marital coercion. I recommend reading the judge's summing up in her first trial (that jury could not agree, and she was re-tried and convicted). It covers both the secrets and lies going on in that case, and much else as well and can be found at: crimeline.info/news/pryce-jury-summing-up

CHAPTER 24

Healthy scepticism:
Identification evidence and other cautionary tales

Anyone who has ever approached a friend in the street only to find that in fact the person was a complete stranger, can easily appreciate the hazards of identification evidence. The risks exist on many levels: eye witnesses' accounts of the same event can differ significantly, an honest witness can believe he saw something he did not, and more than one person can make a credible mistake. At one time, mistaken identity was thought to account for 'by far the greatest cause of actual or possible wrong convictions'.[1]

The law tries to avoid errors in various ways, for example by allowing a witness who identified the accused to reinforce his court testimony by putting into evidence his previous out-of-court identifying statement,[2] and by deprecating so-called dock identifications.[3] Moreover, defendants are protected in two other, important ways: by a Code of Practice governing visual (and other) identification procedures and by a system of judicial warnings to juries.

So far as visual identification is concerned, the relevant code of practice is

1 Criminal Law Revision Committee, Cmnd 4991, 1972, para 196

2 As an exception to the rule against previous consistent statements. See generally Ch. 18

3 Per Hedley J in *R v Brizzalari* [2004] EWCA Crim 310. A 'dock identification' is where an accused is identified for the *first* time when he is in the dock at trial: see BCrP F 19.6

Code D of PACE 1984. These protocols are designed to test a witness's ability to identify the person he saw on the previous occasion and to 'provide safeguards against mistaken identity'. They include making a record of the description first given by the witness *before* any identification procedure takes place, and holding an identification procedure whenever identification is *disputed*, 'unless it is not practicable or would serve no useful purpose'.[4] Breach of Code D may form the basis for a successful application under s 78 PACE 1984 to exclude the identification evidence.

In a jury trial, the judge should stop the case at 'half time' (that is, at the close of the prosecution case) and direct an acquittal if the identification evidence is poor *and* lacking evidential support.[5] But if such evidence goes to the jury, the principal safeguard for the defendant at this point is the *Turnbull*[6] direction which must accompany it. Just as with the *Vye* and *Lucas* directions, by the time of your exams the name *Turnbull* should be indelibly etched on your legal brain.

A *Turnbull* direction is required whenever identification has any significant bearing on the outcome of the case. The words *'wholly and substantially'* were used in the *Turnbull* case, but few judges would risk an appeal by omitting the direction in any case where the prosecution was relying on disputed evidence of identification. Even if the evidence is based on *recognition*, the direction must be given - a failure to direct the jury about the possibility of mistake in the case of recognition can lead to the quashing of the conviction.[7] There will be some circumstances where a full *Turnbull* direction may not be required - for example, where the evidence is one of 'description' rather than identification[8] or where it is the jury itself who is making the identification (from photographs, for instance)[9] or where the accuracy of the identification is not at issue, but the honesty or motivation of the witness is.[10] But judges will always want to err on the side of caution and give a suitably adapted version of the warning whenever there is the risk of mistaken identification - even (perhaps

4 Code D: 1.2 and 3. These provisions are discussed at greater length in Ch. 2

5 See BCrP F 19.18

6 [1977] QB 224. The direction was created for visual identification cases, but can be adapted for analogous risks with other forms of identification.

7 See, e.g., *R v Torme* (D) [2003] EWCA Crim 2322

8 See, e.g., *R v Gayle* [1999] 2 Cr App R 130 vividly recounted in *Practical Guide*, p. 243

9 *R v Blenkinsop* [1995] 1 Cr App R 7, but see also Crown Court Compendium Pt 1 Ch. 15-2

10 See, e.g., *Shand v The Queen* [1996] 1 WLR 67 and generally BCrP F 19.1-19.6

especially) an *honest* mistake - since honestly held views can sound very compelling.

In giving the *Turnbull* direction, the judge *must* do the following:

(i) *Warn* of the *special* need for *caution* when a case against an accused rests on the correctness of visual identification.

(ii) *Explain* the *reason* for the need for caution, *in particular* the fact that *experience has shown* that a person who is *genuinely convinced* of the correctness of his identification may *seem* an impressive witness, but nevertheless may be *mistaken*. This is so even when a *number of witnesses* make the same identification or where a witness purports to *recognise* someone he knows. Mistakes are sometimes made in recognising friends and relatives.

(iii) Examine the *circumstances* in which the identification came to be made, in the case at hand, both as to the *reliability of the observation* (covering things like distance, light, obstructions, whether the suspect was known to the witness, and so on) and the *reliability of recall* (covering things like the length of time between observation and identification, conversations with others, and so on).

(iv) *Identify* any *particular weaknesses* in the identification (for example, fleeting glimpse, poor lighting and so on). Again, these should be *case-specific*, not generic.

(v) *Identify* evidence capable (and when appropriate, not capable) of *supporting* the identification. This can include rejected alibi evidence or the defendant's failure to give evidence at trial or account for himself under police questioning, all of which of course will require their own special directions.[11]

11 For example, *Lucas* or a s 34 direction, as discussed in Ch. 23. See BCrP F 19.13ff

(vi) Explain the *relevance of any breaches* of Code D, where the evidence has, notwithstanding, been admitted into evidence.[12]

Note that the *Turnbull* direction on visual identification can be adapted to cater for more modern methods of identification, for example by CCTV image[13] and voice recognition.[14]

We have now looked at several situations[15] where a jury will need guidance on how to deal with certain kinds of evidence because of the risks that such evidence might be misconstrued or mishandled. Sometimes, the hazard springs not so much from the message, as from the messenger. For many years, evidence from accomplices, complainants in sex offence cases and children required 'corroboration', that is, confirmation from an independent source, because of the inaccuracies which were thought to be inherent in the stories they, in particular, might tell. The result was a prescriptive body of evidential law, which eventually gave way under the weight of modernity, when a more mature approach to the evidence of children began to take shape,[16] and a less chauvinistic view of women. The narrow law of corroboration has now largely been abolished,[17] and replaced with a system of *discretionary* care warnings - to be dispensed, as the need arises, on a case-by-case basis. The leading case is *R v Makanjuola*, in which the following principles were set out.[18]

(a) It is a matter for the trial judge's discretion what, if any, warning should be given to a jury in respect of any witness in whatever type of case. Whether he or she chooses to give a warning and in what terms will depend on the circumstances of the case, the issue raised and the content and quality of the witness's evidence.

12 See, e.g., *R v Forbes* [2001] 1 AC 473

13 See AG's Reference (No 2 of 2002) [2003] 1 Cr App R, p. 321, at p. 327 for a useful summary of how such evidence may be used.

14 See, e.g., *R v Roberts* [2000] Crim LR 183 where the Court of Appeal acknowledged that there are even more hazards with voice identification than with visual identification.

15 E.g., disputed identification evidence, discussed above, and a defendant's 'silence' or 'lies', discussed in Ch. 23

16 This area of evidence and procedure is still evolving. See Ch. 18

17 For the few special cases when corroboration is still required, see BCrP F 5.2

18 [1995] 1 WLR 1384, at p. 1351-52, per Lord Taylor CJ

(b) In some cases it will be appropriate for the judge to warn the jury to exercise caution before acting upon the unsupported evidence of a witness. This will *not simply* be because the witness falls into a particular category of witness (for example, an accomplice). There must be an *evidential basis* for suggesting that the evidence of the witness may be unreliable, and this requires more than mere suggestions by cross-examining counsel.

(c) If any question arises as to whether the judge should give a special warning in respect of a witness, it is desirable that the matter be *discussed with counsel* - in the absence of the jury - before final speeches.

(d) Where the court does decide to give a warning, it will be *for the judge* to determine the strength and terms of the warning, which should be case-specific and given in the context of the evidence as a whole.

(e) The Court of Appeal is unlikely to interfere with the exercise of the judge's discretion, except on the basis of *Wednesbury*[19] unreasonableness.

There are certain identifiable circumstances when the need for special care may arise. One typical instance is when an accused has a 'purpose of his own to serve' in giving evidence against a co-accused. This is particularly apt to be the case when accomplices are running 'cut-throat' defences[20] or the evidence could otherwise be tainted by an improper motive.[21] More recently, it has been said that where experts have entrenched and/or diametrically opposed views on, for example, the cause of an infant's death (that is, whether it was natural or nefarious), the judge should warn of the need to find supporting evidence from an independent source.[22] Where, in any case, the jury is advised to look for supporting evidence, the judge should identify other evidence in the case capable of lending such support.[23]

19 This is a ground of appeal based on the notion that 'no reasonable tribunal' could have made the decision in question: *Associated Provincial Picture Houses Ltd v Wednesbury Corporation* [1948] 1 KB 223

20 See examples in Crown Court Compendium Pt 1 Ch. 10-2

21 See examples set out at *ibid*, para 5 and BCrP F 5.14

22 This is a result of the infamous *Cannings* case [2004] 1 WLR 2607

23 BCrP F 5.10 and examples in Crown Court Compendium.

revision tips

- You must know the *Turnbull* guidelines, understand their function and extent, and be able to apply them to the scenario of any exam question you are given. You may be asked to identify what a judge should say or do in a particular situation.
- Identify some instances where a more generic care warning may be needed - for example, accomplices blaming each other.

It is worth reading ...

R v Brown [2011] EWCA Crim 80. Contract killing, video-ID procedure, escapes from the jurisdiction, references to the famous Barry George case and even a little bad character evidence thrown in for good measure (and useful revision). There is a lot here, but the issues are straightforward. The ID evidence was weak, to say the least, but the accused left behind more telling evidence ...

R v Vasco [2012] EWCA Crim 3004. This is a neat little case, highlighting the need for all the necessary and relevant detail when summing up generally, and giving a *Turnbull* warning in particular - especially if the identification evidence comes in the form of a hearsay statement!

CHAPTER 25

Approaching the exams

Since this book was first published, there have been many changes to the teaching and testing of Criminal Litigation, Evidence and Sentencing on the BPTC. The examinations have been centrally set by the Bar Standards Board (BSB) since 2011/12, and over the last five years there has been much experimentation both with what should be tested, and how. The so-called 'short answer question' (which used to form half the examination) was abandoned in 2016-2017, to be replaced with a new-look form of multiple choice test, known as the 'Single Best Answer' (SBA) test.

The curriculum, meanwhile, is very wide (it is three subjects in one exam for a start!); and the syllabus is now described by means of references to specific paragraphs in Blackstone's Criminal Practice, which contain the 'examinable' material set by the BSB. This means that anything in those paragraphs is 'fair game' insofar as what is tested in that year's examination.

The teaching institutions thus no longer have much (if any) input into the examination process, except to try their best to share their expertise (and keep up) with the BSB and, in particular, to prepare you for the tests, so you should make the most of the guidance, practice and information which your tutors and course leaders give you. It is important to go into the examination hall alert and in a confident frame of mind, knowing what sorts of questions you are likely to find on the paper. Remember that the assessment, although challenging, is designed to allow you to show off what you know and the extent to which you know it - it is not (or shouldn't be) calculated to make you fail. If you are well prepared, there should be a part of you (possibly a very small part) which is looking forward to the test.

1. LEARNING AND REVISION

Learning and revision are very personal things - some people make lists, some people use index cards, some people like mind maps. Vive la difference. Having said that, there is some general guidance which is worth imparting.

First, you need to keep on top of your learning as the year progresses. These are not subjects that you can leave until the last minute to 'swot up'. Prepare and participate as required for lessons, and be willing to listen and learn while you are there. Remember that ultimately you need to get the relevant information into your *head*, not merely onto a piece of paper. This requires thought and effort. It is a good idea, for example, to spend a couple of hours every couple of weeks or so to consolidate and review your knowledge. There is a lot to learn and when you start revising properly, you should not be confronting the material (at least not most of it) for the first time.

When reading judgements as part of your study (or indeed anything from which you are attempting to extract basic information), note the gist and mark up the one or two sentences or sections which *encapsulate the principles and reasoning.* If you find that all you are doing is colouring the entire document in highlighter pen, then you are probably not being discerning enough - you may have just changed it from white to yellow! You must extract, and get to grips with, the essence of the source material.

Similarly, in terms of legislation, rules and so forth (of which there are a lot), always make a note of the *key concepts, words and requirements.* Remember that exceptions can be as important as the general rules. Sometimes the differences between one procedure and another seem rather subtle. When looking at bad character evidence, for example, the court's *permission* must be sought (and granted) before a witness who is *not* a defendant can have his bad character exposed. A prosecutor wanting to do the same to a defendant, on the other hand, must give *notice* that he intends doing so, but if there is no objection from the defence (which there usually is) then no permission from the judge is required. In both cases, there is often an argument in front of the judge about whether the questioning should be allowed, but for different procedural reasons (see Chapter 19). Examiners like to test nuanced distinctions!

Do not, I repeat do not, think you can succeed by trying to 'question spot' for the BPTC examinations. They are not predicated on your demonstrating that you understand some things well, and others not at all. You may find you do not quite get to every nook and cranny of the examinable paragraphs (you are human after all), but you should try your best. These are professional examinations, and you should aim to enter the exam room thinking like a lawyer. You wouldn't be impressed if your GP couldn't help you with your aching knee because she hadn't revised the bit of her syllabus dealing with the causes of joint pain!

The BSB sometimes issues 'guidance' as to the number of questions per topic which might appear in the assessment, but I would not take this too literally. They have been known to change their minds. Clearly if you have a confident grasp, for example, of hearsay evidence and character evidence (in all of their manifestations), this could be good for 10-15 questions or so; but that still leaves a lot left for other topics. You can be asked anything from the 'examinable material', and *more than one* topic may well feature in one question. If you do not have a confident grasp of the syllabus across the board, you could get side-tracked and confused by references in a question which you do not really understand.

Next, I believe it is important to review and consolidate your knowledge 'little and often' and in sensible chunks, giving yourself breaks in between and rewards for what you have accomplished. For example, you might spend a couple of hours in the morning revising bail and then go out for a coffee or go for a run. Then come back and tackle mode of trial. Take a break, in other words, if only a short one. My own view is that the brain (well, certainly mine) can only take in so much in one sitting and it helps to let what you have covered sink in for a while before going on to the next item on the list. Revising just before falling asleep is supposed to be good – maybe because what you have just been working on 'marinates' all night! In any event, whenever you do it, *always* make sure that you really *understand* what you are revising (and *why* the rule or principle is as it is). *It is almost impossible to learn, recall, and especially to apply information you do not fully comprehend.*

As your learning and revision progress, aim towards reducing down to a few pages the fundamentals of each area you are revising, noting key principles, rationale and vocabulary. These in a sense represent a 'snapshot' of the subject matter. Not only will this help you distil the subject matter, but as you approach the exam date you will have a handful rather than a file (or worse, a room) full of revision notes for a last-minute run through.

Think of effective ways to remember detail. For example, knowing that at 14 years of age a child (if competent) can give sworn evidence, might help you remember that this is also the age that a juvenile moves from being a 'child' and becomes a 'young person'. Two birds with one stone!

Last but certainly not least, make sure you are *very clear* about what will be examined on your course and how it will be tested. Always (and periodically) *cross-check* your general knowledge of the various topics you are learning against the *specifics of your examination syllabus.* BPTC students may find that sometimes the BSB seems to have chosen rather random paragraphs in Blackstone's Criminal Practice as 'examinable material.' My own view, therefore, is that it is best to get a good grasp of each topic you are learning, by whatever means, and then narrow or 'drill down' into the examinable paragraphs in Blackstone's for detail as you approach the exam. Blackstone's itself can be a little challenging for beginners to *learn* from, but do what works for you; in any event, all revision roads should lead to those examinable paragraphs! Try crossing them off a list as you go along.

It is also crucial to take *any and all practice tests* which are made available to you, and in particular the mock examinations which the BSB provides, both for the experience and to highlight any weaknesses in your understanding of the subject. It is important to know what you know (and what you still have to learn), and what to expect on the day of the test. The mocks, where possible should be taken in exam conditions, following a revision period. This is, after all, a closed book examination! It is also a good idea to do (or re-do) a mock relatively close in time to the real thing.

As to the assessment itself, do not enter the exam room sleep deprived. My own view is that a good night's sleep the night before the exam is a good thing - what you do not know by 11 pm that night is either not worth knowing, or it is too late. Having said that, I appreciate that many people get exam fever and are too excited to sleep. If you are one of these people, it is especially important that you get plenty of sleep as you approach the exam date. Do not stay up two or three nights in a row. All you are taking into the exam is your brain, and you want that working to full capacity.

For similar reasons, make sure you enter that exam room appropriately fed - you don't want to be faint from hunger or so full that you feel sleepy. Have a reasonably hearty and healthy breakfast (or lunch as the case may be). This would not be a good time for a bag of crisps and a coke. But by all means bring water and some polos (or similar) into the exam, if allowed, to get you through the next 3 hours.

2. THE SINGLE BEST ANSWER QUESTION FORMAT

The Single Best Answer test is a sophisticated form of multiple choice test. If you have not taken even a basic multiple choice test recently, or if you are used to exams where you can get marks for telling the assessor something you know, even if you were not asked, then you need to get used to answering this form of question. No doubt you will be given a lot of information, help and advice about this form of assessment from your tutors and course materials. Make sure you take it all on board, and get as much practice in and exposure to the sorts of questions you will have to answer. You do not have many re-sit opportunities anymore, so make the most of this attempt.

The assessments are intended to test (as the BSB puts it) the 'fundamental principles, key rules and core elements of criminal litigation' expected of a newly qualified lawyer about to embark on a pupillage, training contract or other form of internship. The questions are not directed at historical or academic points of law which a practitioner might need to research, or about which there are intellectual or other differences of opinion. Nor do they test minutiae such as form numbers or the elements of specific criminal offences (you would always be given relevant detail if necessary to answer any procedural question). Similarly, the key requirements of statutory provisions and practice directions are more important than the rule or section numbers in themselves. These may be referred to in a question, but usually as part of the description, not something to be tested as such. Having said that, there are *several cases* which you would be expected to know by name, which have all been mentioned in previous chapters (e.g. *Vye, Turnbull*) and you *would* be expected to know the *most important sections* of the *most important* legislation (e.g. gateways to admissibility of bad character and hearsay evidence under Criminal Justice Act 2003). But it is what such cases and statutes tells us which is what really matters.

The use of SBAs as an assessment format is new; the 2016-2017 academic year was the first time it was used. So all of us (BSB, students and teachers alike) will be on a fairly steep learning curve. The following guidance is intended to help you prepare.

On the BPTC, each SBA is a single question in the form of a (sometimes detailed) factual scenario, followed by a specific question and 4 possible answers [A] to [D]. Only one of these is the correct answer. One mark is awarded for selecting the right answer. No marks are given for choosing the wrong answer (obviously), or marking more than one answer, but no marks are deducted for bad answers. There are 75 questions on the paper, and you have 3 hours to complete the test.

SBAs can come in different permutations, ranging from the traditional MCQ to the pure-form of SBA, with various 'hybrids' in between. Thus, you might encounter any of the following:

- A case scenario, followed by a question asking which of the following is the 'best' answer (or similar form of wording). The four possibilities are all legally or factually possible (if only theoretically), and you have to apply your knowledge and use your judgment to decide which, from a professional lawyer's point of view, is the best of the four. This is the pure SBA, which are well suited for questions involving judicial discretion, counsel's advice, or (non-mandatory) sentencing.

- A case scenario, followed by a question asking you to choose which of the four possibilities is correct. In this type of question, only one answer is right. The other three are wrong. This is the classic multiple choice question, which is most suited to specific time periods, and other 'black or white' rules or requirements (you could also be asked to identify which of the possibilities is 'wrong', but again only one of the four options will meet this description. The BSB does not seem particular fond of this variant).

- A case scenario, followed by a question asking you for the 'best' answer, where only some of the possibilities are clearly wrong. Here you must eliminate the wrong answers, and then use your judgment to select the best of the remaining possibilities. This is something of a hybrid SBA - the best (or worst) of both worlds!

In all cases, you are being tested on your ability to *apply* what you know to a *given* fact pattern and to *select* the correct answer to the question posed.

My advice when tackling these sorts of questions is:

(i) Read any factual scenario carefully and constructively ...

... noting things like type of offence (eg summary, indictable), what court you are in (magistrates' or Crown Court), the age of the defendant or witness (adult or child), is it asking about examination-in-chief or cross examination? - and so forth. Underline or highlight this detail. As you do this you should be able to identify what aspect(s) of procedure or evidence the question is testing; you might even anticipate the question (or answer!). *Often a 'best' answer will be entirely dependent on the circumstances set out in the fact pattern.*

(ii) Read *all* four possible answers

This is so even if the first one seems like the right one. It might well be, but you *must* double check that there is not a better one below it. Sometimes one choice is only *partly* correct, or another choice is more accurately worded. Watch out for words like 'never', 'always' or 'must' in a choice you are given (which leaves no room for exceptions) - this can sometimes be the one thing which makes it wrong. *It is particularly important for the pure SBA question, where you effectively have to make a value judgment about all the possibilities, that you read each one!*

(iii) Be methodical

With a classic multiple choice type question, because you are asked to distinguish between one correct and three incorrect possibilities, it can help to put a mark (e.g. T or F) by each one as you go along (if unsure, put a '?'). This can make it easier to answer the ultimate question accurately. Assuming you can mark all four choices either T or F, the odd one out should be the answer. You could probably invent a similar method to help you 'grade' the best of possible options.

(iv) The process of elimination can help ...

... to get you to the correct answer. This is a useful device no matter which form of SBA you are dealing with. If it is a classic multiple choice type question, you might be a bit doubtful about which answer is correct, but more confident about those which are not. Eliminating the wrong answers will leave you with the one right one. In a hybrid SBA, eliminating the wrong answers narrows down the field, and even when having to select the 'best' answer or course of action, there is no reason why you cannot eliminate the worst (or less good) options first!

There is also a somewhat more complex variation of the classic multiple choice type of SBA which you should be prepared for. The BSB in 2017 claimed not to like this type of question much, but it (or some variant) can crop up so it is worth mentioning. In these you are given a series of three or four statements (possibly numbered, (i) - (iv)) about a particular subject (with or without a factual scenario) and then asked to identify which are correct (these days you might, for example, be given a list of 3 or 4 items of information in the context of a specific fact pattern and then asked which (if any) should be disclosed to the defence). You are then offered a choice of four various permutations (e.g. 'all of them', '(i) and (ii) only' etc), as possible answers [A] to [D]. Again, only one of these will be the right answer and you only get a mark for choosing that one. In respect of this sort of question it is important to be *doubly* systematic. If you are being asked to identify correct propositions, you will need to *first* decide which of the propositions are correct *before* moving down to the list of four possible answers to find the right one. If you are not methodical about these more convoluted questions, you risk getting confused darting back and forth between the initial set of statements and the ultimate choice of four possible answers.

And in respect of *all* of the SBA's:

(v) Record your answers carefully ...

... on the separate answer sheet. Take a second to make sure you are doing this accurately and recording the right answer to the right question. This is especially important if you are tempted to skip a question you are unsure of, so that you can go back to it later. My advice about the latter is not to leave such answers blank, but to record the best answer you can first time round, noting on your question sheet that you want to come back to it. Then, if you do go back and change your mind about the answer, just make sure you erase well and make your revised choice clear. You do not want to get out of sequence!

(vi) Circle the correct answer on your examination paper ...

... before making the appropriate mark on the separate answer sheet - just in case you need to go back and remember what your answer was for recording purposes.

(vii) Treat the examiner as infallible

If your initial reaction when you read a particular question is that there is no correct answer or there are two correct answers or it is impossible to give a correct answer, read it again. If you still feel that way, swallow your pride and choose the *best* answer you can in the circumstances. You can complain later. Mistakes can happen, but they are still more apt to be committed by students than examiners, so have a go at the question whatever you think. If there is an error in the question, it can be taken into account when the questions and answers are all analysed after the examination.

(viii) Keep the momentum going

Do not slow yourself down with unnecessarily time-consuming methods of highlighting detail as you read, or let a question stop you in your tracks. Some questions will be more difficult, and so take you longer to answer than others - the 2 minutes or so for each question is an average. But do not linger too long over any one question or let a question derail you (there are bound to be some 'nasty' ones on the paper) so that you cannot do your best on the rest of the test. Having said that ...

(ix) Do not rush

Remember that 2 minutes is really quite a long time. Just because the factual scenario you are given seems a long one, read it carefully. If you have taken the detail on board (and know the subject matter), it might only take a few seconds to find, circle and record the correct answer. You will not need the full 2 minutes for each question, but do not worry when you do.

(x) If necessary make an intelligent guess

You do not lose marks for a wrong answer, so it is always worth making an educated guess. Narrow down the field as much as you can, make a sensible choice and move on. Remember to think laterally and apply known principles and rationales when guessing - it should be as informed a choice as possible. And don't forget to use your common sense - this can be very handy when choosing 'best' options.

Finally, as I've told my students before their exam, remember:

P repare sensibly (little and often, but thoroughly)
A pply known principles when in doubt (think analogously)
S leep beforehand
S ustenance beforehand

This was known as the PASSword. Many of you, I am sure, can achieve much more than a mere pass. Now go and show them what you can do!